TAKING SIDES

Issues ... icity

D1069321

TAKING·SIDES

Clashing Views on Controversial

Issues in Race and Ethnicity

FOURTH EDITION

Selected, Edited, and with Introductions by

Richard C. Monk
Coppin State College

McGraw-Hill/Dushkin
A Division of The McGraw-Hill Companies

To the memory of my father, Daniel R. Monk (1913–1995), who taught his children to tell the truth and to stand up for their beliefs, and to the brave student writers and researchers of Kaleidoscope: VSC's Journal of Criminal Justice, *who virtually alone stood up for the sororities, both Black and white, and tried to tell the truth.*

Cover image: © 2002 by PhotoDisc, Inc.

Cover Art Acknowledgment
Charles Vitelli

Library of Congress Cataloging-in-Publication Data
Main entry under title:
Taking sides: clashing views on controversial issues in race and ethnicity/selected, edited, and with introductions by Richard C. Monk.—4th ed.
Includes bibliographical references and index.
1. Race awareness. 2. Ethnicity. I. Monk, Richard C., *comp.*
305.8
0-07-243085-0
95-83858

Printed on Recycled Paper

Preface

Do not at the outset of your career make the all too common error of mistaking names for things. Names are only conventional signs for iden- tifying things.... If a thing is despised, either because of ignorance or because it is despicable, you will not alter matters by changing its name. If men despise Negroes, they will not despise them less if Negroes are called "colored" or "Afro-American."

... Your real work... does not lie with names. It is not a matter of changing them, losing them, or forgetting them.

— W. E. B. Du Bois (1928)

When you control a man's thinking, you do not have to worry about his actions.

— Carter G. Woodson, *The Mis-Education of the Negro* (1933)

I have sworn upon the altar of God, eternal hostility against every form of tyranny over the mind of man.

— Thomas Jefferson (1800)

This volume contains 21 controversial issues in race and ethnicity debated in a pro and con format. Each issue is expressed as a single question in order to draw the lines of debate more clearly. The authors of the essays—sociologists, political commentators, historians, and others—reflect a broad range of disci- plines and perspectives. For each issue I have provided an issue *introduction,* which provides some background information and sets the stage for the debate as it is argued in the YES and NO selections, and a *postscript* that summarizes the debate, considers other views on the issue, and suggests additional readings on the topics raised in the issue. In addition, Internet site addresses (URLs) have been provided on the *On the Internet* page that accompanies each part opener, which should prove useful as starting points for further research.

In part, this work grew out of the prodding of my former student Deputy U.S. Marshal Barrett Gay. As a Black American, he wanted to know where he could find a challenging book on controversial issues on racial and ethnic minorities. He challenged me to edit such a work, and he provided many out- standing suggestions. I was delighted both by his encouragement and the op- portunity to work in my favorite area of sociology: ethnic and racial studies.

The reception of the first three editions of *Taking Sides: Clashing Views on Controversial Issues in Race and Ethnicity* by both students and professors has been gratifying. This fourth edition reflects my continuing commitment as a teacher to generating vigorous but informed student dialogue about racial and ethnic issues. At the beginning of the twenty-first century, ethnic and racial

i

understandings and interactions remain highly fluid and increasingly violent in many areas. Just as the patterns of interaction between minorities and the majority groups shift, so do the ways in which sociologists and other scholars as well as the media, politicians, and the general public conceptualize, think about, and evaluate them. Often the changes are dramatic and surprising.

I have attempted to capture as much as possible the shifting empirical realities of increasing ethnic and racial conflicts and the theoretical developments among scholars who are trying to comprehend them. On the one hand, new developments in the mosaic of minority relations around the world as well as how these developments are thought about and taught represent a veritable intellectual feast. On the other hand, there is great angst and a sense of tragedy in many recent minority developments and in some of the current approaches to minority relations. One tragedy that reemerged in the 1990s was genocide. This caught the scholarly community so off guard that many race relations and sociological texts had almost nothing on genocide. Now not only is it well known that at least 2 million people were victims of genocide in Europe, Africa, and other areas, but several prominent individuals and even national leaders are currently being tried for their alleged involvement in these crimes. Unfortunately, neither genocide nor ethnic and racial warfare are close to disappearing.

There are many different issues to explore, think about, and debate in this volume. My primary concern is to get the authors' ideas up front so that you can be immersed in them, fight with them, embrace some of them, and then make your own decisions about the issues. However, now and then my own disdain for or support of certain ideas may be more manifest than on other occasions. Do not be bashful about debating the authors and their ideas, or your editor as well. My students frequently remind me that I could be wrong and need their (and your) critical evaluation. Indeed, it was my students as well as my colleagues who encouraged me to include more of what might be called "contrarian" issues and articles. These reflect ideas that are challenging, logical, and empirically based but, in spite of their relevancy, may be peripheral to or even excluded from mainstream social scientific dialogue. A few may even be on the cutting edge of what scholars and others will be arguing about or framing debates with in the twenty-first century.

Taking Sides: Clashing Views on Controversial Issues in Race and Ethnicity is a tool to encourage critical thinking on important issues concerning racial and ethnic minorities. Although students may find themselves supporting one side of an issue or the other, readers should not feel confined to the views expressed in the selections. Some readers may see important points on both sides of an issue and may construct for themselves a new and creative approach to the issue, which may incorporate the best of both sides or provide an entirely new vantage point for understanding.

I feel that the issues and articles found in *Taking Sides* are representative of what is currently going on in the area of race and ethnic relations. They also allow students to get into this important area of sociology without having old prejudices reinforced or new doctrines internalized. My hope is that students will find these debates stimulating and will use them to clarify their own thinking about issues that are all vital and frequently emotional as well as controversial.

Changes to this edition In response to changes in ethnic and racial controversies, and on the helpful suggestions of those who have used the first three editions, considerable modifications were made to this edition. There are 8 completely new issues: *Are Blacks "Natural Born" Athletes?* (Issue 2); *Does Bilingual Education Harm Hispanic and Other Children?* (Issue 9); *Does Environmental Racism Exist?* (Issue 13); *Should Standardized Tests Be Eliminated From Applicant Processes?* (Issue 15); *Should Inner-City Blacks and Hispanics Be Relocated?* (Issue 16); *Are Reparations a Good Idea?* (Issue 18); *Is Israel the Aggressor in the Israeli-Palestinian Conflict?* (Issue 19); and *Are African Leaders Misguided in Their Fight Against AIDS?* (Issue 20). In addition, an alternative NO selection for Issue 1 (*Should Outsider and Insider Researchers Be Expected to Get Similar Findings?*) has been provided to bring a fresh perspective to the debate. Also, a new section (Part 4) has been added to capture emerging controversies in the area of social justice and hierarchies. In all, there are 17 new selections in this edition. All issue introductions and postscripts have been revised and updated where necessary.

The organization and sections of this book have been changed to reflect emerging conceptual and empirical realities. Part 1 deals with Thinking About and Researching Minorities; Part 2, Constructing Social Identities and Cultural Conflict; Part 3, Immigration, Racism, and Leadership; Part 4, Negotiating Social Justice and Hierarchies; and Part 5, Future Policies and Global Issues.

A word to the instructor An *Instructor's Manual With Test Questions* (multiple-choice and essay) is available through the publisher for the instructor using *Taking Sides* in the classroom. A general guidebook, *Using Taking Sides in the Classroom,* which discusses methods and techniques for using the pro-con approach in any classroom setting, is also available. An online version of *Using Taking Sides in the Classroom* and a correspondence service for Taking Sides adopters can be found at http://www.dushkin.com/usingts/.

Taking Sides: Clashing Views on Controversial Issues in Race and Ethnicity is only one title in the Taking Sides series. If you are interested in seeing the table of contents for any of the other titles, please visit the Taking Sides Web site at http://www.dushkin.com/takingsides/.

Acknowledgments Many people contribute to any worthwhile project. Among those more directly involved in this project whom I would like to thank are the authors of these excellent and stimulating selections. Also, my thanks to the many students over the years who have contributed to the social scientific dialogue. At Coppin State College, these students include Jamilla T. Dickens, Craig Gamble, Tommy McGinnis, Jesse Rosser, Quiana Tarleton, Alicia Flowers, Darnell Coates, Krystal Mattison, Mary Williams, and Avis Selby.

Several colleagues, scholars, and others provided comments and/or support that were immensely helpful and are greatly appreciated. Thanks are extended to John Hudgins and Elias Taylor, in Social Sciences; Evans Eze, in Criminal Justice; Judith Willner, chair of Fine and Communications Arts; Ron Collins, dean of the Honors Program; Tom Terrell and Ruth Petty, of Graduate Studies; and Mary Wanza, director, Robernette Smith, head of Reference Services, and their staff at Parlett Moore Library, all at Coppin State College. Also helpful were Kurt Finsterbusch, of the University of Maryland; Alex Hooke, of Villa Julie College; Tom Gitchoff and Joel Henderson, of San Diego State University; Harv Greisman, of Westchester State University; Daniel B. Monk, of Arlington, Virginia; Kevin Bowman, of Warner Robin, Georgia; Daria Capps, of the Magothy River Middle School in Anne Arundel County, Maryland; Martha Mercer, of San Diego, California; Megan Pedersen, of Silver Spring, Maryland; Rudy Faller, of the Inter-American Development Bank; Ed Tiryakian, of Duke University; Joseph L. Graves, Jr., of Arizona State University; Jon Entine, of Agoura Hills, California; Sandra Ben-Avraham, of Chicago, Illinois; Paul Leighton, of Eastern Michigan University; and Robert P. Engvall, of Roger Williams University. And, once again, to Goober and the memory of Midnight (1991–2000), who, when we dwelled in the land of deceit and duplicity, taught me to love and laugh again, and now to Tommy and little Patti, who make everyone love and laugh.

A special thanks goes to those professors who responded to the questionnaire with specific suggestions for the fourth edition:

Kijna Crawford
Rochester Insitute of Technology

Donald Haydu
El Camino College

Claire Cummings
Newbury College

Guinevere Hodges
Cypress College

John P. Deluca
SUNY at Albany

Virginia Juffer
Century College

Hiroshi Fukurai
University of California, Santa Cruz

Antonio Menendez
Butler University

Finally, someone must have once said that an author or editor is only as good as his or her publisher. Thanks are extended to Ted Knight, list manager, and David Brackley, senior developmental editor for the Taking Sides series, at McGraw-Hill/Dushkin. Naturally, I remain solely responsible for errors.

Richard C. Monk
Coppin State College

Contents In Brief

Contents

Professor of twentieth-century American sociology Robert K. Merton rejects the idea that superior insights automatically result from membership
in a specific group, or being an insider. He argues that outsiders, including
trained scientists and strangers, often understand racial and ethnic groups
better than insiders do. Lelia Lomba De Andrade, an assistant professor of
sociology and Africana studies, draws from both her own ethnic and racial
characteristics and her research as an insider of Cape Verdean Americans
to argue that her identity enables her to acquire significant information that
outsiders could not obtain.

Writer Jon Entine argues that one important way to build bridges is to admit
that racial differences are real and that members of some races are better
than others in certain areas. He notes that Black males from Kenya and
other regions of Africa can run faster, run longer, and jump higher than athletes from other nations, and he maintains that people should not be afraid
to admit it. Sociologist John Hoberman acknowledges that some West
Africans may be endowed with a higher proportion of fast-twitch muscle
fibers than other people. However, he attacks Entine's science as "speculative, selective, and inconclusive," and he rejects the theory that Blacks
are natural athletes.

Professor of arts and sciences Sheila E. Henry argues that in the United States, minorities whose ancestral nations have high prestige are allocated high prestige themselves, while African Americans and others, reflecting both institutional racism and the low status of many African societies, are forced to occupy the bottom rungs of society. Thomas Sowell, a researcher at the Hoover Institute, maintains that dominant theories of racial and ethnic inequality that are based on prejudice, oppression, exploitation, and discrimination are simply wrong.

Daniel Jonah Goldhagen, a political scientist at Harvard University, argues that most writers on the Holocaust have ignored or minimized the role of the police, soldiers, and other "ordinary" Germans as willing executioners of Europe's Jews. Pacific Lutheran University professor Christopher R. Browning rejects Goldhagen's "accusatory approach," which he contends is self-serving, promotes misunderstanding of traditional scholarship, and does little to advance society's understanding of genocide.

Assistant professor of speech communication Olga Idriss Davis links Black identity with Africa. In a moving account based on her visits to Senegal, West Africa, she reveals how she and many other African Americans have benefited from their pilgrimages to Africa. *Washington Post* correspondent Keith B. Richburg contends that it is trendy and foolish for Blacks to attempt to validate themselves through identification with Africa.

Scholar and former political candidate Linda Chavez argues that Hispanics are making it in America. Social scientist Robert Aponte suggests that social scientists have concentrated on Black poverty, which has resulted in a lack of accurate data and information on the economic status of Hispanics. Aponte argues that disaggregation of demographic data shows that Hispanics are increasingly poor.

Professor of curriculum and instruction Jon Reyhner blames the high dropout rate for Native Americans on schools, teachers, and curricula that ignore the needs and potentials of North American Indian students. Educator Susan Ledlow questions the meaning of "cultural discontinuity," and she faults this perspective for ignoring important structural factors, such as employment, in accounting for why Native American students drop out of school.

Dennis R. Martin, president of the National Association of Chiefs of Police, theorizes that rising racial tensions and violence can be attributed to rock music's promotion of "vile, deviant, and sociopathic behaviors." Criminologists Mark S. Hamm and Jeff Ferrell charge that Martin's theory is based on racism and ignorance of both music and broader cultural forces.

The editors of *The New Republic* contend that bilingual education is unpopular among minorities who want their children to be skilled in English to get ahead and that it may actually impede learning. James Crawford, a writer and lecturer who specializes in the politics of language, maintains that bilingual education, although no panacea for inequities between Hispanics and others, does enable non-English-speaking children to learn faster than when they are taught in English only.

Author and *CBS News* consultant Jack G. Shaheen contends that Hollywood's long history of denigrating Arabs as villains and terrorists continues in the film *The Siege.* He maintains that portrayals of Arabs as thugs significantly increase attacks on Muslims in the United States. Lawrence Wright, a staff writer for the *New Yorker* and coauthor of *The Siege,* asserts that the producers of *The Siege* were supportive of Arabs and that the movie's depiction of a heroic Muslim police officer as well as of dangerous, unfair treatment of Arabic Americans indicate that the movie was anything but denigrating.

PART 3 IMMIGRATION, RACISM, AND LEADERSHIP 191

Paul Ruffins, executive editor of *Crisis,* rejects three arguments supporting school segregation in the 1990s and asserts that efforts to achieve school integration should be increased. Glenn C. Loury, director of the Institute on Race and Social Division at Boston University, contends that school racial integration is an untenable goal because schools are more segregated now than they were 30 years ago, the courts and public sentiment no longer support school busing, and enforced integration implies Black inferiority.

Peter Brimelow, senior editor of *Forbes* and *National Review,* links the recent increase in immigration to many of America's major problems, including crises in health care, education, and pollution. David Cole, a professor at the Georgetown University Law Center, maintains that, throughout history, immigrants to the United States have been perceived as a threat by U.S. citizens but that they are beneficial to America.

Professor of sociology Robert D. Bullard attacks corporations, politicians who allow corporations to pollute the environment, and their apologists, including scientists, arguing that their actions primarily harm Blacks and Hispanics and are therefore clearly racist. David Friedman, a writer and an international consultant, contends that charges of environmental racism are a hoax at best and, at worst, lies. He maintains that much of the current debate is spill-over from the many perceived irresponsibilities of the Clinton administration that aims to garner political support and to strengthen muddled agencies such as the Environmental Protection Agency.

Eugene F. Rivers III, founder and pastor of the Azusa Christian Community, notes the many social and economic problems of Black youth in the United States and argues that three types of Black leaders have contributed to the problems rather than the solutions. Emeritus professor of psychology Edmund W. Gordon and researcher Maitrayee Bhattacharyya maintain that intentional neglect and racism by all of society are responsible for the poor state of Black development.

Law professors Susan Sturm and Lani Guinier reject the idea that affirmative action is doing enough to reduce injustices and social hierarchies. They argue that testing candidates either for jobs or for educational slots is inherently unfair and dysfunctional, especially for women and people of color. Sociologist Stephen Steinberg, an internationally renowned authority on race and ethnicity in the United States, questions Sturm and Guinier's contention that hiring, training, and promoting employees on the basis of job performance eliminates possible discrimination and unfairness. He maintains that affirmative action in employment and education should be amended, not eliminated.

Professor of law Owen Fiss contends that the government has historically carried out the wishes of society to discriminate against and mistreat minorities, resulting in many of them being stuck in the modern wasteland of America's inner cities. He argues that justice will be served only when minorities are moved out of the cities and into middle- and upper-middle-class communities. Political scientist J. Phillip Thompson asserts that Fiss's ideas are liable to do more harm than good. In particular, he is bothered by "pretensions of white middle-class moral superiority" that would destroy the African American churches, families, friendships, and neighborhoods.

William G. Bowen, president of the Andrew W. Mellon Foundation, and Derek Bok, former president of Harvard University, contend that the high rate of success of the Black college graduates that they studied would not have happened if they had attended lesser schools. Because admission to the elite schools for many of these students resulted from affirmative action, Bowen and Bok argue that the policy of considering race should be continued. Dinesh D'Souza, the John M. Olin Scholar at the American Enterprise Institute, dismisses the conclusions of Bowen and Bok and asserts that admission to any organization should always be based on merit, not preferential treatment.

PART 5   FUTURE POLICIES AND GLOBAL ISSUES 311

Historian Victoria Barnett contends that paying back African Americans for the horror that many of their ancestors experienced as slaves is both a moral and a possible thing to do, and she cites numerous examples indicating that there is a precedent for reparations. Journalist John V. Brain rejects arguments for reparations because it would be unjust to many Americans whose ancestors did not participate in slavery as well as to the millions of Americans and their descendants who came to the United States after slavery had ended. He maintains that atonement, not reparations, is the sensible action.

Sociologist James Ron, a former Israeli soldier, asserts that Israel is violating treaties, waging an unfair and bloody war against Palestinians, and inaccurately characterizing Muslims as murderers and Jews as victims. Professor of law Kenneth Lasson presents an interview with a colonel in the Israel Defense Forces, who relates several accounts of Palestinians' deliberately having their own children attack Israeli soldiers. The media, Lasson asserts, overlook the aggressiveness of the Arabs, preferring instead to cast the Israelis as the bad guys.

James A. Harmon, chairman of the Export-Import Bank, contends that the "HIV/AIDS pandemic" in sub-Saharan Africa is a moral issue that the rest of the world must address and that humanitarian assistance and loans are needed to fight the problem. He maintains that the Export-Import Bank is trying to do its part by offering extended loan terms and keeping in mind potential debt forgiveness and that such aid will not add to the region's economic woes. Nambian official Kalumbi Shangula, while acknowledging the seriousness of the HIV and AIDS problem in sub-Saharan Africa, rejects the "noble impulse" of the Export-Import Bank and other organizations to loan money to help control it. He argues that antiretroviral drugs only serve to prolong the lives (and expenses) of victims, not cure them; that the drugs are too expensive; and that repayment in most African countries is impossible.

Psychiatrist and psychoanalyst Thomas Szasz maintains that the current drug war harms almost all people, especially Blacks, and that its main function is to increase the power of the medical and criminal justice establishments. James A. Inciardi, director of the Center for Drug and Alcohol Studies at the University of Delaware, surveys several arguments supporting the legalization of drugs and rejects them all, insisting that Blacks and others would be hurt by legalization.

Introduction

Issues in Race and Ethnicity

Richard C. Monk

Modern man finds himself confronted not only by multiple options of possible courses of action, but also by multiple options of possible ways of thinking about the world.

— Peter Berger, *The Heretical Imperative* (1979)

The world is a giant lab waiting for your exploration.

— Robert Park

Bienvenidos (Welcome)! Your intellectual voyage into controversial issues in race and ethnicity is bound to be an exciting one. Some ancient ethnic groups would wish their members: "May you live in interesting times." Every person living in the twenty-first century seems to be a direct recipient of this benediction. This is especially true for students both experiencing and studying the rapidly changing and controversial mosaic of ethnic and racial relations. Since the publication in 2000 of the third edition of this reader, many changes have occurred in race and ethnic relations both in the United States and around the world. While some changes are encouraging, many are not. Indeed, long before the dissolution of the Marxian experiment that was the former Soviet Union in the early 1990s, sociologists and others argued that the greatest flaw in Marx's theory was that he completely underestimated the continued importance of race and ethnicity in both modern and developing societies. For example, in May 2001 two Israeli children were stoned to death allegedly by Palestinians in an act in the continuing Mideast conflict (see Issue 19). In another recent incident, Macedonian Slavs attacked ethnic Albanians (who make up approximately one-quarter of Macedonia's population of 2 million people), resulting in several injured people and the destruction of Albanian stores. And according to the popular media, between September 2000 and May 2001 over 600,000 Rwandans in the Congo—where Rwanda and Uganda are in a bitter fight with soldiers from Zimbabwe, Angola, and Namibia—were displaced.

In Indonesia, ethnic Dayaks attacked the minority Madurese, killing hundreds and parading several dozen enemy heads. In Mexico, a small army of supporters of the Zapatista movement entered Mexico City to show support of Indian rights. And in Burundi, the age-old conflict between Tutsi tribal members and the Hutu flared up again.

In an effort to quell rising neo-Nazi violence, the German government is offering huge incentives for skinheads and Nazis to renounce their hate group membership. These incentives include a new house, a new job, and a new name and identity, as well as cash rewards.

In Japan, right-wing leaders are being elected to office, and youngsters are reading comic books that praise Japan's conquest of Asia (1932–1945) as a war of liberation. Furthermore, many political leaders and scholars continue to deny that Japan used Korean and Chinese women as "comfort women" or exploited and sexually abused them during World War II. Koreans and other victims continue to demand apologies today.

In the United States, hate crimes based on race, ethnic origin, gender, and sexual orientation still occur. In Pittsburgh, Pennsylvania, for example, an assailant was recently found guilty of killing a "Jewish neighbor, a man of Indian descent, two Asians and a black man." Furthermore, a new Black Panthers group is gaining some attention because its leaders are characterizing whites as "crackers" and peppering their speech with anti-Semitism. Meanwhile, both gains and losses in racial and ethnic relations have been recorded in the mass media. In March 2001, for example, an American Society of Newspaper Editors' survey showed that for the first time in 23 years, the number of Blacks in the newsroom had declined, dropping to 11.64 percent from 11.85 percent in 1999. Although this decline is statistically insignificant, symbolically it is worrisome. It reflects the apparent growing disenchantment of minority reporters who feel uncomfortable with the way in which minorities are covered in the media. At another level of minority relations analysis, a U.S. senator reportedly apologized in March 2001 for using the "N" word on national TV.

On a more positive note, since the last edition of this book, minority radio, television, and print media are growing. "Native America Calling," for example, has some 125,000 listeners to 36 radio stations and Web simulcasts. At 2.4 million, Native Americans now make up about 1 percent of the U.S. population. Negative ethnic and racial stereotyping in the media may also be declining.

Perhaps surprisingly, approximately 250 hate crimes on U.S. college campuses are reported each year, with a million or more bias incidents known to occur on campuses. College campuses are among the top three most likely hate crime sites in the nation, according to reports.

Since the last edition of this book, political gains for minorities have been flat. Females, who currently compose 13 percent of the U.S. House of Representatives and Senate, have made small gains, but Blacks and Hispanics made no progress in recent congressional elections. There are still no Black or Hispanic senators, and only 9 percent of the House is Black, while only 4 percent is Hispanic. Three House members are openly gay, and two use wheelchairs.

The 2000 census provided vital new information on race and ethnicity. One in four Americans are now members of a minority group, compared to one in five in 1990. At 35.4 million, the number of Hispanics now almost equal that of Blacks (35.5 million). American and Alaskan natives number 3.4 million, and Asian Americans make up 11.6 percent of the total U.S. population of 281 million. Whites are now a minority in the 100 largest U.S. cities. And America is now the third-largest nation, following China and India. Five percent of U.S. marriages are mixed, with 1.5 million Black-white marriages. Yet 98 percent of married couples on the census identified themselves as members of only one race. Finally, one-half of all immigrants to developed nations came to the United States.

Statistics indicate that as of 2000, women earn only 72.3 percent of what men earn. Moreover, no state has yet met the goal of ensuring that all pregnant women receive prenatal care during the first trimester of pregnancy. Serious racial lags in health care and medical treatment continue as well. For example, Black females have a much higher cholesterol risk than other women, which often results in coronary artery disease, a leading killer.

Although open assaults against affirmative action continue (see Issues 15 and 17), the debate has assumed new parameters. Some scholars and university administrators, for example, now reject SAT scores and other tests as racist. Also, AIDS and its control is now a central issue in minority relations. This is especially so at the global level, where the economic, political, and medical ethics of distributing AIDS medications in Africa and other impoverished areas are debated (see Issue 20).

While several journals clarifying minority relations (such as Wesleyan University's *Meridians,* which emphasizes research on women of color) have recently emerged, in other areas confusions are being generated. One example is the contention that new minority groups now exist that represent the "fourth wave" of the civil rights movement. These groups include transgendered people (individuals that undergo sex change operations) and people who request the removal of one or more limbs. An article in the *Washington Times* (March 17, 2001) reports that this groups' members assert that "they don't feel whole or happy with both arms and legs attached." A Scottish surgeon recently added to this group's membership by amputating the limbs of two healthy individuals. The surgeon was stopped just before he cut off the limbs of a third person. Some argue that such medically induced minority memberships may rival traditional minority groups—those based on race, gender, and ethnicity—or at least those groups whose minority status is based on age, religion, occupation, or region of origin.

At another level of analysis, some prominent African American biologists and sociologists, such as Harry Edwards, are willing to consider new, apparently nonmalignant efforts to link certain biological attributes with behavior. One of these linkages is the alleged connection between ethnic or racial characteristics and success at certain sports (see Issue 2). Many argue, though, that it is a paradox that racially based biological attributes and specific behaviors (such as proficiency in running) are still being made in the wake of the February 2001 release of the entire human genome sequence. Some biologists, such as Joseph L. Graves, argue that if anything, the genome project puts the myth of biological differences between races to rest.

The scholarly world was rocked in October 2000 when allegations were made that anthropologists who researched the Yanomami, an indigenous people in the Amazon basin, seriously abused their subjects. Patrick Tierney, in *Darkness in El Dorado: How Scientists and Journalists Devastated the Amazon* (W. W.

Norton, 2001), charges that Napoleon Chagnon generated dysfunctional conflicts among the Yanomami people and assisted doctors in spreading diseases among the hapless natives. Possibly thousands died as a consequence. Many social scientists maintain that the charges are accurate. Officials in Venezuela have blocked research in the region until protections are provided for the minority subjects. Chagnon reportedly denies the charges against him.

On a more positive note, the Abraham Geiger College opened outside of Berlin, Germany, in November 2000. It is the first rabbinical school in Germany since the Holocaust (1934–1945), when 7 million Jews and hundreds of thousands of Gypsies, handicapped citizens, and others were killed by the Nazis. The graduates of Geiger College, as rabbis, will lead religious services in Jewish communities throughout Europe.

Some ways in which *you* might foster positive ethnic relations would be to invite a foreign student home for Thanksgiving or Christmas (extremely lonely times for "outsiders") or to learn about and appreciate holidays and ceremonies of a culture or religion that is different from your own.

It is obvious from the few examples cited above, as well as from your own experiences growing up in the modern world, that the types, meanings or interpretations, and consequences of minority-based actions and the majority's responses are complex. Moreover, as contemporary sociologist Peter Berger notes, you are confronted not only by different ways of responding to your world, including your interactions with minority members and majority ones, but you also face "multiple options of possible ways of thinking about the world." This includes how you view ethnic and racial groups and the controversies related to their presence, their actions, and the ways in which other members of society respond to them.

The Study of Racial and Ethnic Relations

For generations many social scientists, as trained "people watchers" (a term coined by Berger), have found minority relations to be among the most fascinating aspects of social life. Initially, sociologists and anthropologists tended to have an intellectual monopoly on the formal, systematic study of this area. More recently, historians, economists, and political scientists have increased significantly their studies of minority group relations. Although the work of these people is generally narrower and more focused than that of sociologists (typical subjects for study would be the historical treatment of one region's slave system in a specific time period, attitudes of Italian American voters, or the consumption and marketplace behavior of selected Asian groups), their gradual inclusion of minorities in their research is a welcome addition to the scholarship.

Sociologists and anthropologists have energized research methods, theories, and perspectives within minority scholarship, but the process has been painful and the source of acrimonious controversies among sociologists about proper scholarly work *vis-à-vis* ethnic and racial minorities. Two major events sparked this critical examination of the foundations of concepts and studies: (1) the civil rights movement in the 1960s and the rapid changes that resulted from it; and (2) breakthroughs in the philosophy of science that increased understanding of science, theories, and methods.

The civil rights movement in the United States politicized minority groups, especially Blacks, and moved them onto the public stage. Articulate and militant, they were finally listened to by the majority, including sociologists. Moreover, agents of social control, especially the federal government, assumed a direct role in supporting increasing changes for minorities.

The antiwar protest against the Vietnam War of the same period functioned to undermine both social science characterizations of uniformity and the consensus of American society, as well as the government's claims of fairness and veracity in its justification for the war. Both the civil rights movement and the antiwar protest generated a radical cohort of social scientists who were suspicious of both the political-military and the educational-university establishments, including the establishment teachers and their graduate programs.

Two areas within ethnic and racial minority theories and research that were bitterly attacked during this time were the standard minorities relations cyclical model, which was originally formulated in the 1920s by sociologist Robert Park (1864–1944) and his students at the University of Chicago (hereinafter referred to as "Chicago sociologists"), and the studies that were generated in the 1950s and 1960s by structural functionalists such as Talcott Parsons and Robert Merton and their students. The Chicago model consists of a series of stages that ethnic and racial minorities pass through in their contacts with the dominant group. Partially based on models from plant ecology and from Park's newspaper days—as well as on ideas he learned during the time he was a secretary for Booker T. Washington, founder of the Tuskegee Institute—the model identifies several minority-majority relations processes, such as conflict, accommodation, and eventual assimilation. The latter stage reflects the turn-of-the-century emphasis on the American "melting pot." Up through the 1950s major U.S. institutions simply assumed for the most part that racial and ethnic minorities wanted to and tried to "blend in" with American society. Minorities were encouraged to Anglicize their names, learn and speak English, embrace Anglo middle-class customs and norms, and so on.

Although pluralism (a stage in which a cultural, ethnic, or racial minority group coexists equally within a nation-state while maintaining harmoniously its own values, attitudes, language, and customs) was identified by the Chicago sociologists, it remained a relatively undeveloped concept until the 1940s and 1950s. Then anthropologists and others (such as F. J. Furnival and M. G. Smith) utilized pluralism but primarily to depict social processes in the Caribbean and other areas outside of the United States. However, since conflict, oppression, and exploitation were viewed by radical sociologists in the 1960s and 1970s (and currently) as areas ignored by Park and his followers, the Chicago sociologists' model was dismissed.

Many standard, or liberal, sociologists were horrified at what they viewed as the desecration of Park and his memory. They were especially incensed by the charges of racism against Park and the Chicago race relations theory and research. These supporters argued that the Chicago sociologists were very progressive for their time. The Chicago model clearly allowed for conflict, although Park generally viewed conflict in terms of prejudice and discrimination at the interpersonal level. Because it tended to focus on influences of the individual, Chicago sociology was often more like social psychology. Oppressive institutions and structurally induced and maintained inequalities simply were not part of the vocabulary of most sociologists in the United States until the 1960s. Two important exceptions were the turn-of-the-century writings of Black intellectual W. E. B. Du Bois and the later writings of Professor Oliver Cox (e.g., *Caste, Class, and Race,* 1948), but their work was largely ignored by both the public and sociology.

Structural functionalist theory, which originated at Harvard and Columbia Universities and generally dominated sociology throughout the 1960s, was also bitterly attacked. Structural functionalist theory basically states that a society acquires the characteristics that it does because they meet the particular needs of that society. This theory stresses cohesion, conformity, and integration among the society's members. Some of the charges against this theory were that it was inherently conservative, it celebrated middle-class values while ignoring the pains of the minority status, it excluded contributions of minority scholars, and it relied unduly on the natural science model, omitting systematic efforts to understand the subjective experiences of human beings—including ethnic and racial minorities.

These criticisms (and I only mentioned selected salient points) resulted in a reexamination of sociological work, including ethnic and racial minorities scholarship. Unfortunately, although some of this investigation was infused with sociology of knowledge concepts—that is, sociologists attempted to systematically trace the origins of ideas to the positions that intellectuals held within groups—much of it was largely reduced to name-calling. Many social scientists would argue that hunting down ideological biases in research and theory does not necessarily advance understanding, especially if strengths in the existing work are ignored or no alternative programs are developed. A few would even claim that the social sciences have not advanced significantly in ethnic and racial minority theories beyond the Chicago sociology of the 1920s and 1930s or some of the essays of the structural functionalists of the 1960s, such as Talcott Parsons's *The Negro American* (1968).

Another factor that stimulated change in minority research and theorizing is less direct but possibly as important: breakthroughs in the philosophy of science that occurred in the 1950s and that have continued to occur up to the present. The philosophy of science is generally narrower than the sociology of knowledge. It aims to rigorously identify and explicate the criteria that scientists use to develop and evaluate theory, concepts, and methods. The structures of scientific work and the standards used to accept or reject it are carefully delineated by the philosophy of science.

Before the 1960s the philosophy of science had eschewed "mere" ideology hunting that characterized some variants of the sociology of knowledge. It was considerably more formal and analytic. However, beginning with the works of Thomas Kuhn, especially his *Structure of Scientific Revolutions* (1961), as well as the writings of British philosopher Sir Karl Popper and his student Imre

Lakatos, physical and social scientists became sensitized to the importance of both formal analytical aspects of scholarship *and* communal elements.

Links between variants of the philosophy of science and ethnic-racial minorities issues include analyses of schools of thought within which particular race relations scientific research programs have emerged; the basic terms and their utilizations (e.g., pluralism, and whether or not it is being observed); conflict; and styles of operationalization (how terms are measured). In addition, the kinds of data (information) that are collected—attitudes, consumption patterns, behaviors (observed, implied, elicited from questionnaires, income levels, and so on)—who collects the facts, and how the facts are analyzed (through narrative summaries, tabular presentations, and statistics) have all been subject to scrutiny drawing from the methods of the philosophy of science.

Part of the philosophy of science's influence is expressed directly in some of the more current and influential discussions of theory and theory formation, such as the writings of sociologists George Ritzer and Edward A. Tiryakian. Ritzer combines the sociology of knowledge and the philosophy of science concerns in studying the underlying structure of sociological theory. Tiryakian, taking a tack somewhat closer to traditional sociology of knowledge, has argued for the importance of systematically examining hegemonic, or dominant, schools of thought within the social sciences. Such an examination includes social influences on theory development and the methodological agenda. The former is primarily a sociology of knowledge concern, and the latter is a philosophy of science concern.

Thus far, most contemporary ethnic and racial minority researchers and theorists do not directly draw from Ritzer, Tiryakian, and others; at least not in a systematic, comprehensive fashion. However, they do routinely acknowledge these concerns and often attack other researchers and studies on philosophy of science grounds. Moreover, most introductory racial minorities textbooks raise and briefly discuss underlying assumptions of studies they survey, though frequently in a simplistic manner. Most of the issues in this book indirectly touch on these concerns, and some grapple with them directly.

Additional Basic Concepts and Terms

Many definitions and typologies (classificatory schemes) of minority groups exist. At the very least, it would seem, a scientifically adequate conceptualization ought to take into account both subjective aspects (attitudes, definitions of the situation, and assignment of meanings) and objective ones (proportion, ratio, and quantity of minority members; their income, amount of education, and percentage in specific occupations; and so on).

One definition of *minority* that seems to have hung on since its inception 50 years ago and that remains vital and remarkably serviceable was provided by sociologist Louis Wirth. According to Wirth, a minority is a "group of people who, because of their physical or cultural characteristics, are singled out from the others... for differential and unequal treatment and who therefore regard themselves as objects of collective discrimination. [This] implies the existence of a corresponding dominant group enjoying social status and greater privileges... the minority is treated and regards itself as a people apart." This definition clearly includes ethnic and racial minorities. It does not mean *numerical* minority since, as Wirth points out, frequently a sociological minority group could be a numerical majority (e.g., Blacks in South Africa). The point is that minority members are systematically excluded from certain societal privileges and that they have less power than others.

Although ethnic and racial minorities can be included in Wirth's 50-year-old definition, ethnicity and racism are relatively new concepts. Strict biological classifications of groups by race are scientifically untenable. However, the social construction of images and stereotypes of categories of people based upon attributed racial characteristics are quite real. Although individuals of different racial origins may dress like you do, speak like you do, and have the same attitudes as you, if you view them in terms of their race, then they will be so defined. This is true even if there is absolutely no discernable trait or behavioral characteristic that can be accurately traced to race, as opposed to class, nationality, or region, for example. Unfortunately, while sociologically fascinating, the construction of the myth of race and its perpetuation in terms of attitudes and treatment has had frequently devastating consequences. Ironically, such world-taken-for-granted classifications, along with the concomitant attribution of all kinds of behaviors (often perceived as quite different and negative), are relatively unique to recent history and to the West. Among the ancients there was little or no understanding of the differences of peoples based on race. Nor were there objectionable connotations placed upon peoples of different physiological appearances.

Groups arranged in terms of ethnicity, however, have far more empirical accuracy than those arranged by race. Although negative attributes have been inaccurately and unfairly fixed to different ethnic groups, ethnicity does imply common characteristics such as language, religion, custom, and nationality. Wirth would identify ethnic minority groups as those with distinguishable characteristics who have less power than the dominant group and who are singled out for negative differential treatment.

This reader is restricted to selected controversial issues pertaining to ethnic and racial minorities. I acknowledge that other, equally important minorities exist. Indeed, some argue that the original minority groups were women and children! Certainly they were known to be mistreated and discriminated against long before racial, national, ethnic, or religious groups were on the scene. Nevertheless, the controversial issues in this reader emphasize ethnic and racial minority membership.

Another useful term that students of minority relations will draw from frequently is *ethnocentrism,* which was coined by sociologist William Graham Sumner. He introduced the concept of ethnocentrism in his delightful book *Folkways* (1907). To be ethnocentric is to be group-centered, to take the attitudes, values, customs, and standards of one's group and impose them on the members of another group. To the extent that the latter's behavior differs from the behavior or norms of one's own group, negative connotations are attached to the others' actions. The opposite of this is reverse ethnocentrism, which means to deprecate one's own group and embrace the behaviors and norms of the members of another group, possibly with a blind eye to the problems of that group. An interesting variant of this term is *chronocentrism*, which entails judging people who lived at a different time by the standards of one's own time.

The purpose of much of your training in the social sciences, especially in sociology and minority relations, is to liberate you from ethnocentrism as well as reverse ethnocentrism. In the first issue of the *Journal of Negro History* (1916), Carter G. Woodson, a founder of Black history, warned against controversies that, in the treatment of Blacks, either "brands him as a leper of society" or treats him "as a persecuted saint."

Your goal in reading these controversies, writing about them, criticizing them, and perhaps reformulating them or even eventually resolving them is to learn how to think about and understand major ethnic and racial minority issues.

Part 1, Thinking About and Researching Minorities, consists of four controversial issues pertaining to research, conceptualization, and theories. Before they can think clearly about a problem, students and scholars must learn what the key ideas are, why myths might exist, and what the core problems of researching and theorizing about minorities are. Part 1 will assist you in this task.

Part 2, Constructing Social Identities and Cultural Conflict, addresses the ancient Greek query "Who am I?" from a minority perspective. This leads into the cultural level of analysis. Culture is a societal blueprint for behavior. As a template, it consists of ideas, values, beliefs, attitudes, symbols, and so on. Cultural misunderstandings are often at the core of conflict.

Part 3, Immigration, Racism, and Leadership, reflects some of the most controversial racial and ethnic processes currently being experienced in the United States and elsewhere. Some contend that the goal of achieving school integration (set in 1954) has only increased racism and separation. Also, new and pernicious forms of racism, such as toxic waste dumping in areas in which the waste would primarily harm minorities, are allegedly emerging. Immigration, too, remains a hotly contested issue. The final debate in this section focuses on renewed charges of corruption, race hustling, personal agenda mapping, and hypocrisy against some minority leaders. Some argue that such leaders need to learn the difference between *living for* and *living off* a minority group. Others reject such assertions as groundless and even racist.

Part 4, Negotiating Social Justice and Hierarchies, wrestles with ideas that are central to both philosophy (justice) and the social sciences (hierarchies or inequalities). For many, the latter concerns are the "payoff" of theories and research. That is, what specific actions might be helpful for minorities and the rest of society? Are social scientists successfully pursuing social justice and reducing inequalities, or do they need to go back to the drawing board?

Part 5, Future Policies and Global Issues, first considers whether or not the United States can keep going forward without compensating minorities for past wrongs. Two important international ethnic and racial issues are also debated, casting light on two empirical cases of global conflict (the Israeli-Palestinian conflict and U.S. involvement in easing the AIDS crisis in Africa) as well as on the role of the international community in being either part of the problem or part of the solution of global ethnic and racial issues. Within the United States, the pervasive war on drugs and crime continues to be, at least to some, a not-so-well-disguised war on minorities, especially Blacks. Does the drug war lead to the blaming of victims for society's oppressions, or does it help minorities?

From these arguments, you will learn how to look at controversial issues in a new way. Not only will you learn these new debates and facts pertaining to minorities and society's responses to them, but you will learn—to paraphrase Peter Berger—new ways of thinking about these issues, problems, and possible solutions.

Centre for Research in Ethnic Relations

The Centre for Research in Ethnic Relations is the major academic body in the United Kingdom for the research and teaching of matters concerning racism, migration, and ethnic relations.

http://www.warwick.ac.uk/fac/soc/CRER_RC/

Ethnic Research Guides

This resource of links and titles is a good starting point for researching ethnic history.

http://www.mypahoa.com/ethnic.htm

The Changing Status of the Black Athlete in the 20th Century United States

Black athletes have always been in the news, but their path to fame and fortune has never been easy. Only today are they beginning to gain their rightful place in sport's Hall of Fame. Despite this, problems still remain. In this article, John C. Walter, a professor of American ethnic studies and director of the Blacks in Sports Project at the University of Washington in Seattle, Washington, explains why.

http://www.johncarlos.com/walters.htm

American Civil Liberties Union Racial Equality Reference Site

The sites on this page provide comprehensive or unique resources relating to the work of the American Civil Liberties Union (ACLU) in the area of racial equality.

http://www.aclu.org/issues/racial/irre.html

The Simon Wiesenthal Center

The Simon Wiesenthal Center is an international center for Holocaust remembrance and the defense of human rights and the Jewish people.

http://www.wiesenthal.com

Holocaust

This excellent resource for background reading on the Holocaust is provided by Aish HaTorah, an apolitical, international network of Jewish educational centers that provides "opportunities for Jews of all backgrounds to discover the wisdom and beauty of their heritage in an atmosphere of open inquiry and mutual respect."

http://aish.com/holocaust/

PART 1

Thinking About and Researching Minorities

*W*hat are minority groups? How should research on minority groups be conducted? Do biological theories help standard sociological theories on ethnicity and race, or do they prevent understanding, as they did in the past? How do theories and scholarly research challenge as well as generate myths about minority groups? Do scientific terms, theories, and research sometimes contribute to the oppression of minorities by protecting the oppressors? The debates in this section provide ways to think about and study racial and ethnic relations.

- Should Outsider and Insider Researchers Be Expected to Get Similar Findings?

- Are Blacks "Natural Born" Athletes?

- Do Industrialization and Capitalism Cause Racial and Ethnic Inequalities?

- Have Scholars Ignored the Willing Participation of Germans in Killing Jews During the Holocaust?

ISSUE 1

Should Outsider and Insider Researchers Be Expected to Get Similar Findings?

YES: Robert K. Merton, from "Insiders and Outsiders: A Chapter in the Sociology of Knowledge," *American Journal of Sociology* (July 1972)

NO: Lelia Lomba De Andrade, from "Negotiating From the Inside: Constructing Racial and Ethnic Identity in Qualitative Research," *Journal of Contemporary Ethnography* (June 2000)

ISSUE SUMMARY

YES: Professor of twentieth-century American sociology Robert K. Merton rejects the idea that superior insights automatically result from membership in a specific group, or being an insider. He argues that outsiders, including trained scientists and strangers, often understand racial and ethnic groups better than insiders do.

NO: Lelia Lomba De Andrade, an assistant professor of sociology and Africana studies, draws from both her own ethnic and racial characteristics and her research as an insider of Cape Verdean Americans to argue that her identity enables her to acquire significant information that outsiders could not obtain.

S cientific research, including sociological, anthropological, and psychological, has traditionally been held to standards of objectivity. Such research must be rational, value free, detached, and apolitical. Early sociologists and other researchers of race and ethnicity took pride in their ability to transcend stereotyping, prejudices, and ignorance while much of the rest of the population were denouncing others simply because of their race, ethnicity, and other minority characteristics.

Until the end of World War II, most Americans took for granted what many now realize were stereotypical views of minorities, often because on the surface, these views "made sense." Some examples of these attitudes include "Women can never be doctors or soldiers because they are too frail," "Jews cannot be good farmers because they are city dwellers who cannot function in rural areas," and "Blacks could never run a business or be real leaders because they prefer to allow others to think for them."

Sociologists, anthropologists, and others eventually began to approach minorities scientifically in order to objectively understand them as well as to understand members of dominant groups. Such studies almost always transcended the unfair and inaccurate depictions of racial, religious, ethnic, and gender minorities. For example, studies showed that when women were given the same opportunities as men, they could perform as well as men in the roles of police officer, college professor, and leader. Also, when Blacks and Hispanics had the opportunities, they could perform as well as whites and Anglos economically, socially, and politically. Such findings helped to bring about significant changes in public attitudes, influence legal and economic changes, and legitimize the civil rights movement in the 1960s.

Social scientists were proud of their work, partly because of the contributions that their studies made to reducing misunderstandings and conflict among different racial and ethnic groups. In disseminating their findings, these scientists felt that they had destroyed the mean-spirited myths, superstitions, and ignorance upon which many Americans had based their attitudes toward racial, ethnic, and gender minorities.

Almost all early researchers in sociology, psychology, and anthropology were white males, although the latter discipline did produce several distinguished female scholars early on, such as Ruth Benedict and Margaret Mead. The scientific assumption was that "outsiders" (nonmembers of the group under study) who were properly trained, regardless of their race, gender, or background, could successfully research "insiders," such as members of radically different minority groups. Indeed, as Robert K. Merton suggests in the following selection, insiders will sometimes divulge personal information to sympathetic strangers that they would not share with members of their own group.

In radical contrast, Lelia Lomba De Andrade reflects an emerging variant of feminist epistemology (theory of and approach to knowledge) in the second selection. She rejects Merton's traditional scientific approach to researching minorities, maintaining that insiders are needed to understand others. However, she also tries to go beyond the usual discourse of "insider research is best" and to show that the issue is more complicated than that. De Andrade argues that even insiders have to negotiate with research subjects' mutual identities and understandings. She challenges standard "sympathetic introspection of others" as well as simplistic feminist and other insider strategies.

As you read this controversy, note that it is not only about researching minorities but that it is also a squaring off between the sociology of knowledge perspective of Merton (who significantly shaped its original contours) and emerging contrary epistemologies. Consider Merton's "privileged" view of researchers—their having unique scientific training. Is this perspective still functional? What helpful information does De Andrade's study give about Cape Verdeans as compared to information about herself? Can the two be separated? Whose epistemology is preferable, Merton's or De Andrade's?

Robert K. Merton  **YES**

Insiders and Outsiders: A Chapter in the Sociology of Knowledge

The sociology of knowledge has long been regarded as a complex and esoteric subject, remote from the urgent problems of contemporary social life. To some of us, it seems quite the other way. Especially in times of great social change, precipitated by acute social conflict and attended by much cultural disorganization and reorganization, the perspectives provided by the various sociologies of knowledge bear directly upon problems agitating the society. It is then that differences in the values, commitments, and intellectual orientations of conflicting groups become deepened into basic cleavages, both social and cultural. As the society becomes polarized, so do the contending claims to truth. At the extreme, an active reciprocal distrust between groups finds expression in intellectual perspectives that are no longer located within the same universe of discourse. The more deep-seated the mutual distrust, the more does the argument of the other appear so palpably implausible or absurd that one no longer inquires into its substance or logical structure to assess its truth claims. Instead, one confronts the other's argument with an entirely different sort of question: how does it happen to be advanced at all? Thought and its products thus become altogether functionalized, interpreted only in terms of their presumed social or economic or psychological sources and functions.... In place of the vigorous but intellectually disciplined mutual checking and rechecking that operates to a significant extent, though never of course totally, within the social institutions of science and scholarship, there develops a strain toward separatism, in the domain of the intellect as in the domain of society. Partly grounded mutual suspicion increasingly substitutes for partly grounded mutual trust. There emerge claims to group-based truth: Insider truths that counter Outsider untruths and Outsider truths that counter Insider untruths.

In our day, vastly evident social change is being initiated and funneled through a variety of social movements. These are formally alike in their objectives of achieving an intensified collective consciousness, a deepened solidarity and a new or renewed primary or total allegiance of their members to certain social identities, statuses, groups, or collectivities. Inspecting the familiar list of these movements centered on class, race, ethnicity, age, sex, religion, and

From Robert K. Merton, "Insiders and Outsiders: A Chapter in the Sociology of Knowledge," *American Journal of Sociology*, vol. 78 (July 1972). Copyright © 1972 by University of Chicago Press. Reprinted by permission. References and some notes omitted.

sexual disposition, we note two other instructive similarities between them. First, the movements are for the most part formed principally on the basis of ascribed rather than acquired statuses and identities, with eligibility for inclusion being in terms of who you are rather than what you are. . . . And second, the movements largely involve the public affirmation of pride in statuses and solidarity with collectivities that have long been socially and culturally downgraded, stigmatized, or otherwise victimized in the social system. As with group affiliations generally, these newly reinforced social identities find expression in various affiliative symbols of distinctive speech, bodily appearance, dress, public behavior patterns and, not least, assumptions and foci of thought.

The Insider Doctrine

Within this context of social change, we come upon the contemporary relevance of a long-standing problem in the sociology of knowledge: the problem of patterned differentials among social groups and strata in access to certain types of knowledge. In its strong form, the claim is put forward as a matter of epistemological principle that particular groups in each moment of history have *monopolistic access* to particular kinds of knowledge. In the weaker, more empirical form, the claim holds that some groups have *privileged access,* with other groups also being able to acquire that knowledge for themselves but at greater risk and cost.

Claims of this general sort have been periodically introduced. . . . [T]he Nazi *Gauleiter* of science and learning, Ernest Krieck, expressed an entire ideology in contrasting the access to authentic scientific knowledge by men of unimpeachable Aryan ancestry with the corrupt versions of knowledge accessible to non-Aryans. Krieck could refer without hesitation to "Protestant and Catholic science, German and Jewish science." . . . Nobel laureate in physics, Johannes Stark, could castigate . . . his . . . scientific contemporaries . . . for accepting what Stark described as "the Jewish physics of Einstein."

. . . [W]e need not review the array of elitist doctrines which have maintained that certain groups have, on biological or social grounds, monopolistic or privileged access to new knowledge. Differing in detail, the doctrines are alike in distinguishing between Insider access to knowledge and Outsider exclusion from it. . . .

Social Bases of Insider Doctrine

. . . [W]hite male Insiderism in American sociology during the past generations has largely been of the tacit or de facto rather than doctrinal or principled variety. It has simply taken the form of patterned expectations about the appropriate selection of specialties and of problems for investigation. The handful of Negro sociologists were in large part expected . . . to study problems of Negro life and relations between the races just as the handful of women sociologists were expected to study problems of women, principally as these related to marriage and the family.

In contrast to this de facto form of Insiderism, an explicitly doctrinal form has in recent years been put forward most clearly and emphatically by some black intellectuals.... The argument holds that, as a matter of social episte-mology, *only* black historians can truly understand black history, *only* black ethnologists can understand black culture, *only* black sociologists can under-stand the social life of blacks, and so on.... [T]he Insider doctrine maintains that there is a body of black history, black psychology, black ethnology, and black sociology which can be significantly advanced only by black scholars and social scientists.

... [T]his represents ... the balkanization of social science, with separate baronies kept exclusively in the hands of Insiders bearing their credentials in the shape of one or another ascribed status. Generalizing the specific claim, it would appear to follow that if only black scholars can understand blacks, then only white scholars can understand whites. Generalizing further from race to nation, it would then appear, for example, that only French scholars can understand French society and, of course, that only Americans, not their exter-nal critics, can truly understand American society. Once the basic principle is adopted, the list of Insider claims to a monopoly of knowledge becomes indef-initely expansible to all manner of social formations based on ascribed (and, by extension, on some achieved) statuses. It would thus seem to follow that only women can understand women—and men, men. On the same principle, youth alone is capable of understanding youth.... [O]nly Catholics, Catholics; Jews, Jews, and to halt the inventory of socially atomized claims to knowledge with a limiting case that on its face would seem to have some merit, it would then plainly follow that only sociologists are able to understand their fellow sociologists.

In all these applications, the doctrine of extreme Insiderism represents a new credentialism. This is the credentialism of ascribed status, in which under-standing becomes accessible only to the fortunate few or many who are to the manner born. In this respect, it contrasts with credentialism of achieved status that is characteristic of meritocratic systems.

Extreme Insiderism moves toward a doctrine of *group* methodological solipsism. [The belief that all one *really* knows is one's subjective experience is sometimes described as the "egocentric predicament."] In this form of solipsism, each group must in the end have a monopoly of knowledge about itself.... The Insider doctrine can be put in the vernacular with no great loss in meaning: you have to be one in order to understand one....

We can quickly pass over the trivial version of that rationale; the argument that the Outsider may be incompetent, given to quick and superficial forays into the group or culture under study and even unschooled in its language. That this kind of incompetence can be found is beyond doubt but it holds no principled interest for us. Foolish men (and women) or badly trained men (and women) are to be found everywhere.... But such cases of special ineptitude do not bear on the Insider *principle*. It is not merely that Insiders also have their share of incompetents. The Insider principle does not refer to stupidly designed and stupidly executed inquiries that happen to be made by stupid Outsiders; it maintains a more fundamental position. According to the doctrine of the Insider, the Outsider, no matter how careful and talented, is excluded in principle from gaining access to the social and cultural truth.

In short, the doctrine holds that the Outsider has a structurally imposed incapacity to comprehend alien groups, statuses, cultures, and societies. Unlike the Insider, the Outsider has neither been socialized in the group nor has engaged in the run of experience that makes up its life, and therefore cannot have the direct, intuitive sensitivity that alone makes empathic understanding possible.... [T]o take a specific expression of this thesis by Ralph W. Conant: "Whites are not and never will be as sensitive to the black community precisely because they are not part of that community." ...

A somewhat less stringent version of the doctrine maintains only that Insider and Outsider scholars have significantly different foci of interest.... [T]his weaker version argues only that they will not deal with the same questions and so will simply talk past one another. With the two versions combined, the extended version of the Insider doctrine can also be put in the vernacular: one must not only be one in order to understand one; one must be one in order to understand what is most worth understanding.

Clearly, the social epistemological doctrine of the Insider links up with what Sumner long ago defined as ethnocentrism: "the technical name for [the] view of things in which one's own group is the center of everything, and all others are scaled and rated with reference to it." ...

Theodore Caplow ... examined 33 different kinds of organizations—ranging from dance studios to Protestant and Catholic churches, from skid row missions to ... university departments—and found that members overestimated the prestige of their organization some "eight times as often as they underestimated it" (when compared with judgments by Outsiders).... [W]hile members tended to disagree with Outsiders about the standing of their own organization, they tended to agree with them about the prestige of the other organizations in the same set. These findings can be taken as something of a sociological parable. In these matters at least, the judgments of "Insiders" are best trusted when they assess groups other than their own; that is, when members of groups judge as Outsiders rather than as Insiders.... Ethnocentrism ... becomes intensified under specifiable conditions of acute social conflict. When a nation, race, ethnic group, or any other powerful collectivity has long extolled its own admirable qualities and, expressly or by implication, deprecated the qualities of others, it invites and provides the potential for counterethnocentrism. And when a once largely powerless collectivity acquires a socially validated sense of growing power, its members experience an intensified need for self-affirmation. Under such circumstances, collective self-glorification, found in some measure among all groups, becomes a predictable and intensified counterresponse to long-standing belittlement from without.... What is being proposed here is that the epistemological claims of the Insider to monopolistic or privileged access to social truth develop under particular social and historical conditions. Social groups or strata on the way up develop a revolutionary élan. The new thrust to a larger share of power and control over their social and political environment finds various expressions, among them claims to a unique access to knowledge about their history, culture, and social life.

On this interpretation, we can understand why this Insider doctrine does not argue for a Black Physics, Black Chemistry, Black Biology, or Black Technology. For the new will to control their fate deals with the social environment, not the environment of nature. . . . [T]he black Insider doctrine adopts an essentially social-environmental rationale, not a biologically genetic one. . . .

With varying degrees of intent, groups in conflict want to make their interpretation the prevailing one of how things were and are and will be. The critical measure of success occurs when the interpretation moves beyond the boundaries of the ingroup to be accepted by Outsiders. At the extreme, it then gives rise, through identifiable processes of reference-group behavior, to the familiar case of the converted Outsider validating himself, in his own eyes and in those of others, by becoming even more zealous than the Insiders in adhering to the doctrine of the group with which he wants to identify himself, if only symbolically. He then becomes more royalist than the king, more papist than the pope. Some white social scientists, for example, vicariously and personally guilt ridden over centuries of white racism, are prepared to outdo the claims of the group they would symbolically join. They are ready even to surrender their hard-won expert knowledge if the Insider doctrine seems to require it. . . .

The black Insider doctrine links up with the historically developing social structure in still another way. The dominant social institutions in this country have long treated the racial identity of individuals as actually if not doctrinally relevant to all manner of situations in every sphere of life. For generations, neither blacks nor whites, though with notably differing consequences, were permitted to forget their race. *This treatment of a social status (or identity) as relevant when intrinsically it is functionally irrelevant constitutes the very core of social discrimination.* As the once firmly rooted systems of discriminatory institutions and prejudicial ideology began to lose their hold, this meant that increasingly many judged the worth of ideas on their merits, not in terms of their racial pedigree.

What the Insider doctrine of the most militant blacks proposes on the level of social structure is to adopt the salience of racial identity in every sort of role and situation, a pattern so long imposed upon the American Negro, and to make that identity a total commitment issuing from within the group rather than one imposed upon it from without. By thus affirming the universal saliency of race and by redefining race as an abiding source of pride rather than stigma, the Insider doctrine in effect models itself after doctrine long maintained by white racists.

Neither this component of the Insider doctrine nor the statement on its implications is at all new. Almost a century ago, Frederick Douglass hinged his observations along these lines on the distinction between collective and individual self-images based on ascribed and achieved status:

> One of the few errors to which we are clinging most persistently and, as I think, most mischievously has come into great prominence of late. It is the cultivation and stimulation among us of a sentiment which we are pleased to call race pride. I find it in all our books, papers, and speeches. For my part I see no superiority or inferiority in race or color. Neither the one nor the other is a proper source of pride or complacency. Our race and color are not

of our own choosing. We have no volition in the case one way or another. The only excuse for pride in individuals or races is in the fact of their own achievements.... I see no benefit to be derived from this everlasting exhortation of speakers and writers among us to the cultivation of race pride. On the contrary, I see in it a positive evil. It is building on a false foundation....

Just as conditions of war between nations have long produced a strain toward hyperpatriotism among national ethnocentrics, so current intergroup conflicts have produced a strain toward hyperloyalty among racial or sex or age or religious ethnocentrics. Total commitment easily slides from the solidarity doctrine of "our group, right or wrong" to the morally and intellectually preemptive doctrine of "our group, always right, never wrong." ...

Social Structure of Insiders and Outsiders

... In structural terms, we are all, of course, both Insiders and Outsiders, members of some groups and, sometimes derivatively, not of others; occupants of certain statuses which thereby exclude us from occupying other cognate statuses. Obvious as this basic fact of social structure is, its implications for Insider and Outsider epistemological doctrines are apparently not nearly as obvious. Else, these doctrines would not presuppose, as they typically do, that human beings in socially differentiated societies can be sufficiently located in terms of a single social status, category, or group affiliation—black or white, men or women, under 30 or older—or of several such categories, taken seriatim [in a series] rather than conjointly. This neglects the crucial fact of social structure that individuals have not a single status but a status set: a complement of variously interrelated statuses which interact to affect both their behavior and perspectives.

The structural fact of status sets, in contrast to statuses taken one at a time, introduces severe theoretical problems for total Insider (and Outsider) doctrines of social epistemology. The array of status sets in a population means that aggregates of individuals share some statuses and not others; or, to put this in context, that they typically confront one another simultaneously as Insiders and Outsiders. Thus, if only whites can understand whites and blacks, blacks, and only men can understand men, and women, women, this gives rise to the paradox which severely limits both premises: for it then turns out, by assumption, that some Insiders are excluded from understanding other Insiders with white women being condemned not to understand white men, and black men, not to understand black women, and so through the various combinations of status subsets....

This symptomatic exercise in status-set analysis may be enough to indicate that the idiomatic expression of total Insider doctrine—one must be one in order to understand one—is deceptively simple and sociologically fallacious (just as ... is the case with the total Outsider doctrine). For, from the sociological perspective of the status set, "one" is not a man *or* a black *or* an adolescent *or* a Protestant, *or* self-defined and socially defined as middle class, and so on. Sociologically, "one" is, of course, all of these and, depending on the size of the status set, much more.... [T]he greater the number and variety of group affiliations and statuses distributed among individuals in a society, the smaller, on the average, the number of individuals having precisely the same social configuration....

[I]t is precisely the individual differences among scientists and scholars that are often central to the development of the discipline. They often involve the differences between good scholarship and bad; between imaginative contributions to science and pedestrian ones; between the consequential ideas and stillborn ones. In arguing for the monopolistic access to knowledge, Insider doctrine can make no provision for individual variability that extends beyond the boundaries of the ingroup which alone can develop sound and fruitful ideas....

Yet sociologically, there is nothing fixed about the boundaries separating Insiders from Outsiders. As situations involving different values arise, different statuses are activated and the lines of separation shift. Thus, for a large number of white Americans, Joe Louis was a member of an outgroup. But when Louis defeated the Nazified Max Schmeling, many of the same white Americans promptly redefined him as a member of the (national) ingroup. National self-esteem took precedence over racial separatism. That this sort of drama in which changing situations activate differing statuses in the status set is played out in the domain of the intellect as well is the point of Einstein's ironic observation in an address at the Sorbonne: "If my theory of relativity is proved successful, Germany will claim me as a German and France will declare that I am a citizen of the world. Should my theory prove untrue, France will say that I am a German and Germany will declare that I am a Jew." ...

Insiders as "Outsiders"

... [W]hat some Insiders profess as Insiders they apparently reject as Outsiders. For example, when advocates of black Insider doctrine engage in analysis of "white society," trying to assay its power structure or to detect its vulnerabilities, they seem to deny in practice what they affirm in doctrine. At any rate, their behavior testifies to the assumption that it is possible for self-described "Outsiders" to diagnose and to understand what they describe as an alien social structure and culture....

The strong version of the Insider doctrine, with its epistemological claim to a monopoly of certain kinds of knowledge, runs counter, of course, to a long history of thought....

[First Georg] Simmel and then... Max Weber... adopted the memorable phrase: "one need not be Caesar in order to understand Caesar." In making this claim, they rejected the extreme Insider thesis which asserts in effect that one *must* be Caesar in order to understand him just as they rejected the extreme Outsider thesis that one must *not* be Caesar in order to understand him.... The Insider argues that the authentic understanding of group life can be achieved only by those who are directly engaged as members in the life of the group. Taken seriously, the doctrine puts in question the validity of just about all historical writing.... If direct engagement in the life of a group is essential to understanding it, then the only authentic history is contemporary history, written in fragments by those most fully involved in making inevitably limited portions of it. Rather than constituting only the raw materials of history, the documents prepared by engaged Insiders become all there is to history. But once the historian elects to write the history of a time other than his own, even the most dedicated Insider, of the national, sex, age, racial, ethnic, or religious variety, becomes the Outsider, condemned to error and misunderstanding.

Writing some 20 years ago in another connection, Claude Lévi-Strauss noted the parallelism between history and ethnography. Both subjects, he observed,

> are concerned with societies *other* than the one in which we live. Whether this *otherness* is due to remoteness in time (however slight) or to remoteness in space, or even to cultural heterogeneity, is of secondary importance compared to the basic similarity of perspective. All that the historian or ethnographer can do, and all that we can expect of either of them, is to enlarge a specific experience to the dimensions of a more general one, which thereby becomes accessible as *experience* to men of another country or another epoch. And in order to succeed, both historian and ethnographer, must have the same qualities: skill, precision, a sympathetic approach and objectivity.

... Simmel develops the thesis that the stranger, not caught up in commitments to the group, can more readily acquire the strategic role of the relatively objective inquirer. "He is freer, practically and theoretically," notes Simmel, "he surveys conditions with less prejudice; his criteria for them are more general and more objective ideals: he is not tied down in his action by habit, piety, and precedent." ... It is the stranger, too, who finds what is familiar to the group significantly unfamiliar and so is prompted to raise questions for inquiry less apt to be raised at all by Insiders.

... Outsiders are sought out to observe social institutions and cultures on the premise that they are more apt to do so with detachment. Thus, in the first decade of this century, the Carnegie Foundation for the Advancement of Teaching, in its search for someone to investigate the condition of medical schools, reached out to appoint Abraham Flexner, after he had admitted never before having been inside a medical school. It was a matter of policy to select a total Outsider who, as it happened, produced the uncompromising Report which did much to transform the state of American medical education at the time.

Later, casting about for a scholar who might do a thoroughgoing study of the Negro in the United States, the Carnegie Corporation searched for an Outsider, ... with the quest ending ... with the selection of Gunnar Myrdal [a Swedish social scientist]. In the preface to *An American Dilemma*,* Myrdal (pp. xviii–xix) reflected on his status as an Outsider who, in his words, "had never been subject to the strains involved in living in a black-white society" and who

---

* [*An American Dilemma* (1944) was a benchmark study of race relations.—Ed.]

"as a stranger to the problem . . . has had perhaps a greater awareness of the extent to which human valuations everywhere enter into our scientific discussion of the Negro problem."

Reviews of the book repeatedly alluded to the degree of detachment from entangling loyalties that seemed to come from Myrdal's being an Outsider. J. S. Redding (1944), for one, observed that "as a European, Myrdal had no American sensibilities to protect. He hits hard with fact and interpretation." Robert S. Lynd (1944), for another, saw it as a prime merit of this Outsider that he was free to find out for himself "without any side glances as to what was politically expedient." And for a third, Frank Tannenbaum (1944) noted that Myrdal brought "objectivity in regard to the special foibles and shortcomings in American life. As an outsider, he showed the kind of objectivity which would seem impossible for one reared within the American scene." Even later criticism of Myrdal's work—for example, the comprehensive critique by Cox (1948, chap. 23)—does not attribute imputed errors in interpretation to his having been an Outsider.

Two observations should be made on the Myrdal episode. First, in the judgment of critical minds, the Outsider, far from being excluded from the understating of an alien society, was able to bring needed perspectives to it. And second, that Myrdal, wanting to have both Insider and Outsider perspectives, expressly drew into his circle of associates in the study such Insiders, engaged in the study of Negro life and culture and of race relations, as E. Franklin Frazier, Arnold Rose, Ralph Bunche, Melville Herskovits, Otto Klineberg, J. G. St. Clair Drake, Guy B. Johnson, and Doxey A. Wilkerson. . . .

The cumulative point of this variety of intellectual and institutional cases is not—and this needs to be repeated with all possible emphasis—is *not* a proposal to replace the extreme Insider doctrine by an extreme and equally vulnerable Outsider doctrine. The intent is, rather, to transform the original question altogether. . . . Just as with the process of competition generally, so with the competition of ideas. Competing or conflicting groups take over ideas and procedures from one another, thereby denying in practice the rhetoric of total incompatibility. Even in the course of social polarization, conceptions with cognitive value are utilized all apart from their source. Concepts of power structure, co-optation, the dysfunctions of established institutions and findings associated with these concepts have for some time been utilized by social scientists, irrespective of their social or political identities. . . . Such diffusion of ideas across the boundaries of groups and statuses has long been noted. In one of his more astute analyses, Mannheim (1952) states the general case for the emergence and spread of knowledge that transcends even profound conflicts between groups:

> Syntheses owe their existence to the same social process that brings about polarization; groups take over the modes of thought and intellectual achievements of their adversaries under the simple law of 'competition on the basis of achievement.' . . . In the socially-differentiated thought process, even the opponent is ultimately forced to adopt those categories and forms of thought which are most appropriate in a given type of world order. In the economic sphere, one of the possible results of competition is that one competitor is compelled to catch up with the other's technological

advances. In just the same way, whenever groups compete for having their interpretation of reality accepted as the correct one, it may happen that one of the groups takes over from the adversary some fruitful hypothesis or category—anything that promises cognitive gain....

From Social Conflict to Intellectual Controversy

... Insider and Outsider perspectives can converge, in spite of such differences, through reciprocal adoption of ideas and the developing of complementary and overlapping foci of attention in the formulation of scientific problems. But these intellectual potentials for synthesis are often curbed by social processes that divide scholars and scientists. Internal divisions and polarizations in the society at large often stand in the way of realizing those potentials....

When a transition from social conflict to intellectual controversy is achieved, when the perspectives of each group are taken seriously enough to be carefully examined rather than rejected out of hand, there can develop trade-offs between the distinctive strengths and weaknesses of Insider and Outsider perspectives that enlarge the chances for a sound and relevant understanding of social life....

If indeed we have distinctive contributions to make to social knowledge in our roles as Insiders or Outsiders—and it should be repeated that all of us are both Insiders and Outsiders in various social situations—then those contributions probably link up with a long-standing distinction between two major kinds of knowledge, a basic distinction that is blurred in the often ambiguous use of the word "understanding." In the language of William James (1932, pp. 11–13), ... this is the distinction between "acquaintance with" and "knowledge about." The one involves direct familiarity with phenomena that is expressed in depictive representations; the other involves more abstract formulations which do not at all "resemble" what has been directly experienced (Merton 1968, p. 545)....

These distinct and connected kinds of understanding may turn out to be distributed, in varying mix, among Insiders and Outsiders. The introspective meanings of experience within a status or a group may be more readily accessible, for all the seemingly evident reasons, to those who have shared part or all of that experience. But authentic awareness, even in the sense of acquaintance with, is not guaranteed by social affiliation, as the concept of false consciousness is designed to remind us. Determinants of social life—for an obvious example, ecological patterns and processes—are not necessarily evident to those directly engaged in it. In short, sociological understanding involves much more than acquaintance with. It includes an empirically confirmable comprehension of the conditions and often complex processes in which people are caught up without much awareness of what is going on. To analyze and understand these requires a theoretical and technical competence which, as such, transcends one's status as Insider or Outsider. The role of social scientist concerned with achieving knowledge about society requires enough detachment and trained capacity to know how to assemble and assess the evidence without regard for what the analysis seems to imply about the worth of one's group....

The acceptance of criteria of craftsmanship and integrity in science and learning cuts across differences in the social affiliations and loyalties of scientists and scholars. Commitment to the intellectual values dampens group-induced pressures to advance the interests of groups at the expense of these values and of the intellectual product.

The consolidation of group-influenced perspectives and the autonomous values of scholarship is exemplified in observations by John Hope Franklin who, for more than a quarter-century, has been engaged in research on the history of American Negroes from their ancient African beginnings to the present.... Franklin's application of exacting, autonomous and universalistic standards culminates in a formulation that, once again, transcends the statuses of Insiders and Outsiders:

> ... It takes a person of stout heart, great courage, and uncompromising honesty to look the history of this country squarely in the face and tell it like it is.... And when this approach prevails, the history of the United States and the history of the black man can be written and taught by any person, white, black, or otherwise. For there is nothing so irrelevant in telling the truth as the color of a man's skin.

Lelia Lomba De Andrade

Negotiating From the Inside

This article provides a critical analysis of the role of the "insider" researcher in qualitative fieldwork in race and ethnicity. The analysis is based on research conducted on the construction of racial and ethnic identity in the Cape Verdean American community of southeastern New England. Reflections are presented on the various ways that the researcher's status as an "insider" was evaluated and negotiated during fieldwork. It is suggested that these negotiations reveal the manner in which group members define the boundaries of the group, the attributes they associate with it, and the meaning of the group itself. This interpretation of insider status, as involving complex and ongoing definitions and negotiations of group membership, highlights the way that researchers and participants are simultaneously engaged in the construction of race and ethnicity.

There is a serious disjuncture between qualitative research methodology and the dominant conceptual perspective of race and ethnicity in sociology....

In large part, this concept-method disjuncture can be traced to significant methodological developments in other related disciplines in the academy. In the 1970s and 1980s, prompted mostly by black, Chicano/a and feminist studies, social researchers directed more critical attention to the role of researchers relative to their community of informants. In sociology, and in racial and ethnic studies in particular, this type of analysis emerged as the "insider/outsider" debate.

The insider/outsider debate addressed the qualitative difference between the work conducted by insiders, those who share membership with the social group studied, and outsiders. It was particularly concerned with research conducted on minority communities and focused on issues of power and authority in the field. Working within this framework, the debate addressed the relationship between the researchers and participants in terms of access and rapport in three primary ways. First, it questioned how the race and ethnicity of the researcher vis-à-vis the participants influenced interaction and participation. Second, it examined the impact of this dynamic on the quality of the research conducted, in terms of how the research topic was conceptualized or framed and the interpretation of findings. Finally, it questioned the role of race relations in the discipline itself, calling attention to the predominance of white

From Lelia Lomba De Andrade, "Negotiating From the Inside: Constructing Racial and Ethnic Identity in Qualitative Research," *Journal of Contemporary Ethnography*, vol. 29, no. 3 (June 2000). Copyright © 2000 by Sage Publications, Inc. Reprinted by permission of Sage Publications, Inc. Some notes and references omitted.

researchers in the production of scholarship about minority experiences with race and ethnicity. Because this debate limited analysis to a single dimension of researcher and participant identity, it stalled on the issue of whether these identity relations made research invalid, better, or just different.

Recently, methodological analyses of the relationship between researchers and participants have taken a more critical form. Attention has shifted to examining how the multiple roles and perspective of the researcher shape the research process. Again, feminist methodologists have generated much of this sociological conversation as their scholarship has become more attentive to the multiple realities of women with various class, racial, ethnic, and sexual statuses. From these critiques emerged evaluations of the manner in which the intersecting social statuses of the researcher and the research participant influence what is said, what is heard, and how it is interpreted.

Some feminist scholars have carried this work into their analyses of research methods in racial and ethnic studies. For example, Maxine Baca Zinn and Patricia Hill Collins drew on this perspective to inform their critiques of the insider/outsider debate. They challenged the notion of the insider as a single dimensional status, while emphasizing the significance of race and ethnicity in qualitative research. Since then, other feminist scholars of race and ethnicity ... have drawn on these methodological developments to problematize the role of racial and ethnic identity in research. They too have called attention to the multiple dimensions of identity and its dynamic role in the research process. Unfortunately, apart from these developments, qualitative research methodology in racial and ethnic studies has remained somewhat static and underdeveloped (Stanfield 1993). It continues to give passing recognition to the impact of race and ethnicity in research but has failed to offer a more complex analysis of this phenomenon. Meanwhile, in work focusing specifically on feminist methodology, scholars have continued to take on the issue of how race and ethnicity influence the research process. This work has been particularly useful in recognizing that race and ethnicity are a constant and dynamic presence in fieldwork in ways that may or may not be explicit.

In this article, I extend this line of analysis to research methodology in racial and ethnic studies. More specifically, I use it to examine the status of the insider, which is predicated on the racial and ethnic identity of the researcher in relation to research participants. I argue that because race and ethnicity are ever-present factors in field research, insider/outsider status is also an ongoing presence or dynamic in the research process. Using data from my work as a Cape Verdean American researcher in the Cape Verdean American community, I reflect on how my insider status was negotiated in the course of doing research. I suggest that as participants evaluated my status in relation to the group, they also gave this group membership meaning and used it to define the boundaries of the group. By calling attention to the multiple negotiated dimensions of insider status in racial and ethnic research, I highlight how race and ethnicity, as mediated through insider status, is constructed and becomes a central dynamic in the research process. In this way, I bring the dominant conceptual perspective of race and ethnicity as social constructs into alignment with the methodological trend of examining the role of the insider.

Context: Studying Cape Verdean Identity

I draw my analysis from my experiences doing research on the construction of racial and ethnic identity among Cape Verdean Americans in southeastern New England. In this research, I use an approach informed by symbolic interactionist and social constructionist theoretical perspectives. That is, I view racial and ethnic identity as having complex meanings that are produced in social interaction. They are represented by collections of symbols or signifiers that include such things as physical attributes, as well as behaviors, family relations, group rituals, and even clothing. Social actors read and manipulate these signifiers in the course of interaction as they attempt to categorize themselves and others in a kind of social negotiation. Because race and ethnicity are sensitive to context or situations, social actors may change their selection and presentation of racial and ethnic signifiers as they move into various social contexts. However, social actors do not arbitrarily or freely select the signifiers of race and ethnicity or create them themselves. Rather, the collection of signifiers associated with racial and ethnic categories is itself the product of social forces and is informed by socio-historic and institutional processes. Following this, race and ethnicity are produced through institutional and interactional processes. Social actors "do" racial and ethnic presentations by drawing on and assembling signifiers that are available to them and which they interpret as meaningful to the social context. In doing so, they reinforce, reshape, or construct the meaning of race and ethnicity.

Cape Verdean Americans engage in this process of racial and ethnic identity construction in a very self-conscious or self-aware manner. They perceive their fit into common notions of racial and ethnic categories as problematic. This is in part rooted in their perspective of the origins of Cape Verdean people. The Cape Verdean homeland, Cabo Verde, is an archipelago located about four hundred miles off the northwest coast of Africa. The Portuguese settled the islands with exiles and entrepreneurs from their own country along with members of various other European and West African ethnic groups. The Cape Verdean population emerged out of this multiethnic, multinational setting, and today the majority of the population claims mixed European and African ancestry. This diverse history is the source of many of the signifiers Cape Verdean Americans use to construct their identity. As on the island and in other parts of their diaspora, Cape Verdeans in America employ multiple and shifting methods of labeling themselves in racial and ethnic terms. They select and interpret some combination of elements of Cape Verdean racial and ethnic history to label themselves, such as Portuguese, black, black-Portuguese, white, mulatto, Moreno, mixed, and multiracial, or avoid racial labeling by using terms such as "aracial," or simply Cape Verdean. This richness in modes of self-identification lends a level of complexity to Cape Verdean constructions of identity. . . .

I sought to investigate the manner in which Cape Verdean Americans define and employ these complex notions of racial and ethnic identity. I was interested in how Cape Verdean Americans manage these presentations and negotiate identities that are meaningful to themselves and others in interaction.

In 1991, following a preliminary period of investigation, I moved into a Cape Verdean enclave just outside of Providence, Rhode Island, and began a phase of intensive participant observation. During this period, I attended a range of community cultural events including dances and political functions, such as visits from Cape Verdean dignitaries, and independence celebrations. I also visited various Cape Verdean cultural clubs and organizations, as well as libraries and churches in the core community....

I continued this participant observation while I conducted forty-eight interviews in various Cape Verdean enclaves located in or near the cities of Providence, Rhode Island, and New Bedford, Massachusetts. I interviewed twenty-five women and twenty-three men between the ages of twenty-one and eighty-six. These participants were second and third generation Cape Verdean Americans as well as immigrants who had spent most of their lives in America. The interviews were semi-structured, using open-ended questions that I had developed during the preceding phases of my research. They ranged in length from approximately forty-five minutes to as long as six hours.

Crioula and Sociologist

I entered the field with some trepidation.... I had grown up in the Rhode Island and Massachusetts Cape Verdean enclaves, and both sides of my family had come from Cabo Verde. From these experiences, I had an impression of Cape Verdean racial and ethnic identity as being a popular, but highly controversial and emotional subject. My preliminary interviews and participant observation reinforced this impression. I found that racial and ethnic identity was a common topic of discussion at Cape Verdean gatherings. The Cape Verdeans that I encountered in my fieldwork often approached the topic with very strong opinions and with little flexibility. They reported that this issue was the source of friction in families, ended friendships, and was even the cause of failed marriages.

Of course, with such a sensitive and highly charged topic, I worried about how people in the community would respond to my questions. I thought, however, from my training in qualitative research methods, that my insider status would facilitate this process. I knew that I had insider knowledge about some of the forms that identity issues took in the community. For example, I knew I should never assume that family members shared the same racial and ethnic identity and that each of the islands of Cabo Verde is commonly associated with a distinctive heritage that could be used as shorthand for race (and ethnicity). I expected this knowledge would help me recognize some of the pitfalls or landmarks of this research that an outsider researcher might not see. I also thought that it would be fairly obvious to respondents that I was presenting myself as Cape Verdean; my family names alone would lead many people in the community to recognize me as a member of the group. I assumed that this would make establishing my insider status a bit easier and, by extension, facilitate rapport and comfort around such a sensitive topic.

What I found, however, was that these very things that I imagined would help my research confounded the process in multiple ways. I quickly discovered that my insider status complicated the interview situation in ways that I had not read about or imagined. I learned that my Cape Verdean identity was negotiated and constructed as part of the interview process and that it challenged, changed, and distorted the interview subject in ways that were sometimes visible, sometimes not.

One of the first ways that I became aware of how my insider status would be defined and negotiated in the research process was in the initial response of the participants to the interview. Typically I began the interviews by briefly describing my vision of the research project. I told participants that I was most interested in their experiences as Cape Verdeans and gave details about confidentiality and interview format. . . .

The participants in the research responded in ways that challenged me to reevaluate my interpretation of the significance of my role as a Cape Verdean researcher. In some cases, their responses generally conformed to patterns highlighted in insider literature. Their assessment of my group membership or insider status appeared to include an assumption that I shared their knowledge and experience. This eased our transition into the more sensitive, intimate topic of racial and ethnic identity. What I wasn't prepared for was just how quickly we would move into these topics and the ways in which my identity would become part of the text. . . . [M]y interview with Carlos provides a good example of this pattern of response. Early in the interview, I asked Carlos about the structure of his household and community when he was growing up. . . .

C: . . . [W]hat happens is that most of our parents that came from the old country, they all knew each other even though they came from the different islands. So actually there was no separation. We were all family. And here we are; I'm going to be 66 years old and that hasn't changed. I think that what happens is that something happens, it's a bonding that happens in families. That was our experience and even when we don't see each other for years, you know, when we see each other it's like Christmas all over again. That feeling is always there. If that's what you mean by extended family, we certainly have extended family. . . . So when you walk around and you see another Cape Verdean you say, "Hey, what's happening!" You know, it's nice. That's how it is. That's how it's always been. My hopes are that our kids, like you, my children, my grandchildren, it will rub off, so that we can keep this thing going. Because it's beautiful.

L: Yeah that's great. That's what my research is . . . I'm hoping to do. . . .

C: And not only that, but you see, Cape Verdeans, another thing about Cape Verdeans, we come from black, brown, white, it's a mixed race. Right from the islands, and so we, our parents come over here and they don't have any idea about not being better than anybody else or worse, or lower than anybody else . . . they're people! From day one, sweetheart, you know what I mean? We have an identity. And we know who we are . . . you see? So I think that it made it much easier for Cape Verdeans to assimilate and to be part of what's happening here in this country.

Two features of this excerpt are particularly notable in regard to the influence of insider status on the interview. First, it is obvious from this quote that Carlos recognized me as an insider and incorporated me into his reflections about Cape Verdean racial and ethnic identity. In this and in many other interviews, I was taken aback by the centrality of my identity in the discussions and how the reading of it could influence the direction of the interview. Despite the fact that he had met me only a few minutes prior, Carlos spoke freely and openly about his life and thoughts about being Cape Verdean. He made his recognition of my group membership central to the text and explicit with references to me in his examples and the pronouns he used. The openness and directness of his response seems to be related to his recognition of me as part of this Cape Verdean "family." It was grounded in an assumption that as such we shared experience and perspective.

The second notable element of this excerpt is related to this, although in a subtler dynamic. Clearly, Carlos did more here than simply describe the cultural practices of the community. He also explained his interpretation of the group. In addition to the cultural characteristics of the group, he described Cape Verdeans in racial terms, as a mix of black, brown, and white. With this definition of the group, Carlos constructed his racial and ethnic identity as such. Because he recognized me as a Cape Verdean, he simultaneously defined or constructed my identity. My responses and incorporation in these discussions meant that I was also engaging with him in the construction of the group and our racial and ethnic identities.

In other situations, the participants also incorporated my self-presentation into their construction of the group, but in a somewhat different manner.... My "Cape Verdean-ness" was relatively obvious to participants and it made the appearance of neutrality impossible. Clearly, as a Cape Verdean I had engaged in a similar process. The question, for these participants and for me, was how my understanding of being Cape Verdean related to theirs.

Because of this question, the process of negotiating my identity became a consistent and important theme in the research process. The participants took cues about my interpretation of Cape Verdean racial and ethnic identity from my self-presentation and they reacted to these cues. As a result, I was concerned with how my presentation would influence the interactions in these interviews. For example, their reaction to or interpretation of my physical appearance was a constant concern. Long before I had initiated this research, I had made choices about my physical presentation that challenged some traditional aesthetics of Cape Verdean Americans. I wore my curly, somewhat frizzy, hair in a "natural" style. In addition, I often got quite tanned in the summer and my normally light, coffee-colored complexion darkened to a medium brown color. I knew that participants would interpret this arrangement of physical attributes as a marker of my own understanding of Cape Verdean racial and ethnic identity. Consequently, it could have significant impact on my relationship with them. Participants might read my "dark" skin and "untamed," *cabesa sec* (dry, wild hair) as a more black or African interpretation of Cape Verdean identity. For those who embraced a more European conception of Cape Verdean identity, this might produce some reluctance or barriers in the interview. On the other hand, by wearing my hair straighter and avoiding a tan, I could appear to these participants as one of the same. In that case, I might have more success establishing rapport....

My appearance was not simply used as a passive subtext that influenced my interaction with participants. It became a dynamic part of the text, used as a reference in respondents' stories and descriptions of Cape Verdean life. An example of this process is apparent in my interview with Joe. He described his wife's experiences growing up Cape Verdean and the problematic interaction in his city between the larger African American community and the Cape Verdean community.

> *L:* Did she think of herself as Cape Verdean? Did she call herself Cape Verdean?
>
> *J:* Yes. Her name was Smedo....
>
> *L:* Oh yes ... that's a big Cape Verdean family.
>
> *J:* Yes. And she had the same problem... I don't know if you know... maybe you might have had the same problems... when you get around the blacks... the American blacks... they look at you and treat you differently....
>
> *L:* Mmmm....
>
> *J:* Well, she had that problem. She had that problem in New York, because she had... she was like your complexion with long hair... and she had trouble with black girls....

As these examples suggest, the participants used my appearance as a reference point in their stories. Drawing on their interpretations of my appearance, they solicited my opinions and made assumptions about the experiences and perspectives I might have. In doing so, they made me an active participant in their descriptions of identity construction, and they suggested that they viewed me as an insider.

Obviously, the participants' reading of my presentation and their interpretation of my identity were not simply limited to looking at the way that I wore my hair or my skin color. They read a variety of attributes, such as body type, facial features, manner of speech, and dress as signifiers of my racial and ethnic identity. In addition, they also described using a traditional Cape Verdean cultural perspective to read and interpret these attributes. That is, they associated combinations of attributes with specific islands of Cabo Verde and the particular racial and ethnic character associated with each of them.[1] For example, they may have interpreted my manner of speaking as suggesting that I have a black identity, or they may have associated the combination of my facial features and coloring with the island of Brava and interpreted my identity as relatively Portuguese or white. However, this process of reading and interpreting attributes was far more complicated and subtle than these examples imply. Complex combinations and intersections of multiple attributes gave clues to my interpretation of Cape Verdean identity. The participants read these attributes simultaneously and used them to interpret my racial and ethnic presentation....

Emergent Expertise

In addition to my physical appearance, the participants also interpreted my group membership in terms of who and what I knew in the Cape Verdean community. In almost every interview, we engaged in a process of listing the names of community members or important moments in Cape Verdean cultural history. Often these exchanges extended beyond listing to include related questions about my family. They occurred in various points in the interviews, and it frequently seemed as though they would continue until we finally established that there was some Cape Verdean person or event in common in our lives....

[E]arly in the research process I responded to these questions with vague descriptions of my parents and their history in the community. As the research project developed, however, I sought more information about my family history and social connections in the community and grew more adept at facilitating this locating process. Eventually, I was able to locate myself with more culturally significant and meaningful community referents. I began to refer to myself using the language of Cape Verdean identity.... As a result, the research also included a process of socialization in which I learned to act and eventually became more Cape Verdean in my presentation of self. In this sense, the research project became a collaboration in which the participants evaluated my presentation while teaching me how best to construct it.

Another aspect of this process of locating me within the Cape Verdean community seemed to involve an evaluation of my Cape Verdean identity. Many participants questioned me about my knowledge of the Cape Verdean community, history, and culture. This seemed to me to be another gatekeeping procedure. The participants evaluated my validity as a Crioula researcher and used this evaluation to gage the degree of access to information about Cape Verdeans that they would grant me....

Had I not been able to conform to the participants' expectations of the attributes required of group members, I would have been disqualified. That is, I would have been left in a precarious situation of having an invalid racial and ethnic identity (Omi and Winant 1994). The opportunities for my disqualification seemed to abound in this research project. At times, it seemed to require that I have personal mastery of the very topic that I was investigating, the complexity of Cape Verdean racial and ethnic identity construction.

Insider Status: Turning the Tables on the Research Process

There was also another dimension of risk built into this project, one that I was not prepared for and only became aware of later in the research. As an insider, information about me, my family, and my place in the community became part of the research process. Because it was advocated as part of a feminist methodological strategy, I did not hesitate to disclose considerable amounts of personal information. However, because I had a distinct, previous relationship to the community, this disclosure had implications in terms of my privacy and separateness as a person beyond my role as a researcher. I was very much aware that the evaluation of me as a Cape Verdean by my research participants would reflect on members of my family and me beyond the completion of the project itself.

Disclosure also reinforced the duality of my role in the community, as a kind of outsider-within. My role as a researcher, and thus an outsider, enabled participants to ask me questions about my personal feelings, life, and identity that would not be appropriate in everyday situations in the Cape Verdean community. The outsider role thus required a level of disclosure reserved for more intimate relations. At the same time, my group membership made the information that I was asked to provide significant to the participants in different ways. This information was not about an "other" or an outsider. It was information about another insider, a community member. This dynamic made the research relationship equalizing in a different way than that advocated by feminist methodologists with outsider status. My dual status gave the participants information that would not be available to them in other outsider research situations and, in this way, gave the participants additional power.

As a result, the participants were able to, and often did assume the role of investigator, and shifted me into that of the participant. These role relationships did not remain distinct in the interview process. We engaged in a process of exchange, constantly shifting role positions, and negotiating the norms of these roles. For example, in the following interview excerpt, Joe responded to the completion of the interview with question of his own.

J: Yes. Okay. I feel like asking you some questions now.

L: You can ask me any questions you want.

J: So you felt like an American black or what?

L: Ummmm ... I always just left it up for people to decide because I had friends who were from the Azores, and I would say, "Well, I'm Cape Verdean," and they'd say, "Why are you making such a big deal about being Cape Verdean, we don't tell people we're from the Azores. We're all Portuguese." And then. . . .

J: In other words, they wanted you to just say you're Portuguese. . . .

This is an example of the repositioning and disclosure we engaged in during the interviews. The story I told about my own struggles with race and ethnicity is quite personal and left me feeling vulnerable to evaluations or sanctions about the credibility or "realness" of my racial and ethnic identity. As such, it would not be the kind of information that I would typically share with a new acquaintance in the community. Nor would it be considered polite in the community for another group member to investigate these matters in this manner. During the interviews, however, it seemed acceptable for Joe and other members of the community to prompt me to reveal these rough spots and fluctuations in my presentation. This short story left me professionally vulnerable as well, because I was not sure what kind of reaction it would receive from participants and how it would affect my research experiences. Fortunately, my shared experiences and interpretations did not have a negative impact on my fieldwork. Most of the participants seemed satisfied with the interview and the direction of my research. They responded to my disclosures with agreement or used them as cues to discuss other experiences that they had.

Discussion

I had two primary objectives in presenting this analysis of my research experiences in the Cape Verdean American community. First, I wanted to call attention to the complexity of the ways that insider status operates in qualitative field research. I highlighted the ways that interpretation of my identity was incorporated into the research process and the responses that these interpretations elicited from participants. I found that there were multiple gates that need to be entered and multiple ways that my membership would be read. This demonstrates that my "insider" identity was not one-dimensional or certain, but needed to be negotiated.

The multiple forms and levels of insider status also highlight the complex ways that groups are defined and group membership extended. I perceive these processes as directly related to the construction of racial and ethnic identity. In my research, I found that as my status as an ethnic and racial insider was being evaluated, participants revealed the characteristics they associated with the group and the meanings attributed to the group and group membership. I expect that these processes are not limited to research involving the negotiation of insider status only. With so-called outsider researchers as well as insider researchers, participants will respond to perceptions of difference and/ or similarity, and define the boundaries of the group accordingly (Naples 1996).

Viewed in this way, race and ethnicity appear to be working at another dimension in qualitative fieldwork. Participants are not simply sharing their perspectives of race and ethnicity, they are crafting interpretations in reaction to and through interaction with researchers. That is, race and ethnicity are simultaneously the subject and product of field research. This perspective also helps to blur the line between insider and outsider researcher. The distinction between the two becomes much less significant when both are perceived as fluid, relative positions that are moved into and out of and are equally involved in the process of constructing race and ethnicity.

This brings me to the second point of my analysis. Both of these elements of my analysis bear on a larger critique of the implied conceptualization of race (and to some extent ethnicity) in qualitative research in racial and ethnic studies. Much of the research that addresses researcher and participant identity and how they influence the research process does so with fairly uncritical and problematic perspectives of race. These analyses, at worst, give a cursory inventory of researcher and participant racial identities. At best, they highlight the ways that race affects the process by showing how it appeared in the field. Unfortunately, in these approaches race takes on a static and one-dimensional tone. The effect of this approach has been to present the research process as something akin to home decorating. The racial identity of researchers and participants are like color swatches, selected from within a very limited color pallet, that are matched or contrasted. Framed in this way, it leaves social researchers to analyze the role of race in fieldwork in terms of how white researchers go with black participants and the results of matching a brown researcher with brown participants.

Although this narrow and latently essentialist perspective of race persists in methodological discussions, the conceptualization of race in substantive work in the field has become increasingly attentive of its dynamism and complexity. Much contemporary research on race and ethnicity has focused on the increasing diversity of "colors" in the U.S. population and the many forms and layers of black, Hispanic, and Asian racial identities for contemporary social actors here. At the same time, even notions of "whiteness" have gotten more complicated as more attention has been directed to the racial and ethnic identities of unhyphenated, white social actors. Methodological analysis in qualitative research on race and ethnicity needs to incorporate this conceptualization of race and ethnicity. This is a difficult task, as it calls for researchers to become sensitive to a language of race and ethnicity that is often subtle and complex. However, by paying close attention to how we learn to manage racial and ethnic identities in the field, our understanding of how these identities are constructed will in turn develop.

Note

1. In Cape Verdean cultural tradition, there is a rich mythology or belief system that attributes a distinctive ethnic and racial character, including a typical look and cultural style, to each of the nine islands of Cabo Verde. For example, Brava is considered more Portuguese or white and a Brava "look" includes light, or ruddy, complexions and relatively straight hair. Sao Tiago is described as African and people are typified as having dark skin and more "African features." This is a very complex system, in which the physical attributes associated with an island don't always neatly or obviously correspond with its racial and ethnic character and other attributes like temperament and body type are included in the typologies. For example, the typical look of Sao Vicente is a combination of very dark skin and very straight hair, but the ethnic and racial character associated with the island is a combination of Portuguese and English, rendering it relatively white.

References

Naples, Nancy A. 1996. A feminist revisiting of the insider/outsider debate: The 'outsider phenomenon' in rural Iowa. *Qualitative Sociology* 19:83–106.

Omi, Michael, and Howard Winant. 1994. *Racial formation in the United States: From the 1960s to the 1980s.* New York: Routledge.

Stanfield II, John H. 1993. Methodological reflections. In *Race and ethnicity in research method,* edited by John H. Stanfield II and Rutledge M. Dennis, 3–15. Newbury Park, CA: Sage.

POSTSCRIPT

Should Outsider and Insider Researchers Be Expected to Get Similar Findings?

For generations North American sociologists embraced in their work Max Weber's notion of value-free sociology. That is, they contended that their research was neutral, objective, unbiased, and free of value contamination. Many in minority relations and other areas of the social sciences were caught off guard in 1944 with the publication of the Swedish economist Gunnar Myrdal's *American Dilemma,* arguably the most significant study of its kind in the twentieth century. In this study of the treatment of Blacks in the United States, Myrdal simply said that such treatment was wrong, that it contradicted the creed of the United States, and that he personally opposed exploitation and prejudice.

At about the same time or shortly afterward, a variety of "radical" sociologists, such as Robert Lynd, C. Wright Mills, Howard Becker, and Alvin Gouldner, partially following Myrdal, elected to take stands on issues. Moreover, they contended that a value-free science of human beings was impossible. Just the fact that one elected to research those who are discriminated against instead of the discriminators, for instance, automatically implied a value position.

The sociology of knowledge (which Merton's selection is largely an explication of) can be traced to the German philosopher Karl Marx's assertion that the "ruling ideas of any age are the ideas of the ruling class." The sociology of knowledge pays less attention to formal validity of knowledge claims and pays more attention to the location of intellectuals and their schools within society to account for their research problems, their theories and methods, their findings and interpretations, and how their interpretations are used. The sociology of knowledge parallels the fundamental insight that a person's location within a social structure influences his or her actions. That location also entails occupying several positions based on group memberships that together influence behaviors and attitudes.

Drawing from these insights and Marx's assertion about the ruling class, many scholars have rejected the traditional value-free notion of science. Minority scholars, especially women of color, argue that minority relations theories and methods are used to maintain racist, sexist, and patriarchal domination. They insist that only insiders must research minorities. Beyond this new sociology are radical claims that all science is not only biased but "privileged" and unfair as well. According to this view, intellectuals are elitists who think that their scholarship is superior to the understandings of members of the groups that are being researched. Also, the people in these groups are turned into subjects and are misrepresented and dehumanized by the elitist researchers.

While Merton plainly reflects the traditionalist view, De Andrade's view is ambiguous. On the one hand, she argues strongly for insiderism. Yet she also admits that the issue is far more complicated, in that research entails figuring out not only what is intellectually important (i.e., what is relevant to testing specific hypotheses) but also how the researcher-subject roles are constructed. This goes way beyond simply generating initial reports to obtain cooperation. De Andrade argues that the *meanings* of minority realities are highly problematic and shifting, largely as a function of perceptions of the researcher him- or herself. However, does she prove that an outsider could not have done as well as or even better than she did in her research of Cape Verdean Americans? Moreover, although in many ways she is an insider, isn't she also an outsider, in that she is a young, educated, middle-class female whose interviewees included males, poor individuals, and people who are two or more generations older than her? Should researchers who have close ties with their subjects (as well as stark outsiders) triangle their work (e.g., have at least one other scholar do a mini-survey of the subjects regarding how *they* see that researcher and his or her work)? In Merton's case, isn't it probable that in spite of his calls for the utilization of both insider and outsider knowledge, until very recently understanding of the extent of discrimination and its harms has simply not been captured in traditional research? For example, experts are only now becoming aware of the enormous effects of sexism on women, of institutional racism on all Blacks, and of other forms of discrimination on homosexuals, disabled people, and others. These new insights, some contend, have resulted primarily from "activist" researchers and scholars such as De Andrade.

Although he is in his 90s, Merton (b. 1910) remains a potent intellectual force. Among his more recent contributions is *On Social Structure and Science* (University of Chicago Press, 1996). A helpful reader is *Racing Research Researching Race: Methodological Dilemmas in Critical Race Studies* edited by France Winddance Twine and Jonathan W. Warren (New York University Press, 2000). Empirical cases of insider research by outsiders include "Cultural Autobiography, Testimonial, and Asian American Transnational Feminist Coalition in the 'Comfort Women of World War II' Conference," by Pamela Thoma, *Frontiers* (vol. 21, nos. 1 and 2, 2000); *Struggle for Ethnic Identity: Narratives by Asian American Professionals* edited by Pyong G. Min and Rose Kim (AltaMira Press, 1999); and "Multicultural Conservatism: What It Is, Why It Matters," by Angela D. Dillard, *The Chronicle of Higher Education* (March 2, 2001).

Two works that consider minority faculty members in different contexts are *Faculty of Color in Academe: Bittersweet Success* by Samuel L. Myers and Caroline Sotello Viernes Turner (Prentice Hall, 2000) and *Affirmed Action: Essays on the Academic and Social Lives of White Faculty Members at Historically Black Colleges and Universities* edited by Lenoar Foster, Janet A. Guyden, and Andrea L. Miller (Rowman & Littlefield, 2000). An excellent anthology is *The Gender and Science Reader* edited by Muriel Lederman and Ingrid Bartsch (Routledge, 2001). Finally, see *Global Ethnography: Forces, Connections and Imaginations in a Postmodern World* by Michael Burawoy et al. (University of California Press, 2001) and *Methodology of the Oppressed* by Chela Sandoval (University of Minnesota Press, 2000).

ISSUE 2

Are Blacks "Natural Born" Athletes?

YES: Jon Entine, from *Taboo: Why Black Athletes Dominate Sports and Why We Are Afraid to Talk About It* (PublicAffairs, 2000)

NO: John Hoberman, from "Totem and Taboo: The Myth of Race in Sports," *Skeptic* (Summer 2000)

ISSUE SUMMARY

YES: Writer Jon Entine argues that one important way to build bridges is to admit that racial differences are real and that members of some races are better than others in certain areas. He notes that Black males from Kenya and other regions of Africa can run faster, run longer, and jump higher than athletes from other nations, and he maintains that people should not be afraid to admit it.

NO: Sociologist John Hoberman acknowledges that some West Africans may be endowed with a higher proportion of fast-twitch muscle fibers than other people. However, he attacks Entine's science as "speculative, selective, and inconclusive," and he rejects the theory that Blacks are natural athletes.

In a more perfect world, the debate over whether or not Blacks are natural athletes would be a straightforward biological, physiological, and anthropometric one. That is, discussion would focus on whether or not some groups of people have longer femurs, higher proportions of fast-twitch muscle fibers, longer and thinner legs, and an innate proclivity to breath slower and to relax more than other groups of people. However, as Jon Entine notes in the following selection, such comparisons almost instantly become taboo when they are even partially based on race. And, indeed, such comparisons have been taboo for many years among scholars, especially sociologists.

The alleged biological-racial connection has been advanced in several publications, many of which have been authored by prominent conservative scholars. Among these is *The Bell Curve* (Free Press, 1996), in which the late psychologist Richard Herrnstein and political scientist Charles Murray contend that African Americans are genetically less intelligent than Asians and Caucasians. As a consequence, the authors assert, Blacks are less able to compete in modern society. This, in turn, leads to increasing social breakdown, including rising crime rates.

Scholars in the 1990s were rocked by assertions of natural racial differences not from the Ku Klux Klan, skinheads, neo-Nazis, and the other usual racist suspects but from relatively prominent scholars. To most social scientists, however, no matter how clever or disingenuous the arguments, they were still merely old racism in new bottles. Conservatives countered that critics were afraid to face the difficult truth that racial inequalities based on biology, not discrimination, exist.

In some ways, the debate over whether or not Blacks are natural-born athletes ought to generate as much heat as or even more heat than the debate over racial differences in intellect. After all, slavery and, later, apartheid and segregation were legitimized largely on the grounds that Blacks were not only biologically different from whites but also beastlike, especially males. Inhumane comparisons of Blacks with nonhuman primates were routinely made. In the times of slavery, it was asserted that Blacks were "beasts of burden" because they were stronger than whites; thus, enslaving them was okay. Lynchings in the United States were justified by the ideology that Blacks were animals who were always ready to attack or rape white people. The seemingly compassionate conjugal visitation system for prisoners in Mississippi was created largely for Black inmates because the wardens assumed that providing an animal outlet for Blacks' aggressions would make them more controllable. Furthermore, some classical social theorists, such as Cesare Lombroso (1835–1909), argued that criminals of "inferior" races had lower pain thresholds and were therefore tougher and more dangerous.

In the world of sports, such ignorance and bigotry spilled over into explanations for why Black athletes sometimes seemed more capable than others. For example, claims were made that the ancestors of Black athletes had been bred as slaves to be strong—that they had less intelligence but were better physically—and that these traits had been passed down to modern-day athletes. Some sports commentators and coaches who have restated these fairly commonplace ideas in recent times have received rebuke.

At this level of analysis, the irony is that while Entine is contending that Blacks are indeed natural-born athletes, preeminent African American scholars are either agreeing with him or at least encouraging the dialogue. It is notable that sports sociologist Harry Edwards, who has spent a lifetime researching and fighting racist attitudes toward Black athletes, argues that Entine's ideas may have merit. Even Entine's opponents, while rejecting his arguments, openly admit that genetics may play some significant role in explaining differences between races. Such a claim 30 years ago would have generated a scholarly bloodbath.

Is Entine courageously opening a dialogue that could bring Blacks and whites together as they learn to appreciate and respect each other's strengths and limitations? Or is it old racism in new bottles? In the second selection, John Hoberman rejects Entine's data and interpretations as unconvincing. Is he right?

Jon Entine  **YES**

Taboo

By the Numbers

Biology Circumscribes Possibility

Simply stated, the opposing and incompatible claims that black athletic success can be explained by environmentalism or evolution are equally simplistic. Sports success is a bio-social phenomenon. There is extensive and persuasive research that elite black athletes have a *phenotypic* advantage—a distinctive skeletal system and musculature, metabolic structures, and other characteristics forged over tens of thousands of years of evolution. While people of African descent have spent most of their evolutionary history near to where they originated, the rest of the world's populations have had to modify their African adaptations after migrating to far different regions and climates.

Preliminary research suggests that different *phenotypes* are at least partially encoded in the genes—conferring *genotypic* differences, which may result in an advantage in some sports. But all such differences are mediated through experience, from our prenatal health to the educational opportunities while growing up. In other words, our environment and culture can enhance or diminish whatever tiny variations linked to evolution that may exist. Considering the wide variation within each geographic, racial, and ethnic population, such differences may appear minuscule, but at the elite level, they are the stuff of champions.

These inbred differences influence who does how well and in what sports. Asians, who constitute about 57 percent of the world's population, are virtually invisible in the most democratic of world sports, running, soccer, and basketball. Blacks of sub-Saharan African ancestry comprise approximately 12 percent of the world's 6 billion population, yet their hold on many sports, particularly running, is staggering. In the United States, 13 percent of the population is black. In the mid-1960s the racial breakdown in the National Basketball Association (NBA) was 80 percent white, 20 percent black; today it's almost exactly reversed—the NBA is more than 85 percent black. Women's pro basketball is

75 percent African American. The National Football League (NFL) is 70 percent black. In college, 65 percent of men's basketball players and 50 percent of football players are African Americans.

Becoming a professional athlete is still a long-shot for aspiring teenagers, but it's a lot longer for whites. A black male would have about 1 chance in 4,000 of playing in the NBA, as compared to about a 1 in 90,000 shot for a white. And even as African Americans are abandoning baseball in droves for basketball and football, more than one-third of Major League Baseball and a higher percentage of the top stars are blacks from North and Latin America.

Even these eye-popping numbers grossly understate the trends. Check the NBA statistics: not one white player has finished among the top scorers or rebounders in recent years. White running backs, cornerbacks, or wide receivers in the NFL? Count them on one hand. Roll the calendar back decades, to the 1950s, to find the last time a white led baseball in steals. A white male toeing the line at an Olympic 100-meter final? Not in decades.[1] Don't expect to see a white man set a world record in a road race—any race, at any distance from 100-meters to the marathon. It may happen. In some future decade. But don't hold your breath.

There is a new racial barrier in sports. Positions that require speed and jumping ability are almost exclusively black. In street parlance this phenomenon is blamed on a malady, virulently infectious but apparently limited to Caucasians—white man's disease. "The NBA is perhaps the only arena of American life," opined sports writers Bob Ryan and Terry Pluto in their book *48 Minutes,* "where to be white is to be immediately judged inferior. [It is] not necessary to have a Ph.D. in kinesiology to realize that the average black player can jump higher and run faster than the average white player."

Standing 5 feet, 7 inches tall in high-tops, former NBA guard Spud Webb used to dunk the ball in warm-ups. "Just to keep everybody honest," he would say. Even Mugsy Bogues, at 5 feet, 3 inches, can dunk. White players, many of whom line the bench, wonder what kind of future they have. "White people can't jump as high," sighs Scott Brooks, a white guard who bounced around the league in an undistinguished NBA career. Another itinerant guard, Jon Barry, son of Hall-of-Famer Rick Barry, believes he is the last of a "dying breed." Only the demand for mutant giants of any background is likely to forestall a near total washout of nonblacks in coming years.

This is a worldwide phenomenon. Black athletes are now stars in many western countries, from Europe to Asia. For example, tiny Senegal, population 8 million in a country the size of South Dakota, had seventeen citizens playing college basketball in the United States as of 1998. It has also sent dozens of athletes to play in professional basketball leagues in Greece, France, and Israel. In a nation with just one indoor basketball court, it is a triumph of natural talent and tremendous desire over almost insurmountable odds.

That familiar trend is readily apparent in the world's most popular team sport, soccer. Nigeria won the Olympic gold medal in 1996 and qualified two years later for the World Cup along with Cameroon, Tunisia, and South Africa. With the global hopscotching of top players, Africans have become fixtures in Europe's top clubs, even with sharp restrictions on signing foreign players. The

Netherlands national team, which made it to the semifinals in the '98 World Cup, includes stars from Suriname, and is about one-third black. France, winner of the 1998 World Cup, has a large contingent of players of African descent, including Ghana-born Marcel Desailly, one of the heroes of the World Cup. Even in England, which was slow to allow foreigners and has a black population of less than 2 percent, 1 in 5 professional soccer players in the premier division is black.

As the world playing field continues to level, natural abilities are more likely to come to the fore. East Asians are disciplined and very competitive, yet because of their small stature and natural flexibility—a result of evolutionary forces—they make better ice skaters and gymnasts than basketball players or sprinters. Is it more than just cultural serendipity that Brazilians are time and again the best soccer players, the Chinese among the best divers, black Dominicans among the best baseball players, and African Americans the top basketball and football players? Clearly, "racial" patterns in sports do not lend themselves to a facile black and white explanation.

What About Baseball?

The relative dearth of black players in baseball—about one in six major leaguers —is frequently cited as proof that blacks do not dominate sports. When a "racial report card" published a few years ago by Northeastern University's Center for The Study of Sport in Society noted that the percentage of American black baseball players had fallen slightly, an outraged editorial entitled "A White Man's Place to Be" appeared in the *New York Times*. Warning of an imminent white takeover of the base paths, it expressed "renewed anxiety about the whiteness of players." It noted the sky-high black participation rates in other sports, then quoted a scout as predicting that "African Americans would soon disappear from the game."

In fact African Americans make up approximately 15 percent of top professionals, higher than their 13 percent of the general population. Americans so reflexively expect black domination that anything less than an NBA or NFL-sized black majority is taken as a sign of renewed discrimination—against blacks. To invoke racism for a slight drop in the percentage of American blacks (the raw numbers have actually increased with expansion) shows how deeply the belief in black athletic superiority is ingrained in Americans, black and white.

The racial report card's numbers distort the racial trends. There are actually far more black players in baseball than ever before. Only 60 percent of Major League Baseball players are American-born whites, and the number is decreasing every year. Over the past twenty years, Hispanics, many of whom are black, have jumped from 8 to 24 percent. Today, 40 percent of professional baseball players are of primarily West African ancestry.

By the numbers, black Hispanic ballplayers are the most likely to make it to the big leagues, followed by players of mixed black and white heritage, then whites, with Mexicans (who, according to physical anthropologists, typically have shorter legs and are less muscular in the lower body than Caribbean blacks as a result of their Native Indian heritage) having the toughest time. The largely black Dominican Republic, which currently has more than ninety players in the major leagues, is a baseball hothouse.

Although the overall numbers of blacks in baseball do not approach those in football or basketball, the stars are disproportionately black. A "dream team" recently put together by *USA Today* sports writers included only one white among the position players. This phenomenon is not a recent development. In the fifty years since Jackie Robinson became the first black to be named Most Valuable Player (MVP), a black player has been chosen National League MVP thirty-three times. Since 1963, when Elston Howard of the New York Yankees became the first nonwhite named MVP in the American League, black players have won the honor nineteen times. A clear majority of MVP's are black. Whites are far more likely to be the marginal players filling out a roster.

Baseball historian Bill James, author of dozens of books on the statistical twists of his favorite sport, believes this trend is not a fluke. In an intriguing study conducted in 1987, he compared the careers of hundreds of rookies to figure out what qualities best predict who would develop into stars. He noted many intangible factors, such as whether a player stays fit or is just plain lucky. The best predictors of long-term career success included the age of the rookie, his defensive position as a determinant in future hitting success (e.g., catchers fare worse than outfielders), speed, and the quality of the player's team. But all of these factors paled when compared to the color of the player's skin.

"Nobody likes to write about race," James noted apologetically. "I thought I would do a [statistical] run of black players against white players, fully expecting that it would show nothing in particular or nothing beyond the outside range of chance, and I would file it away and never mention that I had looked at the issue at all."

James first compared fifty-four white rookies against the same number of black first-year players who had comparable statistics. "The results were astonishing," he wrote. The black players:

- went on to have better major-league careers in 44 of the 54 cases
- played 48 percent more games
- had 66 percent more major-league hits
- hit 93 percent more triples
- hit 66 percent more home runs
- scored 69 percent more runs
- stole 400 percent more bases

James compared Reggie Jackson, who began his career as a right-fielder with the Oakland Athletics in 1969, to Bob Allison, who broke in with a splash ten years before with the Washington Senators. A star running back in college, Allison was fast as lightning and strong to boot. The young centerfielder hit a solid .261, smacked a rookie-high 30 homers, knocked in 85 runs, scored almost as many, swiped 13 bases, and led the American League in triples. He also sparkled in centerfield.

Allison's rookie year was remarkably comparable to Jackson's (see Table 1). Like Allison, Jackson was a star football player. Both were speedsters. But

Table 1

Rookie-Year Statistics for Bob Allison and Reggie Jackson

	G	AB	R	H	2B	3B	HR	RBI	SB	AVG
Allison	150	570	83	149	18	9	30	85	13	.261
Jackson	154	553	82	138	13	6	29	74	14	.250

while Jackson got better and better, Allison went into a long decline after a few fine seasons with the Minnesota Twins. By 1965, he had lost his speed and was splitting time between left field and first. A few years later, he was out of the game altogether. Meanwhile, Jackson played on five World Series teams, earning the moniker "Mr. October" before retiring into the Hall of Fame.

Flabbergasted at what he had found, James ran a second study using forty-nine black/white comparisons. Again, blacks proved more durable, retained their speed longer, and were consistently better hitters. For example, he compared Ernie Banks, a power hitting shortstop for the Chicago Cubs, and Bernie Allen, who broke in with Minnesota. They both reached the majors when they were twenty-three years old, were the same height and weight, and were considered equally fast. Over time, Allen bombed and Banks landed in the Hall of Fame.

Or contrast the careers of Gus Bell, who played mostly for Pittsburgh and Cincinnati, and Hank Aaron of the Braves. In their early years, Bell was faster and comparable to Aaron as a slugger. But a few years along in their careers, Aaron was stealing 30-plus bases a year and gunning for Babe Ruth's all time homer record; Bell deteriorated into a part-timer with "wooden legs."

In an attempt to correct for possible bias, James compared players with comparable speed statistics such as the number of doubles, triples, and stolen bases. He ran a study that focused only on players who had little speed. He analyzed for "position bias" and made sure that players in the same eras were being compared. Yet every time he crunched the numbers, the results broke down along racial lines. When comparing home runs, runs scored, RBIs, or stolen bases, black players held the advantage a startling 80 percent of the time. "And I could identify absolutely no bias to help explain why this should happen," said James in disbelief.

James also compared white Hispanic rookies, whom he assumed faced an uphill battle similar to that for blacks, with comparable groups of white and black players. The blacks dominated the white Latinos by even more than they did the white North Americans, besting them in 19 of the 26 comparisons. Blacks played 62 percent more games, hit 192 percent more home runs, drove in 125 percent more runs, and stole 30 percent more bases.

So why have blacks become the stars in baseball far out of proportion to their relative numbers? James eventually concluded that there were only two possible explanations: "Blacks are better athletes because they are born better athletes, which is to say that it is genetic, or that they are born equal and become better athletes." ...

The Most Level Playing Field

... Kenyan domination of distance running, and the virtual takeover of elite-level track by athletes of African descent, is powerful anecdotal evidence of innate physical differences between populations. If there is a level playing field in athletics, it is the earth—literally. "A scientist interested in exploring physical and performance differences couldn't invent a better sport than running," wrote Amby Burfoot, editor of *Runner's World* and former winner of the Boston marathon.

> It's a true world-wide sport, practiced and enjoyed in almost every country around the globe. Also, it doesn't require any special equipment, coaching or facilities. [Ethiopia's] Abebe Bikila proved this dramatically in the 1960 Olympic Games when—shoe-less, little coached and inexperienced—he won the marathon. Given the universality of running, it's reasonable to expect that the best runners should come from a wide-range of countries and racial groups. This isn't, however, what happens. Nearly all the sprints are won by runners of West African descent. Nearly all the distance races are won, remarkably, by runners from just one small corner of one small African country.

For all practical reality, men's world championship events might as well post a sign declaring, "Whites Need Not Apply." Indeed, with the breaking of Sebastian Coe's 18-year-old 1,000-meter world record in 1999 by Kenyan Noah Ngeny, every men's world record at every commonly-run track distance belongs to a runner of African descent.

While Africa is the mother-lode of the running world, talent is not evenly distributed across the continent but is concentrated in three areas: a swath of western African coastal states, notably Senegal, Nigeria, and Cameroon, extending south to Namibia; the northern African countries of Algeria and Morocco; and a long stretch of eastern African states from Ethiopia, Tanzania, and Kenya to mountainous South Africa.

Each sport, or running distance, demands a slightly different mix of biomechanical, anaerobic, and aerobic abilities. Not surprisingly, athletes from each region tend to excel in specific athletic events as a result of both cultural and genetic factors: West Africa is the ancestral home of the world's top sprinters and jumpers; North Africa turns out top middle distance runners; and East Africa is the world distance running capital. Amazingly, whereas only one in every eight of the people in the world are black, more than 70 percent of the top times are held by runners of African origin.

A look at the ancestry (or home country) of the runners holding the top 100 times in eight distances, from the 100 meters to the marathon, makes it clear that African domination is deep as well as broad.

- Blacks who trace their ancestry to West Africa, including African Americans, hold 494 of the top 500 100-meter times and 98 percent of the top sprinting times;
- Whites are virtually absent from the top ranks of sprinting; though whites have traditionally done well in the longer endurance races, particularly the marathon, their ranks have thinned in recent years as Africans entered the sport;
- Athletes from one country, Kenya, make up 40 percent of top times in middle and long distance races; including top performances by other East Africans (most from Ethiopia), that domination swells to more than 50 percent.
- North Africans excel at the middle distances;
- Mexicans, mostly Native Indians, are strong at the longer races, 10,000 meters and the marathon;
- East Asians—Chinese, Koreans and Japanese—are competitive at the event requiring the most endurance, the marathon.

Sprints

Remember the last time a non-black set the men's world record in the 100-meter sprint? One has to go back to 1960, when German Armin Hary won the Olympic gold medal in 10.2 seconds. The best time by a white 100-meter runner is 10 seconds, which ranks below two hundred on the all-time list. There are also no elite sprinters of note from Asia, which has 57 percent of the world's population, even with the Confucian and Tao traditions of discipline and an authoritarian sports system in the most populous country, China.

Today, the 100 meter distance is monopolized by blacks of West African ancestry. They are quicker out of the starting blocks and demonstrate blazing speed. Former "world's fastest human" Donovan Bailey clocked a mind-bending 27 miles per hour at the mid-point of his record-breaking sprint at the Atlanta Olympics. Dozens of blacks have cracked the 10-second barrier.

All of the forty finalists in the last five Olympic men's 100-meter races are of West African descent. The likelihood of that happening based on population numbers alone—blacks with ancestral roots in that region represent 8 percent of the world's population—is 0.000000000000000000000000000000000000000 0001 percent.

There have been a small handful of non-West African 200- and 400-meter runners over the years. In 1979 Italy's Pietro Mennea shattered the 200-meter record, running 19.72 seconds, still the best time by a non-African. Although he ran in Mexico City's 7,300 foot altitude and was aided by a tailwind of 90 percent of the allowable limit, Mennea's moment-in-the-sun is invoked as "proof" that whites can run as fast as blacks of West African ancestry. Mennea's record held for seventeen years before being pulverized in 1996 by Michael Johnson in a stunning 19.32 seconds, an improvement of more than 2 percent, an unheard of breakthrough in sprinting. Intriguingly, many southern Europeans (including Mennea) who are disproportionately stand-outs in running, trace a significant percentage of their genes to Africa as a result of interbreeding.

Middle Distances

Whereas runners of West African ancestry monopolize sprinting from 100 meters to 400 meters, with rare exception, they do not even compete in elite middle distance races. Malvin Whitfield of the United States won gold medals in the 800 meters in the 1948 and 1952 Olympics in times that by today's standards, set by North and East Africans, are pokey. The current list of athletes holding the all-time top 800-meter times includes only two men who might claim West African ancestry: Johnny Gray of the United States and Joaquim Carvalho Cruz of Brazil (although Cruz's racial ancestry, like that of many Brazilians, includes Amerindian/Asian genes).

In contrast, East Africans and North Africans (who have substantial white ancestry, whether Arab or Berber is not certain), who are hapless in the sprints, dominate endurance races. Even tiny Burundi has become a power of sorts, winning a gold in the 5,000-meters and coming in fourth in the 10,000 meters at the Atlanta Olympics, a better showing in distance running than the United States. Not surprisingly, all seven members of the Burundi team were slender Tutsis, of the same Nilotic-Saharan background as athletes from the world's top running superpowers, Ethiopia and Kenya.

As the economic barriers that long limited participation by Africans have eroded, the rest of the world runners, even in some widely-contested races such as the 10,000 meters, drift further and further back in the pack.

Kenya is far and away the world power at 800 meters and the 3,000 meter steeplechase. Excepting two extraordinary North Africans, Noureddine Morceli of Algeria and Morocco's Hicham El Guerrouj, Kenyans set the pace at the other middle distances, the 10,000 meters and the marathon, holding more than half of the top times. Kenyan men have won the World Cross-Country Championships every year since 1986 and are often so dominant that they would have beaten the rest of the world combined.

The depth of the country's talent is so dazzling that Daniel Komen, considered by many to be the world's premier middle-distance runner in 1996, could not make his country's Olympic team. At the World Juniors in 1994, the Rift Valley native took the 5,000- and 10,000-meter titles. But in the Kenyan Olympic Trials two years later, Komen could not finish among the top three in any race. As a result, he ended up watching the Games on television from his summer training base in the London suburb of Teddington, just a few miles from the fields of Harrow, where Roger Bannister had prepared for his assault on the four-minute mile-barrier four decades before, and where Sebastian Coe still lopes through the hills to stay in shape.

Shortly after the Olympics concluded, as if in revenge for not being selected, Komen embarked on one of the great months in running history. In mid-August in Zurich, he crushed then 5,000-meter world-record holder Halle Gebrselassie of Ethiopia. Nine days later in Brussels he took on Morocco's Noureddine Morceli at 3,000 meters and left him sniffing vapors. The next week at Rieti in Italy, he broke the 3,000-meter record, running 7:20:67. Komen moved on to Milan, where he won the 5,000-meter Grand Prix finals. In less than a month, a Kenyan Olympic team also-ran had destroyed three world records at a variety of distances, earning more than $400,000.

The following year, 1997, Komen added the 5,000-meter record, along with two indoor world marks. Still not in his prime, he has run a scintillating 7:58:61 over two miles, the first athlete to cover that distance in less than eight minutes. While the world rightly considers Bannister's sub-four minute mile a momentous accomplishment, Komen ran his first mile in 3:59.2—then turned in a second mile of 3:59.4.

What's most striking about Komen and many other top East African runners is their remarkable range in middle- and long-distance events. Gebrselassie began the 1999 outdoor track season with 15 world records in his career at distances from 2,000- to 10,000-meters. Kenya's Moses Kiptanui, the first athlete to run the 3,000-meter steeplechase in under eight minutes, and countryman Wilson Kipketer, are both capable of record-setting performances over a variety of distances.

Unlikely new stars blossom every season. Ondoro Osoro, who had never previously run a marathon, even in practice, and is primarily a 5,000-meter runner, did nothing less than run the third-fastest marathon in history in Chicago in 1998. "It truly blows me away," says Keith Brantly, a 1996 U.S. Olympian and one of America's top marathoners, of the combination of speed and endurance in East African runners. "It's really nice to be naïve sometimes and run like it's a distance run and sprint at the end."

Is this success just a temporary phenomenon? Not likely. The pipeline is full of young Kenyans, who have captured almost every men's new world junior record in road racing in recent years. Among the females, only a few Chinese women have cracked Kenyan hegemony over the world junior circuit. And the staggering reality is that while Kenyans continue to improve in the middle distances, runners from the rest of the world have stagnated.

The Marathon

Until the mid–1980s, no country dominated marathoning. Africa was an international also-ran. "We were told when we were younger that the marathon was not good for your health, that you might not be able to have children," says Kenya's Moses Tanui, who won his second Boston Marathon with a near-world record run in 1998. That changed with the emergence of the Kenyans, spurred in part by the breakthrough success of Ibrahim Hussein in marathons in Honolulu, Boston, and New York in the late eighties. With Hussein's very visible victories, and as money and prestige washed over the event, such cultural constraints were soon swept away.

Now Kenya is the hands-down best at both middle- and long-distance running. At Boston, considered the world's premier marathon, Kenyan men have not lost since 1990. Even the slow Kenyans leave the rest of the pack behind. Each year, the top fifty fastest Kenyan marathoners can expect to break 2:13, a time out of reach of most whites, and Asians, and blacks of West African ancestry.

Kenya Under the Microscope

Let's turn a high-powered microscope on this tiny powerhouse. Kenya is a diverse country with many ethnic tribes and only a loose and somewhat recent concept of a nation. All told, Kenya has collected forty-five Olympic medals since the 1964 Olympics. That includes fifteen gold in men's races, a haul exceeded by only the sprint-rich United States, with a population ten times larger. At Seoul in 1988 Kenyan men won the 800, 1,500, and 5,000 meters, along with the 3,000 meter steeplechase. Based on population percentages alone, the likelihood that this Texas-sized country could turn in such a remarkable medal performance is *one in 1.6 billion.*

Increase the power on our microscope to focus on the highlands along the western rim of the Great Rift Valley adjacent to Lake Victoria. Three-fourths of Kenyan world-class athletes trace their ancestry to this region, a level of dominance that has remained remarkably consistent over the decades. How remarkable is this juggernaut? Kalenjin runners have won more than seventy percent of Kenya's Olympic medals in world running and all but one of Kenyan-held world records. Over the past decade, athletes from this tiny dot on the world map have won more than 40 percent of all the biggest international distance-running honors available and nearly three times as many Olympic and World Championship distance medals as athletes from *any other nation in the world.*

Yet even these remarkable figures understate what's going on in Kalenjin country. Ratchet the magnification up another notch. One small district, the Nandi, with only 1.8 percent of Kenya's population, has produced about half of the world-class Kalenjin athletes and 20 percent of all the winners of major international distance-running events.

By almost any measure, this tiny region in west-central Kenya represents the greatest concentration of raw athletic talent in the history of sports. "As far as Kalenjin running is concerned," observes John Manners, a former Peace Corps teacher in Kenya and author of two books on Kenyan running, "I think it's unlikely that anyone who spends any time in Kalenjin country and watches what untrained kids can do (especially when compared with other Kenyans of ostensibly similar backgrounds) will come away thinking that anything but genetic factors are paramount in their success. The evidence is impressionistic and anecdotal, but the *prima facie* case is pretty persuasive," he says, though he insists that he remains skeptical of biological theories of athletic success.

Kenyan dominance of international endurance running is so complete that there was a movement afoot by some race directors to limit their number at future races. "They are not only slaughtering the Americans," said Brantly after finishing behind eight Kenyans in the 1998 Cherry Blossom 10-mile race in Washington, "they are slaughtering everybody."

It's gotten to the point where most of the world's best non-Kenyan men have all but given up contesting the middle distances in elite races. "When you are trying to earn your living on the road, it is getting silly," remarked a top British runner. "There are 10 or 15 Kenyans everywhere." Fabian Rancero, the brilliant Spaniard who has run one of the best marathon times ever, is skeptical that anyone can match up against the top Kenyans. "The only athlete capable of going close to 2:05 at this moment is probably [Kenyan] Paul Tergat," he said in 1998. "No white man is capable of running that sort of time."

The best of the non-African runners are dubbed "white Kenyans" in the same slightly patronizing way that Hank Aaron was once called the "black Babe Ruth." Many white runners such as Germany's Dieter Baumann, the surprise gold-medal winner at 5,000-meters in the 1992 Barcelona Olympics, are stunned to find themselves slipping further and further back in the pack. "We Europeans are just as good as them and no less suited for distance running. I don't see myself on the defensive because the Africans are simply normal opponents." Bauman was suspended in 1999 for two years after twice testing positive for the steroid Nandrolone.

Normal, yes. Beatable? That's another story.

"The record-holders used to be athletes from industrialized nations who had access to technology and financial incentives," says Frank Shorter, in search of an explanation. "As more Kenyans and Ethiopians could achieve the same access to agents, money and a lucrative running career, the balance of power changed. The Africans finally got a level playing field. Then, the game was over."

Note

1. Four whites, including the gold and bronze medalists, did compete in the 100-meter final at the 1980 Moscow Olympics, which were boycotted by many nations, including the United States.

NO

John Hoberman

Totem and Taboo: The Myth of Race in Sports

In April 1989 the author of *Taboo* produced an NBC-TV documentary titled *Black Athletes—Fact and Fiction*. The purpose of this program was to examine the question of whether the dominance of black athletes in high-profile sports such as basketball and Olympic running events could be traced to genetic advantages that translated into superior performances. At the conclusion of the show, NBC anchorman Tom Brokaw solemnly announced that the preceding interviews and demonstrations had, indeed, confirmed the biological superiority of the black athlete. In other words, something over an hour of network television put together by a lay enthusiast had managed to resolve one of the great nature-nurture conundrums of modern science.

More than a decade later, *Taboo* is Jon Entine's lengthier attempt to demonstrate that "the scientific evidence for black athletic superiority is overwhelming" (341). The thesis of the book, he says, is "that [racial] populations have evolved functional biomechanical and physiological differences" (83) that can and do determine the outcome of elite athletic competitions. The fact that this argument can only give aid and comfort to "the [potentially harmful] stereotype that blacks are more naturally athletic than whites" (264) has compelled the author to announce that the book has some other, more politically correct purposes, as well. *Taboo* is "out to do some damage" to the "virulent stereotypes" that still lurk in our interracial sports world (8).

Precisely how the documenting of "functional biomechanical and physiological differences" might dissolve racial-athletic stereotypes is never made clear. The achievement of his television program, he says, was to have "stimulated a dialogue about the underlying issue: the destructive categorization of people based simply on their ethnicity or the color of their skin" (7)—a formula that harmonizes well with the 1950 UNESCO *Statement on Race* the author criticizes later in the book (213). Yet it is hardly surprising that not all of the members of NBC's large audience that evening either intuited the shape of the intended dialogue or discerned the producer's humane motives. As one black professional man asked me at the 1990 meeting of the American Psychological Association: "What can we do to keep that kind of programming off the air?"

Whether an exploration of this topic belongs on television is, in fact, an interesting question. Having watched *Black Athletes—Fact and Fiction* several times, both in and out of the classroom, my own view is that it is a textbook example of how the presentation of racial biology to a mass audience can go wrong due to the absence of scientific rigor. Racial anthropology has, after all, been a magnet for amateur speculation over the past two centuries, in part because it is a kind of fantasyland, and it is only natural that an endless stream of books, treatises, and pamphlets on this subject has continued in various electronic forms.

Presenting this material over 340 pages is, however, a more promising strategy, and Entine has worked hard to put together a convincing scientific argument wrapped inside capsule treatments of just about every topic that is relevant to a discussion of race and sport. Here we find chapters on Kenyan runners, black boxers, the Jesse Owens story, the history of racial science and eugenics, the age of Jewish-American prowess in basketball, the East German doping program, and more. While little of this book qualifies as original research, many readers will find it a useful survey that aims at serving a wide readership. Its principal contribution is to have assembled more evidence in favor of the genetic hypothesis than any other previous publication. Whether the book serves scientific inquiry as well as it claims to do is a separate matter that will be examined below.

The author further justifies the publication of this book by claiming that "this is the right time to look at this issue" (8) for two reasons. First, as noted above, it is intended to promote racial understanding by drawing blacks and whites into discussions of an emotionally difficult topic, even as the roadmap to such mutual understanding via the race-biology bramble-bush is never made clear. Second, this is a timely book because science is now in the process of "unlocking the mystery of genes"(8).

Neither of these arguments is as self-evident as the author takes them to be. For while I would agree that peer-reviewed science is preferable to an oral tradition based on folkloric beliefs about racial differences, which can be both wrong and harmful, even this sensible rule may be vulnerable to the law of unintended consequences. For much will depend on what is reported in the scientific literature as well as on how black readers perceive the motivations behind investigations into racial biology. In addition, the therapeutic effect of dialogue anticipated by the author seems to be premised on his conviction that racial athletic aptitude is an almost unbearably painful subject. This is why he refers to "the hotter-than-hot nature of the debate" (78), to "this explosive subject" (271), to "the political bombshells" it might detonate, and to "the provocative and potentially incendiary question" (272) he has tackled in these pages.

In fact, both whites and blacks have had most of a century to adjust to (and even find gratification in) the idea that people of African origin enjoy "natural" advantages. Today, very large numbers of both groups already assume that "black dominance" has a genetic foundation even in the absence of scientific proof. So the idea that *Taboo* contains an "explosive" message is less compelling than the author assumes. Much of the anticipated explosion has already dissipated, having been converted into a bio-racial folklore about athletic ability that is widely accepted in American society. As I have argued elsewhere, we would do well to pay more attention to the social and cultural effects of this folklore quite apart from its scientific dimension.

The claim that *Taboo* has appeared at the right time in relation to the Human Genome Project also strikes me as mistaken. On the contrary, it is clear that our understanding of human genetics will have to make major advances before it will be possible to verify the author's claims about the genetic basis of athletic superiority in a scientifically satisfying way.

Before proceeding to an examination of the author's scientific arguments, I would like to make clear certain of my own positions. First, it should be obvious to any attentive observer that the performance records in quantifiable running events, and especially the sprinting and long-distance events, clearly demonstrate the superior performance levels of athletes of West and East African origin, respectively. In particular, the achievements of male Kenyan runners during the 1990s have been nothing short of phenomenal, and *Taboo* documents this in a convincing way. Second, I do not believe that proposing a genetic basis for such athletic superiority is racism unless scientific curiosity is combined with a racist agenda. As I stated in *Darwin's Athletes: How Sport Has Damaged Black America and Preserved the Myth of Race* (Houghton Mifflin, 1997, 240): "It is possible that there is a population of West African origin that is endowed with an unusual proportion of fast-twitch muscle fibers, and it is somewhat more likely that there are East Africans whose resistance to fatigue, for both genetic and cultural reasons, exceeds that of other racial groups." Contrary to Etine's claim in *Taboo* (77), I am not a dogmatic opponent of the genetic hypothesis.

The scientific argument presented in *Taboo* includes both evolutionary and physiological theses. The "multiregionalist" theory of human origins [one of the two major theories, along with the "Out of Africa" hypothesis, discussed by the author] holds "that all of modern humanity originated from a single ancestor, but millions rather than hundreds of thousands of years ago. Some members of the community of early humans then broke off and migrated to other regions" (82). Entine likes this evolutionary scenario because it allows more time for different racial populations to undergo adaptive resonses to "differing selective pressures" (82) that might result in extra foot speed or endurance. The principal corollaries of this scenario, according to the author, are the genetic dichotomy between Africans and non-Africans (18, 92, 108, 113, 115) and the greater genetic variability of Africans (92, 116), both of which supposedly point to African athletic superiority.

It is hardly necessary to point out that any such theory of human origins remains highly speculative. Paleoanthropologists revise their phylogenetic trees nearly every year as new finds come in from the field, so how and when human populations branched off into different racial groups remains an open question. And it is, of course, the hypothetical status of such theories which gives the author the latitude to assemble favored hypotheses into a developmental scenario that fits the thesis of his book. There are additional problems in Entine's interpretations in this area. Why, for example, does he have the three major racial stocks (Caucasian, Mongoloid, Negroid) splitting as recently as 14,000 years ago (113) after he has argued earlier that this primary racial differentiation is of much greater antiquity (82)? As the author points out, "there is certainly ample wiggle room for ambiguity" (88) when it comes to multiregionalism, and his readers can only agree with one of the few calls for intellectual caution that appear in this book. But after calling for caution, Entine leaps in with both feet anyway.

The author's presentation of the physiological evidence for black athletic superiority (Chapter 19) is the most interesting section of the book. His strategy is to combine into a single model every claim about racial differences for which any support can be found in the published literature or private commentary. If the author can point to a single publication or an interview that supports a favored idea, then it passes muster. This lack of interest in assessing the reliability of his sources is the major deficiency of the book.

The first of several claims about racial physiology is that black babies—African as well as African-American—are physically precocious. Eight published articles, dating from 1953 to 1992, are cited to support this argument, since the author suspects that "precocious infants will end up as athletically skilled adults" (251). Either of these claims is conceivably true. That the author does not distinguish between genetic differences and congenital differences at birth arising from different prenatal environments is one more indication of his advocacy approach to scientific evidence and his lack of interest in environmental factors bearing on human development.

The second claim is that blacks of West African origin have more fast-twitch muscle fibers than whites (253–254). This conclusion is based on a 1986 publication that compared about a dozen sedentary West Africans with an equal number of French Canadians—an inadequate sample on which to base such a generalization. Nor does the author explain to his readers the complexity and potential unreliability of muscle-fiber typing procedures. While information on this subject appears in *Darwin's Athletes* (284–285), the author has chosen not to cite it.

The work of the Swedish physiologist Bengt Saltin on Kenyan and Swedish distance runners is probably the only scientifically credible research on the physiology of elite athletes involving racial comparisons. Saltin found suggestive differences in the cross-sectional area (but not type) of muscle fibers and in physiological variables related to fatigue, both of which might help to explain superior Kenyan performances. Readers of Entine's summary of this work (259–260) will find a less ambivalent and intellectually modest Saltin than the one found in his published papers. Readers may also wish to compare the reviewer's treatment of this work in *Darwin's Athletes* (206–207).

Finally, Entine finds "intriguing data in support of the stereotype that blacks are more relaxed than whites" (265–266), which might translate into an athletic advantage. These "data" consist of stop-action photographs of black and white athletes as described by a scientist in a 1988 issue of *Life* magazine. Once again, readers may want to examine the history of this stereotype in *Darwin's Athletes* (199–201).

In summary, the author's treatment of scientific evidence is speculative, selective, and inconclusive. When the scientists he interviews refuse to speak as categorically as he wishes, he implies they are too faint-hearted to speak their minds (251, 269–270, 271). The author's generally careless approach to genetics is evident in his reference to "significant black-white differences in the prevalence of genetically based hypertension" (288). In fact, one of the mysteries of hypertension is that rural West Africans have much lower rates of hypertension than African Americans, a finding that implicates social factors such as stress rather than genes (Richard S. Cooper, Charles N. Rotimi, and Ryk Ward, "The Puzzle of Hypertension in African-Americans," *Scientific American,* February 1999, 56–63).

In the last analysis, the problem with *Taboo* as a work of science reporting originates in the author's journalistic standards, which are based on a determination to offer "intriguing data" and to be politically incorrect within certain limits. In this regard, his description of Martin Kane's 1971 *Sports Illustrated* article on this subject, "An Assessment of 'Black Is Best'," as being "in the best tradition of journalism, mixing anecdotes with available science," strikes me as unfathomable (see *Darwin's Athletes,* 193–195). I would have thought that the point of a book written 30 years after Kane would be to exceed the scientific standards at *Sports Illustrated,* not to imitate them.

POSTSCRIPT

Are Blacks "Natural Born" Athletes?

Is Hoberman afraid to admit that Entine has proven that Blacks are natural-born athletes, or does Entine play fast and loose with facts, as Hoberman suggests? Neither author considers in-depth the fact that even in sports that currently feature a disproportionately large number of Blacks, they still represent a rainbow. That is, in basketball and football, for example, the skin colors of the Black players range from very light to very dark, indicating that they are not a racially homogeneous group. Entine admits that many baseball players are Hispanic but adds that they are still of Negro descent. Yet Hispanics are also likely to be of white descent.

Do Blacks dominate sports? Clearly, in many sports Blacks remain invisible. Examples are cycling, ice skating, speed skating, hockey, biathlons, boat racing, and until recently, golf (and golf sensation Tiger Woods points out that while he is of African American descent, he is descended from other races as well). And although Entine cites Kenyan runner and two-time Olympic gold medalist Kip Keino as holding that he and other Blacks are born athletes, Keino is quoted in an article in the November 26, 2000, issue of the British newspaper *Observer* as saying, "To me, it is interest and hard work," in dismissing the idea of genetic advantage.

Sports have been an avenue for different ethnic groups to achieve vertical mobility for generations. At one time the Irish dominated football, Jews were disproportionately represented in basketball and produced successful boxers, and Italians and others made significant contributions to baseball and other sports. Moreover, there are places on Earth that are geographically similar to Kenya that have yet to supply an abundance of runners.

Is the issue harmful? Can it be discussed without an invidious or negative connotation being attached to one group or another? Should biology now be used to explain tendencies in other racial and ethnic groups? That is, can one say that Germans are more bellicose, Italians are more musical, and the Irish are more pugilistic because of their genes?

There is a plethora of literature on the issue of Black athleticism and related topics, including Joseph L. Graves, Jr.'s benchmark work *The Emperor's New Clothes: Biological Theories of Race at the Millennium* (Rutgers University Press, 2001). "Breaking the Taboo," by Entine, plus several thoughtful rejoinders on both sides of the debate appear in the summer 2000 issue of *Skeptic*. Also see J. Arlidge's "Black Runners 'Have Speed Genes,'" *Observer* (November 26, 2000), which can be found on the Internet at http://www.observer.co.uk/international/story/0,6903,403113,00.html. Two articles that agree that the issue should at least be gotten up front is A. Barba, "Does Nature

Nurture Speed?" *The Wall Street Journal* (September 20, 2000) and J. Holt, "Nobody Does It Better," *The New York Times Book Review* (April 16, 2000), which is a review of Entine's *Taboo*.

Issues that are related to that of biology-sports connections are addressed in J. Jacobson, "Why Do So Many Female Athletes Enter ACL Hell?" *Chronicle of Higher Education* (March 9, 2001) and M. Lord, "Too Much, Too Soon," *U.S. News & World Report* (July 17, 2000). Jay Schulkin, in *Roots of Social Sensibility and Neural Function* (MIT Press, 2001), looks at neurological bases for emotions. A timely report on a Hispanic athlete is "El Diablo on Ice," by J. Stein, *Time* (June 12, 2000). Finally, two helpful overviews of college sports are *College Football: History, Spectacle, Controversy* by John Sayle Watterson (Johns Hopkins University Press, 2000) and James L. Shulman and William G. Bowen, *Game of Life: College Sports and Educational Values* (Princeton University Press, 2001).

ISSUE 3

Do Industrialization and Capitalism Cause Racial and Ethnic Inequalities?

YES: Sheila E. Henry, from "Ethnic Identity, Nationalism, and International Stratification: The Case of the African American," *Journal of Black Studies* (January 1999)

NO: Thomas Sowell, from "Race, Culture and Equality," *Forbes* (October 5, 1998)

ISSUE SUMMARY

YES: Professor of arts and sciences Sheila E. Henry argues that ethnic and racial inequalities can be understood only in the context of global stratification. She holds that in the United States, minorities whose ancestral nations have high prestige are allocated high prestige themselves, while African Americans and others, reflecting both institutional racism and the low status of many African societies, are forced to occupy the bottom rungs of society.

NO: Thomas Sowell, a researcher at the Hoover Institute, maintains that dominant theories of racial and ethnic inequality that are based on prejudice, oppression, exploitation, and discrimination are simply wrong. He develops an alternative explanation based on geography, which he indicates also has meaningful policy implications.

In all societies some people are better off than others. However, the basis for how society's valued resources (e.g., money, prestige, power, and opportunities) are distributed varies greatly, as does the amount of inequality. Traditional explanations of inequality have been based on genetics (some are born superior to others), theology (it is God's way), and custom (people from one tribe are considered better—or worse—than people from the others).

Most social scientists categorically reject such reasons for inequality. Instead, structural or sociological explanations as well as social psychological factors, such as attitudes and values, are embraced. That is, the environment or social situation within which groups exist accounts for much inequality. For instance, people born in poverty obviously have far less wealth, opportunities, and power than others. Moreover, their speech, body language, clothing, consumption patterns, recreational activities, and even health are sometimes visibly different from those who are better off. This makes it "natural" for others to discriminate against the poor. Prejudice develops, and members of the victimized group often come to agree with the dominant group's definition of them. Quickly, the whole thing becomes a cruel spiral of cumulative causation. Unemployment, lack of formal education, "nonstandard" behavior, and so on are reflected, which reinforces both the low status of the minority group and the perceptions of the dominant group.

While almost all scholars reject the notion that inequality results from biological or religious inferiority, there remains much disagreement about the actual causes. Marxists, for instance, maintain that class or economic factors based on the control of a society's wealth by its elites create social inequalities. Others insist that race and ethnicity are important contributors (that there is discrimination against those with different racial and ethnic backgrounds). Some more recent work has included gender along with race and class as a basis for inequality. Many other variables, such as age and language, also partially account for social differences.

Sheila E. Henry's analysis in the following selection draws heavily from race-based theories and the world system perspective. Following that model, she divides nations into core and peripheral ones. She asserts that the core, or developed, capitalist societies more or less colonize and exploit less developed nations, or those that are peripheral to the world economy. Henry finds parallels between the position of nations within the world economic system and the status of its citizens within the United States. Blacks, for example, were snatched from Africa to function as slaves in the West, and for generations their disadvantaged status has been maintained and even magnified through racism. These chains are still in existence, Henry argues. Moreover, the low international market position of Africa in general helps to reinforce the low status of African Americans.

In the second selection, Thomas Sowell, drawing from once-popular geopolitical theories, contends that it is geography, not race or discrimination, that is destiny. Simply put, folks who are isolated from others are bound to be deprived of cultural stimulation as well as excluded from trade routes. It is not just natural resources that may be lacking but also location. Most African societies, for instance, had a shortage of natural harbors, waterways that were easily navigable, and land routes that were easy to create and use. Thus, they were automatically excluded from contact with others. He cites several similar geographic handicaps among Europeans and others and argues that when these people migrated to the United States, they too could not compete with many other minority members.

Both Henry and Sowell reflect a broad, macrostructural approach to the problem of inequality. Which position seems to have the most empirical validity? Which has the most analytical or theoretic validity? What might the policy implications be for minority members if one or the other viewpoint is accepted?

Sheila E. Henry

Ethnic Identity, Nationalism, and International Stratification

Insofar as Western European nations—in particular Britain, France, and Germany—were among the earliest to industrialize, the imposition of their hegemony on Africa and Asia created a new basis for status allocation within a global stratification system. This article will attempt to explore the relationship between contemporary levels of ethnic or racial inequality within the United States and the global status of country of origin for a number of ethnic groups.

... It will be argued that there are at least two major systemic factors involved: (a) the status of the nation of origin within the global stratification system so that the higher its international status on the criteria of economic, political, and military dominance, the higher the social status accorded group members by the dominant group within the United States; and (b) changes in the international status of the country of origin will be reflected in revisions of status level for such ethnic/racial groups....

Theoretical Explanation of the U.S. Stratification System

The characteristics of social stratification and its bases are well established and documented in the literature. Among scholars, Gerth and Mills (1946), Davis and Moore (1945), Bendix and Lipset (1958), and Kerbo (1983) speak to the institutionalization of unequal access to scarce resources and the differential allocation of rank and prestige to groups bearing specific "valued" characteristics, real or imagined, physical or intellectual. Similarly, proponents of the elitist view of American social structure have demonstrated not only the importance of shared social background and values among the "power elite" but also the degree to which such inherited advantages contribute to the maintenance of elite social status and the opportunity for its members to control the social, political, and economic institutions. The critical contribution of the ascribed status of race/ethnicity is inadequately examined, the privileges of "whiteness" being invisible to those so endowed. Among stigmatized ethnics, Jews have used the survival technique of changing the family name, but African or Asian ancestry with visibly distinguishing characteristics of skin color and texture of hair cannot be so simply discarded or disguised.

These realities contradict or discredit theories of assimilation or the "melting pot" theory, whose basic assumptions held that abandonment of ancestral culture and traditions was the key to entry into mainstream America and access to social, economic, and political opportunity.

European Immigration and Social Stratification

... National status will be shown to be allocated, imposed, and created by the economic relations inherent in imperialism, colonialism, and industrialization. Just as the upper class within a class-based system determines the norms and values of a society—exploiting the labor of the working class for the benefit of the upper classes—so within the international stratification system, the imperial power determines the position of the colonized by exploiting the latter's resources. Informal United States immigration policy has always reflected a preference for immigrants from northwestern Europe, that is, Anglo-Saxons....

Before 1880, about 80% of all immigrants came from the United Kingdom, Ireland, Germany, and Scandinavia. By 1900, immigrants from Italy, Russia, and the Austro-Hungarian Empire accounted for more than one half of the total number of immigrants....

The demand for labor by a rapidly expanding industrial economy and a determination to crush the growing strength of labor unions, the drying up of labor from the preferred countries, together with the effects of World War I had overridden nativism and anti-Popist sentiments and opened the door to previously "undesirable" immigrants from southern and eastern European countries. The "whitening" of southern Europeans had begun, both in response to the freeing of African slaves and the fear of working-class coalitions being formed between former African slaves and the cheap imported European factory laborers and steel and coal mine workers. The possibility of a class struggle evolving was real. The concept of being "White" and privileged took root, yet the preference for immigrants from northwestern Europe persisted with periodic eruptions of nativism at the increasingly visible presence of the "new" immigrants....

Chinese Immigration and the Chinese Exclusion Act of 1882

Although the East Coast and the Midwest were inundated with European immigrants, the West Coast drew its labor from the Pacific Rim, specifically China and Japan. Between 1851 and 1858, more than 200,000 Chinese had emigrated to work on the railroads in California. Ethnic hostility and exclusion took many forms. In 1852, the governor of California wanted restrictions placed on the Chinese on the grounds that Chinese "coolies" were unassimilable, lowered the standard of living, were heathens, and were economic opportunists who would eventually overrun the state. In 1854, a California Supreme Court decision effectively disenfranchised Chinese immigrants by denying them the right to testify against a White man. Violence against Chinese became commonplace. In 1871, some 22 Chinese were lynched in Los Angeles, and in 1885 in Wyoming, 29 Chinese were murdered and their property looted and destroyed....

Chinese immigrants had no recourse, neither could they expect protection from the Chinese Emperor for a number of reasons. As was the case with central and southern Europe, China in the 1840s and until the fall of the Manchu dynasty was [not] a politically united empire.... Chinese identity was framed by family, kinship group, and clan. China's weak political position and low international status is... evidenced by the military defeats she suffered....

The Japanese and the Gentlemen's Agreement: 1908

Japanese immigration followed Chinese, and between 1890 and 1900 approximately 20,000 had arrived on the mainland from Japan and Hawaii where they had already emigrated to work on the sugar cane plantations. Although initially welcomed because of their industry, compliant nature, and willingness to accept low wages, their attempts to improve their economic positions soon aroused the ire of the White American community. Newspaper editorials and legislation record the intensity of anti-Japanese sentiment. The *San Francisco Chronicle* (1910) comments,

> Japanese ambition is to progress beyond mere servility to the plane of the better class of American workman and to own a home with him. The moment that this position is exercised, the Japanese ceases to be an ideal laborer....

Despite [many] obstacles, the Japanese succeeded in securing a significant share of the truck farming market. Their economic success was met with the passing of a more serious restriction, the California Alien Land Act of 1913. Now, as persons ineligible for citizenship, they were prevented from land ownership and could only lease agricultural land up to a period of 3 years.... Although state law and local custom persecuted the Japanese and their children, at the national level an entirely different picture emerges. Attempts to force Japanese children into segregated schools as had been done to the Chinese children were unsuccessful largely as a result of presidential intervention. The furor in Japan at this serious racial insult had the potential to provoke an international incident. President Theodore Roosevelt's concern not to offend the emperor and the Japanese nation could fairly be related to Japan's recent demonstration of its military strength—a convincing defeat of the Russian army in 1904 (an event that had stunned all of Western Europe and the United States)—followed by the conquest of Korea and Manchuria in 1905. Japan had effectively claimed a place within the higher levels of the international stratification system by its military prowess.... And so... the Gentlemen's Agreement of 1908 between the governments of Japan and the United States was a bilateral agreement between political and military equals. Japan agreed to halt immigration to the United

States, whereas the United States undertook to ensure that Japanese citizens in the United States would be protected from discriminatory acts. Unlike China, Japan remained a fully independent nation during the flowering of Western imperialism....

Africa, Colonialism, and the Slave Trade

The history of Africans in the United States as slaves is inextricably tied to the colonization of both the United States and Africa and Britain's rise to supremacy among mercantilist nations in the 17th century.... British ships were supreme on the high seas and had a 30-year monopoly to supply slaves to the Spanish colonies in the West Indies. In West Africa, from which the majority of slaves were brought, kidnapped, or stolen, political structures in 17th and 18th century West Africa broadly resembled that of much of eastern and southern Europe and China—monarchical empires and fragmented communities bound together by traditional tribal social organizations in which tribute was owed and paid to the most powerful military overlord.... Ethnic rivalry fueled continuous raiding parties and warfare, and as was traditional, prisoners were sold as slaves to any willing buyer. Invitations from indigenous chiefs for armed support against an ethnic rival or entry into a temporary strategic alliance with British or French traders were transformed into opportunities for widening economic and political control....

Colonialism and the International Stratification System

In colonial Africa, the imperialists systematically denigrated and partially destroyed indigenous social and political institutions. Most significantly, the economy of the nations in the periphery were distorted to serve those of the core nations, thus the "underdevelopment" of former colonies.... Historians have concluded that whereas in 1879 approximately 90% of the continent was still formally under traditional African sovereignty, by 1900 almost the entire continent was under European rule (Burns, 1929; Oliver & Atmore, 1969)....

The bases for the current system of international and ethnic stratification can be seen to derive from the process of emergent capitalism, the creation and consolidation of nation states in Europe, and imperial expansionism, colonialism, and competition among European nations. The scramble for Africa that occurred between 1880 and 1900 in which Britain, France, and Germany partitioned Africa into spheres of influence resulted in a tumultuous overturning of African sovereignty....

African Americans, Ethnic Identity, and Group Status

What are the consequences of colonialism for Americans of African ancestry or Africans in the diaspora in general? It would appear that the most extreme case of the negative impact of low international status of a country on its members is that of African states for Africans in the diaspora and on African Americans in particular. African Americans find themselves in a qualitatively different situation from either Chinese or Japanese Americans. Arriving as slaves beginning in the 17th century, African slaves and their descendants were not free until the 19th century with the passage of the 13th Amendment (1865). Despite this, they were denied the actual enjoyment of the rights and privileges as evidenced by a series of amendments and Supreme Court decisions—the 14th and 15th Amendments (1868, 1870); *Plessy v. Ferguson* (1892); *Brown v. the Board of Education*, Topeka, Kansas (1954); the Civil Rights Act of 1964; and the Voting Rights Act of 1965. With little authentic knowledge of their ancestral homelands, culture(s), or traditions, they instead widely rejected Africa as ancestral home, with the exception of one state, Ethiopia. The reasons for the rejection should be obvious in the light of the foregoing. On the other hand, Ethiopia was the exception because it was the single African nation that had a long and illustrious history reflected in its international status. It bears comparison with Japan in that it was a politically independent nation that had successfully fended off European intrusion and, in 1896, had inflicted a military defeat on Italy in the decisive battle of Adowa....

The colonial status of Africa continued until the 1950s when political independence was granted or won by most states. But decades of underdevelopment and economic exploitation have made it increasingly difficult to bridge the ever-widening technological gap that reinforces the core/periphery relationship. "Divide and conquer" colonial strategies have sharpened interethnic rivalry into deep political cleavages. In Nigeria, for example, typical of former colonies, the task of creating a single nation with shared values, goals, and a sense of peoplehood from collectivities of linguistically and ethnically diverse peoples (among whom are traditional rivalries) has proved elusive. Rather, the territory has devolved into a myriad of ethnic provinces, a contemporary reversion to precolonial geographic and ethnic homelands. Economic growth resulting from the discovery of extensive oil fields has led to her becoming a significant player in the world market and has had a recognizable psychological impact during the 1960s and 1970s on African Americans, seen in a growth of ethnic pride and awareness. The civil rights movement in the 1960s owed much to the explosion of political and budding economic independence among Africa nations....

International Status, Ethnic Group Status in the United States

How are these sociopolitical historical events and processes reflected in the relationship between the international status of a nation and that of its members within American society? Primacy of place for the British in particular has already been explored. Its imperial power deriving from the resources of its colonial dependents enabled it to confer the highest social status on its members. As "White" came to replace European national origin, all persons of European ancestry have enjoyed a social status higher than those whose origins are non-European. The principle of global economic dominance nevertheless still operates as in the modern-day decline in the status of Britain with loss of empire and economic superiority and its replacement first by Germany during the 1960s and 1970s when the German economy dominated the world market, then by Japan in the 1970s and 1980s. Although Japan's adversarial role in World War II had negative effects for Japanese Americans, its rapid postwar modernization and later domination of the global economy not only restored its status but led to the imitation of its business management strategies....

Chinese Americans, on the other hand, are highly endogamous and retain strong local ethnic communities and associations. Although the two Chinas—mainland China and Taiwan—exist in different relationships with the United States, nevertheless each confers national status benefits on its citizens as a result of its peculiar location within the world system.... Chinese Americans benefit from both sources of international status. African nations, however, have not been able to sustain their initial promise and have, for the most part, declined into a new state of political instability and economic dependency. Today they remain on the periphery of the global economy, of minor strategic interest to the new world system. Despite social and political gains by the African American population, their status as a group remains lower than that of any other ethnic group, even including the most recent immigrants from southeast Asia.

Conclusions

Viewing stratification systems within nations as a reflection of the global economic stratification system offers a perspective that provides greater insight into the origins of internal stratification systems, particularly that of a multi-ethnic society such as the United States. The case studies seem to support the main arguments of this article. The high status held by Britain and other imperial European nations was conferred on their immigrant representatives in the United States, and the possibility of class revolution in the United States led to the inclusion of all persons of European descent under a "White" umbrella. Although some European immigrants were initially excluded, their treatment was still muted compared with that meted out to those who originated from China and Africa. The reasons have been presented. In contemporary times, Japan ranks among the leading capitalist nations of the world, and Japanese Americans may be said to have achieved the status of "honorary" Whites, as Andrew Hacker recently opined. China (mainland, including Hong Kong today and Taiwan) is generally speculated to replace Japan as the next economic giant in the global economy due to the raw potential of its massive populations, its military threat, and the remarkable success (Taiwan and Hong Kong) as semiperipheral societies, and as manufacturers of finished goods for the global market, albeit using the cheap "sweatshop" labor of its citizens. Thus, Chinese Americans as an ethnic group now enjoy a relatively respectable status, although it is by comparison lower than that of Japanese Americans. Africa, by comparison, remains largely noncompetitive within the postindustrial global economy (a peripheral economy in the world system). Its constituent nations remain mired in interethnic wars and unstable political systems reminiscent of mid-19th-century Europe rather than contemporary industrialized societies. Given that the likelihood of any individual African state achieving economic global dominance in the near future appears slim, no revision of ethnic group status appears imminent for African Americans.

References

Bendix, R., & Lipset, S. M. (Eds.). *Class, status and power: A reader in social stratification*. Glencoe, IL: Free Press.

Burns, A. (1929). *History of Nigeria*. London: Allen & Unwin.

Chase-Dunn, C., & Hall, T. D. (Eds.). (1991). *Core-periphery relations in a pre-capitalist world*. Oxford: Blackwell.

Davis, K., & Moore, W. E. (1945). Some principles of stratification. *American Sociological Review, 10*, 243–248.

Gerth H., & Mills, C. W. (1946). *From Max Weber: Essays in sociology*. New York: Oxford University Press.

Kerbo, H. R. (1983). *Social stratification and inequality: Conflict in the U.S.* New York: McGraw-Hill.

Oliver, R., & Atmore, A. (1969). *Africa since 1800*. Cambridge, UK: Cambridge University Press.

Omi, M., Winant, H. (1986). *Racial formation in the United States: From the 1960s to the 1980s*. London: Routledge & Kegan Paul.

NO

Thomas Sowell

Race, Culture and Equality

During the 15 years that I spent researching and writing my recently completed trilogy on racial and cultural issues, I was struck again and again with how common huge disparities in income and wealth have been for centuries, in countries around the world—and yet how each country regards its own particular disparities as unusual, if not unique. Some of these disparities have been among racial or ethnic groups, some among nations, and some among regions, continents or whole civilizations.

In the nineteenth century real per capita income in the Balkans was about one-third that in Britain. That dwarfs intergroup disparities that many in the United States today regard as not merely strange but sinister. Singapore has a median per capita income that is literally hundreds of times greater than that in Burma.

During the recent rioting in Indonesia, much of it directed against the ethnic Chinese in that country, some commentators found it strange that the Chinese minority, which is just 5 percent of the Indonesian population, owned an estimated four-fifths of the capital in the country. But it is not strange. Such disparities have long been common in other countries in Southeast Asia, where Chinese immigrants typically entered poor and then prospered, creating whole industries in the process. People from India did the same in much of East Africa and in Fiji.

Occupational differences have been equally unequal.

In the early 1920s, Jews were just 6 percent of the population of Hungary and 11 percent of the population of Poland, but they were more than half of all the physicians in both countries, as well as being vastly over-represented in commerce and other fields. In the early twentieth century, all of the firms in all of the industries producing the following products in Brazil's state of Rio Grande do Sul were owned by people of German ancestry: trunks, stoves, paper, hats, neckties, leather, soap, glass, watches, beer, confections and carriages.

In the middle of the nineteenth century, just three countries produced most of the manufactured goods in the world—Britain, Germany, and the United States. By the late twentieth century, it was estimated that 17 percent of the people in the world produce four-fifths of the total output on the planet.

Such examples could be multiplied longer than you would have the patience to listen.

Why are there such disparities? In some cases, we can trace the reasons, but in other cases we cannot. A more fundamental question, however, is: Why should anyone have ever expected equality in the first place?

Let us assume, for the sake of argument, that not only every racial or ethnic group, but even every single individual in the entire world, has identical genetic potential. If it is possible to be even more extreme, let us assume that we all behave like saints toward one another. Would that produce equality of results?

Of course not. Real income consists of output and output depends on inputs. These inputs are almost never equal—or even close to being equal.

During the decade of the 1960s, for example, the Chinese minority in Malaysia earned more than a hundred times as many engineering degrees as the Malay majority. Halfway around the world at the same time, the majority of the population of Nigeria, living in its northern provinces, were just 9 percent of the students attending that country's University of Ibadan and just 2 percent of the much larger number of Nigerian students studying abroad in foreign institutions of higher learning. In the Austrian Empire in 1900, the illiteracy rate among Polish adults was 40 percent and among Serbo-Croatians 75 percent —but only 6 percent among the Germans.

Given similar educational disparities among other groups in other countries—disparities in both the quantity and quality of education, as well as in fields of specialization—why should anyone expect equal outcomes in incomes or occupations?

Educational differences are just one source of economic disparities. Even at the level of craft skills, groups have differed enormously, as they have in urbanization. During the Middle Ages, and in some places long beyond, most of the population of the cities in Slavic Eastern Europe were not Slavs. Germans, Jews, and other non-Slavic peoples were the majority populations in these cities for centuries, while the Slavs were predominantly peasants in the surrounding countrysides. Prior to the year 1312, the official records of the city of Cracow were kept in German—and the transition that year was to Latin. Only decades later did Poles become a majority of the population of Cracow. Only over a period of centuries did the other cities of Slavic Eastern Europe acquire predominantly Slavic populations. As late as 1918, 97 percent of the people living in the cities of Byelorussia were not Byelorussians.

Until this long transition to urban living took place among the Slavs, how could the wide range of skills typically found in cities be expected to exist in populations that lived overwhelmingly in the countryside? Not only did they not have such skills in Eastern Europe, they did not have them when they immigrated to the United States, to Australia, or to other countries, where they typically worked in low-level occupations and earned correspondingly low incomes. In the early years of the twentieth century, for example, immigrants to the United States from Eastern and Southern Europe earned just 15 percent of the income of immigrants from Norway, Holland, Sweden, and Britain.

Groups also differ demographically. It is not uncommon to find some groups with median ages a decade younger than the median ages of other groups, and differences of two decades are not unknown. During the era of the Soviet Union, for example, Central Asians had far more children than Russians or the peoples of the Baltic republics, and so had much younger median ages. At one time, the median age of Jews in the United States was 20 years older than the median age of Puerto Ricans. If Jews and Puerto Ricans had been absolutely identical in every other respect, including their cultures and histories, they would still not have been equally represented in jobs requiring long years of experience, or in retirement homes, or in activities associated with youth, such as sports or crime.

Nothing so intractably conflicts with our desires for equality as geography. Yet the physical settings in which races, nations, and civilizations have evolved have had major impacts on the cultures developed within those settings. At its simplest and crudest, the peoples of the Himalayas have not had an equal opportunity to acquire seafaring skills. Nor have Eskimos had an equal opportunity to acquire knowledge and experience in growing pineapples or other tropical crops.

Too often the influence of geography on wealth is thought of narrowly, in terms of natural resources that directly translate into wealth, such as oil in the Middle East or gold in South Africa. But, important as such differences in natural wealth are, geography influences even more profound cultural differences among the people themselves.

Where geography isolates people, whether in mountain valleys or on small islands scattered across a vast sea, there the cultural exposures of those people to the outside world are very limited and so, typically, is their technological advancement. While the rest of the world exchanges goods, knowledge and innovations from a vast cultural universe, isolated peoples have been largely limited to what they alone have been able to develop.

Few, if any, of the great advances in human civilization have come from isolated peoples. As the eminent French historian Fernand Braudel put it, the mountains almost always lag behind the plains—even if the races in the two places are the same. Potatoes and the English language both reached the Scottish lowlands before they reached the highlands. Islam reached North Africa's Rif mountains long after the people in the plains had become Moslems.

When the Spaniards invaded the Canary Islands in the fifteenth century, they found people of a Caucasian race living at a Stone-Age level. So were the Australian aborigines when the British discovered them.

Geographically imposed cultural isolation takes many forms and exists in many degrees. Cities have long been in the vanguard of human progress, all over the world, but cities do not arise randomly in all geographic settings. Most of the great cities of the world have developed on navigable waterways—rivers or harbors—but such waterways are by no means equally or randomly distributed around the world. They are very common in Western Europe and very rare in sub-Saharan Africa. Urbanization has long been correspondingly common in Western Europe and correspondingly rare in sub-Saharan Africa. One-third of the land mass of Europe consists of islands and peninsulas but only one percent of the land mass of South America consists of islands and peninsulas.

Navigable waterways have been economically crucial, especially during the millennia of human history before the development of railroads, trucks and airplanes. Before the transcontinental railroad was built, it was both faster and cheaper to reach San Francisco from a port in China than from Saint Louis. People in the city of Tbilisi bought their kerosene from Texas—8,000 miles away across water—rather than from the Baku oil fields, less than 400 miles away across land.

Such vast differences in costs between water transport and land transport affect what can be transported and how far. Gold or diamonds can repay the costs of transport across thousands of miles of land, but grain or coal cannot. More important, the size of a people's cultural universe depends on how far they can reach out to other peoples and other cultures. No great civilization has developed in isolation. Geography in general and navigable waterways in particular set the limits of a people's cultural universe, broadly or narrowly. But these limits are by no means set equally for all peoples or all civilization.

For example, when the British first crossed the Atlantic and confronted the Iroquois on the eastern seaboard of what is today the United States, they were able to steer across that ocean in the first place because they used rudders invented in China, they could navigate on the open seas with the help of trigonometry invented in Egypt, their calculations were done with numbers invented in India, and their general knowledge was preserved in letters invented by the Romans. But the Iroquois could not draw upon the knowledge of the Aztecs or the Incas, whose very existence they had no way of knowing. The clash was not between the culture created by the British versus the culture created by the Iroquois. It was a clash between cultural developments drawn from vast regions of the world versus cultural developments from a much more circumscribed area. The cultural opportunities were unequal and the outcomes were unequal. Geography has never been egalitarian.

A network of rivers in Western Europe flows gently through vast plains, connecting wide areas economically and culturally. The rivers of tropical Africa plunge a thousand feet or more on their way to the sea, with cascades and waterfalls making them navigable only for stretches between these natural barriers—and the coastal plain in Africa averages just 20 miles. Regular rainfall and melting snows keep the rivers of Western Europe flowing throughout the year, but African rivers have neither—and so rise and fall dramatically with the seasons, further limiting their usefulness. The two continents are at least as dramatically different when it comes to natural harbors. Although Africa is more than twice the size of Europe, it has a shorter coastline. That is because the European coastline continually twists and turns, creating innumerable harbors, while the African coastline is smooth, with few harbors. How surprising is it that international commerce has played a much smaller role in the economic history of Africa than in that of Europe in general and Western Europe in particular?

These particular geographic disparities are by no means exhaustive. But they are suggestive of some of the many ways in which physical settings have expanded or constricted the size of the cultural universe available to different peoples. One revealing indication of cultural fragmentation is that African peoples are 10 percent of the world's population but have one-third of the world's languages.

In controversies over "nature versus nurture" as causes of economic and other disparities among peoples and civilizations, nature is often narrowly conceived as genetic differences. Yet geography is also nature—and its patterns are far more consistent with history than are genetic theories. China, for example, was for many centuries the leading nation in the world—technologically, organizationally and in many other ways. Yet, in more recent centuries, China has been overtaken and far surpassed by Europe. Yet neither region of the world has changed genetically to any extent that would account for this dramatic change in their relative positions. This historic turnaround also shows that geographic limitations do not mean geographic determinism, for the geography of the two regions likewise underwent no such changes as could account for the reversal of their respective positions in the world.

Back in the fifteenth century, China sent ships on voyages of exploration longer than that of Columbus, more than half a century before Columbus, and in ships more advanced than those in Europe at the time. Yet the Chinese rulers made a decision to discontinue such voyages and in fact to reduce China's contacts with the outside world. European rulers made the opposite decision and established worldwide empires, ultimately to the detriment of China. In short, geography sets limits, but people determine what they will do within those limits. In some parts of the world, geographic limits have been set so narrowly that the peoples of these regions have never had the options available to either the Europeans or the Chinese. Isolation has left such regions not only lagging economically but fragmented culturally and politically, making them prey to larger, more prosperous and more powerful nations.

We have seen how cultural handicaps have followed Eastern Europeans as they immigrated overseas, leading to lower levels of income than among immigrants from Western Europe who settled in the same places, whether North America or Australia. If Africans had immigrated voluntarily to the Western Hemisphere, instead of in bondage, is there any reason to believe that their earnings would have achieved an equality that the Slavic immigrants failed to achieve?

There is no question that Africans and their descendants faced the additional barrier of color prejudice, but can we measure its effects by assuming that black people would have had the same income and wealth as white people in the absence of this factor—especially in view of the large disparities among different groups of white immigrants, not to mention the rise of some nonwhite groups such as Chinese Americans and Japanese Americans to incomes above the national average?

Put differently, geography has not only cheated many peoples of equal cultural opportunities, it has also cheated all of us today of a simple criterion for measuring the economic and social effects of other variables, such as prejudice and discrimination. Nothing has been more common in human history than discrimination against different groups, whether different by race, religion, caste or in innumerable other ways. Moreover, this discrimination has itself been unequal—more fierce against some groups than others and more pervasive at some periods of history than in others. If there were not so many other powerful factors creating disparities in income and wealth, it might be possible to measure the degree of discrimination by the degree of differences in economic outcomes. Even so, the temptation to do so is seductive, especially as a means of reducing the complexities of life to the simplicities of politics. But the facts will not fit that vision.

Anyone familiar with the history of race relations in the Western Hemisphere would find it virtually impossible to deny that blacks in the United States have faced more hostility and discrimination than blacks in Latin America. As just one example, 161 blacks were lynched in one year in the United States, but racial lynching was unknown south of the Rio Grande. Perhaps the strongest case against the predominance of discrimination as an explanation of economic disparities would be a comparison of blacks in Haiti with blacks in the United States. Since Haiti became independent two centuries ago, Haitian blacks should be the most prosperous blacks in the hemisphere and American blacks the poorest, if discrimination is the overwhelming factor, but in fact the direct opposite is the case. It is Haitians who are the poorest and American blacks who are the most prosperous in the hemisphere—and in the world.

None of this should be surprising. The fact that discrimination deserves moral condemnation does not automatically make it causally crucial. Whether it is or is not in a given time and place is an empirical question, not a foregone conclusion. A confusion of morality with causation may be politically convenient, but that does not make the two things one.

We rightly condemn a history of gross racial discrimination in American education, for example, but when we make that the causal explanation of educational differences, we go beyond what the facts will support. Everyone is aware of times and places when the amount of money spent educating a black child was a fraction of what was spent educating a white child, when the two groups were educated in separate systems, hermetically sealed off from one another, and when worn-out textbooks from the white schools were then sent over to the black schools to be used, while new and more up-to-date textbooks were bought for the white children. The number of days in school sometimes differed so much that a black child with nine years of schooling would have been in class the same number of days as a white child with only six years of schooling. It seems so obvious that such things would account for disparities in test scores, for example.

But is it true?

There are other groups to whom none of these factors apply—and who still have had test score differences as great as those between black and white children in the Jim Crow South. Japanese and Mexican immigrants began arriving in California at about the same time and initially worked in very similar occupations as agricultural laborers. Yet a study of a school district in which their children attended the same schools and sat side-by-side in the same classrooms found IQ differences as great as those between blacks and whites attending schools on opposite sides of town in the Jim Crow South. International studies have found different groups of illiterates—people with no educational differences because they had no education—with mental test differences larger than those between blacks and whites in the United States. Nor is this necessarily a matter of genetics. During the First World War, black soldiers from Ohio, Illinois, New York, and Pennsylvania scored higher on mental tests than did white soldiers from Georgia, Arkansas, Kentucky, and Mississippi.

What is "the" reason? There may not be any such thing as "the" reason. There are so many cultural, social, economic, and other factors interacting that there was never any reason to expect equal results in the first place. That is why plausible simplicities must be subjected to factual scrutiny.

Back in 1899, when the schools of Washington, D.C. were racially segregated and discrimination was rampant, there were four academic high schools in the city—three white and one black. When standardized tests were given that year, the black academic high school scored higher than two of the three white academic high schools.

Today, nearly a century later, even setting such a goal would be considered hopelessly utopian. Nor was this a fluke. That same high school was scoring at or above the national average on IQ tests during the 1930s and 1940s. Yet its physical plant was inadequate and its average class size was higher than that in the city's white high schools. Today, that same school has a much better physical plant, and per-pupil expenditures in the District of Columbia are among the highest in the nation. But the students' test scores are among the lowest. Nor was this school unique in having had higher academic achievements during a period when it seemingly lacked the prerequisites of achievement and yet fell far behind in a later period when these supposed prerequisites were more plentiful.

This is obviously not an argument for segregation and discrimination, nor does it deny that counter-examples might be found of schools that languished in the first period and did better in the second. The point here is much more specific—that resources have had little or nothing to do with educational quality. Numerous studies of schools in general have shown that, both within the United States and in international comparisons. It should be no surprise that the same applies to black schools.

Politically, however, the disbursement of resources is by no means inconsequential. The ability to dispense largess from the public treasury has for centuries been one of the signs and prerogatives of power in countries around the world. In electoral politics, it is vital as an element in reelection. But the ultimate question is: Does it in fact make people better off? How that question is answered is much less important than that it be asked—that we not succumb to social dogmas, even when they are intellectually fashionable and politically convenient.

It is also important that economic and other disparities be confronted, not evaded. Bestselling author Shelby Steele says that whites in America today are fearful of being considered racists, while blacks are fearful of being considered inferior. Social dogmas may be accepted because they relieve both groups of their fears, even if these dogmas neither explain the past nor prepare for the future.

It should be axiomatic that there is not unlimited time, unlimited re-sources, nor unlimited good will among peoples—anywhere in the world. If we are serious about wanting to enlarge opportunities and advance those who are less fortunate, then we cannot fritter away the limited means at our disposal in quixotic quests. We must decide whether our top priority is to smite the wicked or to advance the less fortunate, whether we are looking for visions and rhetoric that make us feel good for the moment or whether we are seeking methods with a proven track record of success in advancing whole peoples from poverty to prosperity.

In an era when esoteric theories can be readily turned into hard cash from the public treasury, our criteria must be higher than what can get government grants for middle-class professionals. They must instead be what will rescue that youngster imprisoned, not only in poverty, but also in a social and cul-tural isolation that has doomed whole peoples for centuries in countries around the world. When we promote cultural provincialism under glittering labels, we must confront the hard question whether we are throwing him a lifeline or an anchor.

History, geography, and cultures are influences but they are not predesti-nation. Not only individuals but whole peoples have moved from the backwaters of the world to the forefront of civilization. The late Italian author Luigi Barzini asked of Britain: "How, in the first place, did a peripheral island rise from prim-itive squalor to world domination?" The story of Japan's rise from a backward country in the mid-nineteenth century to one of today's leading economic powers has been at least equally as dramatic. Scotland was for centuries known for its illiteracy, poverty, and lack of elementary cleanliness. Yet, from the mid-eighteenth to the mid-nineteenth century, most of the leading intellectual pioneers of Britain were Scots, and Scots also become prominent in business, banking, medicine, and engineering—not only in Britain but around the world.

These and other dramatic and heartening rises of whole peoples came from doing things that were often directly the opposite of what is being urged upon less fortunate groups in the United States today. Far from painting themselves into their own little cultural corner and celebrating their "identity," these peo-ples sought the knowledge and insights of other peoples more advanced than themselves in particular skills, technologies, or organizational experience. It took centuries for the English to absorb the cultural advances brought by such conquerors as the Romans and the Normans and by such immigrants as the Huguenots, Germans, Jews, and others who played a major role in develop-ing the British economy. Their early dependence on outsiders was painfully demonstrated when the Romans pulled out of Britain in the fifth century, in order to go defend their threatened empire on the continent, and the British economy and political structure both collapsed. Yet ultimately—more than a thousand years later—the British rose to lead the world into the industrial revo-lution and controlled an empire containing one-fourth of the land area of the earth and one-fourth of the human race.

Japan's economic rise began from a stage of technological backwardness that was demonstrated when Commodore Perry presented them with a gift of a train. Here was their reaction: "At first the Japanese watched the train fearfully from a safe distance, and when the engine began to move they uttered cries of astonishment and drew in their breath. Before long they were inspecting it closely, stroking it, and riding on it, and they kept this up throughout the day."

A century later, the Japanese "bullet train" would be one of the technological wonders of the world, surpassing anything available in the United States. But, before this happened, a major cultural transformation had to take place among the Japanese people. A painful awareness of their own backwardness spread through Japan. Western nations in general and the United States in particular were held up as models to their children. Japanese textbooks urged imitation of Abraham Lincoln and Benjamin Franklin, even more so than Japanese heroes. Many laments about their own shortcomings by the Japanese of that era would today be called "self-hate." But there were no cultural relativists then to tell them that what they had achieved was just as good, in its own way, as what others had. Instead, the Japanese overcame their backwardness, through generations of dedicated work and study, rather than redefining it out of existence.

Both the British and the Japanese became renowned for their ability to absorb the ideas and the technology of others and to carry them forward to higher levels. So did the Scots. At one time, it was common for Scots to blindly imitate the English, even using an English plow that proved to be unsuitable for the soil of Scotland. Yet, once they had absorbed what the English had to offer, the Scots then surpassed the English in some fields, notably medicine and engineering.

History does not offer blueprints for the present but it does offer examples and insights. If nothing else, it can warn us against becoming mesmerized by the heady visions and soaring rhetoric of the moment.

POSTSCRIPT

Do Industrialization and Capitalism Cause Racial and Ethnic Inequalities?

A mere generation ago, racial and ethnic inequalities were quite peripheral to most social science courses. Efforts to link the international scene with discrimination in specific countries were rare. Now, as shown by this debate, the issue is obtaining a serious hearing. The alleged parochialism of U.S. social science, especially in matters of minority relations, may be less of a problem than it was in the past. To some, the current problem in this area is how to transcend what is seen as reverse ethnocentrism and the bashing of U.S. society. That is, most problems pertaining to racial, ethnic, and gender minorities are seen as terrible. White males of European descent are sometimes seen as the source of all structural strains, if not of evil.

This debate, it seems, considerably raises the level of discourse. Henry presents the "radical" and, some would say, "trendy" position. Yet her argument is deeply rooted in careful historical analysis, she develops meaningful analytical categories, and she leaves at least some room to acknowledge minority achievements. Sowell's ideas are fairly original, and they present a potentially stimulating alternative to most standard theories of racial and ethnic inequalities. Moreover, he attempts to use his analysis to generate meaningful policies that might help minorities.

Can the two sides be synthesized? Is it possible to reformulate Sowell's categories so that his geographical determinism could be seen as generating technological advantages for some who then, in terms of Henry's arguments, turned this achievement into instruments by which to exploit others (such as guns)? Can generations of prejudice and discrimination be discounted simply because a theory identifies initial inequalities as resulting from geographical disadvantages? In today's world, can the geopolitical argument hold up? Also, although they do not yet match the achievements of some Asian Americans in terms of economic and educational gains, haven't African Americans made many significant gains that Henry ignores?

Among Sowell's many books are *The Quest for Cosmic Justice* (Free Press, 1999) and *The Vision of the Anointed: Self-Congratulation as a Basis for Social Policy* (Basic Books, 1995). The founder of the world system approach to inequality, Immanuel Wallerstein, has authored *The End of the World as We Know It: Social Science for the Twenty-First Century* (University of Minnesota Press, 1999). Two useful discussions of the role of geopolitics are *Questioning Geopolitics: Political Projects in a Changing World-System* edited by Georgi M. Derluguian and Scott L. Greer (Greenwood Press, 2000) and *Ethnicity in Contemporary America: A Geographical Appraisal*, 2d ed., by Jesse O. McKee (Rowman & Littlefield, 2000).

Two books that describe successful efforts to modernize while sustaining democracy and equality are Dharam Ghai, ed., *Social Development and Public Policy: A Study of Some Successful Experiences* (St. Martin's Press, 1999) and Richard Sandbrook, *Closing the Circle: Democratization and Development in Africa* (Zed Books, 2000). A challenging work that links Eurocentrism, colonialism, and Western science is Sandra Harding, *Is Science Multicultural? Postcolonialisms, Feminisms, and Epistemologies* (Indiana University Press, 1998).

Other works that lie somewhere between Henry's and Sowell's perspectives are *White Lies: Race and the Myths of Whiteness* by Maurice Berger (Farrar, Straus & Giroux, 1998) and Farai Chideya's *Color of Our Future* (William Morrow, 1999). Two works that address the thesis that capitalism creates racism are Carter A. Wilson's *Racism: From Slavery to Advanced Capitalism* (Sage Publications, 1996) and *How Capitalism Underdeveloped Black America: Problems in Race, Political Economy, and Society* by Manning Marable (South End Press, 1983).

ISSUE 4

Have Scholars Ignored the Willing Participation of Germans in Killing Jews During the Holocaust?

YES: Daniel Jonah Goldhagen, from "The Paradigm Challenged," *Tikkun* (May/June 1998)

NO: Christopher R. Browning, from "Victim Testimony," *Tikkun* (January/February 1999)

ISSUE SUMMARY

YES: Daniel Jonah Goldhagen, a political scientist at Harvard University, argues that most writers on the Holocaust have ignored or minimized the role of the police, soldiers, and other "ordinary" Germans as willing executioners of Europe's Jews.

NO: Pacific Lutheran University professor Christopher R. Browning rejects Goldhagen's "accusatory approach," which he contends is self-serving, promotes misunderstanding of traditional scholarship, and does little to advance society's understanding of genocide.

Human beings are remarkably ingenious at creating barriers between themselves and others. One of the most obvious results of such barrier creation, if maintained, is the classification of an entire group as a "minority." By definition, a minority will, at the very least, have less power than the majority. The actual numbers are usually irrelevant. Frequently, members of the majority are numerically a minority, although they may control the numerical majority economically, politically, and socially.

Various labels and definitions of minorities are created to legitimate their separation and unequal treatment (e.g., they are biologically or intellectually inferior, they are emotional, they are dishonest, they are heathens, and so on). In addition, institutional mechanisms emerge. The former are attitudinal or sociopsychological control variables. Institutional mechanisms include legal and other kinds of structural controls, such as apartheid, segregation, the prohibition of hiring minorities for certain jobs, and the prohibition of teaching minorities to read and write.

More extreme modalities of institutional control include enslavement and genocide. The latter means the systematic killing of the members of a particular group. Usually, efforts at genocide result in mass murder, with many, if not most, members of the targeted group escaping and surviving. Most attempts at genocide in the past, while horrible, failed to wipe out any group of people entirely. The Turks' murder of hundreds of thousands of Armenians in the early part of the twentieth century, the recent carnage in central Europe, the Rwandan and other African massacres, and the killing fields of Cambodia in the 1970s—as terrible as they were and are—fell short of their objectives.

Adolf Hitler's killing machine was far more efficient. Approximately one-third of the world's Jews—between 7 and 12 million—were systematically murdered during the years 1933–1945. If it had not been stopped by the Allied victory, there is little doubt that Germany would have come close to killing most Jews. Ironically, the Jews were arguably the most assimilated minority group in Germany, if not in all of Europe. They held positions of honor, and their scientific, political, economic, social, and legal contributions were enormous. Yet in less than a dozen years the Jews went from being friends and neighbors to being pariahs who were hunted down in Germany and throughout Europe and cast into death camps and gas chambers. Women, children, and grandparents were murdered along with teenage and middle-aged males. How did this happen?

In spite of the fact that many of the Holocaust survivors (as well as Jews in other parts of the world) are among the most educated women and men in their countries, this question has not yet been answered satisfactorily to many. For over 50 years the utter surprise, horror, and enormity of the deed has generated more ink by both Jewish and non-Jewish scholars than any other efforts at minority oppression, including other cases of attempted genocide. Yet it remains a serious *Historikerstreit* (deep conflict between scholars) both in and out of Germany. Unlike the better-publicized Holocaust deniers controversy, in which fringe types maintain that there was no killing of Jews in Germany, the controversy over how the Holocaust could have happened at all has shaken the foundations of traditional scholarship.

As you read the following selection by Daniel Jonah Goldhagen, note the many reasons why he is angry that most scholars (in his eyes) have misunderstood or misrepresented the importance of anti-Semitism in Germany. Are such scholars functioning, however unintentionally, as apologists for the Nazis? What alternative paradigm does Goldhagen seem to provide? Consider how elements from his selection might be useful in researching slavery and in addressing current issues of racism and sexism in the United States.

Note how Christopher R. Browning defends his methodology in the second selection (he relied on survivors' statements in his studies). What is the disagreement between Goldhagen and Browning on the role of interviewing victims? Consider also the reasons why Browning dismisses Goldhagen for misusing facts and engaging in self-promotion. Who is right? Have scholars ignored the willing participation of many in the killing of Jews?

Daniel Jonah Goldhagen  **YES**

The Paradigm Challenged

Imagine a history of American slavery whose authors assert that the testimony of slaves should not be used and where the practice is not to use it, where there is no extensive investigation of whites' conceptions of the enslaved Africans, where it is said that the whites were unwilling slave holders and that few non-slave owning southern whites supported the institutions of slavery, where it is said that those enslaving and routinely brutalizing the slaves were not at all influenced by their conceptions of the victims, where the precept and practice is not to describe the full extent and character of the slave holders' brutality, where it is said furthermore that African American scholars today are suspect because they are African American and the motivation is imputed to them of writing about slavery solely for monetary or political gain or psychological gratification. Imagine what our understanding of American slavery would look like, how skewed it would be, if even only some of these positions prevailed. We would wonder how slavery ever could have existed.

When writing about the Holocaust, many scholars and commentators routinely adopt positions analogous to one or several of these examples. Indeed, some of these positions are a never justified, seemingly unquestioned norm among those who write about the Holocaust. These positions would seem curious—methodologically, substantively, and interpretively—even absurd, if put forward about slavery or about other genocides or mass slaughters such as those in Rwanda or Bosnia. Yet when asserted about the Holocaust, barely an eyebrow is raised. The question naturally arises as to why such manifestly false positions have been frequently adopted? Why until recently were almost no studies, especially no systematic studies, of the perpetrators—namely of those who killed Jews, guarded the camps and ghettos, and deported them to their deaths—to be found among the tens of thousands of books written about the Holocaust, despite the wealth of evidence that had long been available?

The heretofore hegemonic paradigm about the Holocaust has rendered them puppet-like actors, mere pawns whose inner world need not be investigated. It denies the moral agency and assent of the perpetrators and holds that they were compelled to act by forces external to them, such as terror, bureaucratic strictures and modes of behaving, the logic of the system, or social psychological pressure. For a long time, this paradigm diverted attention away from the perpetrators because its logic of external compulsion meant that the perpetrators' internal lives (their beliefs and values) and anything that was sociohistorically particular to them (that they were members of a deeply anti-Semitic political culture) did not influence their actions and that, therefore, the study of them would not contribute much to explaining the Holocaust. The problems with this view and its construction can be indicated by comparing it to the hypothetical, fanciful rendering of slavery above.

The perpetrators are finally being discussed extensively, even if the number of empirical studies remains small. Yet in the last couple of years, a phalanx of scholars and commentators have adopted positions which would make the perpetrators of the Holocaust the only perpetrators of genocide who believed that their victims did not deserve to die, indeed that their victims were innocent. This strange view seems still stranger given that many of the German perpetrators knew explicitly that they had a choice not to kill, and that no German perpetrator was ever killed, sent to a concentration camp, jailed, or punished in any serious way for refusing to kill Jews. That it was possible for many perpetrators to avoid killing Jews, and that some of them availed themselves of this possibility, became known already at the Nuremberg Trials. The related, stunning fact that not a single German perpetrator was ever seriously punished for refusing to kill Jews has been known since 1967 when the jurist Herbert Jager published his pioneering study, *Crime Under Totalitarian Domination*. (I treated both the general issue and presented the case of one man who refused to kill in "The 'Cowardly' Executioner: On Disobedience in the SS" in 1985). Yet this latter fact has remained unmentioned in virtually every work written on the perpetration of the Holocaust since Jager first established it.

Why would Martin Broszat, Raul Hilberg, Eberhard Jäckel, Hans Mommsen and other scholars who wish to explain the Holocaust not discuss these fundamental facts extensively or incorporate their significance into the explanations and interpretations which they put forward? Is it of so little import—that men and women who knew that they could avoid killing children would choose to destroy them anyway—that it is not even worth mentioning this information? Acknowledging these facts would have shaken the foundations of the paradigm to which many scholars are wedded, namely that the perpetrators were compelled by external forces to act against their will. This crucial omission of evidence, for which no justification has been offered, has for decades skewed non-experts' and the public's understanding of the Holocaust.

Similarly, when these writers depict and analyze the events of the Holocaust and particularly when they analyze the motives of the perpetrators, they rarely, if ever, use the testimony of the victims, neither their letters, diaries, memoirs, nor oral testimonies. That is not to say this testimony is never used; certainly, it is used by those writing about the lives and plight of the victims, and by scholars like Yehuda Bauer, Saul Friedlander, and Israel Gutman. But when constructing interpretations of the perpetrators of the Holocaust, it has been the unspoken practice of so many scholars to all but ignore, and certainly not to use systematically, victims' accounts of the perpetrators' actions and the victims' understanding of perpetrators' attitudes towards them. With the sometime exception of a quotation or two from Primo Levi (or some other particularly distinguished memoirist), one searches such authors' works in vain for the instances where they use such evidence seriously or even at all.

Some authors explicitly declare that victim testimony is of little value and an impediment to understanding. Raul Hilberg, who is one of the principal exponents of the conventional paradigm and practice and who often speaks authoritatively for those who are in his school, has written roughly seven pages on survivor testimony in his recent memoir, *The Politics of Memory*, which are highly distorting and almost thoroughly disparaging. He makes not a single positive statement about the victims' testimony as a historical source, except when it shows Jews in a bad light. Even though Hilberg acknowledges in passing, in a strikingly critical vein, that the survivors' "principal subjects are deportations, concentration camps, death camps, escapes, hiding, and partisan fighting"—precisely those themes relevant to learning about and analyzing the perpetrators—his practice and that of those who follow him suggests that they believe that there is little evidentiary or interpretive value in all this testimony.

This widespread devaluation of the testimony of the Jewish victims is peculiar. I know of no other historical or contemporary instance about which it is said that the victims of genocidal onslaughts, sustained violence, or brutality have little of value to tell us about those who victimized and brutalized them. I know of no other crime (e.g., assault, kidnapping), no instance of large scale brutal domination (e.g., slavery, serfdom), no genocide (e.g., Rwanda, Cambodia), nor any other historical instance in which the victims—in the case of the Holocaust a group of eyewitnesses numbering in the millions—are said, as a class, to have little or nothing to tell us about the deeds and attitudes of the men and women who victimized them and whose murderousness and brutalities against others they witnessed. And not only is their testimony silently ignored by many and explicitly devalued by some but it is also sometimes deprecated by writers like Istvan Deak, who began a review of several books on the Holocaust in *The New York Review of Books* (June 26, 1997) by presenting a caricature of and an attack on survivors memoirs. He goes so far as to say that "an accurate record of the Holocaust has been endangered, in my opinion, by the uncritical endorsement, often by well-known Jewish writers or public figures, of virtually any survivor's account or related writings." How have the survivors' writings "endangered" "an accurate record of the Holocaust"? Except to say (correctly) that personal details may be inaccurate or embellished, Deak does not justify his sweeping condemnation.

The invaluable importance of survivor testimony is attested by the crucial, indeed, indispensable part that the survivors have played in the trials of thousands of perpetrators in the Federal Republic of Germany. Many of these trials could not have been held without survivor testimony. The judgment in the most famous of these trials, that of a contingent of guards and administrators of Auschwitz held in 1963, states: "Apart from scattered and not very informative documents, the court had to rely exclusively on witness testimony to help it reconstruct the acts of the defendants" (my emphasis). One thousand three hundred witnesses (among them former guards) gave testimony for that trial.

The Germans' documentation of the killing institutions and operations never record the details of the hundreds or thousands of perpetrators' many actions. Typically, the documents contain, at most, the bare logistics and results of killing operations. So an entire killing operation that might have lasted a full day will appear in a document with nothing more than one line stating that on a given date, the German unit "resettled" (a euphemism) or "shot" some number of Jews.

The accounts of survivors afford a more transparent, more spacious window to the Nazi inferno than the often beclouded and distorting postwar testimonies of the perpetrators who, in order to escape punishment, frequently lie. (Still, some of the perpetrators are surprisingly forthcoming, especially about other perpetrators, and many unwittingly reveal a great deal. Such testimony is invaluable and should be used.) Who would expect to learn from the perpetrators or from contemporaneous German documents a full and accurate account of the texture and details of the Holocaust, of the daily living and dying, of the treatment of the prisoners by the German overlords, including their frequent gratuitous brutality, of the social life of the inmates, their thoughts and feelings, their suffering and their agony? Where can we more fully learn about the character of the perpetrators' actions—the degree to which the perpetrators tortured, brutalized, beat, degraded, and mocked the victims—about the perpetrators' demeanor and attitudes, about whether they acted zealously or reluctantly, about whether they expressed hatred for the victims, and gain insight into the perpetrators' willingness and motivation?

The answer is obvious: from the victims.

Could accurate histories of the Jewish ghettos and of the concentration camps be written without the accounts of the survivors contained in their depositions and memoirs? A perusal of three great books, H. G. Adler's *Theresienstadt, 1941–1945,* Israel Gutman's *The Jews of Warsaw 1939–1943,* and Hermann Langbein's panoramic analysis of Auschwitz, *People in Auschwitz,* shows that the authors have drawn heavily on the accounts of survivors. Are these historical works thereby vitiated? Do they imperil the accuracy of the historical record?

A comparison with the historiography of the Soviet Gulag is instructive. Its scholars do not cast aspersion on the memoirs and accounts of former inmates, whose narratives are indispensable. Aleksandr Solzhenitsyn writes in his Preface to *The Gulag Archipelago:* "This book could never have been created by one person alone. In addition to what I myself was able to take away from the Archipelago—on the skin of my back, and with my eyes and ears—material for this book was given me in reports, memoirs, and letters by 227 witnesses . . . this is our common, collective monument to all those who were tortured and murdered." Evidence of the kind that Hilberg, Deak, Christopher, Browning, and others dismiss, explicitly or tacitly, as unreliable and inessential forms the foundation of Solzhenitsyn's magisterial work. Would Deak argue that Solzhenitsyn has "endangered" "an accurate record" of the Gulag? Or are only survivors of the Holocaust and those who find great value in their testimony prone to such "endangerment"?

It is not because this witness testimony is meager, imprecise, or devoid of insight that it has been ignored. It includes hundreds of memorial volumes, each one containing compilations from survivors of one destroyed Jewish community after another detailing their fates; depositions of many thousands of survivors in the trials of the perpetrators from one camp, killing unit, and ghetto after another; vast amounts of oral testimony; and thousands of memoirs. It would be hard to imagine an instance of mass slaughter, violence, or brutality that would be documented by a greater abundance of rich, detailed, often highly literate testimony that contains penetrating analyses of the events and of the people who perpetrated them. This makes the disparagement of the victims' testimony and its paltry use that much more surprising and indefensible.

Victims' accounts belie the conventional paradigm and the attendant scholarly theories about the perpetrators that have held sway, namely that the perpetrators either explicitly disapproved or at least did not approve of the mass slaughter of Jews and of other victims. The victims know differently. They have testified so again and again. If the proponents of these explanations had incorporated the voices of the victims into their own writings, then they would have undercut immediately and devastatingly their own theories, and the conventional paradigm.

The omission of the survivors' accounts has obscured, among many other aspects of the Holocaust, one of its constituent features. Scholars' failure to use victim accounts has thus, to use Deak's phraseology, "endangered" "an accurate record": the perpetrators' virtually boundless cruelty towards the Jews has been all but ignored by those who purport to explain the perpetrators' actions. If, as many authors do, one relies principally on highly partial and often unrevealing contemporaneous German documents, then, of course, one will not find frequent and detailed recitations of Germans' routine torturing of Jews. These authors construct a distorted portrait of the Holocaust in which the perpetrators' brutality—so frequent, inventive, and willful—is minimized, blurred, or absent. Consequently, it is not surprising that those few authors adhering to the conventional paradigm who do at least say something in passing about the sources of the German perpetrators' brutality to the Jews do not deem the perpetrators to have been moved by hatred of their victims.

Hilberg, for instance, in *Perpetrators, Victims, Bystanders,* puts forward the notion that the German perpetrators' brutality was "most often" an "expression of impatience" with the pace of killing operations. Browning's related view, in *Ordinary Men,* is that the perpetrators' brutality was utilitarian, the consequence of a pragmatic need to be brutal when they were under "pressure" "in terms of manpower ... to get the job done," like rounding up Jews for deportation. When not under such pressure, in Browning's view, they were cruel when under the sway of cruel officers but seemingly not at other times. Hilberg and Browning have failed to present evidence which supports what are ultimately little more than speculations. (How does Hilberg know that they were impatient? He never says. And is the torture of defenseless people, including children, the invariable result of impatience, as Hilberg's quick and casual manner of presenting his speculation suggests?) But that is the least of their problems. Hilberg and Browning's empirical claims are falsified by evidence of the perpetrators' widespread, non-utilitarian cruelty in all manner of circumstances, even when they were not undermanned, even when they were not impatient, even when they were not undertaking killing operations at all.

For example: although the Germans of Police Battalion 101, during one of the ghetto roundups and deportations in Miedzyrzec, Poland, degraded and tortured Jews in the most gratuitous, willful manner, their deeds are entirely absent from their testimony and, therefore, also from Browning's analysis of the killing operation. The accounts of survivors tell a different, more accurate, and more revealing story. Survivors are adamant that the Germans' cruelty that day was anything but instrumental. It was wanton, at times turning into sadistic sport. At the marketplace the Jews, who had been forced to squat for hours, were "mocked" (khoyzek gemacht) and "kicked," and some of the Germans organized "a game" (shpil) of "tossing apples and whoever was struck by the apple was then killed." This sport was continued at the railway station, with empty liquor bottles. "Bottles were tossed over Jewish heads and whoever was struck by a bottle was dragged out of the crowd and beaten murderously amid roaring laughter. Then some of those who were thus mangled (tseharget) were shot." Afterwards, the Germans loaded the dead together with the living onto freight cars bound for Treblinka. One photograph documenting the final stage of what may be this deportation has survived.

Small wonder that in the eyes of the victims—but not in the self-serving testimony of the perpetrators, in contemporaneous German documents, or in Browning's book—these ordinary Germans appeared not as mere murderers, certainly not as reluctant killers dragged to their task against their inner opposition to genocide, but as "two-legged beasts" filled with "bloodthirstiness." (Browning claims that from survivors "we learn nothing about" Police Battalion 101 or, for that matter, about itinerant units in general.) Germans' cruelty towards Jews, as the victims (and also some of the perpetrators after the war) reveal, was voluntary, widespread, sustained, inventive, and gleeful. Such gratuitous cruelty could have been produced only by people who approved of what they were doing.

The vast corpus of the victims' testimony substantiates the conclusion that ordinary Germans degraded, brutalized, and killed Jews willingly because of their hatred of Jews. So profound and near universal was the anti-Semitism during the Nazi period that to the Jewish victims it appeared as if its hold on Germans could be captured and conveyed only in organic terms. As Chaim Kaplan, the trenchant observer and diarist of the Warsaw ghetto, concluded: "A poison of diseased hatred permeates the blood of the Nazis." Once activated, the Germans' profound hatred of Jews, which had in the 1930s by necessity lain relatively dormant, so possessed them, that it appeared to have exuded from their every pore. Kaplan observed many Germans from September 1939 until March 1940 when he penned his evaluation derived from their actions and words:

> The gigantic catastrophe which has descended on Polish Jewry has no parallel, even in the darkest periods of Jewish history. First, in the depth of hatred. This is not just hatred whose source is in a party platform, and which was invented for political purposes. It is a hatred of emotion, whose source is some psychopathic malady. In its outward manifestations it functions as

physiological hatred, which imagines the object of hatred to be unclean in body, a leper who has no place within the camp.

The [German] masses have absorbed this sort of qualitative hatred.... They have absorbed their masters' teachings in a concrete, corporeal form. The Jew is filthy; the Jew is a swindler and an evildoer; the Jew is the enemy of Germany, who undermines its existence; the Jew was the prime mover in the Versailles Treaty, which reduced Germany to nothing; the Jew is Satan, who sows dissension between one nation and another, arousing them to bloodshed in order to profit from their destruction. These are easily understood concepts whose effect in day-to-day life can be felt immediately.

Significantly, this characterization is based on the words and acts of Germans—of SS men, policemen, soldiers, administrators, and those working in the economy—*before* the formal genocidal program of systematic killing had begun. It is the masses, the ordinary Germans, not the Nazi ideologues and theoreticians, whom Kaplan exposes. The causal link between the Germans' beliefs and actions is palpable, so that the Jews feel the effect of their "concepts" "in day-to-day life." In the more than two-and-a-half years of subsequent concentrated observation of the Germans in Warsaw, Kaplan saw no reason to alter this evaluation, an evaluation confirmed by a German police official, who states plainly that those serving alongside him in the Cracow region of Poland "were, with a few exceptions, quite happy to take part in shootings of Jews. They had a ball!" Their killing was motivated by "great hatred against the Jews; it was revenge...." The revenge was not for any real harm that the Jews had visited upon Germans, but for the figmental harms for which the perpetrators believed, in their anti-Semitically-inflamed minds, the Jews were responsible.

Effectively extinguishing the voices of the victims, and sometimes suggesting that they do little more than glorify themselves, is not only indefensible methodologically but also a deep affront to survivors. Most victims want to do nothing more than convey what the perpetrators did to them, their families, and to others. Victims of such crimes can never gain full restitution for their losses and suffering. What they generally seem to want is to have the truth be told, particularly so that the perpetrators will acknowledge their crimes. Survivors often express bewilderment that their experience has been generally ignored by the scholarship that treats the perpetration of the Holocaust. Many survivors have told me that they are thankful for my book, *Hitler's Willing Executioners[,]* and for its detailed analysis of the German perpetrators, including their gleeful cruelty and brutality, which the survivors attest was almost always voluntary. They say my interpretation of the Holocaust accords with what they and so many others witnessed and experienced.

꿍

A new way of approaching the study of the Holocaust is implicit in much of the unparalleled, widespread public discussion about various aspects of the Holocaust that has been taking place [recently]. The old paradigm consists of abstract, faceless structures and institutions (bureaucracy, the greatly exaggerated "terror apparatus" that was supposedly directed at ordinary Germans, the

SS, the Nazi Party, the gas chambers) and allegedly irresistible external forces (totalitarian terror, the exigencies of war, social psychological pressure). This paradigm effaces the human actors and their capacity to judge what they were doing and to make moral choices. It is ahistorical. All of this implies that any people from any era with any set of beliefs about Jews (even non-anti-Semites) would have acted in exactly the same manner as the perpetrators, with the same brutality, zeal, and Mephistophelean laughter. This is being challenged by a view that recognizes that the Holocaust was brought about by human beings who had beliefs about what they were doing, beliefs which they developed within a highly specific historical context, and who made many choices about how to act within the institutions in which they worked and which brought them to their tasks in the first place. The human beings are finally at the center of the discussion. The heretofore dominant question of "What compelled them to act against their will?" is being replaced by the question of "Why did these people choose to act in the ways that they did?"

As a result, powerful myths are crumbling: the myth that the Swiss or the Swedes acted as they did only because of the German threat; the myth that the peoples in different occupied countries did not do more to thwart the Germans or less to help in the killing of the Jews merely because of their fear of the occupying Germans; the official Allied governmental myths that they could not reasonably have attempted to do much more to save the victims; the myth that those who procured Jewish property, including art, generally did so innocently; the myth that the perpetrators, by and large, disapproved of what they were doing but were coerced, were being blindly obedient, or were pressured to act as they did; and the three related myths that the German people more broadly (all the exceptions notwithstanding) did not know that their countrymen were killing Jews en masse, did not support the Nazi regime even though its many brutal policies (forced sterilization, so-called "euthanasia," the violent persecution of the Jews and others, the reintroduction of slavery into the European continent) were widely known, and did not approve of the general eliminationist persecution of the Jews.

Not surprisingly, many people who have either been comforted by such views or whose careers have been made by adopting positions that buttress them, and who find the new, powerful challenges to these views to be politically undesirable or personally threatening, are extremely unhappy and have let that be known. The frequent response is to attack, often in the most vitriolic and unprincipled ways, the messengers—whether they be scholars, institutions like the Hamburg Institute for Social Research which produced the exhibit, "War of Extermination: The Crime of the Wehrmacht, 1941–1944" that has been traveling around Germany, the World Jewish Congress for forcing the issue of Swiss gold onto the agenda, or the witnesses, namely Jewish survivors, whose testimony has always been a devastating threat to many of the myths.

It would be beneficial if certain basics could become widely accepted which the crumbling paradigm has obscured. They include:

1. The discarding of the caricature of individual Germans as having had no views of their own about the rightness of what they or their coun-

trymen were doing, which included slaughtering children. We need to know how these views were distributed among Germans, and how they, singly or in interaction with other factors, influenced Germans' actions during these years. The same applies to the peoples of other countries, those where the Germans found many willing helpers and those where the populace worked to thwart (sometimes successfully) the program of extermination.

2. The rejection of the myth that the large scale, mass killing of Jews remained unknown to the broader German public. Germans themselves are becoming more candid: twenty-seven percent of those who were at least fourteen years old at the end of the war now admit that they knew of the extermination of the Jews *when it was taking place.* (The survey which determined this stunning new finding, which the chief pollster of the German wire service, dpa, says is still clearly a substantial underreporting of the real figure, was conducted for the German television network ZdF in September 1996. Yet in the flood of articles written about the Holocaust since then, I have seen no mention of this finding, perhaps because it explodes a central element of the conventional paradigm—even though the survey's results were announced and discussed on German national television during a panel discussion on the Holocaust and reported by the dpa.)

3. The acknowledgment that Germans who were not members of specifically targeted groups (Jews; Gays; the Sinti and Roma peoples, who are commonly known as gypsies; the mentally infirm; the Communist and Social Democratic leadership) were not so terrorized as the totalitarian terror model posits. The enormous amount of dissent and opposition that Germans expressed against so many policies of the regime and the regime's responsiveness to public sentiment and action makes this clear. So a new understanding of the relationship between state power, regime policy, and popular consent needs to be worked out. The comparative question of why Germans expressed different degrees of dissent and opposition to different policies, yet virtually no principled dissent against the eliminationist persecution of the Jews, becomes central. More generally, all models that posit that irresistible external forces compelled people—Germans, French, Poles, Swiss, or the Allies—to act as they did need to be replaced by views that acknowledge the existence of human agency. If the vast majority of the German people had genuinely been opposed to the radical eliminationist persecution of the Jews, then Hitler would have never been able to pursue it as he did.

4. The adoption of a comparative perspective on genocide, so that those who study the Holocaust do not adopt methodological practices or causal claims that are at odds with how we study and what we know of other analogous phenomena. All available evidence (contemporaneous documents and the testimony of perpetrators, victims, and bystanders) that is not rendered suspect according to clearly articulated, standard social scientific principles is to be used. Regarding the use of

the testimony of Jewish survivors, for example, the reasons given for excluding it must be defensible if one changed the word "Jews" to Tutsis, Bosnians, Cambodians, Armenians, the victims of the Gulag, or enslaved Blacks in the American South. The methods of the social sciences present rules regarding research design and the structure of inference, including when generalization is allowed and even required. A major research project might be undertaken using all available evidence to catalogue what is known of the backgrounds, actions, and attitudes of every perpetrator in every ghetto, camp, and other institution of killing—those who victimized Jews and non-Jews—so that a general portrait and systematic analysis of them can be composed.

5. The recognition that the Holocaust had *both* universal and particular elements. Its universal aspect is that all people have the capacity to dehumanize groups of others so intensely that their hatred can impel them to commit genocide. Its particular aspect is that such views do not come to exist in equal measure in every society about every group, and when they do, it is not every society that has a state which mobilizes those who hold such views in a program of mass annihilation. The universal capacity to hate does not mean that all people actually do hate and hate all others in the same way, or that all hatreds will motivate people to treat the object of their aggression similarly. Real existing hatreds, as opposed to the capacity to hate, are primarily socially constructed and historically particular.

The Holocaust is not "beyond human comprehension." In principle, it is as explicable as every other genocide. No one says that the Rwandan or Cambodian genocide cannot be explained. What so many people simply do not want to accept is that the victims of the Holocaust have a great deal to tell us about their victimizers (no less than do the victims in Rwanda and Bosnia); and that the German perpetrators were like the perpetrators of other mass slaughters: the vast majority of these Germans were also willing executioners. That people automatically accept these facts about non-Jewish victims of genocide and about African or Asian perpetrators but not about Jews and "civilized" white Christian Europeans respectively is disturbing. Does anyone think for a moment that the Turkish, Hutu, or Serbian perpetrators did not believe that slaughtering Armenians, Tutsis, or Muslims was right? Does anyone for a moment believe that the testimony of these genocides' victims should not be used extensively in order to learn about the texture of the genocides, including the attitudes of the perpetrators? Indeed, in the Armenian genocide, in Bosnia, Cambodia, Rwanda, and other instances of mass slaughter, such testimony is eagerly used by scholars and has provided the principal knowledge of the perpetrators' deeds and attitudes.

As ever more Germans themselves have come to realize, one can acknowledge that many Germans were virulent anti-Semites during and before the Nazi period, that many supported the brutal persecution of the Jews, and that the murderers of European Jewry came from the ranks of ordinary Germans, without it leading either to the indictment of those Germans who resisted the prevailing norms and practices of the time, or to a condemnation of today's Germany. This seems so obvious that it bears mentioning only because some commentators continue to put forward two fallacies: they pretend that demonstrating that *individual* culpability for crimes was far more widespread in Nazi Germany than had previously been presumed is the same as maintaining that Germans are guilty as a *collectivity*. They also react as if plain talk about the Germany of the past defames the Germany of the present. Such notions can be maintained only by people who themselves deny individual responsibility, are beholden to the insupportable notion of a timeless "national character" (Hilberg has declared in his recent memoir that a German "national character" exists and is critical of others for not accepting this), or believe in some kind of collective, inheritable guilt. Individual Germans during the Nazi period should be judged according to the same legal and moral principles that we use for people in our own societies. The Federal Republic of Germany, like all other countries, should be assessed in the light of its own character and practices, achievements and shortcomings, and not according to a period of Germany's history that is now over fifty years in the past.

Much of what I write here finds an echo in a private letter written in 1946 by a German to a priest, in which the author was plainly speaking his mind:

> In my opinion the German people as well as the bishops and clergy bear a great guilt for the events in the concentration camps. It is perhaps true that afterwards not a lot could be done. The guilt lies earlier. The German people, including a great part of the bishops and clergy, accepted the National Socialist agitation. It allowed itself to be brought into line (*gleichgeschaltet*) [with Nazism] almost without resistance, indeed in part with enthusiasm. Therein lies its guilt. Moreover, even if one did not know the full extent of the events in the camps, one knew that personal freedom and all the principles of justice were being trampled underfoot, that in the concentration camps great atrocities were being perpetrated, and that the Gestapo and our SS and in part also our troops in Poland and Russia treated the civilian population with unexampled cruelty. The pogroms against the Jews in 1933 and in 1938 took place in full public view. The murders of the hostages in France were officially announced by us. One cannot therefore truly assert that the public did not know that the National Socialist government and army command constantly and as a matter of principle violated natural law, the Hague Convention, and the most simple laws of humanity. I believe that much could have been prevented if all the bishops together on a certain day from their pulpits had publicly protested against all this. This did not occur and for this there is no excuse. If for this the bishops had been sent to prison or concentration camp, then this would not have been a loss, on the contrary. All this did not occur, therefore it is best to be silent.

The author of this letter was no less a personage than Konrad Adenauer, the long time and, by many, revered post-War Christian Democratic Chancellor of Germany who, more than anyone else helped to reintegrate Germany into the community of nations. No one would accuse Adenauer of condemning every last German (even though he wrote of "the German people"), of being anti-German, of maintaining that Germans could never change and would therefore eternally share the views which led them to support Nazism, so why do some deem the speaking today of Adenauer's plain truths to be indications of such attitudes and to be impermissible?

Anyone who knows today's Germany, the Germany which Adenauer worked so steadfastly to forge, knows that it is remarkably different from Nazi Germany. Indeed, it is only by acknowledging the depths to which Germany had sunk, and not just that it somehow had the misfortune to have been captured by a brutal, murderous dictatorship, that one can appreciate the enormous accomplishments of Germans after the war. By denying how Germany really was, we will never fully understand the great effort Germans have made and the good that has occurred after the war. By being false to the past, the conventional, scholarly paradigm which denies the agency of the actors is also false to the present. When one acknowledges that it was culturally-constructed racist beliefs and values which led many Germans to take part in, and so many more—though decidedly not all Germans—to support, the annihilation of the Jews and the killing and brutalizing of many other Europeans deemed racially inferior, it becomes more comprehensible why Germany has been able to change so much. Political culture can be transformed.

Just as the beliefs which led American whites to enslave Blacks and then to impose legal segregation have changed profoundly, so too—as the survey data demonstrate unequivocally—have the dominant beliefs in Germany *gradually* changed about Jews, humanity, and democracy. (In 1933, most Germans voted for parties openly dedicated to destroying the country's democratic institutions. Today, virtually everyone in what was West Germany sincerely supports democracy.) Such profound, positive changes in beliefs and values are hopeful —though, of course, both in the United States and in Germany prejudice and ethnic hatred have by no means been completely eradicated. Over the period of a generation or two, a society can greatly remake its prevailing views, making its people less bigoted and less prone to engaging in discrimination and violence. But this is not accomplished easily. How such changes occur are little studied and little understood. Perhaps people should devote more attention to examining such transformations, instead of working so hard to deny that in Germany any transformation was necessary.

My view of the mentality of the vast majority of Germans during the Nazi period is similar to that of one of the most esteemed of German historians of this century, Friedrich Meinecke (though our understandings of what produced this mentality differ). Meinecke remained in Germany but he kept his distance from the Nazi regime, retreating into "internal emigration" from which he observed the regime's policies and the people's attitudes, sentiments, and conduct. Soon after the war, he wrote a book, *The German Catastrophe*, seeking to explain the origins and character of Nazism. He was severely critical of Germans' conduct during the Nazi era and held that certain traits and traditions common in Germany had contributed to the emergence and success of the Nazi movement. His was a rare candor. Meinecke acknowledged that it is a "shocking" and "shameful" fact that a "criminal gang succeeded for twelve years in compelling the allegiance of the German people and in imparting to a great part of this people the belief that it was following a great 'Idea'." Germany had fallen, but it was not beyond redemption. Its moral corruption was curable. For "the German people had not become diseased to the core with a criminal mentality but suffered only a unique grave infection caused by a poison that had been administered to it. The case could have become hopeless if the poison would have wrought its effect in the body for long." The young generation would have then become incurably afflicted with moral degeneration. "That was the gloomiest thought that tormented me during the twelve years, that the party could remain in power in perpetuity and instill in the entire younger generation its own degenerate character."

His gloomy moments notwithstanding, Meinecke knew that Germany would be defeated. The prospect of that defeat filled him with mingled trepidation and hope. Germany would suffer grievous external, material destruction but it would be liberated spiritually and mentally. The poisons which he and the Warsaw ghetto's diarist, Kaplan, each identified as having infected so many Germans—so that each one chose to write in collective, corporeal terms—would, in Meinecke's view dissipate and Germany's "soul" and "conscience" would "breathe again." A new day could and would dawn.

Meinecke's depiction of the mentality of most Germans during the Nazi period could hardly be bettered. His prophecy could hardly have been more true.

NO

Christopher R. Browning

Victim Testimony

In his recent TIKKUN article ("The Paradigm Challenged." July/August 1998), Daniel Goldhagen directly attacks my work as well as that of the larger community of Holocaust scholars. In doing so, he misrepresents and distorts what he attacks in order to achieve a hollow victory over his own easily demolished strawmen.

Goldhagen states that I "dismiss" survivor testimony "explicitly or tacitly, as unreliable and inessential" and that I have allegedly written that "from survivors 'we learn nothing [sic] about' Police Battalion 101 or, for that matter, about itinerant units in general. What in fact I wrote in the preface of *Ordinary Men* is the following: "... unlike survivor testimony about prominent perpetrators in the ghettos and camps, where prolonged contact was possible, survivor testimony can tell us *little* about an itinerant unit like Reserve Police Battalion 101" (xvii–xviii, emphasis added). In a subsequent panel exchange with Goldhagen, I expanded as follows:

> Jewish testimony was indispensable to my study in establishing the chronology of the fall of 1942. What became a blur of events for the perpetrators remained quite distinct days of horror for the victims. Also, while survivor testimony may be extremely valuable in many regards, it does not illuminate the internal dynamics of an itinerant killing unit. It would be difficult for the victim of such a unit to provide testimony concerning the various levels of participation of different perpetrators and any change in their character over time. Where long-term contact between victims and perpetrators did occur, survivors are able to and in fact do differentiate on such issues.

Thus Goldhagen misquotes from the preface of *Ordinary Men,* changing "little" to "nothing," and furthermore takes my remarks from our subsequent exchange entirely out of context. I do not "dismiss" survivor testimony either "explicitly or tacitly" as "unreliable and inessential." I do insist that survivor testimony, like any other evidence, be used cautiously and with due regard for what any particular witness was in a position to know. Quite simply, Goldhagen's summary of my position is a gross distortion; his misquotation violates accepted academic standards.

Moreover, I have noted that in rare cases where survivors had worked as translators or menial laborers in German police stations they were indeed in a position to give invaluable testimony precisely on the question of the attitudes and mindset of middle-aged reserve policemen like those in Reserve Police Battalion 101. Such a rare witness was Oswald Rufeisen, whose story was told by Nechama Tec in her book *In the Lion's Den*. According to Rufeisen, among the thirteen policemen at Mir, one stood out as a "beast in the form of a man," three did not participate in Jewish actions at all, and most of the remainder considered the killing of Jews as something "unclean" about which they did not wish to talk. This is a far cry from Goldhagen's portrayal of middle-aged German reserve policemen, according to which they were uniformly possessed of a "lethal, hallucinatory view of the Jews" and viewed their killing of Jews as a "a redemptive act" to be celebrated and enjoyed.

Tec's book was published in 1992, the same year as *Ordinary Men*, and thus Rufeisen's unique testimony was not available to me and could not be cited in my book. It was available to Goldhagen before he published *Hitler's Willing Executioners* four years later, but he did not cite it. It appears that this self-styled champion of survivor testimony can be quite selective himself when survivor testimony fails to support the hypothesis he is trying to prove.

In my opinion, Goldhagen's accusatory approach to the issue of survivor testimony disserves scholarship because it diverts attention from the real issue, namely what the historian can learn from a systematic use of concentrated survivor testimony. I am currently engaged in researching the Starachowice ghetto and labor camps in the Radom district in central Poland; my work is based primarily on more than one hundred written and videotaped survivor testimonies given over a period of more than four decades. Several conclusions relevant to this discussion have already emerged.

The first concerns the itinerant unit involved in the ghetto roundup and deportation action on October 27, 1942. This was the notorious *Vernichtungs-batallion* or "destruction battalion" of Erich Kapke that travelled from ghetto to ghetto throughout the Radom district. When asked by German investigators desperate for witnesses and evidence, not one survivor could recognize either the name or picture of Kapke, much less anyone else in the unit. They knew that the battalion consisted of foreign auxiliaries but disagreed on nationality. Different witnesses suggested Lithuanians, Latvians, Ukrainians, or Estonians. The survivors had extremely vivid and precise memories about many aspects of that traumatic day, but not about the itinerant police unit that dispatched their families to Treblinka. Given the horrific circumstances of that brief event, it is no reproach of survivors or devaluation of their testimony to note that there are some things they cannot tell us about it.

Goldhagen's second strawman is an "old" or "hegemonic paradigm" that is now allegedly crumbling in the face of public discussion "that has been taking place for the last two years" (which is to say since the publication of *Hitler's Willing Executioners* in 1996). According to Goldhagen, this "old paradigm" consists of "abstract, faceless structures and institutions" and "irresistible external forces"; it renders perpetrators into "puppet-like actors" and "effaces" them as human beings making moral choices because it portrays these perpetrators as "compelled by external forces to act against their will."

For the past twenty years, I have been publishing various case studies about particular groups of perpetrators—the so-called "Jewish experts" of the German Foreign Office, the motor pool mechanics who designed and constructed the gas van, the military administration of occupied Serbia, the personnel of the Semlin death camp, the ghetto administrators of Lodz and Warsaw, the public health doctors of the General Government, and the men of Reserve Police Battalion 101. It has been my goal throughout to put human faces on the perpetrators and assess their motivation. Never did I suggest or conclude that they had been "compelled... to act against their will" in ways that precluded moral or legal judgment.

How has Goldhagen constructed this pernicious discourse that casts himself as the pioneer hero of a morally-sensitive history and attempts to delegitimize the generations of pre-1996 historians as morally obtuse? He does so by inventing an artificial dichotomy between actions motivated by allegedly "internal" factors permitting moral judgment (namely beliefs and values, which in effect Goldhagen limits to anti-Semitic or racist convictions) and actions "compelled" by what he terms "external" factors that, because of the compulsion, are devoid of a moral dimension involving choice. In reality, of course, there are numerous "values and beliefs" that motivate people other than racist ones, such as perceptions of authority, duty, legitimacy, and loyalty to one's unit and country in wartime. And there are other personality traits such as ambition, greed, and lack of empathy that shape people's behavior without absolving them of individual responsibility. Indeed, in the penultimate paragraph of my book, *Ordinary Men,* I conclude that "The reserve policemen faced choices, and most of them committed terrible deeds. But those who killed cannot be absolved by the notion that anyone in the same situation would have done as they did. For even among them, some refused to kill and others stopped killing. Human responsibility is ultimately an individual matter" (188).

The issue between Goldhagen and the "phalanx of scholars" whom he dismisses has never been the "willing" participation of "ordinary Germans" from virtually every segment of society, as would be clear to anyone who has read with an open mind Raul Hilberg's *The Destruction of the European Jews,* first published in 1961. Nor is it an issue that "culturally-constructed racist beliefs and values... led many Germans to take part in" the annihilation of the Jews, even though the debate over the relative roles of ideological and cultural factors on the one hand and situational, organizational, and institutional factors on the other has been continuous, spirited, and fruitful. Indeed, most elements of Goldhagen's proposed new paradigm, to say nothing of the passages from [Konrad] Adenauer and [Friedrich] Meinecke that he quotes approvingly, have been commonplace in virtually any course on modern German history or the Holocaust taught in the United States in the past two decades or more.

What then is all the fuss about, and why did Goldhagen's book arouse such a negative reaction among so many scholars? It is useful to remind ourselves of what he actually wrote and said in 1996. In several interviews promoting the book, Goldhagen flatly proclaimed that German culture was a "genocidal culture." In the book itself, he urged historians to rid themselves of the notion that Germans in the Third Reich were "more or less like us" or that "their sensibilities had remotely approximated our own" (27, 269). He recommended that scholars approach the Germans as they would the Aztecs, who believed human sacrifice was necessary to cause the sun to rise (28).

Goldhagen wrote emphatically that "with regard to the motivational cause of the Holocaust, for the vast majority of the perpetrators, a monocausal explanation does suffice"—namely "a demonological antisemitism" that "was the common structure of the perpetrators' cognition and that of German society in general" (416, 392). Accordingly, "equipped with little more than the cultural notions current in Germany," ordinary Germans "wanted to be genocidal executioners" (185, 279). And when given the chance, the vast majority killed with "gusto" and "for pleasure" (241, 451). In contrast, they killed Poles with "obvious distaste and reluctance" (241). A major transformation in German political culture after the war was duly noted, though the possibility of a similar or even greater transformation of German political culture under the impact of the Nazi regime between 1933 and 1941 was denied.

When I presented these quotations at the symposium of the U.S. Holocaust Memorial Museum in April 1996 as representing the core of his argument, Goldhagen acknowledged that I had read his book carefully and did not dispute that I had summarized his argument correctly. If he has muted his sweeping generalizations and fiery accusations and embraced the likes of Adenauer and Meinecke, we are witnessing not the crumbling of some "hegemonic paradigm," but the repositioning of Daniel Goldhagen.

POSTSCRIPT

Have Scholars Ignored the Willing Participation of Germans in Killing Jews During the Holocaust?

If Goldhagen is correct, why haven't Jewish concentration camp survivors been interviewed frequently by Holocaust scholars? Would German witnesses and perpetrators provide better information? Does Browning's contention that the oppression of Jews was largely done by ordinary men reflect psychological studies such as Stanley Milgram's obedience research, in which subjects delivered what they believed to be extreme electric shocks to Milgram's confederates, despite the screaming protests of the confederates, because an authority figure told them that they must do so? That is, is it accurate to suggest that anyone, under the right circumstances, would be willing to harm minority group members?

Many Marxists in Germany have attacked Goldhagen's thesis. They reject his assertion that post–World War II capitalist Germany has successfully reeducated Germans so that they are no longer capable of doing a Hilter's bidding or of having the entrenched hatred of Jews. Does Goldhagen's thesis strongly support the teaching of multicultural courses and diversity training? Jan T. Gross's book *Neighbors: The Destruction of the Jewish Community in Jedwabne* (Princeton University Press, 2001) seems to support both Browning's and Goldhagen's thinking. Meanwhile, despite the reemergence of Nazis, skinheads, and other racist groups, it seems clear that Germany has taken pains to at least partially atone for the Holocaust. In contrast, some countries seem to remain in denial about atrocities committed against others—Japan's refusal to acknowledge how it treated Koreans and the Chinese during World War II, for example.

An important work that clarifies genocide is *Governments, Citizens and Genocide: A Comparative and Interdisciplinary Analysis* by Alex Alvarez (Indiana University Press, 2001). Norman Finkelstein, *The Holocaust Industry: Reflections on the Exploitation of Jewish Sufferings* (Verso, 2000) and Stanley Cohen, *States of Denial: Knowing About Atrocities and Suffering* (Polity Press, 2000) provide arguments not considered by Browning or Goldhagen. Among the many entries into the debate over the IBM Corporation's complicity in the Holocaust is *IBM and the Holocaust: The Strategic Alliance Between Nazi Germany and America's Most Powerful Corporation* by Edwin Black (Random House, 2001). For works that straddle Goldhagen's and Browning's views, see *Bystanders: Conscience and Complicity During the Holocaust* by Victoria J. Barnett (Greenwood, 2000) and *Rethinking the Holocaust* by Yehuda Bauer (Yale University Press, 2001).

On the Internet . . .

Academic Info: African American History and Studies

This is a thoroughly annotated directory of Internet resources on Black history. It links to meta-indexes and general directories, digital libraries, online publications, exhibits, and much more.

http://www.academicinfo.com/africanam.html

The National Council of La Raza (NCLR)

The National Council of La Raza (NCLR) is a private, nonprofit, nonpartisan, tax-exempt organization established in 1968 to reduce poverty and discrimination and to improve life opportunities for Hispanic Americans.

http://www.nclr.org/index.html

American Indian Research and Policy Institute (AIRPI)

The American Indian Research and Policy Institute (AIRPI), founded in 1992, is a nonprofit center for research, policy development, and education on critical American Indian issues.

http://www.airpi.org

Urban Think Tank, Inc.

Urban Think Tank, Inc., is a community-based home for a body of thinkers that is committed to repositioning hip hop culture by providing platforms that encourage public discourse and that uses multimedia strategies to influence public policy in the areas of politics, economics, and culture.

http://www.urbanthinktank.org

National Association for Bilingual Education (NABE)

Promoting educational excellence and equity through bilingual education, the National Association for Bilingual Education (NABE) is the only national organization exclusively concerned with the education of language-minority students in American schools.

http://www.nabe.org

Council on American-Islamic Relations (CAIR)

This is the home page of the Council on American-Islamic Relations (CAIR). In addition to news releases, publications, and action alerts, CAIR provides a "media watch" page that reports on anti-Arab and anti-Muslim representations and stories in the media.

http://www.cair-net.org/main.html

PART 2

Constructing Social Identities and Cultural Conflict

*S*cientifically identifying, enumerating, and analyzing minorities is only the first step toward understanding. It is also necessary to explore both how the majority constructs its attitudes toward minorities and how minorities, in turn, interpret themselves. Discrepancies in the construction of identities often lead to cultural conflict. What aspects of the broader culture are accepted or rejected by minorities? How do the labels that are applied to minorities by members of the dominant group, the media, and others influence their identities? How and why do romantic myths sometimes harden into ideologies, creating cultural conflicts that are both functional and dysfunctional?

- Do the Identities of Blacks Lie in Africa?

- Are Hispanics Making Significant Progress?

- Do Cultural Differences Between Home and School Explain the High Dropout Rates for American Indian Students?

- Does Rap Music Contribute to Violent Crime?

- Does Bilingual Education Harm Hispanic and Other Children?

- Are Arabs and Other Muslims Portrayed Unfairly in American Films?

ISSUE 5

Do the Identities of Blacks Lie in Africa?

YES: Olga Idriss Davis, from "The Door of No Return: Reclaiming the Past Through the Rhetoric of Pilgrimage," *The Western Journal of Black Studies* (vol. 21, no. 3, 1997)

NO: Keith B. Richburg, from "Continental Divide," *The Washington Post Magazine* (March 26, 1995)

ISSUE SUMMARY

YES: Assistant professor of speech communication Olga Idriss Davis links Black identity with Africa. In a moving account based on her visits to Senegal, West Africa—the departing point to America for thousands of slaves, almost none of whom ever saw their homes again—she reveals how she and many other African Americans have benefited from their pilgrimages to Africa.

NO: *Washington Post* correspondent Keith B. Richburg contends that it is trendy and foolish for Blacks to attempt to validate themselves through identification with Africa. He is personally thankful that his forefathers were enslaved and transported to America so that he did not grow up in Africa.

Historically, the United States has been a nation of immigrants that continuously generates new Americans and new minorities. The country of origin of individual newcomers, or at least their descendants, is generally considered irrelevant. Yet most minorities frequently went through generational metamorphosis: people of the first generation worked extremely hard to make it in the "promised land," and they were very proud that their children were born U.S. citizens, spoke English, and acted like typical Americans. While the members of the first generation were not necessarily ashamed of their origins, their main interest was to be assimilated into American society. Their own children, however, were sometimes ashamed of their immigrant parents because they wore outlandish clothing, spoke broken English, or reflected customs that other children made fun of. However, by later generations, the stigma, the hardships, and the outsider status had evaporated. The initial hurts of the old country and the prejudice and bigotry of the new one became distant memories. People began to search for their roots, sometimes hiring genealogists or attending meetings of ethnically or racially based organizations. Eventually, interested people embarked on individual treks and organized pilgrimages back to the old country. Citizens of the old countries point out to these people sites known to have been frequent places of disembarkation from which the American tourists' ancestors may have begun their journeys to America. Religious sites, sometimes neglected or even shunned as pagan monuments by locals, assume new importance if they capture the interests of tourists seeking their roots.

Although many Blacks in the United States are racially mixed (as are whites), when they search for their roots, they almost always look toward the African continent. This is largely because the social (and, until recently, the legal) construction of citizens with significant African ancentrage was "Negro" citizenship status.

Historically, next to women and children, African Americans are by far the oldest minority group in the United States. In spite of the vast majority having been forced to come here as slaves beginning in 1619, and in spite of enforced segregation, some argue that Black Americans are the "most American" of all minorities. Regardless, Blacks have experienced painful ambivalences about their identity. For generations, African Americans have gone to great pains to distance themselves from all things African, partially because the media and historians portray less developed countries, especially African ones, negatively. Although there have always been members of the Black avant-garde who proudly display African artifacts in their homes or who have traveled to Africa, the vast majority of Blacks have minimized any linkage, even historical, to Africa. This is partially a function of the stigma of Africa and partially the typical desire of most minorities to be considered American.

The situation is now quite different. Black intellectuals, the affluent, and the middle class are transcending the stigma attached to Africa. In the United States they are identifying with political liberation (and have for many generations), and in Africa they are identifying with the "homeland." Afrocentrism is very much in fashion. Over the past 30 years America's core values have been challenged by the civil rights movement, the antiwar movement, the feminist movement, and other movements. A variant of reverse ethnocentrism has been achieving prominence, if not dominance, among some. That is, what is foreign is viewed positively, while what is American, especially that associated with the elite, is viewed negatively. Accomplishments of Blacks both in the United States and elsewhere are now greatly celebrated. African American leaders, even when found corrupt, are usually forgiven. To many, such allowances are functional because the main thing is that Blacks are finally allowed to excel and to be proud.

As you look over the following very different interpretations of the African experience by Olga Idriss Davis and Keith B. Richburg, consider the relevancy for minority groups (and others) of myths. In what ways might returning to one's area of origin be similar or dissimilar for Blacks as it would be for Asians or white Europeans? Would Americans from Serbia or Bosnia, for instance, visiting after generations, experience similar disappointments to those of Richburg? Does the identity of any American lie outside of the United States?

Olga Idriss Davis  **YES**

The Door of No Return

Abstract. Placed against the backdrop of Senegal, West Africa, this essay explores the symbolic meaning of pilgrimage as a re-encountering of self. By examining the role of social drama, Goree Island becomes a ritual site of meaning and lived experience. Employing Victor Turner's theory of pilgrimage, language serves as a framework for discussing the journey to Africa by many African-Americans. This essay enhances understanding of how African-Americans use discursive means to claim identity with Africa and locate a collective oneness with its people and cultures. The inquiry asks, what is the symbolic nature of African-American pilgrimage?

But watch, watch where you walk, forgotten stranger—this is the very depth of your roots: Black. Walk proud. Watch, listen to the calls of the ancestral spirits, prodigal son—to the call of the long-awaited soil. They welcome you home, home. In the song of birds the winds whisper the golden names of your tribal warriors, the fresh breeze blown into your nostrils floats their bones turned to dust. Walk tall. The spirits welcome their lost-son-returned.

— excerpt from *Home-Coming Son* by Tsegaye Gabre Medhen

Throughout the United States African-Americans are taking tours to a variety of countries on the continent of Africa. It is as though they are searching for something; attempting to fill a void that is not easily squelched by the celebratory month of Black history, Kwaanza rituals or holidays of slain civil rights leaders. The notion that African-Americans are reclaiming their identity by locating a cultural past informs the rhetorical dimensions of place as a symbolic representation of survival in the culture of pilgrimage.

The purpose of this essay is to examine how a rhetoric of pilgrimage reveals African Americans' search for identity and cultural collectiveness. Reclaiming the past through pilgrimage points to the slave castle of Goree Island off the coast of Senegal, West Africa, which serves as a site of sacred recollection through the symbolic means of the narrative. The narratives of African-Americans who travel to this island reveal the complexity of social and cultural

From Olga Idriss Davis, "The Door of No Return: Reclaiming the Past Through the Rhetoric of Pilgrimage," *The Western Journal of Black Studies*, vol. 21, no. 3 (1997). Copyright © 1997 by *The Western Journal of Black Studies*. Reprinted by permission.

performance of which social dramas of historical significance emanate. The metaphor of pilgrimage illuminates the social ritual of returning to Africa to claim self, redefine culture, and reclaim the social reality of life in America. First, the concepts of pilgrimage and social drama are defined. Second, the way in which language provides a framework for symbolic action of transformation and empowerment is explored. The essay concludes by discussing the implications of pilgrimage for explicating the deep structures of cultural memory and self-healing through a reclamation of the past.

The rhetoric of pilgrimage for the African-American is a language deeply rooted in the quest for self-identity. From the time of slavery the African-American has inquired, *Who am I? Why am I here? How do I return home?* According to historian John Henrik Clarke (1985):

> Self-identity for African-Americans is a search for the lost identity that the slave system had destroyed. The search for an identity in America has been a search for an identity in the world ... as a human being with a history, before and after slavery....(p. 157)

This search I contend, ruminates within the center of the African-American spirit. The inner conflict of what it means to be an American and at the same time what it means to be an African-American places one in a double bind both psychologically and politically. How do I negotiate my Africanness with my American character? Where do the two ideologies meet? How do they co-exist if they can at all? It is within the spiritual and cultural transformation of self through sojourning to locate the African consciousness that this secular pilgrimage becomes a unique phenomenon for study. Thus, travelling to a geographical place affectionately termed as the *homeland* or *motherland* is not the essence of the experience, but rather the process by which the African-American comes to know the self within an African context. More importantly, many African-Americans discover the place of pain and suffering deeply embedded in the spiritual consciousness through an encounter of place. They come to know and understand its legacy in the historical, cultural, sociological, and political matrix of world consciousness. It is my contention that a *return home* for African-Americans reaffirms a sense of self by recognizing Western-imposed alienation on the psyche, yet simultaneously reclaiming identity as a lost entity of African heritage.

For many African-Americans, the notion of heritage and ancestral roots are a mystery. Because of the vast pillaging of women, separation of families, and attempts to erase the culture of predominantly West African villages during the fifteenth through the seventeenth centuries by the English, Dutch, Portuguese, French, and Spanish, the African-American of contemporary day knows little if any of the familiar ties to Africa nor of the intellectual and cultural greatness the continent produced. Furthermore, the Western educational system and American culture with its varied media have corroborated extensively to present African people and iconic images as non-beings genetically predisposed to violence on one hand, or extraordinarily talented in the realm of athletics or entertainment on the other. Generationally, myths and folklore of the inferiority of the African have become internalized by African-Americans resulting in the schism of self-identity.

The popular notion of pilgrimage is one of a sacred journey to come in contact with a higher or greater spiritual source. It symbolizes a spiritual awakening elicited by a journey, an escape, a gestalt from which a higher level of consciousness is achieved. Pilgrimage serves as a guide for understanding the contours of human social behavior. Individuals disparate in age, occupation, gender, ethnicity, social class, power, and wealth temporarily come together to journey to sacred shrines. Victor Turner (1974) explains that pilgrimages "are 'functional equivalents' in complex cultures dominated by the major historical religions partly of 'rites de passage' and partly of 'rituals of affliction' in preliterate, small-scale societies." He suggests in the following statement that pilgrimages function both:

> ... as occasions on which communitas is experienced and as journeys toward a sacred source of communitas which is also seen as a source of healing and renewal. (p. 203)

As a result, pilgrimages function as community-building efforts to perpetuate a sense of oneness, collectiveness, and unity. The notion of pilgrimages as social dramas enables rhetorical scholars to explain the homologies of narrative form and symbolic content within African-American experience. Such a lens informs that African-American pilgrimages claim a lost consciousness and serve the same individual and societal functions as Turner's corporeal pilgrimages do.

It is suggested here that while the Turnerian theory of pilgrimage asserts an anthropological purview, the African-American experience of pilgrimage is a re-awakening, a connection with the center of being-ness, an often-untapped space of yesterday in the subconsciousness of the here and now. In the poem by Tsegaye Gabre Medhen, homecoming of Africa's children is depicted much differently. It is a return to self, hidden in the mysteries of pre-slavery, slave castles, the middle passage, and the rich culture of the African heritage of which there is gross miseducation (Clarke, 1985). The pilgrimage is a recognition of the psyche, a replenishing of the reality of Blackness not celebrated in the Westernized conception of its banality, but rather Blackness as pride, strength, revelation of traditions, and recognition of greatness within.

The idea of returning to self is reflected by the late educational theorist Paulo Freire's experience of "being at home on African soil" expressed as he first stepped on African soil in Tanzania:

> ... I make this reference to underline how important it was for me to step for the first time on African soil, and to feel myself to be one who was returning and not one who was arriving. In truth, five years ago, as I left the airport of Dar es Salaam, going toward the university campus, the city opened before me as something I was seeing again and in which I re-encountered myself. The color of the skies; the blue-green of the sea; the coconut, the mango and the cashew trees; the perfume of flowers; the smell of the earth; the bananas and, among them, my very favorite, the apple-banana; the fish cooked in coconut oil; the locusts hopping in the dry grass; the sinuous body movements of the people as they walked in the streets, their smiles so ready for

life; the drums sounding in the depths of night; bodies dancing and, as they did so, expressions of their culture that the colonialists, no matter how hard they tried, could not stamp out—all of this took possession of me and made me realize that I was more African than I had thought. Naturally, it was not only these aspects, considered by some people merely sentimental, that affected me. There was something else in that encounter: a re-encounter with myself. There is so much I could say of the impressions that continue and of the learning I have done on successive visits to Tanzania only to emphasize the importance for me of stepping on African soil and feeling as though I were returning somewhere, rather than arriving. (Freire, 1974)

Re-encountering self is the foundation to the social reality of African-American pilgrimage. Language shapes the meaning of the past and provides a symbolic discourse for liberating and empowering self of an historical past.

On the island of Goree, social dramas create a language of pilgrimage where place is fused with past and present horrors.

Pilgrimage as Social Drama

According to Turner, social dramas are created out of an urgency to become reflexive about the cause and motive of action damaging to the social fabric (Turner, 1988). Reflexivity refers to the way in which a sociocultural group reflects back upon themselves or other sociocultural components which make up their public selves (p. 24). As African-Americans at the end of the twentieth century reflect back upon the actions, symbols, meanings, roles, social structures, and ethical and legal rules of the peculiar institution of slavery and subsequent ramifications, there still remains a plethora of questions surrounding the damaging effects of such a social system. That history prior to slavery serves as a source for cultural identity illuminates the symbolic meaning of self and provides a context for exploring the socio-political continuum of Black struggle in American society.

As a rhetorical critic, I am intrigued by the way in which symbolic discourse reveals the dynamics of culture and identity in the process of altering reality. In narrative, rhetoric locates a self of the past by revealing an identity of oppression. Through identification with oppression, the self of the present is empowered by the past. Experiencing the place in which Africans were brutally taken from their land never to return, and setting foot at the very spot from which they left, is a chilling realization of the resilience of the human spirit and of one's place in the historical continuum. The symbolic nature of social dramas point to the rhetorical situation in African-American pilgrimage.

Bitzer (1968) contends that a situation is rhetorical when discourse comes into existence as a response to an obstacle, a defect, an exigency. The exigence of slavery and a coming to terms with the historical implications of past and present invites the creation of discourse in the form of social dramas. Rhetoric provides a symbolic means of altering reality. The narratives of African-American visitors reveal the four phases of social dramas in the creation of public action identified by Turner as breach, crisis, redressive action, and reintegration (Turner, 1974).

For many African-Americans, the reality of oppression, domination, and control continue to plague their definition of national character and racial identity. Often, the rhetorical response is to travel to Africa, particularly Goree Island, to redefine the rhetorical situation of slavery. Crafted within the ritual of the African-African-American Summit, pilgrimage becomes a public discourse of social dramas and a symbolic action of claiming identity. As a delegate to the Third African-African-American Summit, the social drama began as a community of one, preparing me to redefine community through self-reclamation.

The Breach

Turner (1988) identifies this phase of social drama as a breach of regular norm-governed social relations. Leaving from a small, predominately-white midwestern town in which I live, to travel to a continent embellished with people diverse in color, hues, and cultures, without knowing the language nor other travellers presents a challenge for social coordination and situational adjustment.

As I departed from my home and family, it struck me quite emphatically, how it must have felt for the African women to be taken from their families. While I was not forced to board the airplane and leave, I still experienced the sorrow of leaving my family, being separated from them across a continent, and the fear of not knowing what to expect in Africa; *Would it be safe? Will I return to my family?* I knew I would be seeing from the eyes of a different culture and would connect to something deeply rooted within me. Yet, I had no expectations, only that I knew I would be transformed in such a way that I would never be the same.

Later that day, I arrived in Philadelphia, the place of our departure. The Concourse for international departures was a place of hustle-and-bustle of approximately 1200 African-American "delegates" checking baggage, obtaining boarding passes, showing passports, and greeting former acquaintances who attended the first two African-African-American Summits in Cote D'Ivoire and Gabon, respectively. I was struck by the number of students preparing to attend and their excitement to see such dignitaries as the Reverend Jesse Jackson, comedian and social activist Dick Gregory, former United States Secretary of Agriculture Mike Espy, former President of the NAACP Benjamin Chavis, Mayors Marion Berry and Johnny Ford, and United States Secretary of Commerce, the late Ron Brown.

Such an event was history in the making. The Summit was to be a symbolic reunion to unify Africa's "children" around a common ideal. That common ideal was to build a bridge of connectedness between the cultures of Africa and of African-Americans and Friends of Africa.... [T]he children of slaves were returning to build bridges of economic, cultural, and human development in Africa for the twenty-first century and beyond. A personal journal entry reveals such sentiment:

> We boarded the plane for SENEGAL! What a wonderful experience—meeting
> all new people, some with whom I've already made a warm connection in

Philadelphia. We are going to see our HOME; A home we have never known —YET WE KNOW. An anticipation like this I've *never* felt before. . . .

As the door opened at Dakar International Airport, we were greeted from the airplane by dignitaries from several of the African countries to be represented at the Summit. From the moments of descending the ramp, there was a sense of meeting family. Hugs, embraces, handshakes, and loving smiles were exchanged and a sense of returning rather than a sense of arrival accompanied these early moments in, for many of us, our first trip to Africa. The Summit in Dakar, Senegal, brought together persons of African ancestry and of American nationality, many of whom did not know each other, yet we were embraced such as are cousins whom one knows of but has never met. Thus, new social relationships were born out of an identity with world history of being separated from the land and the peoples of Africa.

. . . By redefining the social relations between Africans and African-Americans, the breach becomes a symbolic transgression from the contradictions of a lack of cohesiveness between the two cultures.

The Crisis

Social drama in the crisis phase stresses the dialectic between the temporalization of space and the spacialization of process (Turner, 1988). Framed within the postmodern turn in anthropology, Turner suggests that performance of the self in everyday life moves to the center of observation and hormeneutical observation (p. 77). In so doing, the factors which bring about inner conflict and sociocultural crises are revealed through the human communication process of symbolic action. Rhetorical discourse, then, provides the vehicle by which African-Americans come to know the meaning of identity and find a context in which to talk about their experience as orphans, pilgrims, children of Africa, dispersed of Ethiopia. The crisis of African-American pilgrimage is a dialectic between the political realities of past and present oppression and locating self-identity within the symbolic reality of both. Turner's notion of the temporalization of space points to a return to the past to an island off the coast of Senegal; Goree Island's slave castle:

> At the dawn of the 16th century, a small strip of land on the tip of the West African coast became a bustling shipping port. Humans were the main export. They were weighted, chained, dehydrated, sold, and forced to suffer the final indignity of walking through the door of no return. (Martin, 1995)

The limitations of time and space are collapsed as African-Americans are transported back in time as they explore cave dungeons which held thousands of African men, women, children, and infants in preparation for their Transatlantic voyage known as The Middle Passage.

The island of Goree, was a re-encountering of myself in a very emotional way. Here is where an estimated 15 to 20 million Africans were held captive before being shipped to America and other parts of the world. I re-encountered myself as I stood alone in the slave caves, as I touched the stones surrounding me and the earth beneath me; as I stood and gazed out of a little slither of a opening in the wall of rocks. I thought of the many African women my ancestors who also gazed out of the same slither only to be assured they would never return to their tribe, their families again. Not to know what lay beyond the vastness of the Atlantic Ocean is an emotional and psychological turmoil one can only contemplate upon the visit to Goree Island.

I re-encountered myself when I stood in "The Door of No Return" and thought of my ancestors who were forced to either go through the door and walk the plank to the slave ship, or meet his or her death among sharks. Knowing I was standing in the very place sent chills up my spine. As I looked at the foamy waves crashing beneath the door, I realized in essence, I was standing on holy ground.

Many African-Americans return yearly to the last piece of Africa their ancestors ever saw, Goree Island. I experienced grown men and women after more than 400 years, pay their respects to their ancestors by grieving for their suffering and rejoicing in their strength to survive. Of his trip to Goree Island, an African-American respondent from Ohio comments:

> I stood in the door of no return. When a man went through this door, he would either go to America and become a slave or meet his death among the sharks. Nothing can describe the feeling of knowing our ancestors had to walk through that door.

Perhaps for the first time, this journey can begin to heal the wounds of slavery. For African-Americans, a return to the slave castle presents an inner crisis to negotiate the inconsistencies of Western history with an ancestral identity in the dungeons of yesteryear.

Several narratives of African-Americans returning to Goree Island reveal the crisis phase of pilgrimage. Selma Dodson, a radio sales manager explains:

> There is still the impression among many Americans, she said, that Africa is mostly jungles, filled with primitive people and a chest-thumping Tarzan. . . . We had our history and our heritage stripped from us. But as a saying I read goes: "I am African, not because I was born in Africa, but because Africa was born in me. I'm going back to find that Africa born in me." (Martin, 1995)

. . . Ferdinand Dennis, a Jamaican-born, British-educated writer/broadcaster who lives in London spoke of the inner crisis faced by African-Americans to find identity thus:

> The enslaved Africans lost their myths, their gods, their rituals of celebration, their languages, their names. . . . A search for those things lost, to cease feeling like orphans of history—that's why some of us come back to Africa again and again. But sometimes I do fear that these losses are irretrievable. (Charles, 1993)

African-Americans are attempting to re-claim their African identity while redefining their American identity through the narrative discourse of pilgrimage.

Redressive Action

The redressive action to resolve the historical crises of African identity and the socio-political crises of being Black in America is ritualized in the symbolic action of pilgrimage. The call to heal African-Americans of this lost identity is being addressed in Senegal. Here, Goree Island stands as a place for healing, and as a sacred site for memorializing those who because of their indomitable spirit, endured for the hope of tomorrow's children.

At the Third African-African-American Summit, the host country's President Abdou Diouf of the Republic of Senegal eluded to a redressive action in his opening address to the Summit:

> Goree, an island present like a burning ember in our collective memory. Goree, an island of history, a witness to a time when man chose to silence the calling of his higher destiny, and denied his own humanity through the suffering and humiliation he inflicted on his fellow beings. If Goree is to preserve that memory for present and future generations, it is also the symbol of an Africa resolutely turned towards the future. Hopefully, a future world of justice and solidarity. A world which will transcend the prejudices of race and murderous tribalism.

The hope for tomorrow is ever-present in the rhetorical discourse of African culture....

Reintegration

The delegation to the Third African-African-American Summit experienced reintegration into American society with a social recognition of the tenacity of their ancestors and through a legitimation of the human character and spirit revealed on Goree Island. It is my contention that the reintegration phase signifies a process of empowerment occurring during pilgrimage. Empowerment was the recognition that healing took place and transcended us to another level of resilience upon returning to America.

Connecting with others who grieve the past atrocities and look for an escape from the pain of slavery through the knowledge of cultural and self identity is an empowering experience. My personal narrative states that:

> This journal is a chronicle, a compilation, and a "journeying" back to the Africa of my past. The Summit is an opportunity to reconnect with the ancestors whose spirits provide the linkages of Africans throughout the Diaspora. (Davis, 1995)

Throughout the week-long experiences filled with workshops, plenary sessions, and visits to markets and historical sites, a spiritual connection between and among African-Americans and Africans became more and more pronounced. It was as though a presence was around us continuously. We were told it was the ancestral spirits welcoming us home and protecting us during our stay.

As the Summit was nearing its closing ceremony, we prepared for our journey back to the United States. Many brothers and sisters from many countries implored us to return to Africa saying, *You are not a stranger, you are one of us. Senegal is your home now, Come back soon.* We said our goodbyes to many of our African family and reflected on the week-long experiences as our plane entered the beautiful blue skies. As we took leave for our journey back to America, the cabin was quiet, some were weeping, others were in silent reflection. All of us however, had been transformed. We would never be the same.

References

Bitzer, Lloyd F. (1968). "The Rhetorical Situation." *Philosophy and Rhetoric.* Vol 1:1, 1–14.

Charles, Nick. (1993). "Back to Africa: Call is Deep-Rooted in Blacks Worldwide." January 31. *The Plain Dealer,* p. G1.

Clarke, John Henrik. (1985). "African-American Historians and the Reclaiming of African History," In *African Culture: The Rhythms of Unity.* Asante, Molefi K. and Kariamu W. Asante. Westport: Greenwood Press.

Davis, Olga I. (1995). *Personal Journal.*

Diouf, Abdou. (1995). *Opening Ceremonial Address to the Third African/African-American Summit.* Senegal, West Africa.

Freire, Paulo. (1974). *The Pedagogy of Liberation.* South Hadley: Bergin and Garvey.

Martin, Norma. (1995). African-Americans Plan Trip to Africa for Heritage, Healing. February 13. *The Houston Chronicle,* p. A13.

Turner, Victor. (1974). *Dramas, Fields, and Metaphors.* Ithaca: Cornell UP.

___. (1988). *The Anthropology of Performance.* Baltimore: John Hopkins UP.

Continental Divide

I watched the dead float down a river in Tanzania.

Of all the gut-wrenching emotions I wrestled with during three years of covering famine, war and misery around Africa, no feeling so gripped me as the one I felt that scorching hot day [of] April [1994], standing on the Rusumo Falls bridge, in a remote corner of Tanzania, watching dozens of discolored, bloated bodies floating downstream, floating from the insanity that was Rwanda.

The image of those bodies in the river lingered in my mind long after that, recurring during interminable nights in desolate hotel rooms without running water, or while I walked through the teeming refugee camps of eastern Zaire. And the same feeling kept coming back too, as much as I tried to force it from my mind. How can I describe it? Revulsion? Yes, but that doesn't begin to touch on what I really felt. Sorrow, or pity, at the monumental waste of human life? Yes, that's closer. But the feeling nagging at me was—is—something more, something far deeper. It's a sentiment that, when uttered aloud, might come across as callous, self-obsessed, maybe even racist.

But I've felt it before, that same nagging, terrible sensation. I felt it in Somalia, walking among the living dead of Baidoa and Baardheere—towns in the middle of a devastating famine. And I felt it again in those refugee camps in Zaire, as I watched bulldozers scoop up black corpses, and trucks dump them into open pits.

I know exactly the feeling that haunts me, but I've just been too embarrassed to say it. So let me drop the charade and put it as simply as I can: *There but for the grace of God go I.*

Somewhere, sometime, maybe 400 years ago, an ancestor of mine whose name I'll never know was shackled in leg irons, kept in a dark pit, possibly at Goree Island off the coast of Senegal, and then put with thousands of other Africans into the crowded, filthy cargo hold of a ship for the long and treacherous journey across the Atlantic. Many of them died along the way, of disease, of hunger. But my ancestor survived, maybe because he was strong, maybe stubborn enough to want to live, or maybe just lucky. He was ripped away from his country and his family, forced into slavery somewhere in the Caribbean. Then one of his descendants somehow made it up to South Carolina, and one of those descendants, my father, made it to Detroit during the Second World

War, and there I was born, 36 years ago. And if that original ancestor hadn't been forced to make that horrific voyage, I would not have been standing there that day on the Rusumo Falls bridge, a journalist—a mere spectator—watching the bodies glide past me like river logs. No, I might have instead been one of them—or have met some similarly anonymous fate in any one of the countless ongoing civil wars or tribal clashes on this brutal continent. And so I thank God my ancestor made that voyage.

Does that sound shocking? Does it sound almost like a justification for the terrible crime of slavery? Does it sound like this black man has forgotten his African roots? Of course it does, all that and more. And that is precisely why I have tried to keep the emotion buried so deep for so long. But as I sit before the computer screen, trying to sum up my time in Africa, I have decided I cannot lie to you, the reader. After three years traveling around this continent as a reporter for The Washington Post, I've become cynical, jaded. I have covered the famine and civil war in Somalia; I've seen a cholera epidemic in Zaire (hence the trucks dumping the bodies into pits); I've interviewed evil "warlords," I've encountered machete-wielding Hutu mass murderers; I've talked to a guy in a wig and a shower cap, smoking a joint and holding an AK-47, on a bridge just outside Monrovia. I've seen some cities in rubble because they had been bombed, and some cities in rubble because corrupt leaders had let them rot and decay. I've seen monumental greed and corruption, brutality, tyranny and evil.

I've also seen heroism, honor and dignity in Africa, particularly in the stories of small people, anonymous people—Africans battling insurmountable odds to publish an independent newspaper, to organize a political party, usually just to survive. I interviewed an opposition leader in the back seat of a car driving around the darkened streets of Blantyre, in Malawi, because it was then too dangerous for us even to park, lest we be spotted by the ubiquitous security forces. In Zaire, I talked to an opposition leader whose son had just been doused with gasoline and burned to death, a message from dictator Mobutu Sese Seko's henchmen. And in the Rift Valley of central Kenya, I met the Rev. Festus Okonyene, an elderly African priest with the Dutch Reformed Church who endured terrible racism under the Afrikaner settlers there, and who taught me something about the meaning of tolerance, forgiveness, dignity and restraint.

But even with all the good I've found here, my perceptions have been hopelessly skewed by the bad. My tour in Africa coincided with two of the world's worst tragedies, Somalia and Rwanda. I've had friends and colleagues killed, beaten to death by mobs, shot and left to bleed to death on a Mogadishu street.

Now, after three years, I'm beaten down and tired. And I'm no longer even going to pretend to block that feeling from my mind. I empathize with Africa's pain. I recoil in horror at the mindless waste of human life, and human potential. I salute the gallantry and dignity and sheer perseverance of the Africans. But most of all, I feel secretly glad that my ancestor made it out—because, now, I am not one of them.

❦

... I grew up as a black kid in 1960s white America, not really poor, but not particularly rich either. Like most blacks who settled in Detroit, my father had come up from the South because of the opportunities offered in the automobile plants....

There were actually two black Detroits while I was growing up, the east side and the west. The dividing line was Woodward Avenue, our own version of Beirut's infamous Green Line. But the division was more psychological than geographic, centering mainly on black attitudes, the strange caste system in black America at the time, and where you could place your roots in the South. Roughly put, the split was between South Carolina blacks on the west side and Alabama blacks on the east. These were, in a way, our "tribes."

It sounds strange even to me as I look back on it. But those divisions were very real to the black people living in Detroit when I was young, at a time when the city was transforming itself from predominantly white to predominantly black. It was drummed into me that South Carolina blacks, like my family, owned their homes and rarely rented. They had small patches of yard in the front and kept their fences mended. They came from Charleston, Anderson, Greenville, sometimes Columbia. They saved their money, went to church on Sunday, bought their kids new clothes at Easter and for the start of the school year. They kept their hair cut close, to avoid the nappy look. They ate turkey and ham and grits and sweet potato pie. They were well-brought-up, and they expected their children to be the same.

Don't cross Woodward Avenue, we were told, because those blacks over there came up from Alabama. They talked loudly, they drank heavily, and they cursed in public. They had darker skin and nappier hair. They didn't own homes, they rented, and they let the grass in the front run down to dirt, and their fences were all falling apart. They ate pigs' feet, and often had more than a dozen relatives, all from Alabama, stacked up in a few small rooms. They were, as my father would have called them back then, "niggers"—South Carolina blacks being good colored people. The greatest insult was: "He ain't nothin'— he just came up here from Alabama!"

Detroit can get oppressively hot in the summers, and those little houses that black families owned then didn't have anything like air conditioning. So to stay cool, my brother and I would walk (you could walk in those days) down Grand River Avenue to the Globe Theater, where for less than a buck you could sit all day, watching the same movie over and over in air-conditioned splendor until it was time for dinner. I especially remember when the movie "Zulu" was playing, and we watched Michael Caine lead a group of British soldiers against attacking Zulu tribesmen in what is now South Africa. We took turns cheering for the British side and the Zulus. But neither of us really wanted to cheer for the losers. Whoever was rooting for the Africans would usually sit sullenly, knowing what fate held in store. Then came the credits and the heady knowledge that when the movie played again, after a cartoon break, you would be able to cheer for the British once more.

Beyond what I learned from "Zulu," I can't say I had much knowledge of Africa as a kid. I probably couldn't have named a single African country until high school. The word "black" came into vogue in the 1960s, thanks to, among others, James Brown. In 1967, Detroiters burned a large part of the city to the ground, and then all the white people I knew in my neighborhood starting moving out to suburbs that seemed really far away. A lot of the people my father called "black radicals" took to wearing African-style dashikis, and stocking caps in red, black and green, the colors of African liberation. But, when you were a kid from a quiet, South Carolina family growing up on the west side, these seemed like frightening symbols of militancy, defiance, even violence. Any connection to a strange and unknown continent seemed tenuous.

◦◦◉◦◦

... What does Detroit more than a quarter-century ago have to do with contemporary Africa? Maybe I'm hoping that bit of personal history will help explain the attitude of many black Americans to the concept of their own blackness, their African-ness.

You see? I just wrote "black Americans." I couldn't even bring myself to write "African Americans." It's a phrase that, for me, still doesn't roll easily off the tongue, or look natural on the screen of the computer terminal. Going from "colored" to "black" took some time to get used to. But now "African American"? Is that what we really are? Is there anything African left in the descendants of those original slaves who made that long journey over? Are white Americans whose ancestors came here as long ago as the slaves did "English Americans" or "Dutch Americans"? Haven't the centuries erased all those connections, so that we are all now simply "Americans"?

But I am digressing. Let's continue with the story at hand.

Somewhere along the line, I decided to become a journalist. It was during my undergraduate years at the University of Michigan, while working on the school newspaper, the Michigan Daily. My father would have preferred that I study law, then go into politics. Blacks in the 1970s were just coming into their own in politics, taking over city halls across the country and winning congressional seats in newly defined black districts. And that's what articulate, well-educated black kids did: They became lawyers and politicians.

But I wanted to write, and to travel. The travel urge, I think—a longing to cross an ocean—is shared by a lot of midwesterners. I became a reporter for The Post, and would take trips overseas whenever I could save up the money and vacation time. Paris. Morocco. Brazil. London for a year of graduate school. Train journeys across Europe. Trips to Hong Kong, Taiwan, later Japan and China.

But never sub-Saharan Africa (defined as "black Africa"). Whenever friends asked me why, in all my travels, I had avoided the continent of my ancestry, I would usually reply that it was so big, so diverse, that it would take many weeks if not months. I had studied African politics in school, even written a graduate school thesis on the problem of single-party states in Africa. I considered myself a wide-eyed realist, not given to any romantic notions about the place.

The real reason I avoided Africa had more to do with my personal reaction —or, more accurately, my fear of how I would react. I knew that Africa was a continent with much poverty and despair. But what would it be like, really like, to see it as a black person, knowing my ancestors came from there? What if I found myself frightened or, worse, disgusted or repulsed?

And what would it be like, for once in my life, not to stand out in a crowd? To be just one of a vast number of anonymous faces? For better or for worse, a black man in America, or a black man in Asia, stands out.

A friend of mine in Hawaii, a fourth-generation Japanese American, told me once of her fear of traveling to Japan. "I don't know what it would be like to be just another face in the crowd," she said rather innocently. It was a sentiment I immediately shared. When, in early 1991, my editors at The Post asked me if I wanted to cover Africa, that same feeling welled up inside me. I was in Asia on vacation when I got the assignment, and I sought out a Reuter reporter named Kevin Cooney, who was based in Bangkok but had spent several months working in Nairobi. He put it to me bluntly. "In Africa," he said, after we both had a few too many beers, "you'll be just another nigger."

It was a well-intentioned warning, I would find myself recalling often over three sometimes-tumultuous years.

❧

"Where are you from?" the Zairian immigration officer asked suspiciously in French, fingering through the pages of my passport.

I found the question a bit nonsensical, since he was holding proof of my nationality in his hand. I replied in French, "United States."

"I think you are a Zairian," he said, moving his eyes from the passport photo to me to the photo again. "You look like a Zairian."

"I'm not a Zairian," I said again. I was tired, it was late, I had just spent the day in the Rwandan border town of Cyangugu, just across from Bukavu in Zaire. And all I wanted to do was get back to my room at the Hotel Residence, where, at least if the water was running, a shower awaited. "Look," I said, trying to control my temper, "that's an American passport. I'm an American."

"What about your father—was he Zairian?" The immigration man was not convinced.

"My parents, my grandparents, everybody was American," I said, trying not to shout. "Maybe, 400 years ago, there was a Zairian somewhere, but I can assure you, I'm American."

"You have the face of a Zairian," he said, calling over his colleague so they could try to assess which tribe, which region of Zaire, I might spring from.

Finally, I thought of one thing to convince him. "Okay," I said, pushing my French to its limit. "Suppose I was a Zairian. And suppose I did manage to get myself a fake American passport." I could see his eyes light up at the thought. "So, I'm a Zairian with a fake American passport. Tell me, why on earth would I be trying to sneak back into Zaire?"

The immigration officer pondered this for a moment, churning over in his mind the dizzying array of possibilities a fake U.S. passport might offer; surely, using it to come into Zaire was not among the likely options. "You are right," he concluded, as he picked up his rubber stamp and pounded in my entry. "You are American—black American."

And so it went around Africa. I was constantly met with raised eyebrows and suspicions upon explaining that I really was, really am, an American. "I know you're a Kenyan," said one woman in a bar—a hooker, I think, in retrospect. "You're just trying to pretend you don't speak Swahili."

"Okay," I told her, "you found me out. I'm really a Kenyan."

"Aha!" she said. "I knew it!"

Being able to pass for an African had some advantages. In Somalia, for example, when anti-Americanism was flaring as U.S. Cobra helicopters were bombing militia strongholds of Gen. Mohamed Farah Aideed, I was able to venture into some of the most dangerous neighborhoods without attracting undue attention. I would simply don a pair of sunglasses and ride in the back seat of my beat-up white Toyota, with my Somali driver and AK-47-toting bodyguard up front. My biggest worry was getting caught in the cross hairs of some U.S. Army marksman or helicopter gunner who would only see what, I suppose, we were: three African-looking men riding around Mogadishu's mean streets in a car with an automatic weapon sticking out one of the windows.

But mostly, I concluded, being black in Somalia was a disadvantage. This came home to me late in 1993. I was one of the reporters at the first public rally Aideed had held since coming out of four months of hiding. The arrest order on him had been lifted, and the Clinton administration had called off the humiliating and futile manhunt that had earlier left 18 U.S. soldiers dead in a single encounter. The mood at the rally was, predictably, euphoric. I was among a group of reporters standing on the stage awaiting Aideed's arrival.

Suddenly, one of the Somali gunmen guarding the stage raced up to me and shoved me hard in the chest, forcing me down onto my back. I looked up, stunned, into his wild eyes, and he seemed to be pulling his AK-47 off his shoulder to take aim at me. He was shouting in Somali, and I couldn't understand him. A crowd gathered, and there was more shouting back and forth. Finally, one of Aideed's aides, whom I recognized, helped me to my feet. "I apologize," the aide said, as others hustled my attacker away. "You look like a Somali. He thought you were someone else."

Being black in Africa: I had to fight myself to keep my composure, to keep from bursting into tears.

⋘⊙⋙

Many months later, I found out it wasn't only black Americans who felt the way I did. That was when I ran across Sam Msibi, a black South African cameraman for Britain-based Worldwide Television News....

Msibi knew better than I what it was like to be a black journalist amid Africa's violence; he had been shot five times, in Tokoza township, and managed to live to tell the tale. "It's a problem in Africa," he said, as he navigated the winding mountain road. "When you're black, you have to worry about black-on-black violence."

"Sometimes I want to stop to take pictures," he said, surveying the scene of refugees on the move toward the border, often with their herds of cattle and goats in front, always with small children trailing behind. "But I don't know how these people will react." I explained to him, naively, that I had just traveled the same road a week or so earlier with a Belgian TV crew that had no problem filming along the highway. "Yeah, but they're white," Msibi said. "These people might think I'm a Hutu or something."

I grew quite fond of Msibi during that nearly four-hour drive; I found that he, a black South African, and I, a black American, were thinking many of the same thoughts, venturing together into the heart of an African tragedy that was about as different from downtown Johannesburg as it was from Detroit or Washington, D.C.

"Africa is the worst place—Somalia, Zaire," Msibi said, more to himself than to me. "When you see something like this, you pray your own country will never go this way. Who wants to see his children walking like that?" . . .

✦

Are you black first, or a journalist first?

The question succinctly sums up the dilemma facing almost every black journalist working for the "mainstream" (read: white) press. Are you supposed to report and write accurately, and critically, about what you see and hear? Or are you supposed to be pushing some kind of black agenda, protecting black American leaders from tough scrutiny, treating black people and black issues in a different way?

Many of those questions were at the heart of the debate stirred up a decade ago by my Post colleague, Milton Coleman, when he reported remarks of Jesse Jackson referring to Jews as "Hymie." Coleman was accused of using material that was off the record; more troubling, he was accused of betraying his race. For being a hard-nosed journalist, he suffered the wrath of much of the black community, and even had to endure veiled threats from Louis Farrakhan's henchmen.

I have had to deal with many of the same questions over the years, including those asked by family members during Thanksgiving or Christmas gatherings in Detroit. "Let me ask you something," my favorite cousin, Loretta, began once. "Why does the media have to tear down our black leaders?" She was referring to Marion Barry and his cocaine arrest, and to Coleman Young, the longtime Detroit mayor who was always under a cloud for something or other. I tried to explain that journalists only do their job and should expose wrongdoing no matter if the wrongdoer is black or white. My cousin wasn't convinced. "But they are the only role models we have," she said.

It was an argument that couldn't be won. And it was an argument that trailed after me as a black reporter covering black Africa. Was I supposed to travel around looking for the "good news" stories out of the continent, or was I supposed to find the kind of compelling, hard-hitting stories that I would look for any other place in the world? Was I not to call a dictator a dictator, just because he happened to be black? Was I supposed to be an apologist for corrupt, ruthless, undemocratic, illegitimate black regimes?

Apparently so, if you subscribe to the kind of Pan Africanism that permeates much of black American thinking. Pan Africanism, as I see it, prescribes a kind of code of political correctness in dealing with Africa, an attitude that says black America should bury its head in the sand to all that is wrong in Africa, and play up the worn-out demons of colonialism, slavery and Western exploitation of minerals. Anyone who does, or writes, otherwise is said to be playing into the old "white conspiracy." That attitude was confirmed to me in Gabon, in May 1993, when I first met C. Payne Lucas of Africare, a Washington-based development and relief organization. "You mean you're a *black* man writing all of that stuff about Africa?" he said.

Lucas was in Gabon for the second African-American Summit, a meeting bringing black American civil rights activists and business leaders together with African government officials and others. It was an odd affair, this "summit," for at a time of profound change across Africa—more and more African countries struggling to shed long-entrenched dictatorships—not one of the American civil rights luminaries ever talked about "democracy" or "good governance" or "political pluralism" in my hearing. These same American leaders who were so quick off the mark to condemn injustice in South Africa, when the repression was white-on-black, suddenly lost their voices when the dictatorships were black.

Instead, what came out was a nauseating outpouring of praise from black Americans for a coterie of some of Africa's most ruthless strongmen and dictators. There were such famous champions of civil rights as Jesse Jackson heaping accolades on the likes of Nigeria's number one military thug at the time, Gen. Ibrahim Babangida, who had just shut down a critical newspaper and was about to renege on his pledge to transfer his country to democratic rule. There was speaker after speaker on the American side complimenting the host, Omar Bongo, a corrupt little dictator in platform shoes who at that very moment was busy shutting down his country's only private (read: opposition) radio station.

But the most sickening spectacle of all came when the baby dictator of Sierra Leone entered the conference hall. Capt. Valentine Strasser, a young tough in Ray-Ban sunglasses, walked in to swoons and cheers from the assembled American dignitaries, who were obviously more impressed by the macho military figure he cut than by the knowledge that back home Strasser was summarily executing former government officials and opponents of his new military regime.

I had seen that kind of display before around Africa: black Americans coming to the land of their ancestors with a kind of touchy-feely sentimentality straight out of Roots. The problem is, it flies smack into the face of a cold reality.

[In] March [1994] in the Sudanese capital of Khartoum, I ran into a large group of black Americans who were also staying at the Khartoum Hilton. They were there on some kind of a fact-finding trip, and being given VIP treatment by the Sudanese regime. Some of the men went all-out and dressed the part, donning long white Sudanese robes and turbans. Several of the women in the group covered themselves in Muslim wrap.

The U.S. ambassador in Khartoum had the group over to his house, and the next day, the government-controlled newspaper ran a front-page story on how the group berated the ambassador over U.S. policy toward Sudan. Apparently, some members of the group told the ambassador that it was unfair to label the Khartoum regime as a sponsor of terrorists and one of the world's most violent, repressive governments. After all, they said, they themselves had been granted nothing but courtesy, and they had found the dusty streets of the capital safer than most crime-ridden American cities.

I was nearly shaking with rage. Couldn't they see they were being used, manipulated by one of the world's most oppressive regimes? Human Rights Watch/Africa—hardly a water carrier for U.S. policy—had recently labeled Khartoum's human rights record as "abysmal," and reported that "all forms of political opposition remain banned both legally and through systematic terror." And here were these black Americans, these willing tools, heaping praise on an unsavory clique of ruling thugs. I wanted to confront them, but instead I deliberately avoided them....

Do I sound cynical? Maybe I am. Maybe that's because, unlike some of the African American tourists who have come out here on a two-week visit to the land of their roots, I've *lived* here.

Do you think I'm alone in my view? Then meet Linda Thomas-Greenfield, and hear her story.

⋅⟐⋅

Thomas-Greenfield is a black American diplomat at the U.S. Embassy in Nairobi, her third African posting; she spent three years in Gambia and $2\frac{1}{2}$ in Nigeria. After completing her studies at the University of Wisconsin, she had spent time in Liberia, and she remembers how elated she felt then making her first voyage to her ancestral homeland. "I remember the plane coming down," she said. "I couldn't wait to touch down."

But when I talked to Thomas-Greenfield last summer, she had just finished nine months in Kenya. And she was burned out, fed up and ready to go home.

Her house in Nairobi had been burglarized five times. She had had an electric fence installed. "When they put up the electric fence, I told them to put in enough volts to barbecue anybody who came over." When she continued to complain that even the fence didn't stop the intruders, the local Kenyan police station posted two officers on her grounds. But then the police began extorting payment for their services. "I've gotten to the point where I'm more afraid not to give them money," she said. "They're sitting outside with automatic weapons." ...

In April, Thomas-Greenfield traveled to Rwanda for an embassy assignment. She had been in the country only a day when the presidential plane was shot down and an orgy of tribal bloodletting began. Most of the victims were Tutsi, and Thomas-Greenfield, a towering 6-foot-plus black woman, was immediately mistaken for a Tutsi. She recalls cowering in fear with machine guns pointed in her face, pleading repeatedly: "I don't have anything to do with this. I'm not a Rwandan. I'm an American."

In the end, it was not just the crime and her close call in Rwanda but the attitude of the Africans that wore down even this onetime Africa-lover. Thomas-Greenfield had never been invited into a Kenyan home. And doing the daily chores of life, she had been met constantly with the Kenyans' own perverse form of racism, under which whites are granted preferential treatment over blacks.

"There's nothing that annoys me more than sitting in a restaurant and seeing two white people getting waited on, and I can't get any service," she said. . . .

"I think it's an absolute disadvantage" being black in Africa, said Thomas-Greenfield, who, at the time we talked, said she was considering cutting short her assignment. "Here, as anywhere else in Africa, the cleavages are not racial, they are ethnic. People think they can tell what ethnic group you are by looking at you. And if there's any conflict going on between the ethnic groups, you need to let them know you're an American."

She added, "I'd rather be black in South Africa under apartheid than to go through what I'm going through here in Kenya."

◦⟨◎⟩◦

This is not the story I sat down to write. Originally, I had wanted to expound on Africa's politics, the prospects of freedom and development, the hopes for the future. My tour in Africa, after all, came during what was supposed to be the continent's "decade of democracy"—after the fall of one-party communist states of Eastern Europe, the argument went, and the consolidation of democracy in Latin America, could Africa's one-party dictatorships and military regimes be far behind? At least this was the view of many Africa analysts, and of hopeful African democrats themselves, when I began the assignment.

But three years of following African elections, in countries as diverse as Nigeria, Cameroon, Kenya, Ethiopia, Malawi and Mozambique, has left me—and many of those early, hopeful African democrats—far less than optimistic. I've seen elections hijacked or stolen outright, elections canceled, elections bought and elections that have proved to be essentially meaningless. How can you talk about elections in countries where whole chunks of territory are under the sway of armed guerrillas? Where whole villages get burned down because of competing political loyalties? And where traditional belief runs so deep that a politician can be charged in public with casting magic spells over poor villagers to force them to vote for him?

African autocrats are proving far more entrenched, far more brutal and far more adept at the manipulation of state machinery than their Eastern European communist counterparts. Africa's militaries—as compared with those in, say, South America—are proving less willing to return to the barracks and bow to the popular will. In country after country, even oppositionists demonstrate themselves to be grasping, quarrelsome and in most cases incapable of running things if they ever do manage to make it to power. Politics in Africa is about lucrative spoils and fresh opportunities for corruption, and much of opposition politics across the continent consists of an out group wanting its turn at the feeding trough.

It's become a cliche to call tribalism the affliction of modern Africa, but, unfortunately, my years of covering African politics has convinced me that it is true. Tribalism is a corrosive influence impeding democratic change and development....

Even in places where opposition parties have managed to overcome the odds and win power in democratic elections, the results so far have been mixed. In Zambia's case, the 1991 election of Frederick Chiluba was supposed to herald a beginning of a new democratic era. But what I found there last year was a country reeling from corruption and incompetence. Government officials have been implicated in drug dealing, others have resigned in disgust claiming the old democratic movement has lost its direction....

And finally, finding hope becomes even more difficult when you look at the basket cases—places like Zaire, which is in perpetual meltdown; Liberia, still carved up between competing armies; Sudan, ground down by seemingly endless civil war; Rwanda, which was convulsed by one of the worst episodes of tribal genocide in modern times; and Somalia, poor Somalia, which has virtually ceased to exist as a nation-state.

My final journey in Africa was to Somalia—fittingly, I thought, because it was the place I spent most of my time over the past three years. I found it fascinating to cover a country in which all forms of government had collapsed....

❧

In trying to explain Africa to you, I needed first to try to explain it to myself. I want to love the place, love the people. I can tell you I see hope amid the chaos, and I do, in places like Malawi, even Mozambique. But the Rwandas and Somalias and Liberias and Zaires keep intruding into my mind. Three years— three long years—have left me cold and heartless. Africa is a killing field of good intentions, as Somalia alone is enough to prove.

And where does that leave the black man who has come "home" to Africa? I write this surrounded by my own high fence, protected by two large dogs, a paid security guard, a silent alarm system and a large metal door that I bolt shut at night to keep "Africa" from coming across the yard and bashing in my brains with a panga knife for the $200 in my desk drawer. I am tired and, like Linda Thomas-Greenfield, ready to go.

Another black American, writer Eddy L. Harris, the author of *Native Stranger*, ventured into the dark continent, to discover that the place where he felt most at home was South Africa, that most modern, most Western of African countries....

So, do you think I'm a cynic? An Africa-basher? A racist even, or at least a self-hating black man who has forgotten his African roots? Maybe I am all that and more. But by an accident of birth, I am a black man born in America, and everything I am today—culture, attitudes, sensitivities, loves and desires—derives from that one simple and irrefutable truth.

POSTSCRIPT

Do the Identities of Blacks Lie in Africa?

It is worth noting that Richburg's selected case studies were all of war-torn societies or those recovering from difficult political turmoil (e.g., South Africa). Davis, meanwhile, bases her glowing discussion on a pilgrimage to a single country (Senegal) that might be considered remarkable and unusual anywhere. Does Richburg provide enough data to establish his case? Does Davis's rich and moving experience in a single society establish her case that Black identities may lie in Africa?

Scholars theorize that when groups experience sharp ambiguities, disjunctions, and changes, their identities may become problematic. One logical response is to look outside for understanding. For example, prior to and during the breakup of the former Soviet Union into competing ethnic groups, reports of flying saucer sightings were widespread. Some speculated that these reports reflected a search for some higher intelligence to somehow structure the chaotic, ambiguous situation in the former Soviet Union.

Are the many Black influentials who praise African leaders and societies self-serving hypocrites? Or are they acting on the realization that African Americans, like all people, need a sense of the past to provide continuity into the future and to make sense out of the present? Considering the hideous efforts to obliterate Blacks' ties with their families, religions, and institutions, might the identities of Black Americans at least partially lie in Africa?

What ties, perceived or otherwise, do your friends, relatives, and fellow students seem to have to their countries of origin? What does it mean for them to be Americans? What does it mean for them to be members of the racial, gender, or ethnic majority or minority?

Among the many excellent, recently published books highlighting the continuing racism in the United States and justifying, at least indirectly, Davis's position are Maurice Berger's *White Lies: Race and the Myths of Whiteness* (Farrar, Straus & Giroux, 1999); Leonard Steinhorn and Barbara Diggs-Brown's *By the Color of Our Skin: The Illusion of Integration and the Reality of Race* (Dutton, 1999); and Farai Chideya's *The Color of Our Future* (William Morrow, 1999). For a helpful sociopolitical history of Africa on disk, see Microsoft's *Encarta Africana* (1999).

For discussions of identity in broader contexts, see *Fires of Hatred: Ethnic Cleansing in Twentieth-Century Europe* by Norman M. Naimark (Harvard University Press, 2001) and *Shopping for Identity: The Marketing of Ethnicity* by Marilyn Halter (Schocken Books, 2000).

ISSUE 6

Are Hispanics Making Significant Progress?

YES: Linda Chavez, from *Out of the Barrio: Toward a New Politics of Hispanic Assimilation* (Basic Books, 1991)

NO: Robert Aponte, from "Urban Hispanic Poverty: Disaggregations and Explanations," *Social Problems* (November 1991)

ISSUE SUMMARY

YES: Scholar, business consultant, and former political candidate Linda Chavez documents the accomplishments of Hispanics and asserts that they are making it in America.

NO: Social scientist Robert Aponte suggests that social scientists, following an agenda driven by government policy, have concentrated on Black poverty, which has resulted in a lack of accurate data and information on the economic status of Hispanics. Aponte argues that disaggregation of demographic data shows that Hispanics are becoming increasingly poor.

For years almost all minority relations scholars reflected a social psychological approach to the study of ethnic and racial minority relations. That is, they were interested in explaining attitudes and values and lifestyles of minorities. Sociologists were also interested in patterns of interaction, especially stages of assimilation of immigrants.

Scholarly interest in the dominant group was concentrated on dominant group attitudes toward, stereotypes of, and prejudices and discrimination against minorities. The distinction between prejudice (an attitude) and discrimination (behavior) was developed. Studies of institutional power arrangements, including systematic racism in the marketplace, government, education, religion, and so on, were largely nonexistent until the 1960s. Most scholarly works on racial and ethnic relations concentrated on the values, beliefs, and attitudes among the white majority that were inconsistent with American ideals of equality.

But since the 1960s, race and ethnicity has come to be seen not as just the working out of individual attitudes and lifestyles but as a fundamental dimension of social stratification. Minority conflict was reconceptualized not as simply a clash of cultures and myths but as conflict that results when one group attempts to obtain greater equality and another group acts to maintain its advantageous position.

Understanding poverty came to be seen as important to understanding the effects of inequality, and data on poverty was needed as a basis for policy formulation. Unemployment rates, degree of residential segregation, percentage receiving welfare assistance, percentage in managerial positions, and so on came to characterize the questions asked by sociologists, economists, and politicians about minorities. The very idea of "poverty" found its way back into mainstream sociology and public discourse. The benchmark for this shift was probably in the early 1960s with the publication of Michael Harrington's *The Other America.*

In the following selections, both Linda Chavez and Robert Aponte acknowledge methodological and definitional problems inherent in researching poverty. And neither one assumes a zero-sum model of minority-majority economic relations. That is, economic gains of ethnic minorities, including Hispanics, are not viewed as "taking something away from" the majority. As minorities obtain economic success, all of society gains. The 2000 census showed that there are 35.3 million Hispanics (up from 22.4 million in 1990) widely distributed across the United States, especially in cities. Thus, the potential for either significant gains or losses is great.

In almost every other respect, however, Chavez and Aponte disagree. They clearly have a different definition of poverty. Chavez argues that Hispanic leaders dishonestly inflate the extent of poverty in order to create political capital for themselves and their group. She feels that government research and programs encourage some minority groups to jockey for entitlements by exaggerating the types and extent of Hispanic poverty.

Aponte also feels that significant, nonscientific factors have structured poverty research and policies. However, his interpretation is quite different. He feels that government policies based on identifying and partially correcting Black poverty, as commendable as they may be, have sometimes functioned to neglect the equally serious problem of Hispanic poverty. He is also incensed that researchers who ought to know better have generally collapsed Hispanics into one homogeneous ethnic group. He suggests that analytically and empirically there are huge differences in life chances and quality of life among various Hispanic groups.

As you review the following selections, note that the authors sometimes draw from the same data sets but reach very different conclusions. How can that be? According to Aponte, how might thinking about and viewing every member of an ethnic group as the same be misleading?

Out of the Barrio

In the Beginning

Before the affirmative action age, there were no *Hispanics,* only Mexicans, Puerto Ricans, Cubans, and so on. Indeed, few efforts were made to forge an alliance among the various Hispanic subgroups until the 1970s, when competition with blacks for college admissions, jobs, and other rewards of affirmative action made it advantageous for Hispanics to join forces in order to demand a larger share of the pie. In addition to having no common history, these groups were more or less geographically isolated from one another. Mexican Americans lived in the Southwest, Puerto Ricans in the Northeast, mostly in New York, and Cubans in Florida; . . .

The Second World War marked a turning point for Hispanic activism. Hispanics served with great distinction in the war, earning more Congressional Medals of Honor per capita than any other group. Moreover, unlike blacks, Hispanics served in integrated military units, which brought them into contact with other Americans and introduced them, for the first time, to Americans who lived outside the Southwest. More than 100,000 Puerto Ricans served in the military during the war; later, many of these men and their families decided to migrate from the island in search of greater economic opportunity in the United States. Hispanics returned from the war expecting better treatment than was the standard fare for Mexican Americans and Puerto Ricans in most places. Hispanics wanted to increase their earnings and social standing, live where they wanted, and send their children to better schools. Indeed, there was significant upward mobility for Mexican Americans in the period, especially in California and other areas outside Texas, and for the Puerto Ricans who migrated to New York City. . . .

"Each decade offered us hope, but our hopes evaporated into smoke. We became the poorest of the poor, the most segregated minority in schools, the lowest paid group in America and the least educated minority in this nation." This view of Hispanics' progress by the president of the National Council of La

Raza, one of the country's leading Hispanic civil rights groups, is the prevalent one among Hispanic leaders and is shared by many outside the Hispanic community as well. By and large, Hispanics are perceived to be a disadvantaged minority—poorly educated, concentrated in barrios, economically impoverished; with little hope of participating in the American Dream. This perception has not changed substantially in twenty-five years. And it is wrong.

Hispanics have been called the invisible minority, and indeed they were for many years, largely because most Hispanics lived in the Southwest and the Northeast, away from the most blatant discrimination of the Deep South. But the most invisible Hispanics today are those who have been absorbed into the mainstream. The success of middle-class Hispanics is an untold—and misunderstood—story perhaps least appreciated by Hispanic advocates whose interest is in promoting the view that Latinos cannot make it in this society. The Hispanic poor, who constitute only about one-fourth of the Hispanic population, are visible to all. These are the Hispanics most likely to be studied, analyzed, and reported on and certainly the ones most likely to be read about. A recent computer search of stories about Hispanics in major newspapers and magazines over a twelve-month period turned up more than eighteen hundred stories in which the word *Hispanic* or *Latino* occurred within a hundred words of the word *poverty*. In most people's minds, the expression *poor Hispanic* is almost redundant.

Has Hispanics' Progress Stalled?

Most Hispanics, rather than being poor, lead solidly lower-middle- or middle-class lives, but finding evidence to support this thesis is sometimes difficult. Of course, Hispanic groups vary one from another, as do individuals within any group. Most analysts acknowledge, for example, that Cubans are highly successful. Within one generation, they have virtually closed the earnings and education gap with other Americans. (For a broad range of social and economic indicators for each of the major Hispanic groups, see table 1.) Although some analysts claim that the success of Cubans is due exclusively to their high socioeconomic status when they arrived, many Cuban refugees—especially those who came after the first wave in the 1960s—were in fact skilled or semiskilled workers with relatively little education. Their accomplishments in the United States are attributable in large measure to diligence and hard work. They established enclave economies, in the traditional immigrant mode, opening restaurants, stores, and other émigré-oriented services. . . . But Cubans are as a rule dismissed as the exception among Hispanics. What about other Hispanic groups? Why has there been no "progress" among them?

The largest and most important group is the Mexican American population. . . . [I]ts leaders have driven much of the policy agenda affecting all Hispanics, but the importance of Mexican Americans also stems from their having a longer history in the United States than does any other Hispanic group. If Mexican Americans whose families have lived in the United States for generations are not yet making it in this society, they may have a legitimate claim to consider themselves a more or less permanently disadvantaged group, like

Table 1

Characteristics of Hispanic Subgroups and Non-Hispanics

	Mexican-Origin*	Puerto Rican	Cuban	South/Central American	Other Hispanic	Non-Hispanic
Total population (in millions)	13.3	2.2	1.0	2.8	1.4	246.2
Median age	24.1	27.0	39.1	28.0	31.1	33.5
Median years of schooling (1988)	10.8	12.0	12.4	12.4	12.7	12.7
Percentage in labor force						
Male	81.2%	69.2%	74.9%	83.7%	75.3%	74.2%
Female	52.9%	41.4%	57.8%	61.0%	57.0%	57.4%
Percentage of unemployed	9.0%	8.6%	5.8%	6.6%	6.2%	5.3%
Median earnings (1989)						
Male	$12,527	$18,222	$19,336	$15,067	$17,486	$22,081
Female	$8,874	$12,812	$12,880	$10,083	$11,564	$11,885
Percentage of married-couple families	72.5%	57.2%	77.4%	68.7%	69.8%	79.9%
Percentage of female-headed families	19.6%	38.9%	18.9%	25.0%	24.5%	16.0%
Percentage of out-of-wedlock births	28.9%	53.0%	16.1%	37.1%	34.2%	23.9%**
Percentage of families in poverty	25.7%	30.4%	12.5%	16.8%	15.8%	9.2%

*Mexican-origin population includes both native- and foreign-born persons.
**Includes black out-of-wedlock births, 63.1% and white births, 13.9%.

Source: Bureau of the Census, *The Hispanic Population in the United States: March 1990,* Current Population Reports, ser. P-20, no. 449; median years of schooling are from *The Hispanic Population of the United States: March 1988,* Current Population Reports, ser. P-20, no. 438; out-of-wedlock births are from National Center for Health Statistics, *Advance Report of Final Natality Statistics, 1987.*

blacks. That is precisely what Mexican American leaders suggest is happening. Their proof is that statistical measures of Mexican American achievement in education, earnings, poverty rates, and other social and economic indicators have remained largely unchanged for decades. In 1959 the median income of Mexican-origin males in the Southwest was 57 percent that of non-Hispanics. In 1989 it was still 57 percent of non-Hispanic income. If Mexican Americans had made progress, it would show up in improved education attainment and earnings and in lower poverty rates, so the argument goes. Since it doesn't, progress must be stalled.

In the post–civil rights era, the failure of a minority to close the social and economic gap with whites is assumed to be the result of persistent discrimination. Progress is perceived not in absolute but in relative terms. The poor may become less poor over time, but so long as those on the upper rungs of the economic ladder are climbing even faster, the poor are believed to have suffered some harm, even if they have made absolute gains and their lives are much improved. However, in order for Hispanics (or any group on the lower rungs) to close the gap, they must progress at an even greater rate than non-Hispanic whites; their apparent failure to do so in recent years causes Hispanic leaders and the public to conclude that Hispanics are falling behind. Is this a fair way to judge Hispanics' progress? In fact, it makes almost no sense to apply this test today (if it ever did), because the Hispanic population itself is changing so rapidly. This is most true of the Mexican-origin population.

In 1959 the overwhelming majority of persons of Mexican origin living in the United States were native-born, 85 percent. Today only about two-thirds of the people of Mexican origin were born in the United States, and among adults barely one in two was born here. Increasingly, the Hispanic population, including that of Mexican origin, is made up of new immigrants, who, like immigrants of every era, start off at the bottom of the economic ladder. This infusion of new immigrants is bound to distort our image of progress in the Hispanic population, if each time we measure the group we include people who have just arrived and have yet to make their way in this society.

... In 1980 there were about 14.6 million Hispanics living in the United States; in 1990, nearly 21 million, an increase of about 44 percent in one decade. At least one-half of this increase was the result of immigration, legal and illegal.... [T]his influx consists mostly of poorly educated persons, with minimal skills, who cannot speak English. Not surprisingly, when these Hispanics are added to the pool being measured, the achievement levels of the whole group fall. It is almost inconceivable that the addition of two or three million new immigrants to the Hispanic pool would not seriously distort evidence of Hispanics' progress during the decade. Yet no major Hispanic organization will acknowledge the validity of this reasonable assumption. Instead, Hispanic leaders complain, "Hispanics are the population that has benefitted least from the economic recovery." "The Myth of Hispanic Progress" is the title of a study by a Mexican American professor, purporting to show that "it is simply wrong to assume that Hispanics are making gradual progress toward parity with Anglos." "Hispanic poverty is now comparable to that of blacks and is expected to exceed it by the end of this decade," warns another group.

Hispanics wear disadvantage almost like a badge of distinction, as if groups were competing with each other for the title "most disadvantaged." Sadly, the most frequently heard complaint among Hispanic leaders is not that the public ignores evidence of Hispanics' achievement but that it underestimates their disadvantage. "More than any group in American political history, Hispanic Americans have turned to the national statistical system as an instrument for advancing their political and economic interests, by making visible the magnitude of social and economic problems they face," says a Rockefeller Foundation official. But gathering all Hispanics together under one umbrella obscures as much information as it illuminates, and may make Hispanics—especially the native-born—appear to suffer greater social and economic problems than they actually do.

In fact, a careful examination of the voluminous data on the Hispanic population gathered by the Census Bureau and other federal agencies shows that, as a group, Hispanics have made progress in this society and that most of them have moved into the social and economic mainstream. In most respects, Hispanics—particularly those born here—are very much like other Americans; they work hard, support their own families without outside assistance, have more education and higher earnings than their parents, and own their own home. In short, they are pursuing the American Dream—with increasing success.

Work

Hispanic men are more likely to be members of the labor force—that is, working or looking for work—than non-Hispanic whites. Among all Mexican-origin men sixteen years old or older in 1990, for example, participation in the labor force was substantially higher than it was for non-Hispanic males overall—81 percent compared with 74 percent. This fact bodes well for the future and is in marked contrast to the experience of black men, whose labor force participation has been steadily declining for more than twenty years. Most analysts believe that low attachment to the labor force and its correlate, high dependence on welfare, are prime components of underclass behavior. As the political scientist Lawrence Mead writes in his book *Beyond Entitlement: The Social Obligations of Citizenship,* for many persons who are in the underclass, "the problem is not that jobs are *unavailable* but that they are frequently *unacceptable,* in pay or condition, given that some income is usually available from families or benefit programs." In other words, persons in the underclass frequently choose not to work rather than to take jobs they deem beneath them.... The willingness of Hispanic men to work, even at low-wage jobs if their skills qualify them for nothing better, suggests that Hispanics are in no immediate danger of forming a large underclass.

... During the 1980s, 3.3 million new Hispanic workers were added to the work force, giving Hispanics a disproportionate share of the new jobs. Hispanics benefited more than any other group in terms of employment growth in the last decade. By the year 2000, they are expected to account for 10 percent of the nation's work force.

Earnings

... Hispanic leaders charge that Hispanics' wages have failed to keep pace with those of non-Hispanics. Statistics on average Hispanic earnings during the decade appear to bear this out, but they should be viewed with caution. The changing composition of the Hispanic population, from a predominantly native-born to an increasingly immigrant one, makes an enormous difference in how we interpret the data on Hispanic earnings. Since nearly half of all Hispanic workers are foreign-born and since many of these have immigrated within the last ten years, we should not be surprised that the average earnings of Hispanics appear low. After all, most Hispanic immigrants are semi-skilled workers who do not speak English, and their wages reflect these deficiencies. When huge numbers of such workers are added to the pool on which we base average-earnings figures, they will lower the mean.…

When earnings of native-born Mexican American men are analyzed separately from those of Mexican immigrants, a very different picture emerges. On the average, the weekly earnings of Mexican American men are about 83 percent those of non-Hispanic white men—a figure that cuts in half the apparent gap between their earnings and those of non-Hispanics. Even this gap can be explained at least in part. Schooling, experience, hours worked, and geographical region of residence are among several factors that can affect earnings. When we compensate for these variables, we find that Mexican American men earn about 93 percent of the weekly earnings of comparable non-Hispanic white men. English-language proficiency also plays an important role in the earnings of Hispanics; some economists assert that those who are proficient in English experience "no important earnings differences from native-born Anglos."…

Education

Contrary to popular opinion, most Mexican American young adults have completed high school, being nearly as likely to do so as other Americans. But the popular press, the federal government, and Hispanic organizations cite statistics that indicate otherwise. They claim that about 60 percent of all Mexican-origin persons do not complete high school. The confusion stems, as it does with earnings data, from lumping native-born Hispanics with immigrants to get statistical averages for the entire group.…

Traditionally, Hispanics, like blacks, were more likely to concentrate in fields such as education and the social sciences, which are less remunerative than the physical sciences, business, engineering, and other technical and professional fields. Recently this trend has been reversed; in 1987 (the last year for which such statistics are available), Hispanics were almost as likely as non-Hispanic whites to receive baccalaureate degrees in the natural sciences and were more likely than they to major in computer sciences and engineering.

Occupational Status

Fewer Hispanic college graduates will mean fewer Hispanics in the professions and in higher-paying occupations, but this does not translate into the doomsday predictions about their achievement that advocacy organizations commonly voice. It does not mean, for example, that there will be a "a permanent Hispanic underclass" of persons "stuck in poverty because of low wages and deprived of upward mobility," as one Hispanic leader suggested in a *New York Times* article. It may mean, however, that Hispanics will be more likely to hold jobs as clerks in stores and banks, as secretaries and other office support personnel, as skilled workers, and as laborers.… Only in the managerial and professional and the service categories are there very large differences along ethnic lines: 11 percent of all Hispanic males are employed in managerial or professional jobs compared with 27 percent of all non-Hispanics; conversely, 16 percent of the Hispanic males compared with only 9 percent of the non-Hispanic males are employed in service jobs. But these figures include large numbers of immigrants in the Hispanic population, who are disproportionately represented in the service industry and among laborers.

An increasing number of Hispanics are self-employed, many in owner-operated businesses. According to the economist Timothy Bates, who has done a comprehensive study of minority small businesses, those owned by Hispanics are more successful than those owned by blacks. Yet Mexican business owners, a majority of whom are immigrants, are less well educated than any other group; one-third have completed less than twelve years of schooling. One reason why Hispanics may be more successful than blacks in operating small businesses, according to Bates, is that they cater to a nonminority clientele, whereas blacks operate businesses in black neighborhoods, catering to black clients. Hispanic-owned businesses are concentrated in the retail field; about one-quarter of both Mexican and non-Mexican Hispanic firms are retail businesses. About 10 percent of the Mexican-owned firms are in construction.

Poverty

Despite generally encouraging economic indicators for Hispanics, poverty rates are quite high; 26 percent of all Hispanics live below the poverty line. Hispanics are more than twice as likely to be living in poverty than are persons in the general population. Two factors, however, distort the poverty data: the inclusion of Puerto Ricans, who make up about 10 percent of Hispanics, one-third of whom live in poverty; and the low earnings of new immigrants. The persistence of poverty among Puerto Ricans is one of the most troubling features of the Hispanic population. . . .

An exhaustive study of the 1980 census by Frank Bean and Marta Tienda, however, suggests that nativity plays an important role in poverty data, as it does in earnings data generally. Bean and Tienda estimate that the poverty rate among U.S.-born Mexican Americans was nearly 20 percent lower than that among Mexican immigrants in 1980. Their analysis of data from the 1970 census, by contrast, shows almost no difference in poverty rates between Mexican Americans and Mexican immigrants, with both groups suffering significantly greater poverty in 1970 than in 1980. This implies that while poverty was declining among immigrants and the native-born alike between 1970 and 1980, the decline was greater for Mexican Americans.

The Public Policy Implications of Such Findings

For most Hispanics, especially those born in the United States, the last few decades have brought greater economic opportunity and social mobility. They are building solid lower-middle- and middle-class lives that include two-parent households, with a male head who works full-time and earns a wage commensurate with his education and training. Their educational level has been steadily rising, their earnings no longer reflect wide disparities with those of non-Hispanics, and their occupational distribution is coming to resemble more closely that of the general population. They are buying homes—42 percent of all Hispanics owned or were purchasing their home in 1989, including 47 percent of all Mexican Americans—and moving away from inner cities. . . .

❦

There is much reason for optimism about the progress of Hispanics in the United States. . . . Mexican Americans, the oldest and largest Hispanic group, are moving steadily into the middle class, with the majority having established solid, working- and middle-class lives. Even Mexican immigrants and those from other Latin American countries, many of whom have very little formal education, appear to be largely self-sufficient. The vast majority of such immigrants—two-thirds—live above the poverty line, having achieved a standard of living far above that attainable by them in their countries of origin.

There is no indication that any of these groups is in danger of becoming a permanent underclass. If Hispanics choose to (and most *are* choosing to), they will quickly join the mainstream of this society. . . . [T]he evidence suggests that Hispanics, by and large, are behaving much as other ethnic groups did in the past. One group of Hispanics, however, appears not to be following this pattern. Puerto Ricans occupy the lowest rung of the social and economic ladder among Hispanics, and a disturbing number of them show little hope of climbing higher.

. . . Puerto Ricans are not simply the poorest of all Hispanic groups; they experience the highest degree of social dysfunction of any Hispanic group and exceed that of blacks on some indicators. Thirty-nine percent of all Puerto Rican families are headed by single women; 53 percent of all Puerto Rican children are born out of wedlock; the proportion of men in the labor force is lower among Puerto Ricans than any other group, including blacks; Puerto Ricans have the highest welfare participation rate of any group in New York, where nearly half of all Puerto Ricans in the United States live. Yet, on the average, Puerto Ricans are better educated than Mexicans and nearly as well educated as Cubans, with a median education of twelve years. . . .

Some Hopeful Signs

Despite the overall poor performance of Puerto Ricans, there are some bright spots in their achievement—which make their poverty seem all the more stark. While the median family earnings of Puerto Ricans are the lowest of any Hispanic groups, *individual* earnings of both male and female Puerto Ricans are actually higher than those of any other Hispanic subgroup except Cubans. In 1989 Puerto Rican men had median earnings that were 82 percent of those of non-Hispanics; Puerto Rican women's median earnings were actually higher than those of non-Hispanic women. Moreover, the occupational distribution of Puerto Ricans shows that substantial numbers work in white-collar jobs: nearly one-third of the Puerto Rican males who are employed work in managerial, professional, technical, sales, or administrative support jobs and more than two-thirds of the Puerto Rican females who work hold such jobs.

Moreover, Puerto Ricans are not doing uniformly poorly in all parts of the country. Those in Florida, Texas, and California, for example, perform far better than those in New York. . . .

In fact, as their earnings attest, Puerto Ricans who hold jobs are not doing appreciably worse than other Hispanics, or non-Hispanics, once their lower educational attainment is taken into account. The low overall achievement of Puerto Ricans is simply not attributable to the characteristics of those who work but is a factor of the large number of those—male and female—who are neither working nor looking for work. . . .

Where Do Puerto Ricans Go From Here?

Many Puerto Ricans are making it in the United States. There is a thriving middle class of well-educated professionals, managers, and white-collar workers, whose individual earnings are among the highest of all Hispanic groups' and most of whom live in married-couple families. These Puerto Ricans have done what other Hispanics and, indeed, most members of other ethnic groups have: they have moved up the economic ladder and into the social mainstream within one or two generations of their arrival in the United States. . . .

The crisis facing the Puerto Rican community is not simply one of poverty and neglect. If anything, Puerto Ricans have been showered with too much government attention. . . . The fact that Puerto Ricans outside New York succeed proves there is nothing inevitable about Puerto Rican failure. Nor does the existence of prejudice and discrimination explain why so many Puerto Ricans fail when so many other Hispanics, including those from racially mixed backgrounds, are succeeding.

So long as significant numbers of young Puerto Rican men remain alienated from the work force, living by means of crime or charity, fathering children toward whom they feel no responsibility, the prospects of Puerto Ricans in the United States will dim. So long as so many Puerto Rican women allow the men who father their babies to avoid the duties of marriage and parenthood, they will deny their children the promise of a better life, which has been the patrimony of generations of poor immigrants' children. The solution to these problems will not be found in more government programs. Indeed, government has been an accomplice in enabling fathers to abandon their responsibility. Only the Puerto Rican community can save itself, but the healing cannot begin until the community recognizes that many of its deadliest wounds are self-inflicted.

. . . Hispanics have not always had an easy time of it in the United States. Even though discrimination against Mexican Americans and Puerto Ricans was not as severe as it was against blacks, acceptance has come only with struggle, and some prejudices still exist. Discrimination against Hispanics, or any other group, should be fought, and there are laws and a massive administrative apparatus to do so. But the way to eliminate such discrimination is not to classify all Hispanics as victims and treat them as if they could not succeed by their own efforts. Hispanics can and will prosper in the United States by following the example of the millions before them.

NO

Robert Aponte

Urban Hispanic Poverty: Disaggregations and Explanations

Nearly a quarter century since the passage of the Civil Rights Act and the initiation of the massive War on Poverty effort, substantial proportions of inner city minorities appear more hopelessly mired in poverty than at any time since these efforts were undertaken (Tienda 1989, Wacquant and Wilson 1989b, Wilson 1987). The poverty rate among central city blacks, for example, stood at about one person in three in 1989, having risen from a rate of one in four two decades earlier (U.S. Bureau of the Census 1980, 1990). Equally ominous is the poverty rate of central city Latinos (Hispanics), some three in ten, which exceeds that of central city whites by a factor of nearly two and one half (U.S. Bureau of the Census 1990). Associated with these indicators of deprivation among urban minorities have been other signs of potential distress. Available evidence indicates that minorities are experiencing rates of joblessness, welfare receipt, and female headship substantially in excess of the rates prevailing among whites (Tienda 1989, Tienda and Jensen 1988, Wacquant and Wilson 1989b, Wilson and Neckerman 1986).

These important issues have not escaped research attention, but until the 1980s, this research focused almost exclusively on blacks among the minority groups and how they compared to whites (Wilson and Aponte 1985). Indeed, prior to the 1980s, empirical research on the poverty of Hispanics in the United States beyond small scale studies was difficult to perform for lack of data. Hence, as we enter the 1990s, far too little is known about the complex configuration of factors underlying Latino poverty. In addition, while the various reports from the Current Population Survey began producing detailed information on "Hispanics" in the 1970s, often presenting the trends alongside those of blacks and whites, it was not until the mid 1980s that we began to consistently receive detailed, individualized data on the major ethnic groups within the hybrid category of "Hispanic." What little systematic research has been done on the topic has far too often treated the hybrid category as a single group.

Any reliance on the aggregate category "Hispanic" is fraught with a high potential to mislead. For analytic purposes beyond the most superficial generalizations, it is crucial that social and economic trends among Hispanics studied

From Robert Aponte, "Urban Hispanic Poverty: Disaggregations and Explanations," *Social Problems,* vol. 38, no. 4 (November 1991), pp. 516–528. Copyright © 1991 by The Society for the Study of Social Problems. Reprinted by permission of University of California Press/Journals. Notes and references omitted.

be as fully disaggregated as possible if an inquiry is to reveal rather than obscure the dynamics underlying the statistical indicators.* The major current streams of research on minority poverty have produced precious few paradigms with relevance to the Latino population, in part because of the lack of research directed toward the group as a whole, but also because of the failure to consider the individual national groupings separately. Even those analyses incorporating disaggregated indicators need to be interpreted with careful attention paid to the appropriate historic and contemporary circumstances surrounding the various Hispanic groups' incorporation into the mainland United States society.

In the relatively short period that the detailed data have been available, much of significance has been revealed that is consistent with the perspective advanced here. It has been shown, for example, that poverty among Puerto Ricans, the most urban and second largest Latino group, has hovered at a rate averaging over 40 percent in the last several years—a rate second to none among the major ethnic or racial groups for which there is data, and one substantially higher than that of the other Hispanic groups (cf. U.S. Bureau of the Census 1985a, 1986, 1987b, 1988, 1989b). In addition, the rate of poverty for all Hispanics has grown far more rapidly in recent years than that of whites or blacks, as dramatically shown in an important recent report by the Center on Budget and Policy Priorities (Greenstein et al. 1988).

The report notes that the 1987 Hispanic poverty rate of slightly greater than 28 percent is less than 5 percentage points lower than that of blacks, traditionally the poorest group, and nearly three times that of whites, despite the fact that the labor force participation rate of Hispanics is somewhat higher than that of these other groups. Moreover, the increase in Hispanic poverty over the 1980s shown in the Policy Center Report has been fueled largely by increases in poverty among two parent families. Thus, it cannot be blamed on the relatively modest rise in Hispanic single parent families over this particular period, nor can it easily be pinned on sagging work efforts, given the higher than average participation in the workforce of the group.

Importantly, the patterns outlined above appear to defy common sense interpretations. For example, the idea that discrimination can account for the patterning of such indicators falls short of explaining why Puerto Ricans are poorer than blacks even though they almost certainly experience far less discrimination (Massey and Bitterman 1985). Likewise, a human capital perspective by itself cannot explain why Mexicans, who speak poorer English than Puerto Ricans and are less educated than whites and blacks as well as Puerto Ricans, are more often employed than persons of the other three groups (U.S. Bureau of Labor Statistics 1990)....

Disaggregations and Context

To speak of Hispanic poverty in urban America at present is to speak of the two largest groups, those of Mexican and those of Puerto Rican extraction,

---

* [Disaggregation is the process of breaking data down into smaller, more meaningful parts to better understand the information.—Ed.]

who together account for roughly three-fourths of all U.S. Hispanics. Together these two groups accounted for over 80 percent of all 1987 Hispanic poor within metropolitan areas, their central cities taken separately, or the continental United States as a whole (U.S. Bureau of the Census 1989a). Cubans, the next largest group, have accounted for only about five to six percent of all Hispanics during the 1980s and have significantly lower rates of poverty (U.S. Bureau of the Census 1987a, 1989b; see also U.S. Bureau of the Census 1989b). Hence, this article focuses on Latinos of Mexican or Puerto Rican extraction.

While the diverse groups that comprise the remainder of the Latino population have not yet been numerous enough to have a great impact on the indicators for all Hispanics, it does not follow that their experiences have been trouble free. As noted by the Policy Center Report (Greenstein et al. 1988), available data suggests that many of these other groups are experiencing substantial poverty....

Contrasting sharply with the Cuban experience, the processes whereby Mexicans and Puerto Ricans entered the mainstream urban economy entailed a number of common features. Characteristics shared by these incoming groups include mother tongue, economic or labor migrant status, relatively low levels of skill, inadequate command of English, and little formal education. In addition to their relatively modest social status upon entry, these groups generally received no special government assistance, and each sustained a fair amount of discrimination.

Though the urban settlement of Puerto Ricans on the mainland occurred rapidly, was highly concentrated in a major northern city, and began largely after the Second World War, among Mexicans the process transpired throughout much of the 20th century, was far more gradual and diffuse, and was contained largely within the southwest section of the country. Indeed, in only a few midwestern cities—notably Chicago—where small proportions of each group have settled, do Mexicans and Puerto Ricans maintain any substantial co-residence. In addition, the Puerto Ricans entered as citizens and were thereby entitled to certain rights that were available to only some Mexicans.

From less than 100,000 at the end of the Second World War, the Puerto Rican population on the mainland grew to well over 1 million by 1970, at which time a solid majority were residents of New York City (Moore and Pachon 1985). Although by 1980 the city no longer contained a majority of the nearly two million members of the group, most of those living elsewhere still resided in large metropolitan cities, and mainly in the Northeast....

While rapid immigration by Puerto Ricans is no longer evident, Mexican immigration into both urban and rural areas has continued in recent years. The estimated population of nearly 12 million Mexican-origin Hispanics in 1988 accounted for nearly 63 percent of all mainland Latinos and was about five times the size of the estimated 2.3 million Puerto Ricans (U.S. Bureau of the Census 1989b). If present trends continue, the gap in population size separating these groups will further widen.

These settlement differences may affect social mobility in several ways. First, the economic well-being of Puerto Ricans can be expected to hinge heavily on economic conditions *inside* the major cities of the eastern end of the snowbelt, especially New York, and be particularly dependent on the opportunity structure confronting the less skilled in those areas. Such conditions have not been favorable in recent decades due to the widely documented decline in manufacturing, trade, and other forms of low skilled employment that was most evident in northern *inner cities* beginning with the 1950s and accelerating during the 1970s (Kasarda 1985, Wacquant and Wilson 1989b). Moreover, such jobs have not returned to these places, even where sagging economies have sharply rebounded (as in New York and Boston), since the newer mix of jobs in such areas still tend to require more skills or credentials than previously (Kasarda 1983, 1988).

By contrast, Mexican Hispanics are more dependent upon the opportunity structures confronting less skilled labor in southwestern cities and their suburbs but without heavy reliance on only one or two such areas or on *central city* employment. These areas are believed to have better job prospects for the less skilled than northern cities because of the continued employment growth in low skilled jobs throughout the entire postwar period (Kasarda 1985, Wacquant and Wilson 1989b).

A second important distinction concerns social welfare provisions. Specifically, Puerto Ricans have settled into the *relatively* more generous states of the North, while their counterparts populate a band of states with traditionally low levels of assistance. A notable exception to this is California—the state with the largest number of Mexican Hispanics. However, many among the group in that state are ineligible for assistance due to lack of citizenship. At the same time, many eligible recipients likely co-reside with undocumented immigrants subject to deportation if caught. No doubt many of the impoverished among both such groups will not apply for assistance for fear of triggering discovery of the undocumented in their families or households.

As of 1987, *no state* in the continental U.S. provided enough AFDC [Aid to Families with Dependent Children] benefits to bring families up to the poverty line.... Recent research by Jencks and Edin (1990) demonstrates conclusively that very few AFDC families can survive in major cities on just the legally prescribed income; most are forced to cheat, many turn to petty crimes for supplementary income, and some even slip into homelessness (cf. Ellison 1990, Rossi and Wright 1989).

However, this was not always so (Tobier 1984, National Social Science and Law Center 1987). For example, in New York city during the late 1960s, the maximum AFDC benefit package for a family of three, discounting food stamps, could raise the family's income to *97 percent* of the poverty line (Tobier 1984). The payment levels declined gradually during the first part of the 1970s....

The statistical indicators on these groups are consistent with such expectations. For example, among men aged 20 years and over, Puerto Ricans had a labor force participation rate 10 percentage points lower than that of Mexican origin men in 1987 (U.S. Bureau of Labor Statistics 1988), representing a widening of the respective 1977 gap of only five percentage points. The employment-to-population ratios exhibited a similar gap, but they remained unchanged over the ten year period, with the Puerto Rican ratio trailing that of the Mexican origin group by 10 percentage points (Newman 1978), suggesting that the Mexican unemployment rate is catching up to the Puerto Rican rate (Greenstein et al. 1988). Although these are national level trends, they should reflect urban conditions since both groups have become highly urbanized. As expected, Puerto Ricans are also poorer than Mexicans. The central city poverty rate for Puerto Ricans in 1987 was 46 percent, with the corresponding rate for Mexicans 30 percent. The metropolitan area rates were similarly distributed. Likewise, the proportion of families headed by women among central city Puerto Ricans was 49 percent, while only about 21 percent of the Mexican origin families were so headed (U.S. Bureau of the Census 1989a).

Finally, the Current Population Survey reveals that employed Puerto Ricans, on average, earn more than employed Mexicans (U.S. Bureau of the Census 1989b). The survey also reveals that many more Mexican families in poverty have members in the work force than do poor Puerto Rican families, while a substantially higher proportion of the latter group receive government assistance. For example, in 1987, 72 percent of all Mexican origin families in poverty had at least one member in the work force compared to only 24 percent of the Puerto Rican families. Conversely, 72 percent of Puerto Rican families in poverty that year received all of their income from some form of assistance or transfer compared to 25 percent of the Mexican families (U.S. Bureau of the Census 1989a). In spite of the "assistance," not one of these needy families was brought over the poverty line, and many were left with incomes well below the designated level!

It seems likely that the kind of approach urged here, one that maximizes sensitivity to the varying conditions of the individual Latino groups' plights, can help in interpreting trends among data that are largely aggregated. For example, the Policy Center Report reached a number of findings that can be pushed further. The report concluded that recent increases in Hispanic poverty are associated only weakly, if at all, with recent increases in female headship or joblessness within the group. Rather, the poverty increases were strongly associated with declining real wages. The report also noted that the increase in poverty occurred mainly among Mexicans and in the Sunbelt and Midwest. However, the report did *not* make a connection between these factors.

Attending to Latino subgroup differences provides an explanation. We would expect declining real wages to bring more Mexicans into poverty than Puerto Ricans because proportionately more Mexicans hold very low wage jobs. In turn, Mexican dominance in the three regions outside of the Northeast helps explain why those regions, but *not* the Northeast, were more affected by the rise in poverty traceable to real wage declines, even as the Puerto Rican dominated northeastern region maintained the highest level of poverty.

Finally, consideration of the continuation of Mexican immigration leads to a second hypothesis about their vulnerability to falling real wages: Mexicans are employed in regions plagued by labor market crowding resulting from continued immigration, especially since much of it consists of "undocumenteds," a group that clearly constitutes cheaper labor. This especially hurts those with lower levels of education, since they are most likely to compete directly with the latest newcomers. Indeed, the Report singles out the lesser educated Hispanics as the group sustaining the most increased hardship. . . .

Explanations of Urban Poverty

Most current popular theories about urban poverty fall short of fully accounting for the plight of the Hispanic poor because of a narrow focus on blacks. In spite of the apparent deficit, disaggregating the Hispanic figures allows us to apply some of this work to at least one of the two major groups under study.

The culture of poverty. The idea of a "culture of poverty" generally traces back to the work of Oscar Lewis (1959, 1966) who coined the phrase, although others have advanced similar notions. Lewis developed the core ideas of the argument while studying Mexican and Puerto Rican families. The work suggests that culturally-based attitudes or predispositions such as "present mindedness" and "obsessive consumption" are the major barriers to economic mobility for many of the poor, implying that providing opportunities to the poor will not be enough: some will need "cultural uplifting" as well. The major strength of the idea for my purposes is that it can apply equally well to the poor of any of the Latino groups.

However, the theory is largely discredited within academic circles.... In fact, numerous subsequent studies of poor people's values and attitudes have found little support for the theory (Corcoran et al. 1985, Goodwin 1972, Irelan et al. 1969)....

The welfare-as-cause argument. In his book *Losing Ground,* Charles Murray (1984) argues that the liberalization of welfare during the late 1960s and early 1970s made work less beneficial than welfare and encouraged low-income people to avoid work and marriage, in order to reap the benefits of welfare, and that this is a primary source of the rise in female headship and, indirectly, poverty itself....

We might ask if welfare payments were so lucrative, why did the poor fail to escape poverty, at least while "on the dole," but Murray does not address this issue.... Moreover, studies on the effects of welfare availability to changes in family structure have produced few results supporting a connection, the overall consensus being that such effects as they exist are relatively weak (Wilson and Neckerman 1986. U.S. General Accounting Office 1987).... Thus, welfare appears unlikely to be a major cause of female headship or joblessness among Hispanics, as among blacks. However, it may properly be seen as a major cause of Latino poverty insofar as so many of the Hispanic impoverished who are legally entitled to assistance are left destitute by miserly benefit levels while many other equally needy Hispanics are denied benefits altogether.

The mismatch thesis. This explanation... focuses mainly on older, northern, industrial towns. It finds recent urban poverty rooted in the movement of manufacturing and other blue-collar employment away from snowbelt central cities where blacks and Hispanics make up increasingly larger proportions of the population. As blue-collar industry moved from the cities to the suburbs and from the Snow Belt to the Sun Belt, central city job growth occurred primarily in white-collar jobs for which the black and Hispanic central city residents often did not qualify for lack of skills or credentials.

... While studies based on data for 1970 or earlier have tended to disconfirm the hypothesis, work on more recent periods has largely produced supporting results (Holzer 1991). Hence, the argument remains a viable hypothesis about joblessness in northern central cities. Once again, however, the idea offers no explanation for the poverty of Mexicans since relatively few live in those areas....

Labor market segmentation theories (dual labor market theory). According to early versions of labor market segmentation theories, racial and ethnic minorities were intentionally relegated to the "secondary" sector of the labor market characterized by highly unstable work with low pay and little room for advancement (Cain 1976). More recent versions often suggest that disadvantaged native workers all but openly shun such jobs because of their undesirable characteristics and that immigrants are therefore "imported" to fill the positions (Piore 1979)....

Though clearly of important explanatory potential, the segmentation theory falls short of providing a complete explanation for the patterns in question.... Thus, the argument would appear to operate better in cities such as New York which have received large numbers of immigrants in recent years than in places such as Buffalo, Cleveland, Philadelphia, or Rochester with proportionately fewer such persons. (Waldinger 1989). Yet, Puerto Ricans in these cities appear as plagued by poverty and joblessness as those in New York (U.S. Bureau of the Census 1985b)....

The underclass hypothesis. The underclass argument, proposed by William Julius Wilson (1987, 1988), begins with the observation that declining housing discrimination and rising incomes among some blacks have enabled many to leave the older central city ghettos. Their departure from the highly segregated and traditionally underserviced areas, characterized by higher than average rates of physical deterioration, exacerbates the purely economic problems confronted by the remaining population....

Ghetto residents subjected to the described conditions constitute Wilson's underclass. The combined material and environmental deprivation confronted by the group anchors them firmly to prolonged poverty, welfare dependence, and assorted illicit enterprises.... Once again, among Hispanics, only the Puerto Rican poor are as geographically isolated as poor blacks and, therefore, appear to be the only Hispanic population for which this explanation can hold.

Conclusion

... The data and discussions presented here, while far from providing a definitive analysis of Hispanic poverty, provide support to a number of generalizations about the problems and potential solutions. Decreased employment opportunities for the less skilled and educated, severely depressed wages among the employed, and restricted or nonexistent welfare benefits comprise the major causes of urban Hispanic poverty. Expanding employment, increasing wages, providing a better living to those unable to work, and promoting higher levels of human capital attainment are major public policy imperatives if these problems are ever to be adequately addressed.

POSTSCRIPT

Are Hispanics Making Significant Progress?

In 2001, 35.3 million people out of a total U.S. population of 281 million were Hispanic, almost tying Hispanics with Blacks as the largest minority group, according to demographers. As Aponte shows, a major problem in understanding Hispanic poverty, which for some is so intense that they are considered an underclass, is the large variations in income, education, and status among groups of Spanish-speaking Americans.

As Chavez shows, many Hispanics have paralleled other ethnic and racial minority success stories of making it in the United States. Yet her data ignore significant pockets of poverty.

Are Hispanics making significant progress? Or is it an illusion, already crumbling in the face of America's recent economic downturns? Do all racial minorities require the same government programs? For instance, how should the $185 billion in available federal funds be distributed among minorities?

Neither Chavez nor Aponte address in detail the issue of continuing resistance toward Hispanics. See, for example, "Hispanic Diaspora," by B. Yeoman, *Mother Jones* (July/August 2000) and Samuel P. Huntington's *Clash of Civilizations and the Remaking of World Order* (W. W. Norton, 1996), in which the author attacks Hispanics as "immigrants" as opposed to earlier "settlers," who helped to build U.S. culture rather than threaten it. Many critics have bitterly attacked Huntington's thesis. See, for example, "Cultural Pressures Undoing Our Unity," by P. Roberts, *The Washington Times* (February 26, 2001). Other works document both the contributions of and the problems faced by Hispanics. See *Magical Urbanism: Latinos Reinvent the U.S. City* by Mike Davis (Verso, 2000) and Lawrence Bobo et al., eds., *Prismatic Metropolis: Inequality in Los Angeles* (Russell Sage Foundation, 2000).

For two different kinds of empirical analyses of the issue of Hispanic progress in the United States, see *Puerto Ricans in the United States* by María Pérez y González (Greenwood Press, 2000) and *Encyclopedia of the Mexican American Civil Rights Movement* by Matt S. Meier and Margo Gutiérrez (Greenwood Press, 2000). A more general study of the measurement of economic progress is *The International Glossary on Poverty* edited by David Gordon and Paul Spicker (Zed Books, 1999). An additional salient issue is discussed in "The Continual Significance of Skin Color: An Exploratory Study of Latinos in the Northeast," by C. Gomez, *Hispanic Journal of Behavioral Studies* (February 2000).

ISSUE 7

Do Cultural Differences Between Home and School Explain the High Dropout Rates for American Indian Students?

YES: Jon Reyhner, from "American Indians Out of School: A Review of School-Based Causes and Solutions," *Journal of American Indian Education* (May 1992)

NO: Susan Ledlow, from "Is Cultural Discontinuity an Adequate Explanation for Dropping Out?" *Journal of American Indian Education* (May 1992)

ISSUE SUMMARY

YES: Professor of curriculum and instruction Jon Reyhner argues that the school dropout rate for Native Americans is 35 percent, almost double that of other groups. He blames this on schools, teachers, and curricula that ignore the needs and potentials of American Indian students.

NO: Educator Susan Ledlow argues that data on dropout rates for American Indians, especially at the national level, is sparse. She questions the meaning and measurement of "cultural discontinuity," and she faults this perspective for ignoring important structural factors, such as employment, in accounting for why Native American students drop out of school.

One of the things that is striking about the following arguments of Jon Reyhner and Susan Ledlow is the immense difference in what might be called the skeptical factor. Reyhner without doubt or hesitation embraces and cites the highest available statistic on American Indian school dropout rates: 35 percent. Ledlow, by contrast, begins by stating that reliable statistics simply do not exist.

Reyhner is highly skeptical of most schools and teachers. He doubts if many really have Native American students' interests at heart. He blames the problem on the discontinuity between the backgrounds of the students and those of their white teachers. He does not believe that non-Indians, especially those whose training has been primarily or exclusively in subject content and not in Indian ways, can effectively teach Native Americans.

Formal education for Native American children has long been problematic and controversial, in part because much of it has been directed by the federal government as part of the management of reservation life. There have been many efforts in the past to replace Native American children's heritage with the skills and attitudes of the larger, white society, and the earliest formal schooling efforts placed great emphasis on Anglo conformity. Reyhner takes a detailed look at the schools today and the ways in which they are run, and he argues that the discontinuity between the life experiences of Native American schoolchildren and the schools and the curricula they teach explains the high dropout rates.

While she admits that some schools and some teachers may be inadequate in teaching Native American children, Ledlow seriously doubts if the cultural discontinuity theory is sound. She contends that we must look elsewhere for a more plausible and empirically correct explanation of high dropout rates. She even questions if the rates are indeed as high as the accepted wisdom says they are. She asks, Are those high rates derived from misinformation or misinterpretation of the data and then repeated by the mass media and Native American lobbying groups? She suggests that, in some cases, the rates may be greatly inflated and/or statistical anomalies. As you consider this debate, compare other instances in which data have been misused to support political agendas. Examples might be the assertions that domestic abuse increases significantly on Super Bowl Sunday, that gay teenagers are more likely to commit suicide, and that there is a new law that will disenfranchise Black citizens, ending their right to vote.

Ledlow is also concerned with the assumption of Reyhner and others that a "culturally relevant" curriculum is superior to alternative ones. What is such a curriculum to begin with, she wonders? Even more important, where is the research that demonstrates that it is superior?

After providing a critique of cultural discontinuity theorists, Ledlow advances an alternative theory. Her explanation is largely derived from the neglected (at least within sociology circles) Marxist anthropologist John U. Ogbu. Hers is basically a structural explanation. She emphasizes the importance of political and economic structures, especially the latter, in accounting for Native American dropout rates.

As you read these two selections, think back to when you were in high school. Were your "best" teachers necessarily warm and supportive? Were good teachers ever from radically different backgrounds than your own? Was your education geared to any specific minority group's needs? Would it have been more effective if it had been?

Extrapolate from Ogbu's typology as presented by Ledlow. Which minorities that you have studied so far or that you are otherwise familiar with would fit into which part of his classification? Does it appear to be a sound one?

Jon Reyhner  **YES**

American Indians Out of School:
A Review of School-Based Causes
and Solutions

During the summer of 1991, I taught a dropout prevention seminar at Eastern Montana College. In initial class discussions, the students, mostly members of Montana Indian tribes, blamed dysfunctional families and alcohol abuse for the high dropout rate among Indian students. If this allegation is correct, and Indian families and the abuse of alcohol are to be held responsible, then the implication exists that teachers and schools are satisfactory and not in need of change. However, the testimony given at the Indian Nations at Risk (INAR) Task Force hearings, held throughout the United States in 1990 and 1991, and other research reviewed, indicate that, both on and off the reservation, schools and teachers are to be held accountable as well. Academically capable American Indian students often drop out of school because their needs are not being met. Others are pushed out because they protest, in a variety of ways, how they are being treated. This article examines various explanations for the high dropout rate which oppose the dysfunctional Indian family and alcohol abuse resolution so popularly accepted.

American schools are not providing an appropriate education for Indian students who are put in large, factory-like schools. Indian students are denied teachers with special training in Indian education, denied a curriculum that includes their heritage, and denied culturally appropriate assessment. Their parents are also denied a voice in the education of their children....

Extent and Background of the Problem

The National Center for Education Statistics (1989) reported that American Indian and Alaska Native students have a dropout rate of 35.5%, about twice the national average and the highest dropout rate of any United States ethnic or racial group [cited].... Regional and local studies gave similar rates (see for example Deyhle, 1989; Eberhard, 1989; Platero, Brandt, Witherspoon, & Wong, 1986; Ward & Wilson, 1989). This overall Indian dropout rate (35%) is not much higher than the 27.1% of Indians between the ages of 16 and 19 living on reservations who were found by the 1980 Census to be neither enrolled in school nor high school graduates. However, the Census figures also showed wide variation among reservations as to how many Indian teenagers between 16 and 19 were not in school. One New Mexico Pueblo had only 5.2% of those teenagers not getting a high school education whereas several small Nevada, Arizona, Washington, and California sites had no students completing a high school education (Bureau, 1985).

A recent compelling explanation as to why Indian students do poorly in school in the United States involves the cultural differences between Indian cultures and the dominant Euro-American culture [see Jacob and Jordan (1987) for an interesting discussion of explanations for the school performance of minority students]. As Estelle Fuchs and Robert J. Havighurst reported from the National Study of American Indian Education in the late 1960s, "many Indian children live in homes and communities where the cultural expectations are different and discontinuous from the expectations held by school teachers and school authorities" (1972, p. 299). In the INAR Task Force hearings several educators and community members testified on the need for Indian teachers and Indian curriculum to reduce the cultural conflict between home and school (Indian Nations at Risk Task Force, 1991).

Positive identity formation, as the psychiatrist Erik Erikson (1963) pointed out, is an ongoing, cumulative process that starts in the home with a trusting relationship established between mother and child and develops through the child's interaction with other children and adults. To build a strong positive identity, educators that the child interacts with in school need to reinforce and build on the cultural training and messages that the child has previously received. If educators give Indian children messages that conflict with what Indian parents and communities show and tell their children, the conflicting messages can confuse the children and create resistance to school (Bowers & Flinders, 1990; Jacob & Jordan, 1987; Spindler, 1987). In the words of John Goodlad, ethnic minority children are "caught and often savaged between the language and expectations of the school and those of the home" (1990, pp. 6–7).

Too often, well-meaning remedial programs focus on finding the reason for failure in students and their homes thus, "blaming the victims." The idea that Indian students are "culturally disadvantaged" or "culturally deprived" reflects ethnocentrism rather than the results of educational research. When schools do not recognize, value, and build on what Indian students learn at home, the students are given a watered-down curriculum (meant to guarantee student learning) which often results in a tedious education, and their being "bored out" of school. . . .

Students do not have to assimilate into the dominant Euro-American culture to succeed in school. Two studies (Deyhle, 1989; Platero et al., 1986) of Indian dropouts found that a traditional Indian orientation is not a handicap in regard to school success. The Navajo Students at Risk study reported that "the most successful students were for the most part fluent Navajo/English bilinguals" (Platero, 1986, p. 6). Lin (1990) found that Indian college students with traditional orientations outperformed students with modern orientations.

Tradition oriented students are able to learn in school, in spite of negative characteristics of the schools, because of the strong sense of personal and group identity their native cultures give them.

Why Students Leave School

Research indicates a number of factors associated with higher student dropout rates. Particularly critical factors for Indian students include large schools, uncaring and untrained teachers, passive teaching methods, inappropriate curriculum, inappropriate testing/student retention, tracked classes, and lack of parent involvement....

1. Large Schools

The increasing size of American schools, especially the large comprehensive high schools with more than one thousand students, creates conditions conducive to dropping out. Goodlad (1984) criticized large schools for creating factory-like environments that prevent educators from forming personal relationships with students. He recommended that high schools maintain no more than 600 students....

Smaller schools can allow a greater percentage of students to participate in extra-curricular activities. Students participating in these activities, especially sports when excessive travel is not required, drop out less frequently (Platero, et al., 1986). However, many reservation schools do not have drama clubs, debate teams, and other non-sport extra-curricular activities which would help develop Indian student leadership and language skills.

The Navajo Students at Risk study (Platero, et al., 1986) reported that students who travel long distances to get to school are more likely to drop out. Large consolidated high schools in rural areas, in contrast to smaller more dispersed high schools, increase the distance some students must travel, and thus increase their risk of dropping out. Students who miss the school bus often cannot find alternative transportation, and many high schools today maintain strict attendance policies causing students who miss 10 days of school or more to lose their credit for the semester.

2. Uncaring and Untrained Teachers and Counselors

In an ethnographic study of Navajo and Ute dropouts that included both interviews with students and classroom observations, Deyhle (1989) reported that students "complained bitterly that their teachers did not care about them or help them in school" (1989, p. 39). Students who "experienced minimal individual attention or personal contact with their teachers" interpreted this neglect as "teacher dislike and rejection" (p. 39).

In comparison to other racial or ethnic groups, few Indian students report that "discipline is fair," that "the teaching is good," that "teachers are interested in students," and that "teachers really listen to me" (National, 1990, p. 43)....

It can be argued that in an attempt to improve the quality of teaching in the United States, changes have been made in teacher preparation programs and certification standards that aggravate rather than solve the problem of recruiting well-qualified caring teachers for Indian children. Increased certification standards are preventing Indian students from entering the teaching profession because [of] the National Teachers Examination (NTE) and similar tests that neither measure teacher commitment to educating Indian children nor their knowledge of Indian cultures, languages, and teaching practices.

Indian students can successfully complete four or more years of college and receive a Bachelors Degree in education at an accredited college or university and be denied a license to teach Indian students on the basis of one timed standardized examination, usually the NTE, that does not reflect Indian education at all. At the same time, a non-Native who has never seen an Indian student, never studied native history, language, or culture, and whose three credit class in multicultural education emphasized Blacks and Hispanics, can legally teach the Indian students that the Indian graduate cannot.

The Winter 1989 issue of the *Fair Test Examiner* reported how teacher competency tests barred nearly 38,000 Black, Latino, Indian, and other minority teacher candidates from the classroom. In addition, teacher preparation and certification programs are culturally and linguistically "one size fits all," and the size that is measured is a middle-class, Western-European cultural orientation. Recent research (see for example, Reyhner, 1992) identifies a wide body of knowledge about bilingual education, Indian learning styles, and English-as-a-Second-Language (ESL) teaching techniques that teachers of Indian students need to know. In addition, teachers of Indian students should have an Indian cultural literacy specific to the tribal background of their students. But teachers often get just one generic multicultural course in accredited teacher education programs.

This lack of job-specific training is a factor in the high turnover rates among teachers of Indian children. Bureau of Indian Affairs (BIA) professional staff have a 50% turnover rate every two years (Office, 1988). When teaching, those instructors who are not trained to educate Indian children, as most teachers are not with our present teacher training system, tend to experience failure from the beginning. As these teachers often become discouraged and find other jobs, the students are left to suffer from continued educational malpractice.

Proper training and screening of teachers could solve this problem, especially the training of Indian teachers. However, today's commonly used screening devices of test scores and grade point averages do not measure teacher personality. The Kenney Report (Special, 1969) found that one-fourth of the elementary and secondary teachers of Indian children admitted not wanting to teach them.

These teachers also need to use interactive teaching strategies... to develop positive relationships with their students, because related to the high turnover is the fact that Indian students think worse of their teachers than any other group (Office, 1988). Studies (Coburn & Nelson, 1989; Deyhle, 1989; Kleinfeld, 1979; Platero et al., 1986) clearly show the Indian student's need for warm, supportive teachers....

3. Passive Teaching Methods

Too often educators of Indian students use passive teaching methods to instruct Indian children. Cummins (1989) argued that most teachers in the United States use a passive "transmission" method of instruction in which knowledge is given to students in the form of facts and concepts. These teachers, according to Bowers and Flinders (1990), view language simplistically as a conduit for the transmitting of information rather than as a metaphorical medium through which the teacher and students mutually build meaning through shared experiences and understandings. They expect students to sit passively, to listen to lectures, or to read and memorize the information they receive so that they can answer worksheet, chapter, or test questions (Deyhle, 1989). Students who refuse to sit quietly for long periods of time are considered discipline problems who, over time, are gradually encouraged in a variety of ways to drop out of school.

Although it is popularly assumed that students who drop out are academic failures, the Navajo Students at Risk study (Platero et al., 1986) showed that the academic performance of dropouts is not that different from students who remain in school. Forty-five percent of the Navajo dropouts are B or better students (Platero et al., 1986). Navajo students most frequently give boredom with school, not academic failure or problems with drugs and alcohol, as their reason for dropping out or planning to drop out.

Indian and other minority students are most likely to be the recipients of passive teaching strategies, and they are commonly placed in low track classes.... In a study of Alaskan education (Senate, 1989), seniors included the following reasons for their classmates dropping out of school: not being good at memorizing facts, boredom, larger class sizes, and unsupportive teachers.

4. Inappropriate Curriculum

In addition to inappropriate teaching methods, Indian schools are characterized by an inappropriate curriculum that does not reflect the Indian child's unique cultural background (Coladarci, 1983; Reyhner, 1992). Textbooks are not written for Indian students, and thus they enlarge the cultural gap between home and school. In the INAR Task Force hearings, many Indian educators pointed out the need for teaching materials specially designed for Indian students. Despite vast improvement in the past two decades, there are still reports that "too many textbooks are demeaning to minorities" (Senate, 1989, p. 28)....

Related to the lack of Indian-specific curriculum and multicultural curriculum, which increases the cultural distance between the Indian student and school, is the use of standardized tests to measure how well students learn that inappropriate curriculum. The use of these tests, which do not reflect either Indian subject matter or ways of learning, is discussed below.

5. Inappropriate Testing/Student Retention

The way tests are designed in this country, with an emphasis on standardized testing, a built-in failure is produced (Oakes, 1985; Bloom, 1981). In addition to the built-in sorting function of standardized tests, they have a cultural bias that has yet to be overcome (Rhodes, 1989). Some of the changes made to improve education in American schools recommended in *A Nation at Risk* (National, 1983) and other studies have hurt rather than helped Indian students.

The use of standardized tests to measure school success leads to more Indian students being retained in a grade, and retention leads to over-age students who drop out of high school. The National Education Longitudinal Study of 1988 (NELS:88) reported that 28.8% of Indian students have repeated at least one grade, the highest percentage of any racial or ethnic group reported (National, 1990, p. 9). The research on failing students (retaining them in grade for another year) indicates that it only creates more failure and more dropouts (Weis, et al., 1989). Even retention in kindergarten does not help students who are having academic problems (Shepard & Smith, 1989). With current practices, schools can make themselves look better by pushing out Indian students since they are evaluated on their average test scores. The more "at risk" students educators push out, the higher the schools' average test scores (Bearden, Spencer, & Moracco, 1989).

Without realizing they are comparing bilingual students' test scores with monolingual English student norms, school administrators and teachers use the California Test of Basic Skills (CTBS) and other standardized test scores to show that their present curriculum is not working. It is also common sense that achievement tests given to Indian students be aligned with what they are being taught in their schools. Testimony given at the INAR/NACIE joint issue sessions in San Diego gave instances of the inappropriate use of tests in schools. For example, tests designed for state mandated curricula were used on students who were not taught using those curricula in BIA schools....

The result of this misuse of tests is that educators keep changing the curriculum in a futile attempt to get Native language speaking students in the early grades to have English language test scores that match the test scores of students of the same age who have spoken English all their lives. Research indicates that it takes about five to seven years for non-English speaking students to acquire an academic proficiency in English which will give them a chance to match the English language test scores of students whose native language is English (Collier, 1989; Cummins, 1989).

6. Tracked Classes

Teachers often have low expectations for Indian students and put them in a non-college-bound vocationally-oriented curriculum. This "tracking" of students is a common practice in secondary schools. The study body is divided into high achievers, average achievers, and low achievers, and each group is put in separate classes. Oakes (1985) described the negative effects of tracking in our nation's high schools and how ethnic minority students are disproportionately represented in the lower tracks where they receive a substandard education. She documented how, in tracked classrooms, "lower-class students are expected to assume lower-class jobs and social positions as adults" (p. 117) and that "students, especially lower-class students, often actively resist what schools try to teach them" (p. 120). Data from the NEL:88 show that less than 10% of Indian students are in the upper quartile of achievement test scores in history, mathematics, reading, and science whereas over 40% are in the lowest quartile (National, 1989). The low expectations of teachers for low track students, already unsuccessful in school, make a serious problem worse. . . .

7. Lack of Parent Involvement

The last factor to discuss is parent involvement. Greater Indian parent involvement can reduce the cultural distance between home and school. Often school staff say they want parent involvement, but what they really want is parents to get after their children to attend school and study. . . .

Although getting parents to get their children to school is important, parent involvement also means educating parents about the function of the school and allowing parents real decision making power about what and how their children learn. Cummins (1989) noted that "although lip service is paid to community participation through Parent Advisory Committees (PAC) in many school programs, these committees are frequently manipulated through misinformation and intimidation" (p. 62). He goes on to list a number of studies supporting the need for minority parent involvement in schools.

Promising Remedies

Both educational literature and testimony at INAR hearings recommend solutions to the problems that result in Indian student failure. The following suggestions for improving Indian schools are targeted at the seven factors described above and involve restructuring schools, promoting caring teachers, using active teaching strategies, having culturally-relevant curriculum, testing to help students rather than to fail them, having high expectations of all students, and promoting community involvement. . . .

Time and again in the INAR Task Force hearings Indian parents testified about the need for more Indian teachers who will stand as role models for their children. These instructors would offer students a unique cultural knowledge and would maintain the ability to identify with the problems their students face.

Active Teaching Methods

Obviously, just caring is not enough. Teachers also need to learn culturally appropriate teaching strategies in their teacher training and inservice programs and use these instructional methodologies in their classrooms. . . . Other studies of Indian students show the need for teachers to know more about the home culture of their students. . . .

ぐ◎や

Beyond using active and culturally-appropriate teaching strategies, research (see for example Reyhner, 1992) showed the need for a culturally-appropriate curriculum. Extensive material exists to produce elementary and secondary culturally appropriate curriculum for Indian students, however, there is little incentive for publishers to produce material for the relatively small market that Indian education represents. Books such as Jack Weatherford's (1988) *Indian givers: How the Indians of the Americas transformed the world* indicate the wealth of information that could positively affect Indian students' understanding and self-concept. This information, however, does not seem to be reaching Indian students at the elementary and secondary level....

The best way to get schools to reflect parent and community values and to reduce cultural discontinuity between home and school is to have real parent involvement in Indian education. At many successful Indian schools, the school board, administrators, and teachers are Indian people. The extensive parent involvement at Rock Point Community School in Arizona is one example of how parents can come to feel ownership in their children's school and to translate that feeling into supporting their children's attendance and academic performance. Parent involvement at Rock Point includes quarterly parent-teacher conferences, a yearly general public meeting, and an eight-member elected parent advisory committee that formally observes the school several times a year (Reyhner, 1990). In addition, the Indian school board conducts its meetings in the Navajo language and each classroom has special chairs reserved for parents.

Parents need to have effective input as to how and what their children are taught. This is best achieved through Indian control of schools. However, curriculum restrictions placed by states on public schools, and even the BIA on BIA-funded schools, limit the effectiveness of Indian parent involvement. State and BIA regulations force Indian schools to use curriculum and textbooks not specifically designed for Indian children and to employ teachers who, though certified, have no special training in Indian education.

Conclusions

Supplemental, add-on programs such as Indian Education Act, Johnson-O'Malley (JOM), Bilingual Education, Special Education, and other federal programs have had limited success in improving the education of Indian children. However, add-on programs are only a first step in making schooling appropriate for Indian children....

If educators continue to get inadequate or inappropriate training in colleges of education, then local teacher-training programs need to provide school staff with information on what works in Indian education and information about the language, history, and culture of the Indian students. Tribal colleges are beginning to develop teacher training programs to fill this need. Parents and local school boards also need on-going training about what works in Indian education and what schools can accomplish. Head Start, elementary, and secondary schools need the support of tribal education departments and tribal colleges to design and implement effective educational programs that support rather than ignore Indian cultures.

Much testimony was given in the INAR Task Force hearings on the importance of self-esteem for Indian students. It is sometimes unclear that self-esteem is not an independent variable but is a reflection of how competent an Indian child feels. Having students memorize material to show success on standardized tests, a common element of the transmission model of teaching previously described, is a poor way to develop self-esteem. However, if students interact with caring, supportive adults, if students are allowed to explore and learn about the world they live in, including learning about their rich Indian heritage, if they are allowed to develop problem solving skills, if they are given frequent opportunities to read and write and to do mathematics and science in meaningful situations, and if they are encouraged to help improve the world they live in through community service, it is likely that Indian students will feel good about themselves and will be successful in life....

Teachers of Indian students need to have special training in instructional methodologies that have proven effective with Indian students and in using curriculum materials that reflect American Indian history and cultures. They also need to build on the cultural values that Indian parents give their children if teachers want to produce a strong positive sense of identity in their students.

Attempts to replace Indian identity with a dominant cultural identity can confuse and repel Indian students and force them to make a choice between their Indian values or their school's values. Neither choice is desirable or necessary. Students can be academically successful and learn about the larger non-Native world while at the same time retaining and developing their Indian identity. Indian students need to attend schools that reinforce rather than ignore or depreciate Indian cultural values.

Is Cultural Discontinuity an Adequate Explanation for Dropping Out?

American Indian Dropout Research

On the national level, there is little information about overall rates for American Indian dropouts. Most national level educational research does not differentiate American Indian students as a separate cohort as with Blacks, Whites, or Hispanics....

There are a number of sources in the educational literature which discuss the issue of American Indian dropouts either directly or indirectly. A comprehensive review of the educational literature regarding American Indian dropout rates disclosed, literally, hundreds of reports; evaluation or annual reports; local, state, or national government reports; senate hearings; task force proceedings; or descriptions of dropout intervention programs. Some reports provided actual dropout rates for local areas or states. These reports suffer from the same weaknesses as many national studies: they define and count dropouts variously and, often, inaccurately (see Rumberger 1987 for a discussion of the problems with dropout research). What is most noteworthy is that there is very little research which specifically address the causes of American Indian students dropping out.

In spite of this dearth of knowledge about the causes for so many Indian students' decision to leave school, many of the reports commonly cite the need for making the school curriculum more "culturally relevant" or adding some type of Indian studies component to the regular curriculum in order to solve the problem. Cultural relevance is rarely defined and almost always assumed to be significant. With no evidence to support the claim and no definition of what a culturally relevant curriculum is, many of the school district and special program reports recommend that a culturally relevant curriculum will ameliorate Indian students' difficulties in school. How and why a relevant curriculum will solve the problems is rarely addressed; one assumes that the proponents of such solutions believe them to be based on some body of empirical knowledge, most probably the cultural discontinuity hypothesis, which originated in the ideas of anthropologists such as Dell Hymes (1974).

The Cultural Discontinuity Hypothesis

The cultural discontinuity hypothesis assumes that culturally based differences in the communication styles of the minority students' home and the Anglo culture of the school lead to conflicts, misunderstandings, and, ultimately, failure for those students. The research focuses on the process, rather than the structure of education and concludes that making the classroom more culturally appropriate will mean a higher rate of achievement. Erickson offered three reasons for this. He stated that cultural adaptation may reduce culture shock for students, it may make them feel that the school and teacher hold a positive regard for them, and it simplifies learning tasks, in that students do not have to master a culturally unfamiliar way of behavior at the same time that they are expected to master academic content.

Susan Philips' research on children at the Warm Springs Reservation in Oregon is the premier example of this type of research. She focused on the differences in communication and interaction patterns in the school and in the Warm Springs community. Her argument is that

> the children of the Warm Springs Indian Reservation are enculturated in their preschool years into modes of organizing the transmission of verbal messages that are culturally different from those of Anglo middle-class children. I argue that this difference makes it more difficult for them to then comprehend verbal messages conveyed through the school's Anglo middle-class modes of organizing classroom interaction. (1982, p. 4).

Philips indicated that the hierarchical structure of the classroom, with the teacher as the focus of all communication is fundamentally at odds with the Warm Springs children's understanding of appropriate communication patterns. For example, teachers often assumed that Indian children were not paying attention because they did not look directly at the teacher or provide behavioral feedback that indicated they were listening (p. 101). These behaviors, however, are appropriate in their own community. She also noted that of four possible participant structures—whole class, small group, individual work, and one-to-one with the teacher—Indian students, when allowed to control their own interaction, most actively participated in one-to-one with the teacher and in small group work. Warm Springs students showed little enthusiasm for teacher-directed whole class or small group encounters or for individual desk work, which are the most commonly employed participant structures. The implication of her research is that more Indian teachers, culturally relevant materials, and teaching methods which emphasize appropriate participant structures will allow Indian students to experience greater success and achievement in school.

The Kamehameha Elementary Education Project (KEEP) is another well known example of research supporting the cultural discontinuity hypothesis. KEEP originated in response to the relative lack of success experienced by Native Hawaiian children compared with Japanese, Chinese, and haole (of northern European ancestry) children. The project used research on socialization practices in Hawaiian homes, and how these differed from the patterns of interaction in the school, to develop a "K-3 language arts program that is culturally compatible for Hawaiian children, and that, both in the lab school and public schools, produced significant gains in reading achievement levels for educationally at-risk Hawaiian children" (Vogt, Jordan, and Tharp, 1987, p. 278).

Anticipating that the gains experienced by KEEP children might be interpreted as the result of better teaching methods, rather than culturally specific methods, the Rough Rock Community School on the Navajo reservation in Arizona replicated the KEEP project. Many of the strategies developed for use with Hawaiian children were found to be ineffective or actually counterproductive with Navajo students (Vogt, Jordan, and Tharp, 1987, pp. 282–285). Vogt, Jordan, and Tharp concluded that the KEEP research strongly supports the argument that cultural compatibility between home and school can enhance the likelihood of students' success, and conversely, cultural discontinuity is a valid explanation for school failure (1987, p. 286).

These two research projects are often cited in the field of Indian education and do seem to provide strong evidence that cultural discontinuity plays a role in some minority students' lack of success in school. Unfortunately, however, this hypothesis is now accepted as fact by many researchers and has become an underlying assumption rather than a research question in Indian education. I argue that the unquestioning acceptance of the cultural discontinuity hypothesis by many educators, as a cause for dropping out of school, is misguided for two reasons. First, the body of research on the causes of American Indian students' dropping out does not specifically support the hypothesis, and, second, the focus on cultural discontinuity precludes examination of macrostructural variables which may, in fact, be far more significant.

Why American Indian Students Drop Out

There are relatively few specific research studies which seek to identify the reasons why American Indian students drop out (Giles, 1985; Coladarci, 1983; Eberhard, 1989; Chan and Osthimer, 1983; Platero, Brandt, Witherspoon, and Wong, 1986; Milone, 1983; Deyhle, 1989), and those few certainly do not explicitly support the cultural discontinuity hypothesis. In fact, few directly address the issue as a research question, although they do contain both explicit and implicit assumptions about the importance of cultural relevance in curriculum.

Giles' (1985) study of urban Indian dropouts in Milwaukee is the only study which explicitly employed (but did not critically examine) the cultural discontinuity hypothesis. She stated that,

> Considering the disproportionately high Native American dropout rate, one can reasonably assume that certain culturally-based Indian characteristics exist that clash with the urban public school environment (p. 2).

Based upon this assumption, Giles assigned the eight students she interviewed a place on a continuum between a "Native American value orientation" and an "American middle class value orientation." She reported that "it was evident that the more assimilated an Indian student is into the American middle class value orientation, the more likely that person is to complete high school" (p. 14). She goes on to discuss the implications of this finding with extensive reference to Susan Philips' (1982) work in a Warm Springs, Oregon reservation elementary school. She concluded by recommending that school counselors target those "traditional" students for dropout prevention programs, that Indian cultural values (such as a preference for cooperation) be incorporated into curricula, that Indian cultural activities be provided at the schools, and that teachers be trained to more effectively serve Indian students (pp. 26–27).

Giles' research, although undoubtedly inspired by the best of intentions, typifies the problem with assuming that cultural discontinuity between Indian students' culture and the culture of the school causes their academic difficulties (in this case dropping out), and that creating a congruence between the two cultures will solve the problems. There is no critical examination of this premise; the report attempted to show **how** this is true, rather than **if** this is true. In addition, Giles assumed that there is such a thing as a "Native American value orientation" and an "American middle class value orientation." She further assumed that the findings of Philips' ethnographic research into the communication styles of elementary school students on the Warm Springs reservation in Oregon is directly applicable to the situation of urban high school students in Wisconsin.

Several studies reported interviews with students specifically about the importance of cultural relevance or sensitivity. Coladarci (1983) supervised interviews of American Indian students who dropped out of a Montana school district. Student interviews indicated five factors which significantly influenced their leaving school: 1) the lack of relevance of the school curriculum both in terms of future employment and native culture; 2) the perceived insensitivity of teachers; 3) the peer pressure to leave school; 4) having to remain in school for the full senior year when needing only a few classes to graduate; and 5) the problems at home (pp. 18–19). Coladarci recommended that the district critically examine the curriculum in terms of its relevance to both future job opportunities and sensitivity to American Indian culture (pp. 19–21). There is no independent verification of the student self reports, and Coladarci noted that the results should be considered cautiously and should be supported by ethnographic research.

Eberhard (1989) followed and interviewed four cohorts of urban American Indian students. Low test scores and GPAs were found to be significant to students' dropping out. Family constellation was not statistically significant, but more stay-ins came from two parent homes. Little gender difference was found, but family mobility was very significant (p. 37). Interviews indicated that both parents and students found the schools "culturally insensitive" (p. 38). Students also reported that they need more support from their parents. Again, there is no explicit research into cultural relevance and no supporting evidence which defines culturally insensitive.

Some researchers also related students' participation in or ties to traditional culture to their propensity to drop out. In a case study of Navajo students from public schools, Chan and Osthimer (1983) hired Navajo community researchers to interview nine college bound students, nine graduates with no immediate plans for continuing their education, and six dropouts. In addition, the project used school and community documents, interviews with "experts" on Navajo students, and student records.

Chan and Osthimer found that the student's first language was not as important a determinant to their success in school as the successful transition into English. Students who were English dominant or bilingual were less likely to drop out, regardless of their first language. Bilinguals were most likely to be college bound (pp. 24–27). Of particular interest is their finding that students from less traditional homes dropped out at higher rates. Students who reported their families as "moderate," meaning they observed Navajo traditions while having adopted certain Anglo conveniences, were most likely to be college bound (pp. 27–30). Achievement and attendance were not clear critical markers (perhaps due to the fact that these data were often incomplete), whereas high absenteeism was significant in predicting dropping out (pp. 30–36). Students who travelled long distances to school dropped out more (pp. 36–40), and students who had specific career goals/ambitions tended to persist (p. 42).

In a study commissioned by the Navajo tribal government, Platero, Brandt, Witherspoon, and Wong (1986) calculated the Navajo Nation's dropout rate to be 31%. They used a combination of school records and student questionnaires. They examined student demographic variables, socioeconomic variables, cultural variables, home support for education, transportation factors, academic expectations and performance, future orientation, extracurricular activities, school support programs, and behavioral problems (pp. 23–43). In addition, they included dropouts' own reports of why they left school. One of their most significant findings was that many students who were assumed to have dropped out had transferred to other schools (p. 63). There was little difference in grades or retention rates between dropouts and persisters (p. 66). Living a long distance from school was a significant factor in dropping out but "absenteeism was likely to be more of a symptom of dropping out, rather than a cause" (pp. 70–72). Having reliable backup transportation was important to students who missed the bus. Stayers were more likely to live within walking distance of their schools or to be driven to school (p. 81). Students themselves reported boredom, social problems, retention, and pregnancy or marriage as the most significant factors in their dropping out (p. 73). Although many of the problems experienced by the students in Platero et al. (1986) seemed to be economic or social, the authors nonetheless noted that,

> There is ample evidence from the student and dropout survey that dropouts have not acquired the cultural drives and behavioral molds the school systems wish to develop in their students.... This is obviously in part due to the variance these cultural values and social codes have with those of traditional Navajo culture and society (p. 74)....

The report makes a number of recommendations to the Navajo tribal government (pp. 182–186) including the development of a system for tracking dropouts in a more systematic manner, the development of prevention programs, and an improvement in transportation systems for students in remote areas. They also recommended that schools incorporate more Navajo cultural values into the school curriculum and daily operations....

Deyhle's 1989 study of Navajo and Ute school leavers represents a welcome departure from the current state of the art in educational research.... [S]ignificant numbers of students she interviewed mentioned the economic necessity of finding a job, long distance commutes to school, pregnancy, and academic problems as contributing to their decisions to leave school.

Particularly interesting in Deyhle's work is her discussion of the curricular issues which dominate other studies. She found that those students who came from the most traditional Navajo homes, spoke their native language, and participated in traditional religious and social activities (who, according to the prevailing assumptions, would experience the greatest cultural discontinuity) did not feel that the school curriculum was inappropriate to them as Indians (p. 42). Ute students who came from the least traditional homes felt that the curriculum was not important to them as Indians. These students experienced the highest dropout rates and most problems academically and socially in school. Deyhle concluded, "A culturally non-responsive curriculum is a greater threat to those whose own cultural 'identity' is insecure." (p. 42).

Deyhle noted, however, that the relevance of the school curriculum to the economic reality of the community is an important issue. There are few jobs in the community and fewer that require a high school diploma. There is no tangible economic benefit to students to remain in school.

Deyhle also reported specifically the issues of racism and cultural maintenance as important factors influencing students to leave school. She noted that there is considerable conflict between a number of factions in the school: between Anglos and Indians, Utes and Navajos, traditional Navajos and more acculturated Navajos, and Mormons and non-Mormons. These conflicts create an atmosphere of social unease in the school which, when coupled with academic difficulties, leave students with few positive experiences to encourage them to stay in school. In addition, many Indian students who were successful were berated by their peers for trying to act like Whites or for being perceived as looking down on their friends and families (pp. 48–49). Deyhle noted that there is some basis for this attitude; given the lack of jobs on the reservation, those who get more education and training frequently must move away to find jobs for which their training prepares them.

Discussion of Data

It is difficult to draw any firm conclusions from the data available on American Indian dropouts. Dropping out is a serious problem for American Indian students, but there is little consensus as to the cause. Virtually all research indicate that Indian students drop out of school at very high rates—invariably at higher rates than Anglos and Asians, and often at higher rates than all other minorities. These rates vary from school to school, year to year, tribe to tribe, male to female, BIA to public school or, in other words, from study to study.

I argue that there is simply not enough evidence to conclude that cultural discontinuity plays a significant role, but there is overwhelming evidence that economic and social issues which are not culturally specific to being Indian (although they may be specific to being a minority) are very significant in causing students to drop out of school. Milone (1983) noted that

> many of the reasons given by Indian students for dropping out of school—
> such as pregnancy, drugs, wanting to be with friends, and boredom in school
> —are the same as those of non-Indians (p. 56).

Long commuting distances and the lack of relevance of school to reservation students' economic future may be the only differences between Indian and non-Indian students' reasons for dropping out. In the case of urban Indian students, are the problems they encounter which lead to their dropping out of school any different than the problems encountered by African-American or Hispanic students? Chances are, they are not. If there is a cultural discontinuity, it is not unique to their situation. If there is institutional racism, it is also not unique to them (although the lack of general awareness about American Indians is probably greater than for other groups). Poverty, discrimination, poor health care, and other problems may be more a result of the general status of being a minority in this country than the type of minority that you are. Reservation students may be in an economically and socially different situation. High unemployment rates and menial work opportunities in a community must certainly influence a student's perception of the value of school.

Most research has yet to look beyond the classroom and home to the wider influences of the economic and political environment of the community as a whole. How do the attitudes that teachers from the dominant culture have about Indian students' abilities contribute to their treatment of the students and the students' perceptions of their school experience? How does the curriculum prepare students for the political and economic opportunity structure that they experience when they graduate, especially on the reservation? Do some Indian students consciously avoid academic achievement because it means peer opposition for "acting White?" If so, how can schools hope to separate the two ideas? These questions have rarely been addressed and may point to more profitable areas of inquiry. A promising avenue of inquiry into the dropout problem among Indian students is the macrostructural or Marxist perspective.

Macrostructural Explanations of Minority Schooling

Marxist anthropological theorists, principally John Ogbu (1974, 1978, 1981, 1982, 1983, 1985, 1987), found the "structured inequality" of American society to be the cause of minority student failure. Because of racism and discrimination, minority students have a lower "job ceiling" than do Anglo, middle-class students. The idea that hard work and achievement in school lead to economic success is contradicted by the circumstances of poverty in which the members of their communities live, leaving them with "disillusionment and lack of effort, optimism, and perseverance" (1982, p. 21). Ogbu believed that "children's school learning problems are ultimately caused by historical and structural forces beyond their control" (1985, p. 868).

Ogbu recognized that not all minority groups in the United States experience difficulty in school. He makes a distinction between autonomous, immigrant, and castelike (originally labeled subordinate) minorities (1974, 1978, 1982, 1983). Autonomous minorities are groups such as the Jews or the Amish in the United States who are "not totally subordinated by the dominant group politically or economically" (1983, p. 169), whereas immigrant minorities

> are people who have moved more or less voluntarily to their host societies.... As strangers they can operate psychologically outside established definitions of social status and relations. They may be subject to pillory and discrimination, but have not usually had time to internalize the effects of discrimination or have those effects become an ingrained part of their culture (1983, pp. 169–170).

The home country is the frame of reference for immigrant minorities who, although experiencing discrimination, may still feel themselves to be better off in the United States than in the political or economic situations they left behind.

Ogbu noted that, as a group, autonomous and immigrant minorities do not experience failure in schools; his concern is the experience of the castelike minorities:

> Castelike minorities are distinguished from immigrant and other types of minorities in that (1) they have been incorporated into the society involuntarily and permanently, (2) they face a job and status ceiling, and (3) they tend to formulate their economic and social problems in terms of collective institutional discrimination, which they perceive as more than temporary. Examples of castelike minorities in the United States include blacks, Indians, Chicanos, and Puerto Ricans (1982, p. 299)....

Castelike minorities... experience secondary cultural discontinuities which "develop *after* members of two populations have been in contact or *after* members of a given population have begun to participate in an institution, such as the school system, controlled by another group" (1982, p. 298). Castelike minority cultures may define themselves in opposition to Anglo culture and include "coping behaviors" which develop in response to systematic oppression. Coping behaviors, although effective in the social and economic context, may actually work against student achievement in school. In addition, defining oneself in opposition to Anglo culture may mean that the student will actively resist the attempts of the school to impart knowledge and values which are seen to be important to Anglo culture. In other words, to say that minority students experience failure merely due to cultural differences between their homes and the school is to deny the historical and structural context in which those differences are embedded.

Ogbu saw the shortcomings of the cultural discontinuity explanation as inherent to the microethnographic approach used so often to study minority student failure. He noted that many of these studies are poorly done in that they are not true ethnographies. The researcher may spend little time, if any, outside of the classroom, and the period of study is often inadequate. Ogbu also criticized the sociolinguistic bias in much of the research which sees schooling as a transmission of culture with little regard for the larger societal context in which it takes place....

Conclusions

Much more research is needed to understand the complex problem of American Indian dropouts. The cultural discontinuity hypothesis has played the strongest role in influencing the direction of research, or is, at least, used as an underlying assumption guiding the research questions, though it has not been convincingly demonstrated to be true. This exclusive focus on culture and curricular innovation draws attention from the very real possibility that economics and social structure may be more important. According to Ogbu, the castelike status of Indians and Mexican Americans are far more significant factors than their languages and cultures. He stated that

> This does not mean that cultural and language differences are not relevant; what it does mean is that their castelike status makes it more difficult for them to overcome any problems created by cultural and language differences than it is for immigrant minorities (1978, p. 237).

Although "culture" itself may truly be a significant factor in student success in school, it may be that the culture in the student's background, not in the school curriculum, is significant. There is some evidence from the research, especially in Deyhle (1989) but also in Chan and Osthimer (1983), that a strong sense of traditional cultural identity (as defined by speaking the native language fluently and engaging in traditional religious and social activities) provides a student with an advantage in school. The idea that traditional Indian students may have an academic advantage over more "acculturated" students is an important issue. This would seem to contradict the idea that the more different the culture of the home and school, the more problems students will experience. Traditional American Indian students might then be seen as more like Ogbu's immigrant minorities in that they have strongly developed identities and do not need to "resist" White culture to have an identity. They, therefore, do better in school. That traditional students do better in school does not necessarily mean that providing non-traditional students with traditional cultural information will make them achieve (even if it could be done). American Indian students from homes with little participation in traditional social or religious activities or little use of the native language may fit more closely into Ogbu's classification of castelike minorities. Those students' resistance to school seems to be a far more significant factor.

The assumption that schools have control over the critical variables affecting any student's success is yet unproven. This is not to say that many schools could not do a much better job, or that some schools are not now doing an excellent job in educating American Indian students. This is merely to note that the relationship between the microlevel and macrolevel variables in schooling remain largely unexplored. I would not argue that research into cultural discontinuities is inappropriate or irrelevant, but that it is surely insufficient to fully explain the problems that American Indian students experience in school.

An understanding of minority school failure cannot be captured by focusing on children's "home environment," on their unique cultural background, or on their genetic makeup or idiosyncratic personal attributes (Ogbu, 1981, p. 23)....
Further research into the problem of American Indian dropouts must test implicit notions about the importance of culture and devote equal attention to variables outside the boundaries of the school itself.

POSTSCRIPT

Do Cultural Differences Between Home and School Explain the High Dropout Rates for American Indian Students?

This debate deals with a relatively recent concern within minority studies, that of having sensitivity toward ethnic cultural needs, even if it means maintaining separation. Historically, both social scientists and the general public simply assumed that assimilation was the proper goal for everyone. And assimilation demanded that minorities not only conform to the dominant cultural values and practices but also subordinate their own ideas of desirable conduct. This was most pronounced in public schools, which were clearly supposed to function to socialize ethnic groups into the American mainstream.

In the past, the primary concerns for public schools were that a teacher should know his or her subject matter, know how to teach it—that is, be organized and present the concepts and assignments clearly in English—and be fair in grading. To many scholars socialized in the more recent generation of minority group theory—or those such as Reyhner, who have been teaching for several years and who have embraced the newer perspective—the above description of "good teaching" is barbaric. To them, the idea of a teacher's not worrying about students' cultural values but instead being concerned primarily or even exclusively about course content is outmoded.

A useful discussion of the current tensions between economic development and cultural maintenance is *Modern Tribal Development: Paths to Self Sufficiency and Cultural Integrity in Indian Country* by Dean Howard Smith (Rowman & Littlefield, 2000). Critiques of Native American education can be found in Duane Champagne, ed., *Contemporary Native American Cultural Issues* (AltaMira Press, 1999). A discussion of teaching American history that emphasizes the role of minorities is E. Foner's "Teaching American History," *American Scholar* (October 1998). One of the many books documenting the abuse of Native Americans is *The Earth Shall Weep: A History of Native America* by James Wilson (Grove/Atlantic, 2000). The late Paulo Freire, who revolutionized educational theory, provides a pedagogical platform that in many ways parallels the assumptions of Reyhner in *Pedagogy of Freedom: Ethics, Democracy and Civic Courage* (Rowman & Littlefield, 2001). Finally, a work that delineates a major style of learning and knowledge transmission is *The Native American Oral Tradition: Voices of the Spirit and Soul* by Lois J. Einhorn (Praeger, 2000).

ISSUE 8

Does Rap Music Contribute to Violent Crime?

YES: Dennis R. Martin, from "The Music of Murder," *ACJS Today* (November/December 1993)

NO: Mark S. Hamm and Jeff Ferrell, from "Rap, Cops, and Crime: Clarifying the 'Cop Killer' Controversy," *ACJS Today* (May/June 1994)

ISSUE SUMMARY

YES: Dennis R. Martin, president of the National Association of Chiefs of Police, theorizes that since "music has the power both to 'soothe the savage beast' and to stir violent emotions," then rising racial tensions and violence can be attributed to rock music's promotion of "vile, deviant, and sociopathic behaviors."

NO: Criminologists Mark S. Hamm and Jeff Ferrell reject Martin's analysis of the relationship between music and violence, charging that the theory is based on racism and ignorance of both music and broader cultural forces.

Traditionally, science has been about ascertaining causal relations between two or more variables. The producing, contributing, influencing, forcing, or cause variable is known as the *independent variable,* symbolized as X. The result, effect, outcome, produced, or caused variable is known as the *dependent variable,* or Y. In the social sciences, independent variables have generally been traced to specific social factors (e.g., gender, wealth, education, neighborhood, family, race, religion, age, and so on). Such objective factors have been used to predict or explain individuals' and groups' attitudes and behaviors.

Throughout the twentieth century, however, many philosophers of science have questioned the value and validity of causal analysis. This is especially true in the social sciences, including criminology. Drawing from the sixteenth-century philosopher David Hume, questions have been asked about how one can ever "know" causes. Frequently, cause cannot be seen. In addition, in human behavior one must often take into account subjective attitudes, feelings, motivations, and such. There are no isomorphic relationships in criminology as there are in the physical sciences. That is, there are no one-to-one relationships, such as that at sea level, water will freeze at temperatures below 32 degrees or that what goes up on Earth must come down. Instead, there are only contingencies, or probabilities, such as that living in an impoverished area and having a parent and several siblings in prison will probably result in a younger brother becoming a criminal as well. In such a situation there may be a *high probability*, but there is hardly a certain link between environment and behavior.

Not only is there no inevitable relation between background factors and outcomes (such as crime) but people's behavior usually has multiple causes: positive or negative parental role models, area of residency, types of and relations with peers, and so on. Sometimes influencing factors on subsequent behaviors lie dormant or gradually accumulate. Poverty, for instance, can demoralize individuals; coupled with racism, it can lead to low self-esteem and self-destructive behaviors such as alcoholism, partially resulting in medical problems, preventing working when jobs become available, which can lead to reinforcing prejudiced people's negative stereotyping that "poor people do not want to work anyway."

Due to these and other reasons, some social scientists eschew searching for causal relations. Instead, they search for correlations. For instance, when there is poverty, racism, declining jobs, and so on, there is usually more crime. All of the identified variables would be examined to determine if they correlate with crime and, if so, what type.

Ascertaining the causes of most things, especially human behavior, is remarkably difficult, and many view such a search as a waste of time. When there are widespread perceptions that serious problems are upon us and that things are "out of control" (such as the current views toward violent crime), people demand immediate solutions. Often the entire scientific process and even reason itself are short-circuited because powerful figures—or those wanting to become powerful—formulate "self-evident" explanations of the problem.

Although scholars trained in scientific methodology can see the fallacies and dangers of glib explanations (and concomitant glib solutions), for others it makes sense to blame some misunderstood phenomenon or even categories of people for societal problems. In its extreme version, this is scapegoating.

In the following selections, Dennis R. Martin provides many examples through history of how music has been linked with violence. He also discusses the marketing of some gangsta rap albums, which he maintains generate hostilities toward police officers and others because of their lyrics and strident sounds. Mark S. Hamm and Jeff Ferrell dismiss Martin's linking of rap music and violence as bad sociology, bad history, and worse criminology. They also attack Martin's historical analysis of current music as being racist because he does not mention the positive contributions of Black musicians.

What bearing do you think the murders of rappers Biggie Smalls (the Notorious B.I.G.) and Tupac Shakur have on this debate? How does the recent spate of school slayings affect the debate? What role might the popularity of the white performer Eminem play in expanding violence against women, gays, and others?

Dennis R. Martin

 **YES**

The Music of Murder

In my career in law enforcement I have weathered the rough seas of society, first as a patrol officer, then as a director of police training, shift commander, police chief, and now as the President of the National Association of Chiefs of Police. As tumultuous as contemporary society is, it could not exist without the foundation of law. We Americans are fortunate to live under a government of laws, not of men.

The United States Constitution is a remarkable and unique compact between the government and its people. The First Amendment, in particular, states a once revolutionary concept with great power and simplicity: "Congress shall make no law... abridging the freedom of speech". In our three-branched system of government, the will of the people is expressed through duly elected legislators in Congress and enforced by an elected executive; the Constitution finds its voice in the judicial branch. What are the people to do when the laws that are meant to ensure their freedom are abused in a manner that erodes the very foundation of law?

Early First Amendment cases sanctioned restrictions on speech where its free exercise created a clear, existing danger, or where a serious evil would result. In two centuries, First Amendment law has evolved to the point where practically the only prohibited speech involves the mention of God in public assemblies.

The misuse of the First Amendment is graphically illustrated in Time-Warner's attempt to insert into the mainstream culture the vile and dangerous lyrics of the Ice-T song entitled *Cop Killer*. The *Body Count* album containing *Cop Killer* was shipped throughout the United States in miniature body bags. Only days before distribution of the album was voluntarily suspended, Time-Warner flooded the record market with a half million copies. The *Cop Killer* song has been implicated in at least two shooting incidents and has inflamed racial tensions in cities across the country. Those who work closely with the families and friends of slain officers, as I do, volunteering for the American Police Hall of Fame and Museum, are outraged by the message of *Cop Killer*. It is an affront to the officers—144 in 1992 alone—who have been killed in the line of duty while upholding the laws of our society and protecting all its citizens.

Is it fair to blame a musical composition for the increase in racial tensions and the shooting incidents? Music has the power both to "soothe the savage beast" and to stir violent emotions in man. Music can create an ambiance for gentle romance, or unleash brutal sensuality. It can transcend the material world and make our hearts soar to a realm of spiritual beauty. Yet the trend in American rock music for the last decade has been to promote ever more vile, deviant, and sociopathic behaviors. Recognition, leading to fame and fortune far exceeding merit, propels performers and the industry to attack every shared value that has bound our society together for more than two centuries.

The power that music works on the human mind can be seen throughout history; it has existed in every known society. The Bible contains numerous references to music. Music is found in the ancient tales of China, as well as in the traditions of Native Americans. In the beginning of human history, music stood at the center of life, acting as an intermediary between the natural and supernatural. It was both handmaiden to religion and the cornerstone of education. While there may be music without culture, culture without music is unthinkable.

The earliest music consisted of a vocal melody with rhythmic, regular beats kept by the hands and feet. In time, the pattern of beats evolved into more complicated rhythms. Formal music found its roots in China, beginning around 2000 BC. Ritualistic music emerged around 1900 BC among the Israelites during the reign of the Canaanites. By setting stories and teachings to music, preliterate Hebrew leaders were able to memorize and recite long passages, and to entertain and instruct their audience with greater impact than words alone could convey. One generation handed down to the next Hebrew laws, traditions, and important historic events in song, often accompanied by a simple harp.

Folk music is the basis for formal music. The march, for example, dates from the Roman Empire. Its insistent rhythm, powerful major chords, and strong simple melody were designed to ignite courage in the hearts of those preparing for battle (and, possibly, fear in the enemies' camp).

Led by St. Benedict, the early Christian Church developed the art of choral singing. Over the centuries, sacred choral music has provided us with a view of the world to come. A branch of choral music evolved into opera, a form of music more than once credited with inciting riots. In 1830, the Brussels premiere of *La Muette de Portici* by Daniel Esprit Auber ignited the Belgian independence movement against the Dutch. In 1842, Giuseppe Verdi achieved overnight fame after the debut of his third opera, *Nabucca,* which inspired rioting in Milan. One of the choruses, *Va Pensilero,* so touched the Italian soldiers that it was adopted as the Italian anthem.

Perhaps the greatest composition combining choral and symphonic modes is the *Ninth Symphony* of Beethoven. An utterly revolutionary work, both musically and politically, it proclaims that all men will be brothers when the power of joy resides in their hearts, binding together the fabric of society torn asunder by different cultural mores. This was not a popular sentiment to express in Vienna, the seat of power of the reactionary Austrian Empire.

The twentieth century brought new sounds to America: atonal classical music, the big band era, jazz, and country and western, among others. History recorded two world wars in which Germanic leaders preyed upon human society; the American musical response, spearheaded by George M. Cohan, was proudly defiant, full of valor and resolve. Across the Atlantic, German composer Paul Hindemith was charged with a war crime because his compositions reflected spiritual ideas and themes of renewal. He was barred from performing music.

The 1950s and '60s ushered in a new era for music in which elements of jazz, bluegrass, and country music combined to create early rock and roll. Bill Haley, of Bill Haley and the Comets, holds the distinction of being the country's first composer of rock and roll, in 1955. With the rise of "the King of Rock and Roll," Elvis Presley, rock and roll forever changed the world. For the first time, contemporary music did not reflect the values of society but glamorized rebelliousness and adolescent sexuality.

Later, lyrics of the 1960s and '70s espoused drug abuse. Heavy metal bands of the '70s, '80s, and even into the '90s with bands such as Guns 'N' Roses, promote a panoply of anti-social behaviors and attitudes. The common denominator of their music is that self-gratification and self-expression excuse aggressively violent and sexual behavior inflicted on others.

The new kid on the popular music scene has stretched the fabric of our First Amendment like none before. Rap music is a culmination of the course charted by Elvis Presley. Put his rebellion, swagger, and sexuality into the pressurized cauldron of a black ghetto and the resulting music explodes with rage. It is primitive music—stripped of melodic line and original chord progressions. The beat alone propels the street smart rhyming verse lyrics through topics of deprivation, rebellion, poverty, sex, guns, drug abuse, and AIDS.

Since the Rodney King incident* and the subsequent riots in Los Angeles, the media has contributed to a climate wherein police bashing is socially and politically correct. Ignored is the role police play in safe-guarding the lives and liberties of all law-abiding citizens. The ingrained hatred of police authority, already prevalent in poor urban "hoods" is easily mobilized by the suggestive lyrics of rap.

The framers of the Constitution lived in a world far different from our own. Could they have imagined a day when music would become a tool to destabilize a democratic society by provoking civil unrest, violence, and murder? Yet, the lyrics of rapper Ice-T's *Cop Killer* do precisely that by describing steps to kill a cop. Time-Warner's recording company not only defended the "instructional" song, but marketed the album by shipping it in miniature body bags, complete with a three by four foot poster graphically depicting a cop killer. The company flooded the United States market with an additional half-

---

* [This refers to the severe beating of black motorist Rodney King by four white Los Angeles police officers in 1991, which was captured on videotape by a bystander and broadcast on national television. The later acquittal of the officers sparked public outrage and touched off the 1992 Los Angeles riots.—Ed.]

million copies just prior to Ice-T's announcement that distribution would be suspended voluntarily.

While on patrol in July 1992, two Las Vegas police officers were ambushed and shot by four juvenile delinquents who boasted that Ice-T's *Cop Killer* gave them a sense of duty and purpose, to get even with "a f—king pig". The juveniles continued to sing its lyrics when apprehended.

Notwithstanding the predictability of police being ambushed after such a rousing call-to-arms, Time-Warner continues to defend the song. In a letter addressed to Chief Gerald S. Arenberg, Executive Director of the National Association of Chiefs of Police, Time-Warner Vice Chairman Martin D. Payson gave his rationale for Warner Bros recording and mass-marketing *Cop Killer:*

> Ice-T is attempting to express the rage and frustration a young black person feels in the face of official brutality and systematic racism. Though the incidents of brutality may be perpetrated by a small number of police, the impact on the black community is intense and widespread. The anger that exists is neither an invention of Ice-T's nor a figment of the creative imagination. It is real and growing. Our job as a society is to address the causes of this anger, not suppress its articulation.

This last sentence is disingenuous at best. Is Time-Warner addressing the causes of black anger, or is it magnifying isolated instances of anger into a fashionable popular sentiment and reaping handsome profits in the process?

Would Thomas Jefferson have advocated using the First Amendment as a shield to publish a step-by-step guide on how to ambush and murder the police? The *Body Count* album also contains *Smoked Pork,* a song describing how Ice-T murders two police officers, with dialogue so graphic the lyrics were not printed with the album. Freedom of speech ought to end short of advocating violent physical harm to fellow members of society. If Ice-T had, instead, produced a song describing how to sexually abuse and torture young children, perhaps there would be an appropriate public outcry. A full measure of consideration ought to be given to the lives and welfare of our nation's police officers and their families.

Safety and order in any community requires a partnership of a type that can exist only in a functioning democracy. Public attitudes toward the police may play a part in the frightening rise in crime rates. Disrespect for the law enforcement officer breeds disrespect for the law. A child who is raised to laugh at cops is not likely to grow up with any great respect for the laws that the police enforce. Youthful experimenters, confused by adolescent anxiety, look up to Ice-T as a powerful role model who supports hatred, racism, sexual abuse, and vile crimes that he depicts through dialogue in his lyrics.

Decades of misrepresentation and abuse of law enforcement in entertainment and education have left their mark. Society is now finding that it cannot ridicule the enforcers of the law on one hand and build respect for the law on the other. You cannot separate the two, any more than you can separate education from teachers, justice from judges, and religion from the ministry.

It is a sad irony that, in our society, scandal breeds financial gain. Sales of *Cop Killer,* and the *Body Count* album on which it appears, have soared since law enforcement officers from around the country rallied behind police organizations like the National Association of Chiefs of Police, CLEAT (Combined Law Enforcement Officers of Texas), and the American Federation of Police.

Ice-T is but one rapper encouraging violent reaction to the presence of law enforcement. Rap group Almighty RSO defiantly sings *One in the Chamber*, referring to the bullet they would use to kill a cop. Kool G-Rap and DJ Polo's song *Live and Let Die* describes how G-Rap brutally murders two undercover police officers as he tries to complete a drug deal.

Tragically, this violent message is too often followed by its young audience. On April 11, 1992, Trooper Bill Davidson, formerly with the Texas Department of Public Safety, was killed in cold blood as he approached the driver of a vehicle he had stopped for a defective headlight. The trooper's widow, Linda Davidson, described to me an account of the events surrounding the killing and the impact of this tragedy on the Davidson family. The teen-age killer, Ronald Howard, explained to law enforcement authorities that he felt hypnotized by the lyrics of six songs by the rap group 2 Pac, from their album *2 Pacalyypse Now*, which urge the killing of police officers. Howard claims that the lyrical instructions devoured him like an animal, taking control over his subconscious mind and compelling him to kill Trooper Davidson as he approached Howard's vehicle. The rap's influence, however, apparently continues to affect Howard's judgment. Two psychiatrists found that the music still affects his psycho-social behavior. In a meeting with Linda Davidson, Howard expressed his desire to completely carry out the rap's instruction by putting away a pig's wife and dusting his family. Howard's reaction has left Linda dumfounded, confused, bewildered, and most of all, angry.

The Davidsons' anger is aimed not solely at Howard, but has also expressed itself in a civil lawsuit against Time-Warner, the company that promotes 2 Pac. Again, Time-Warner claims the First Amendment protects its right to promote songs that advocate the killing of police. In preparation for trial, the corporation's lawyers are closely observing the criminal trial of Ron Howard. Given the current state of American law, one can only hope that Time-Warner will tire of the expense of defending state court actions prompted by such lyrics and attacks on police.

With growing lawlessness and violence in our society, every American is at risk of losing his property and his life to criminals. Police officers risk their lives daily to preserve peace and property rights for all Americans. The officers deserve protection from abusive speech when that abuse imperils not only their ability to protect citizens, but also their ability to protect their very lives.

NO

Mark S. Hamm and Jeff Ferrell

Rap, Cops, and Crime: Clarifying the "Cop Killer" Controversy

Perhaps the most enduring feature of the ACJS [Academy of Criminal Justice Sciences] is that it routinely brings practitioners and researchers together in a public forum where they can debate the current state of criminal justice. In this spirit, we offer a counterpoint to the attacks made by Dennis R. Martin, President of the National Association of Chiefs of Police, on rapper Ice-T's song "Cop Killer" and its alleged relationship to violent acts ("The Music of Murder," *ACJS Today*, Nov/Dec 1993).

"Cop Killer" in Cultural Context

As a starting point, Martin offers a truncated and distorted description of rap's gestation that largely misses the music's social and cultural meanings. To suggest, as does Martin, that rap is "a culmination of the course charted by Elvis Presley" is to commit a double fallacy. First, Martin's characterization of Elvis Presley as the founder of rock 'n' roll, and Bill Haley as "the country's first composer of rock and roll," constitutes a racist and revisionist rock history which curiously excludes Louis Jordan, Chuck Berry, Bo Diddley, and a host of other black musicians and musical traditions which established the essentials of rock 'n' roll. (This sort of myopic ethnic insensitivity echoes in Martin's subsequent claim that rap is "primitive" (!) music.)

Second, Martin compounds these sorts of mistakes by tracing rap's lineage to rock 'n' roll—or, apparently, white Southern rockabilly. Rap artists have in fact explicitly denied this lineage. Early rappers, for example, sang "no more rock 'n' roll," and rappers Public Enemy have attacked Elvis Presley, and his racist attitudes, specifically. To draw a parallel between white Southern rockabilly of the mid-1950's and today's black urban rap is therefore analogous to comparing Joshua's trumpets at the battle of Jericho with the Wagnerian operas of Nazi storm troopers, or to equating the horn-calls which led Caesar's troops into England with the thrash metal of Slaughter and Megadeth absorbed by US Air Force pilots prior to bombing raids during the Persian Gulf War. Other than to say that militaries have routinely used music to lead soldiers into battle, the analogies have little heuristic value. What Martin's analysis lacks is the crucial historical specificity and sociological contextualization, the framework of conceptual clarity and appreciation necessary to explain the complex relationship between particular forms of music, popular culture dynamics, and incidents of violence.

Most commentators, in fact, locate the beginnings of rap (or, more broadly, hip-hop) in the funkadelic period of the mid–late 1970s, a la George Clinton, Parliament, P-Funk, Kurtis Blow, and Grandmaster Flash and the Furious Five. Evolving from this musical base, rap gained its popular appeal in the grim ghettos of New York City—first in the Bronx, and then in Harlem and Brooklyn. Rap caught the sounds of the city, capturing the aggressive boasts and stylized threats of street-tough black males. By the mid-1980s, rap was injected into the American mainstream via Run-D.M.C.'s version of Aerosmith's "Walk this Way" and other cross-over hits. MC Hammer, Tone Loc, Public Enemy, Ice-T, NWA (Niggers with Attitude), De La Soul, and a legion of others soon followed, infusing rap with R and B, jazz, and other influences, and introducing rap to world-wide audiences of all ethnicities.

In ignoring this rich history, Martin misunderstands both the aesthetics and the politics of rap. Martin, for example, leaps to the extraordinary conclusion that rap is a "vile and dangerous" form of cultural expression, a "primitive music" that attacks "every shared value that has bound our society together for more than two-hundred years." From within this sort of uncritical, consensus model of contemporary society, Martin then locates this portentous social threat in a wider cultural crisis. "[T]he trend in American rock music for the last decade," he argues, "has been to promote ever more vile, deviant, and sociopathic behaviors." And if this trend is not reversed, Martin concludes, "every American is at risk of losing his [sic] property and his life to criminals." A careful analysis of rock's lyrical diversity and social effects would, of course, undermine these sorts of hysterical generalizations. A careful analysis of rap music's lyrical content and cultural context likewise reveals a very different social dynamic.

"Message Rap" (or "Gangster Rap," the focus of the remainder of this essay) deals head-on with universal themes of injustice and oppression—themes which have both bound and divided US society from its inception. But at the same time, gangster rap is proudly localized as "ghetto music," thematizing its commitment to the black urban experience. (This is also, by the way, part of what constitutes rap's appeal for millions of middle-class white kids who have never been inside a black ghetto.) In fact, rap focuses on aspects of ghetto life that most adult whites, middle-class blacks, and self-protective police officers and politicians would rather ignore. Rappers record the everyday experiences of pimping, prostitution, child abandonment, AIDS, and drugs (as in Ice-T's *anti-drug* song, "I'm Your Pusher"). Other rappers deal with deeper institutionalized problems such as poverty, racial conflict, revisionist history books, the demand for trivial consumer goods, the exploitation of disenfranchised blacks through military service, and black dislocation from Africa. And still other rap songs lay bare the desperate and often violent nature of ghetto life, as played out in individual and collective fear, sadly misogynistic and homophobic fantasies, street killings, and, significantly, oppressive harassment by police patrols.

These themes are packed in the aesthetic of black ghetto life, an aesthetic which features verbal virtuosity as a powerful symbol in the negotiation of social status. Rap is developed from US and Jamaican verbal street games like "signifying," "the dozens," and "toasting." Rap in turn encases this verbal jousting in the funky beat of rhythms reworked through the formal musical devices which give birth to the rap sound: "sampling," "scratch mixing," and "punch phrasing" (hardly the "primitive" or "stripped" music which Martin describes). The result of this complex artistic process is a sensual, bad-assed gangster who "won't be happy till the dancers are wet, out of control" and wildly "possessed" by the rapper's divine right to rhyme the ironies, ambiguities, and fears of urban ghetto life (Ice-T, "Hit the Deck"). Musically, rap certainly emerges more from studio funk and street poetry than the blues; but like Sonny Boy Williamson, Muddy Waters, Willie Dixon and a host of other great postwar US bluesmen, Ice-T and other rappers twist and shout from within a world of crippling adversity.

"Cop Killer" on Trial

Because he misses this cultural context, it is no surprise that Martin attempts to "kill the messenger" by attacking rap music as itself a social problem. His choicest blows are saved for Ice-T, whose album *Body Count* integrates rap and "metal" styling, and includes a trilogy of protest sirens on police brutality written "for every pig who ever beat a brother down": "Smoked Pork," "Out in the Parking Lot," and "Cop Killer." Martin argues that one of these, "Cop Killer," is a "misuse of the First Amendment" because it has been "implicated in at least two shooting incidents and has inflamed racial tensions in cities across the country."

Here, though, is the available evidence on "Cop Killer": Since its release in early 1992, an unknown number of persons have heard the song. Martin claims that Time-Warner shipped 500,000 copies of *Body Count* upon its *initial* release. This number is important because subsequent pressings of *Body Count* did not contain "Cop Killer." It was pulled by Time-Warner after US Vice-President Dan Quayle, Parents' Music Resource Center spokeswoman and future Vice-Presidential associate Tipper Gore, and a host of influential media personalities and "moral entrepreneurs" leveled a highly organized and well-publicized campaign of "moral panic" against the song (see Becker, 1963; Cohen, 1972).

But our repeated inquiries to Time-Warner revealed that no such sales figures are available. We were told that Ice-T has since left Time-Warner and is now under contract with Profile records. Yet Profile cannot document sales figures for the first *Body Count* album either, claiming that these figures are known only to Ice-T himself—who, despite our attempts to reach him, remains unavailable for comment. We simply don't know—and neither does Martin— how many young Americans have heard "Cop Killer."

Setting all this aside, let's assume that the President of the National Association of Chiefs of Police is correct: some 500,000 persons have heard "Cop Killer" via the music recording industry. Because popular music is a highly contagious commodity (especially among the young), we may cautiously estimate that three times that number have listened to this song (each buyer sharing the song with just two others). From this very conservative estimate, then, it is not unreasonable to conclude that at least 1.5 million young Americans have heard "Cop Killer."

According to Martin, 144 US police officers were killed in the line of duty during 1992. This is indeed a tragic fact, the seriousness of which we do not wish in any way to diminish. But the fact also remains that there is no evidence to show that the perpetrators of these 144 homicides were influenced by "Cop Killer." Martin bases his argument on a brief review of four juveniles arrested in Las Vegas (NV) for wounding two police officers with firearms, allegedly behind the emotional impetus of "Cop Killer." Put another way, while some 1.5 million persons may have listened to this song, only four may have acted on its message. Thankfully, none were successful.

In summary, Martin claims that "Ice-T's *Cop Killer* [sic] gave [the Las Vegas youths] a sense of duty and purpose, to get even with a f—king pig." If so, we should expect this same "sense of duty and purpose" to influence the behavior of some of the other 1.5 million listeners. Martin, in fact, describes popular music as "a tool to destabilize a democratic society by provoking civil unrest, violence, and murder," and argues that "the lyrics of rapper Ice-T's 'Cop Killer' do precisely that...". He further notes the "predictability of police being ambushed after such a rousing call-to-arms...". But we cannot, in fact, find another "predictable" case. The relationship between listening to "Cop Killer" and committing subsequent acts of violence appears to more closely resemble a statistical accident than a causal equation. (The probability of attacking a police officer with a loaded firearm after listening to "Cop Killer" is, according to Martin's count, less than 1 in 375,000). Treating this relationship as one of cause and effect therefore not only misrepresents the issues; it intentionally engineers self-serving moral panic around rap music, and obstructs solutions to the sorts of problems which rap portrays.

"Cop Killer," Culture, and Crime

Ice-T is not the first artist to embed a "cop killer" theme in United States popular culture. This theme has been the subject of countless cinematic and literary works, and has appeared many times before in popular music. During the Great Depression, for example, musicians celebrated Pretty Boy Floyd and his exploits, which included the murder of law enforcement personnel. Similarly, the highly respected fiddler Tommy Jarrell wrote and sang "Policeman," which begins, "Policeman come and I didn't want to go this morning, so I shot him in the head with my 44." But perhaps the best-known case is Eric Clapton's cover version of Bob Marley and the Wailers' "I Shot the Sheriff," which reached the top of the US music charts in the mid-1970s (a feat not approached by Ice-T). "I Shot the Sheriff," though, never suffered the sort of moral and political condemnation leveled at "Cop Killer." How do we account for this difference?

First, "I Shot the Sheriff" was released by a white artist, and in an era when the availability and allure of firearms and ammunition had not reached the saturation point we see today. Clapton's white bread portrayal of an armed and heroic Jamaican "rudeboy" was therefore comfortably abstract and romantic. In contrast, Ice-T's shotgun-toting black US gangster is all too concrete, stripped of romantic pretense and lodged uncomfortably in everyday life. Firearms and ammunition are now prevalent in the black community, and are the leading cause of death among young black males. Within the context of gangster rap, artists like Ice-T portray, with chilling clarity, this tragic obsession with lethal weapons.

Second, the social aesthetic of rap music creates a key cultural and political difference. Because rap constitutes a strident form of cultural combat and critique, it generates in response organized censorship, blacklisting, arrests, and the police-enforced cancellation of concerts. Rap's cultural roots and primary audience are among the impoverished, minority residents of US inner cities. While many of these citizens are unable or unwilling to speak out—for lack of access to cultural channels, for fear of reprisal—rappers invoke a militant black pride, and portray and confront social injustice in ways that threaten the complacent status quo of mainstream society. And as part of this critique, rappers lay bare the daily reality of police violence against minority populations, and remind us how many Rodney Kings haven't made it onto videotape.

For these reasons, Dennis Martin and other defenders of the status quo are loath to acknowledge or appreciate rap on any level—as innovative music, verbal virtuosity, or cultural critique. In fact, their discomfort with rap's politics intertwines with their displeasure over its style and sound. Gangster rap is frequently raunchy, sometimes violent, and often played loud, with a heavy emphasis on the staccato, thumping back beat. By artistic design, it is meant to be "in your face" and threatening. This, in combination with the evocative power of rap's imagery, generates loud and urgent condemnations of rap from those who benefit, directly and indirectly, from contemporary social arrangements. For them, personal offense becomes a measure of political superiority.

Finally, the remarkable attention given to "Cop Killer" reflects a growing concern, among both criminologists and the general public, over the intersections of popular culture and crime. Our own studies in this area have led us to conclude that contemporary music can in some cases be significantly linked to criminality—but only when particular forms of music take on meaning within the dynamics of specific subcultures like neo-Nazi skinheads (Hamm, 1993) or hip-hop graffiti artists (Ferrell, 1993). And in this regard, we end by commending Martin for an important discovery. The fact that four youths may have in fact used the cultural material of "Cop Killer" as an epistemic and aesthetic framework for attacking two police officers is cause for serious criminological concern. And to demonstrate *how* this song may have changed the social and political consciousness of these would-be cop killers, within the dynamics of their own subcultural arrangements, is of paramount importance for understanding the situated social meanings of gangster rap.

But this sort of research requires something more than Martin offers in his essay. It demands an attention to ethnographic particulars, in place of Martin's wide generalizations and blanket condemnations. It calls for a sort of criminological *verstehen,* a willingness to pay careful attention to the lyrics of gangster rap and to the lives of those who listen to it, in place of Martin's dismissive disregard. Ultimately, it requires that criminologists confront and critique the kinds of social injustices which rap exposes, rather than participating, as does Martin, in their perpetuation.

POSTSCRIPT

Does Rap Music Contribute to Violent Crime?

In many ways the twentieth century is unique in that much of the popular music sharply divides generations. In the past, it was rare to think about "old people's music," "teenagers' music," and so on. Today's popular music often functions to divide generations as well as regions, races, and ethnic groups. Yet it also brings together millions of youngsters, as rich teens and poor, inner-city teens alike rap and gyrate to the same music. Young Chicanos, Jews, Italians, Asians, and WASPs seem equally likely to purchase the proliferating rap CDs.

Both sides of this issue are highly selective in their sensitivities. Martin is offended because police are treated with contempt on some rap albums. Hamm and Ferrell are indignant that racism and poverty are facts of life. Neither side of the controversy considers the fact that rates of violence and homicide committed by young Blacks against other Blacks is skyrocketing. Might teenagers in inner cities who listen to messages of violence turn heightened hostilities on each other instead of the police or whites? Note that the alleged criminal acts of performers such as Snoop Doggy Dogg, Dr. Dre, Marion "Suge" Knight, and others involved Black, not white, victims.

Some Blacks resent what they see as whites' justifying rap lyrics because they allegedly speak for poor (or any) Blacks. Moreover, the slayings of innocent children caught in the crossfires of drug battles as well as the many recent homicides on school grounds have fueled calls for a decrease in violence in music, movies, and television programs, as well as increased monitoring of the Internet. Some complain that people get worried about violence in the media only when rich, white kids get killed; when Black youths kill Black youths, violent lyrics are considered merely expressions of a way of life or defended as protected free speech.

For a different formulation of this debate, see "Raprehensible: Must I Push My Son Away From Black Music?" by A. Thomas-Lester, *The Washington Post* (November 5, 2000) and "Rap's Appeal Not Lost on 'Older' Critic," by C. Passey, *The Washington Times* (August 19, 2000). An attack on rap music can be found in "Your Children Are Rap Victims," by J. Delingpole, *The Spectator* (December 2000). An outstanding historical overview of the centrality of music is *All Shook Up: Music, Passion, and Politics* by Carson Holloway (Spence, 2001). The role of women in music is considered by Shelia Whiteley in *Women and Popular Music: Sexuality, Identity, and Subjectivity* (Routledge, 2001). And a scientific overview of global teen violence can be found in Allan M. Hoffman and Randal W. Summers, eds., *Teen Violence: A Global View* (Greenwood Press, 2001).

ISSUE 9

Does Bilingual Education Harm Hispanic and Other Children?

YES: Editors of *The New Republic*, from "Tongue Twister," *The New Republic* (June 22, 1998)

NO: James Crawford, from "Does Bilingual Ed Work?" *Rethinking Schools* (Winter 1998/1999)

ISSUE SUMMARY

YES: The editors of *The New Republic* contend that bilingual education is unpopular among minorities who want their children to be skilled in English to get ahead and that it may actually impede learning.

NO: James Crawford, a writer and lecturer who specializes in the politics of language, maintains that bilingual education, although no panacea for inequities between Hispanics and others, does enable non-English-speaking children to learn faster than when they are taught in English only.

Some social critics have argued that for generations the public school system in the United States functioned primarily to acculturate foreigners and the poor into mainstream middle-class values. According to this view, the manifest function of the schools was to teach all children so that America would have happy, enlightened citizens who would be capable of participating in a democratic society in an informed manner.

Critics of this view argued that the real purpose of public education was to force all youngsters into a mold so that they could become efficient workers in an industrializing, capitalist society. The indoctrination entailed tracking students so that the poor, the new arrivals, and ethnic and racial minorities would be in bottom-tier educational programs. The emphasis of these programs was not on learning truth, beauty, and critical thinking skills but on being trained in basic English, reading and writing, and basic computational skills. These were all skills needed by workers to staff factories, warehouses, department stores, and, more recently, fast-food chains.

All courses were taught in English. To facilitate the creation of a homogeneous cadre of workers, so this argument went, middle-class U.S. values were given primacy over the values, languages, identities, and customs of students who immigrated from other countries. Moreover, until the Supreme Court ruling in *Brown v. Board of Education of Topeka, Kansas* (1954), the segregation of students by race was legal. School segregation also remained *de facto* in many states, and since 1972 a growing number of schools have become resegregated. Despite its 1954 ruling on desegregation, the Supreme Court was never directly involved with school curricula and other pedagogical matters until 1968. That year, Congress passed the Education Act and provided funds for bilingual education programs. Clearly, the United States had come a long way from its insistence on cultural and language hegemony. However, many people worry that the schools are still highly politicized and that competing interest groups are bootlegging their own agendas as "humane," "scientifically based," or "best for students."

Spanish is by far the most common language spoken by students whose first language is not English. Yet research indicates that most Hispanic parents in the United States do not want their youngsters in bilingual programs. They want their children to learn in English so that they can become employable and successful more quickly in the United States.

More recently, there have been sharp reactions to bilingual education. In 1998 Californians voted in favor of Proposition 227, which abolished bilingual education. Activists and some educational experts bitterly denounced this action. The former contended that students of different backgrounds are being dehumanized by this action. The latter argued that research shows that non-English-speaking students in bilingual programs learn English faster and perform better in most areas than those who are not in bilingual programs.

One major aspect of this issue is that bilingual education, while costly for the public, generates more jobs and more grants for educators. It also provides proponents with moral capital. That is, in their view, opponents of bilingual education are guilty of dehumanizing youngsters by failing to recognize their unique cultural identities. Hence, supporters of bilingual education are morally superior. On the opposite side, critics of bilingual education maintain that it is simply another effort to drive a wedge between Americans.

In addition to the ideological controversy, there is a scientific one. In the following selections, both the editors of *The New Republic* and James Crawford draw from experts and research to prove their cases. But nowadays science is never value-free, and the political subtext in educational research is even more stark. To begin with, teaching fads rapidly come and go, often depending on the political shifts of the day. Most fads are backed by research; however, a careful examination of the samples, design, and findings of much of this work indicates little substance and highly exaggerated claims of success. Some argue that public education, considered by many to be America's most vital institution, has the most poorly trained teachers, poorest scholarship, and most politicized staff possible. Others reject this viewpoint, maintaining that America has the best public school system possible by far. Crawford contends that bilingual education contributes to that system.

Tongue Twister

Let us begin with what's regrettable about the victory of Proposition 227, the ballot initiative that will effectively end bilingual education in California public schools. As a general rule, statewide referenda are not the best means for making nuanced decisions about pedagogical policy. Once again, initiative-happy California voters have tied the hands of their policymakers, this time in a way that may also curtail the freedom of local school districts to respond flexibly to the challenges of teaching children with limited English skills. Among the options they might need is carefully designed bilingual education, which, in certain circumstances, may be the best way to involve some immigrant parents in the education of their kids or to meet the needs of a sudden influx of refugees. Under the new initiative, however, children with limited English will get no more than one year of what is called "sheltered English" instruction—in which they are taught mostly in English but the pace is gentler and the language used is simpler. Though the "sheltered English" method is untested as a means of moving large numbers of kids into mainstream classes, it is now the law.

Still, it might never have come to this if not for the intransigence of bilingual education's supporters. Proposition 227, for all its flaws, was provoked by the fact that, in recent years, bilingual education had acquired one of those halos of political virtue that made criticizing it—much less reforming it—a taboo for elected officials. "Since the seventies," writes Gregory Rodriguez, a research fellow at the Pepperdine Institute for Public Policy and an acute observer of Latino politics in California, "a mixture of blind faith and administrative arrogance had not only kept bilingual education afloat but made it unassailable." More and more, Rodriguez argues, the program was debated "in cultural rather than pedagogical terms."

For opponents, the idea that children of immigrants should receive up to several years of instruction in their native language, delaying their "mainstreaming" into English classes, was a blow to the American tradition of assimilation. For supporters, meanwhile, bilingual ed had become not so much a way of improving the educational prospects of children as a way of instilling a brand of ethnic pride that bordered on nationalism. As Rodriguez puts it: "Lost in this racialized hubbub was the only question that should have mattered: Is bilingual education helping or hurting limited-English speakers in U.S. public schools?"

And, while both sides in the debate sometimes assumed that most Latinos themselves wanted bilingual education as much as their ostensible leaders did, this assumption was unfounded. Though Prop 227 was written by Ron Unz, a Republican multimillionaire from Silicon Valley, he took his inspiration from a group of Mexican-American parents, most of them garment workers in downtown Los Angeles, who had decided that bilingual teaching was holding their children back and were engineering a boycott of it. "Parents do not want their children working in sweatshops or cleaning downtown office buildings when they grow up," Alice Callaghan, an Episcopal priest and community organizer who worked with the parents, told *The Boston Globe*. "They want them to get into Harvard and Stanford, and that won't happen unless they are truly fluent and literate in English." Polls taken before Tuesday's election indicated that anywhere between 30 and 60 percent of Latino voters in California approved of the measure. This was not the son of Proposition 187; Latino voters did not see it as another round of immigrant-bashing.

And they were right not to. After decades of research, there is no good evidence that bilingual education has been successful in meeting its original goal: helping students with limited English to master the language and to make it through school. In part, this is a function of inadequate research. Many of the relevant studies have simply been too tendentious in spirit and methodology to yield reliable results. A report released last year by the National Research Council concluded that most evaluations of bilingual education were not reliable. But, in part, it's because, at the broadest level, the results of the bilingual experiment have not been encouraging. Bilingual ed has done nothing to reverse the strikingly high dropout rate among Hispanics (17.9 percent for those born in the U.S. and 46.2 percent for immigrants compared to 12.2 percent for blacks and 8.6 percent for whites). Hispanic students in bilingual programs are no less likely to drop out than are those in English-only programs.

Moreover, although bilingual instruction may work for students who have just arrived in the U.S. with some experience of good schooling in their native countries, it doesn't seem to work at all for students who haven't had decent schooling. Nor does it seem to work for those who were born in the U.S. to parents who speak Spanish at home. As Charles L. Glenn, a professor of education policy at Boston University, told *The New York Times*: "Someone who plays soccer will learn to play American football faster than someone who has never played a sport. But that does not make it more efficient to teach soccer first if the goal is football. We should build on academic skills if a child already has them in another language, but we should not make developing new ones in that language a priority." And, at least one well-designed recent study has confirmed what many Latino parents have apparently begun to suspect—that bilingual schooling can actually impede social mobility. Two Mexican-American economists, Mark Lopez of the University of Maryland and Marie Mora of New Mexico State University, found that first- and second-generation

Latinos who went through bilingual ed earned significantly less in the job market than otherwise similar peers who got their instruction in English only.

It's time for a fundamental rethinking of bilingual education. With any luck, parents, teachers, and local legislators in other states will learn from California's experience and radically reform the program before somebody circulates a ballot initiative that takes the decision out of their hands altogether.

NO

James Crawford

Does Bilingual Ed Work?

Bilingual education is counterintuitive. Most people wonder: How could teaching students in their native tongue help them learn English?

Many assume the idea of bilingual education is to go easy on limited-English-proficient (LEP) children, to postpone the pain and confusion of acquiring a new language. They wonder if it wouldn't be better to teach the students English quickly—through "total immersion"—so they can get on with their schooling. Won't it lessen their motivation to learn by prolonging reliance on the first language?

Such attitudes sustained generations of "sink or swim" schooling. LEP students were placed in English-only classrooms, with no special help in learning the language and no access to the curriculum until they did so. Inevitably they fell behind English-speaking peers. Some caught up, but many failed and dropped out.

By the 1960s, a critical mass of educators and policymakers recognized the English-only approach was failing. Bilingual education seemed like a promising, if untested, alternative.

Three decades later, research has confirmed the wisdom of this view. Over the long term, programs that develop children's native-language skills show beneficial effects on their English-language development and overall academic achievement.

Yet skepticism persists. During the Proposition 227 campaign, journalists repeatedly asked: "If bilingual education is effective, why are language-minority students—Latinos in particular—continuing to fail and drop out at alarming rates?" There are several answers.

First, the shortage of trained staff has grown increasingly acute in states like California, where LEP enrollments have risen rapidly. As a result, well-designed bilingual programs have been provided to only a tiny minority of English learners.

Second, research shows that students drop out for many reasons. Those who received bilingual education are more likely to stay in school.

Finally, native-language instruction is hardly a panacea for the academic problems of Latino or Asian students—any more than it is for Anglo students. It

From James Crawford, "Does Bilingual Ed Work?" *Rethinking Schools*, vol. 13, no. 2 (Winter 1998/1999). Copyright © 1998 by James Crawford. Reprinted by permission. Notes omitted.

is merely one variable among many that determines the success or failure of an educational program.

Nevertheless, bilingual education can be a crucial variable for many students learning English. Stephen Krashen, a linguist at the University of Southern California, explains how it works: We acquire language by understanding messages, by obtaining *comprehensible input*. When we give children quality education in their primary language, we give them two things:

1. Knowledge, both general knowledge of the world and subject-matter knowledge, [which] helps make the English they hear more comprehensible. This results in more English acquisition. . . .
2. Literacy, which *transfers* across languages. Here is a simple, three-step argument: (1) We learn to read by reading, by making sense of what we see on the page. (2) If we learn to read by reading, it will be much easier to learn to read in a language we already understand. (3) Once you can read, you can read. The ability to read transfers across languages.

Thus, time spent studying in the native language is not time wasted in learning English. To the contrary, it supports English acquisition.

Like other researchers in the field, Krashen advocates English instruction from day one in bilingual programs, but at a level students can understand. Beginners acquire conversational English from hearing it used in simple, real-life contexts, such as music, art, and physical education.

Intermediate learners can benefit from "sheltered instruction" in English, lessons in science or social studies that are tailored to their level of second-language proficiency. Gradually, they acquire the complex English skills required to make a successful transition to the mainstream—typically by the fourth or fifth grade.

The key point is that language acquisition is a natural, developmental process that cannot be rushed. Indeed, placing children in incomprehensible classrooms and drilling them in meaningless exercises is likely to slow them down.

Still, hopes for a shortcut to English die hard—as shown by Californians' vote to mandate a one-year "English immersion" approach that has no support in educational research.

Critics say bilingual education has no support either, citing mixed results in program evaluation studies. It is true that such findings are less clear-cut than conclusions from basic research on second-language acquisition.

Scientific comparisons of program effectiveness, which must track student outcomes over several years and control for differences among experimental groups, are difficult to design and costly to execute. Relatively few such studies exist. The best examples, however, confirm hypotheses about the benefits of bilingual instruction.

Last year, using a sophisticated technique known as meta-analysis, a University of Texas study reviewed the scientific literature and found a small but significant edge for programs that used students' native language over those that did not. Researcher Jay Greene determined that the more rigorous the evaluation, the more support it provided for bilingual education. This was true even though many of the comparisons were short-term and little was known about program design.

The last large-scale evaluation, released by the U.S. Department of Education in 1991, took a more controlled approach. It compared the outcomes of three distinct program types: English-only immersion, quick-exit (transitional) bilingual education, and late-exit (developmental) bilingual education. Students' academic progress, charted in nine school districts over a four-year period, was most dramatic in the program that stressed fluent bilingualism. In the late-exit model, their achievement accelerated over time—almost catching up with that of English-speaking peers. In the other models, it leveled off well below national norms.

Wayne Thomas and Virginia Collier, of George Mason University, recently reported similar patterns in a larger group of school districts. They found that LEP children fared best in "two-way" bilingual programs, learning alongside English-speakers acquiring Spanish. Thus far, however, the researchers have released limited data to support their conclusions—an issue that critics have been quick to seize upon.

In 1997, the National Research Council condemned the "politicized" debate over language of instruction. It recommended greater emphasis on "finding a set of program components that works for the children in the community of interest, given the community's goals, demographics, and resources."

Nevertheless, the "what works" controversy is unlikely to subside anytime soon—at least not before policymakers support more extensive and rigorous studies comparing the range of program alternatives for LEP students.

POSTSCRIPT

Does Bilingual Education Harm Hispanic and Other Children?

Even as state legislatures curtail bilingual education programs, the controversy continues. One related issue that is not addressed by either the editors of *The New Republic* or Crawford is that of "diversity fatigue." Many people are exhausted by the many rapid changes that have been demanded to achieve multicultural diversity, which is compounded by the lack of proof that many are better off because of those changes. Many Americans also feel that if their ancestors survived and prospered without the aid of special programs such as bilingual education, then why do recent arrivals and their children need such consideration?

At the same time, however, the mass media and scholarly investigations routinely reveal the pervasiveness and depth of terrible discrimination and hurt to society's racial, ethnic, and gender minorities. Some suggest that even if bilingual education does not improve educational scores, the programs do help to reverse the years of humiliation and scorn that were built into early schooling (as well as other institutions). According to this view, this belated respect for the importance of others' languages and cultures in itself justifies the expense and controversy.

The literature on bilingual education and related topics has become a cottage industry. Among Crawford's contributions to the debate is *Bilingual Education: History, Politics, Theory, and Practice,* 4th ed. (Bilingual Education Services, 1998). Also, the journal *Rethinking Schools* frequently addresses this issue. See, for example, the special report on multiculturalism in the Fall 2000 issue, including Priscilla Pardini's "Down But Not Out."

A classic work on language codes as a function of group membership is *Pedagogy, Symbolic Control and Identity* by Basil Bernstein (Rowman & Littlefield, 2000). For a debate over the necessity of being bilingual in the field of journalism, see "Talking the Talk," by Gigi Anders, *American Journalism Review* (November 2000). A formal review of the literature that finds that bilingual education programs are helping is the Tomas Rivera Policy Institute report *A Meta-Analysis of the Effectiveness of Bilingual Education* by Jay P. Greene (March 2, 1998). A shorter debate on the issue is "Bilingual Education Fails Test, Exposing Deeper Problem" and "Bilingual Method Works," both in *USA Today* (August 28, 2000). An important study is Ronald Schmidt, Sr., *Language Policy and Identity Politics in the United States* (Temple University Press, 2000).

For a pointed attack on a collateral issue, see chapter 6, "African-American Self-Sabotage in Action: The Ebonics Controversy," of John McWhorter's book *Losing the Race: Self-Sabotage in Black America* (Free Press, 2000). Finally, among the many attacks on bilingual education are Sandra Stotsky's *Losing Our Language: How Multicultural Classroom Instruction Is Undermining Our Children's Ability to Read, Write and Reason* (Free Press, 1999) and John J. Miller's *The Unmaking of Americans: How Multiculturalism Has Undermined the Assimilation Ethic* (Free Press, 1998).

ISSUE 10

Are Arabs and Other Muslims Portrayed Unfairly in American Films?

YES: Jack G. Shaheen, from "We've Seen This Plot Too Many Times," *The Washington Post* (November 15, 1998)

NO: Lawrence Wright, from "Open Your Mind to the Movie We Made," *The Washington Post* (November 15, 1998)

ISSUE SUMMARY

YES: Author and *CBS News* consultant Jack G. Shaheen contends that Hollywood's long history of denigrating Arabs as villains and terrorists continues in the film *The Siege*. He maintains that portrayals of Arabs as thugs significantly increase attacks on Muslims in the United States.

NO: Lawrence Wright, a staff writer for the *New Yorker* and coauthor of *The Siege*, acknowledges that films in the past have portrayed minorities, including Arabs, unfairly. However, he asserts that the producers of *The Siege* were supportive of Arabs and that the movie's depiction of a heroic Muslim police officer as well as of dangerous, unfair treatment of Arabic Americans indicate that the movie was anything but denigrating.

The role of the mass media in creating misunderstandings, prejudice, and hate has long been noted by researchers. The epic 1915 film *Birth of a Nation*, which legitimized the emergence of the Ku Klux Klan as a necessary organization to control the "blood-thirsty" and "savage" former slaves in the South of the 1860s and 1870s is a notorious example. In the 1920s Hollywood films had an ambivalent relation with Arab stereotyping. For instance, the heartthrob of the silent film era, Rudolph Valentino, portrayed an Arab sheik waiting to snatch a blonde, white girl to carry her off to his tent to have his way with her. To some, such films were sexist, anti-Arab, and anti-foreigner. To others, they were great fun—just plain, old-fashioned make-believe entertainment.

Throughout the 1930s Hitler's minister of propaganda, Joseph Goebbels, raised films as avowed political propaganda to unprecedented levels. His productions effectively sold Germans the lies about *untermenschen* (inferior "races," such as Jews and Eastern Europeans). They also presented the Nazi leaders as God-like heroes whose only aim was to bring a pure German "race" to its rightful destiny. Many prominent individuals, both inside and outside of Germany, participated in this cinematic cultural carnage.

Critics argue that throughout its history, Hollywood has helped to maintain America's bigotry, if not to create it. Most minorities have been presented unfavorably as a group, and minority actors and actresses have been locked into demeaning roles, such as servants, half-wits, the "lovable oaf," and the butt of jokes. The early ritual of actors and actresses' being assigned new names was partly to eliminate foreign-sounding names that might offend theatergoers. Although some minority actors were allowed to maintain their original names (such as the Cuban Cesar Romero), they were almost always locked into roles as tokens.

To be fair, many important films have aimed to create understanding and tolerance, such as *Gentlemen's Agreement* (1947), which addressed religious discrimination. However, it seems fair to say that, until recently, much of Hollywood's thrust has been to maintain society's prejudices against minority groups in its hiring, casting, and story lines.

In the following selection, Jack G. Shaheen traces the celluloid depiction of Arabs since 1970 and finds that American movies, including the 1998 film *The Siege,* are full of anti-Muslim, anti-Arabic biases. In his rebuttal, Lawrence Wright contends that *The Siege* is quite different from traditional depictions of Arabic peoples for several reasons.

Much of Shaheen and Wright's disagreement reflects the difficulties of agreeing on what is meant by "negative portrayals." For example, some assert that the charges of racism that are currently being leveled against *Gone With the Wind* (1939) are highly chronocentric, or unfairly based on contemporary values. Some accuse the Black actresses and actors who starred in that film of selling out by playing roles that are demeaning to Blacks. Others counter that at least the film offered many jobs for Black actors. It is also argued that many of the Black characters in the film had dignity and decency, in contrast to the notorious white heroine, Scarlett O'Hara. Further controversy related to *Gone With the Wind* arose in early 2001, when a federal judge in Atlanta, Georgia, blocked from publication Alice Randall's parody of the book, entitled *The Wind Done Gone,* which is a retelling of the events from *Gone With the Wind* from a slave's perspective. Although the ruling was based on interpretations of copyright laws, some suggest that it is a reflection of the sensitivities of white southerners.

To many, the blanket dismissal of some films as racist or unfair can be based on misunderstanding or standards that distort reality instead of clarifying it. As you review the debate, relate the disagreements over *The Siege* and its treatment of the Arab characters—both terrorists (a few) and nonterrorists (the vast majority)—to other movies with which you are familiar. Are they unfair toward minorities? Are they unfairly criticized for their treatment of minorities?

Jack G. Shaheen
 **YES**

We've Seen This Plot Too Many Times

After all these years, Hollywood still doesn't get it. Since 1970, more than 300 major films have vilified Arabs. They have featured Arab curs drawing sabers ("Paradise"), abducting blondes ("Sahara"), buying America ("Network"), siding with the Nazis against Israel ("Exodus") and tossing bombs—even nuclear ones—at the West ("True Lies").

Now we have "The Siege," in which Arab terrorists methodically lay waste to Manhattan. The movie not only reinforces historically damaging stereotypes, but promotes a dangerously generalized portrayal of Arabs as rabidly anti-American.

I don't mean to deny or diminish the horror of recent acts of Arab terrorism, nor even to suggest that movies should exclude Arab terrorists from their stories. But it troubles me that almost *all* Hollywood stories about Arabs are about bad ones. History teaches painful lessons about how bigoted images such as these can tarnish our judgments of another culture.

I became involved with "The Siege" [in] March [1998] after a group of Muslim-American extras alerted the Council on Arab-Islamic Relations (CAIR) of the movie's focus. Because my specialty is analyzing stereotypical images of racial and ethnic groups—notably Arabs and Muslims—CAIR asked me to comment on the screenplay, which I read immediately.

The scenario troubled me profoundly. Arab immigrants, assisted by Arab-American auto mechanics, university students and even a college teacher, kill more than 700 innocent New Yorkers. The extremists blow up the city's FBI building, murdering scores of government agents; they blast theatergoers, and detonate a bomb in a crowded bus.

So, on April 2, accompanied by two CAIR officials, I met with director Edward Zwick and producer Lynda Obst. Given how vulnerable Arab and Muslim Americans are to defamation in the wake of recent violence, we wanted to know: Why single them out as terrorists? "The Siege" lumped our country's 6 million to 8 million hard-working and law abiding doctors, construction workers, police women and artists together with the lunatic fringe. And it failed to reflect the world's 1.1 billion Arabs and Muslims accurately. We reminded Zwick and Obst of a 1995 Los Angeles Times report, stating that of 171 people indicted in the United States for terrorism and related activities that year, just "6 percent were connected to Arab groups."

Zwick pointed out that he and Obst were willing to make minor changes, which—to their credit—they did. Dozens of offensive words and gratuitous scenes (such as a segment showing an Arab cab driver refusing to pick up an African-American FBI agent, portrayed by Denzel Washington) ended up on the cutting room floor as a result of our meeting.

But we could never agree on a major issue. Zwick argued that, because some scenes in the movie show innocent Arab Americans being tossed indiscriminately into detention centers, the film would make American moviegoers examine their reactions to terrorism, that it would "provoke thought." I countered that it was more likely to provoke violence: After seeing Arab thugs murder hundreds of New Yorkers, some viewers may think that Arab Americans belong in those camps. The film may be fiction, but the terrorists' on-screen killings take place in a real city, the Arabs are rounded up in Brooklyn, where many peace-loving Arab Americans reside.

Zwick argued that he had created a balance in the film, that actor Tony Shalhoub plays a decent Arab-American FBI agent. The director's token good guy reminded me of how film producers of the past tried to justify their hostile depiction of American Indians by pointing to Tonto in movies that focused on savage Indians massacring settlers.

In my opinion, minor edits would not suffice. Unless the major plot line linking religion—Muslims and Islamic prayers—with violence was changed, the film could advance hatreds, I felt. I offered possible alternatives, suggesting "The Siege" could work well if Arab-Muslim heavies were replaced with generic or multicultural terrorists. Why not making radical militia men or renegade military/government agents the villains?

Looking back now, I realize I was asking them to change the very essence of the film. It was a story about evil Arabs, and it was naive of me to think I might be able to get them to change that.

After our meeting, I reiterated my concerns to Obst and Zwick in three faxes. On April 30, Obst wrote CAIR, saying my story ideas were "impractical and frankly comical," and that my creative suggestions were "inappropriate," "border[ing] on sophistry." She pointed out that our viewpoints were at odds, saying "you [CAIR] are in the business of educating and enlightening, and we are in the business of storytelling." We do not have "a monolithic view of the Middle East," she wrote, nor do we have a "political agenda."

Obst may believe that, but not much has changed since movie mogul Darryl F. Zanuck declared in the 1940s that motion pictures are "the greatest political fact in the world today." The truth is that stereotypical images gain force by repetitive play. Film can be used as a powerful propaganda tool. Persisting in defiance of all evidence, movie images can affect the way people think and behave. You only have to look back to the way Jews were portrayed in Nazi-inspired German movies ("The Rothschilds' Shares in Waterloo" and "The Eternal Jew") to realize how effective the big screen can be in provoking hatred. Today, no other group is so flagrantly vilified by the film industry as Arabs. And, as Hollywood culture is the dominant culture, today's films are distributed in more than 100 countries worldwide.

Stereotypes do not exist in a vacuum. As Attorney General Janet Reno said to those attending an American-Arab anti-discrimination committee conference in Washington in June, "There is a direct link between false perceptions of the Arab American community and harassment." The most troubling examples of this followed the 1995 bombing of Oklahoma City's Alfred P. Murrah Federal Office Building, which killed 169 people. Speculative reporting encouraged, according to CAIR, more than 300 hate crimes against Arabs and Muslims in America. Several mosques were trashed around the country; community members received bomb threats; children were mocked at schools.

I am not suggesting that the cinema exclude portrayals of Arab terrorists. I am suggesting that Hollywood cease uniformly projecting Arabs and Muslims as having a monopoly on terrorism, that the industry being projecting them as they do other people—no better, no worse. The time is long overdue for Hollywood to end its undeclared war on Arabs and Muslims.

Open Your Mind to the Movie We Made

$\mathbf{A}$ll over the country, Muslims have been leafleting and protesting the opening of "The Siege," a movie I co-wrote (with Menno Meyjes and director Edward Zwick). The protesters assert that it perpetuates Hollywood stereotypes of Arabs as terrorists. They even say they will hold the filmmakers responsible for hate crimes that may be committed against Arab Americans because of the reaction to this movie.

Well, the protesters must be seeing a different movie than the one I see. I see a movie that takes as its subject the danger of stereotyping and scapegoating groups for the crimes of individuals. On one level, "The Siege" is a thriller. On another, it is a story of what we might do to our constitutional liberties if we reacted to terrorist threats with the same hair-trigger mentality that was evident, for instance, in the Waco catastrophe.

I can understand why the plot—which depicts the imposition of martial law, the suspension of civil rights and house-to-house searches for people of Arab descent who are then interned in detention camps—would frighten some Arab and Muslim citizens. Many of them thought that a similar contingency plan was prepared by the Department of Defense during the Gulf War. The movie is intended as a cautionary tale about what might happen in this country if terrorism were to escalate to the point that has already been reached in Israel, France and Great Britain. In such a scenario there is little doubt that we would be debating our responses for real, just as the movie causes us to debate them now, hypothetically.

I also see a movie that has an Arab-American hero in the character of Frank Haddad, an FBI agent, who is played by the Lebanese-American actor Tony Shalhoub. In all the talk about how Arabs are portrayed in this film, little is said about the fact that this is the first fully rounded, positive role for an Arab American in modern Hollywood history—maybe ever. Yes, he drinks and cusses, but he's not meant to be a paragon of Islamic virtue—he's a copy. He's also the only character in the movie whose family life, and to some extent his religious life, is approvingly explored. The anxiety, the torn loyalties, the weight of prejudice that are part of the daily experience of life in Muslim and Arab-American communities are embodied in the character of Frank Haddad.

But the critics of the movie want to make it pay for the sins of Hollywood's past. Those sins are mighty, no doubt. Hollywood has stereotyped Arabs in cartoonish movies simply because they make easily accepted villains. The filmmakers of "The Siege" went out of their way to make a movie that is not simplistic, but one that is grounded in the frightening reality of modern terrorism. Some of the people who are now criticizing the movie acted as advisers during the making of it; indeed, they had an unprecedented degree of access to the director and the producer, and many of their suggestions about the script and the characters were heeded. But in the end they wanted one change that the filmmakers would not accommodate: that the terrorists be made "generic"—i.e., something other than Arabs.

Frankly, this demand still distresses me. After the bombing of the World Trade Center, the subsequent trials of Sheik Omar Abdul Rahman and Ramzi Ahmed Yousef and other Islamic extremists, the destruction of two American embassies in Africa and the retaliatory U.S. strikes in Afghanistan and Sudan, it would be disingenuous to say that the United States is not engaged in a worldwide struggle against Arab terrorism. There are certainly other sources of terrorism within our own country, and it would be absurd to suggest that all Arabs are terrorists. Indeed, the whole point of the movie is to demonstrate that in overreacting to the crimes of a few, we may punish an innocent but vulnerable minority. This point is made so explicitly in the movie that the misreading of "The Siege" by its critics seems entirely willful.

Moreover, there is also a connection between terrorism and fundamentalist religious beliefs. I've explored this connection in religions other than Islam —most recently, in a New Yorker article ("Forcing the End," July 20) about evangelical American Christians, and Israeli ultra-Orthodox Jews who would like to blow up the mosques on top of the Haram al-Sharif, or Temple Mount, in Jerusalem. Islam has no monopoly on violence. The enemy is not Islam. It is fanaticism—in whatever religious guise it chooses to hide behind.

The critics have charged that "The Siege" is too real and too sophisticated for audiences to take on the level that it is intended. I admit that I, too, have been jarred by the coincidence of events in real life that seem shockingly similar to elements in the film. For instance, the opening sequence depicts the U.S. abduction of a sheik who is accused of sponsoring terrorism. Now we learn that the CIA had a similar plan to capture alleged terrorist godfather Osama bin Laden. Such eerie parallels are bound to resonate with anyone who reads the news.

The subject of terrorism is frightening precisely because we know how vulnerable we are. Terrorists have already changed our lives. We see the barricades around our monuments and public buildings. We read about the establishment of counterterrorist task forces in our major cities. The question is whether any serious movie can be made about this vital subject that does not invite the kind of campaign of vilification to which this movie has been subjected. The reason most Hollywood movies are so bland or cartoonish is that they steer away from controversy. And yet movies that draw deep from the well of reality can do us the favor of approximating actual experience. They allow us as a society to address questions about ourselves that we hope we don't ever have to face in real life.

The very act of posing these questions in a genuine and hard-edged drama is one of the highest callings of art. Even the critics would have to admit that this movie has opened a debate—more than one, in fact—about how Arabs are treated in America, about the danger terrorism poses to our civil liberties, about the connection between violence and fundamentalism, and finally about what kind of country we might become in the post-Cold War world. The question that the movie asks is: How do we avoid becoming the enemy we are fighting against?

POSTSCRIPT

Are Arabs and Other Muslims Portrayed Unfairly in American Films?

$\mathbf{A}$s both authors indicate, the United States had been extremely lucky until recently in that it had been relatively free of the pains of terrorism, unlike many other nations. Prior to the 1993 bombing of the World Trade Center, Americans could only imagine what terrorists on a large scale looked like when operating in the United States. For many Americans, political cartoon depictions of Palestine Liberation Organization chairman Yasser Arafat before he was redefined as an acceptable Arabic statesman provided their only perception of Arab or terrorist leaders. The fact that such mental baggage was inaccurate mattered little.

Because of the World Trade Center bombing and the destruction of a federal office building in Oklahoma City in 1995, massive effects of terrorism are no longer a Hollywood fiction. The World Trade Center bombing was apparently done by Arabs, which resulted in many members of this minority being attacked throughout the United States. Immediately after the Oklahoma City bombing, Muslims were again attacked. As Attorney General Janet Reno warned, "There is a direct link between false perceptions of the Arab American community and harrassment."

It might be expected that anti-Arab sentiments in Hollywood films would expand even more after the bombings. However, it was quickly discovered that the bombers of the federal building were working-class, right-wing Americans. Wright maintains that he and others' purpose in making *The Siege* was to warn Americans of the dangers of overreacting to anti-Arab sentiments. He points out that the Arab American FBI agent is depicted as a hero, and he cites the moving account of Arab citizens' being confined to concentration camps. Shaheen insists that the overall thrust of this and other movies is to depict Arabs unfairly and inaccurately.

Neither protagonist seems to consider the broader issue that even if a film is grossly unfair in its treatment of minorities, should it be censored? Does expanding the definition of and laws against hate crimes to include one-sided treatments of minorities in films risk preventing potentially important ideas from being shown? Should the artistic merits of *The Siege* and other controversial films be completely neglected in favor of debating its ideological position?

Shaheen argues that films dealing with terrorism should portray the terrorists as a multicultural, ethnically, racially, and gender diversified sort of UN. Does such a recommendation have merit? Is the fact that a scene showing an

Arab taxicab driver refusing to pick up a Black man was cut from *The Siege* ostensibly because it might inflame Black-Arab relations be a cause to celebrate? Or should this act be condemned as racist because it denies the fact that many Black males are ignored by taxi drivers of many different nationalities?

Does *The Siege* fairly present many different aspects of modern life, including some of the great strengths of Muslims? If, as Shaheen insists, it hurts innocent Arabs and other Muslims, what, if anything, should be done to punish the film's producers? How could Hollywood minimize the chances of this happening again? Would the advantages of keeping all material that might be offensive to minorities out of films equal the potential disadvantages?

For a biting attack on Muslim Americans' claims of unfair treatment, see D. Pipes, "Are Muslim Americans Victimized?" *Commentary* (November 2000). For opposing perspectives reflecting the difficulties that Muslim Americans face as a consequence of the Israeli-Arab conflict in the Middle East, see "Torn Between Two Worlds," by L. Ali, *Newsweek* (November 27, 2000) and "On Becoming an Arab," by L. Ahmed, *Boston Review* (February/March 1999).

Shaheen further addresses the issue in *Arab and Muslim Stereotyping in American Popular Culture* (Georgetown University Press, 1997). A book that is critical of Muslim sociological scholarship is *Arab World: Questions From Arab Societies* edited by Abdelkader Zghal and Ahmed Iadh Ouederni (International Sociological Association, 1998). An excellent reader on media stereotyping of minorities is Coramae Richey Mann and Marjorie S. Zata, eds., *Images of Color, Images of Crime* (Roxbury, 1998).

An interesting take on the issue from the perspective of Muslim travelers to the United States can be found in *America in an Arab Mirror: Images of America in Arabic Travel Literature: An Anthology, 1895–1995* translated and edited by Kamal Abdel-Malek (St. Martin's Press, 2000). A helpful book that considers the 85 percent of the Muslim population that resides outside the Arab world, including those in the United States, is *Islam Outside the Arab World* edited by David Westerlund and Ingvar Svanberg (St. Martin's Press, 1999). Finally, for discussions of how others are treated by Hollywood, see "On Sports and on Screen, the British Don't Get No Respect," by S. Lyall, *The New York Times* (July 2, 2000) and *Hollywood and Anti-Semitism: A Cultural History, 1880–1941* by Steven Alan Carr (Cambridge University Press, 2001).

On the Internet . . .

Immigration, Racism, and Leadership

The Brookings Institution presents this April 2001 report on current Black/non-Black segregation levels, authored by Edward L. Glaeser and Jacob L. Vigdor.

http://www.brook.edu/es/urban/census/glaeserexsum.htm

In Focus: The Immigration Debate

This discussion of the immigration debate is part of U.S. Foreign Policy in Focus: A Project of the Institute for Policy Studies and the Interhemispheric Resource Center. It includes sources for more information, including organizations, publications, and Web links.

http://immigration.about.com/gi/dynamic/offsite.
htm?site=http%3A%2F%2Fwww.theodora.com%2Fdebate.html

What Is Environmental Justice & Environmental Racism?

This resource offers definitions and readings on environmental justice and racism.

http://www.ejnet.org/ej/

Black Leadership Forum, Inc.

The mission of the Black Leadership Forum is to promote creative and coordinated Black leadership, diverse in its membership but clear on its priority: the empowerment of African Americans to improve their own lives and to expand their opportunities to fully participate in American social, economic, and political life.

http://www.blackleadershipforum.org

PART 3

Immigration, Racism, and Leadership

*T*he world's population has changed dramatically in the past dozen years, as people have been displaced by wars, upheavals, and migrations. The United States, however, remains the world's foremost nation of immigrants. Yet the melting pot success story of America is rarely told today without frequent qualification. Some maintain that not only have African Americans not been allowed to assimilate but they and other minorities should be discouraged from making assimilation their goal at all. Minorities are encouraged to maintain their own ethnic and racial cultural identities. Others maintain that pluralism, assimilation, and integration are preferable to the alternatives: separation, balkanization, imperialism, and even genocide. Has the road toward integration in the United States become so bumpy that it should be abandoned? Has any other nation been as just to as many diverse peoples? Are minorities being unfairly subjected to toxic atmospheres and living areas? And are minority leaders, like many majority ones, living off their constituents instead of for them? These questions are addressed in this section.

- Is Racial Segregation Necessarily Bad?

- Is Immigration a Problem in the United States?

- Does Environmental Racism Exist?

- Are Black Leaders Part of the Problem?

ISSUE 11

Is Racial Segregation Necessarily Bad?

YES: Paul Ruffins, from "Segregation Is a Sign of Failure," *Crisis* (December/January 1998)

NO: Glenn C. Loury, from "Integration Is Yesterday's Struggle," *Crisis* (December/January 1998)

ISSUE SUMMARY

YES: Paul Ruffins, executive editor of *Crisis,* identifies three arguments supporting school segregation in the 1990s: it is possible to make separate equal, court decisions make further integration impossible, and segregation does not really harm anyone. He rejects these arguments and asserts that efforts to achieve school integration should be increased.

NO: Glenn C. Loury, director of the Institute on Race and Social Division at Boston University, contends that school racial integration is an untenable goal because schools are more segregated now than they were 30 years ago, the courts and public sentiment no longer support school busing, and enforced integration implies Black inferiority. It is better, he says, to increase support services in the schools.

In *Plessey v. Ferguson* (1896) the Supreme Court upheld the right of states to create and maintain racial segregation in virtually all areas of public life, including restaurants, theaters, public transportation, parks and recreation facilities, jobs, and schools. The stipulation for the latter was that schools could be segregated if they were "separate but equal." In parts of the deep South, this served to legitimate all but a return to the pre–Civil War status of Blacks as slaves. It certainly allowed passage of the notorious Jim Crow laws in the 1870s and 1880s, which banned Blacks from almost all public interactions with whites.

The Jim Crow laws denied most Blacks constitutional rights as U.S. citizens. The forced separation was not only insulting, but it greatly hampered the newly freed slaves and their children from participating in American life and from gaining the knowledge and skills needed to compete in a rapidly developing industrial society. "Colored schools," as they came to be known, were almost never "equal" to white schools. When they had books and other supplies at all, they were dated hand-me-downs from white schools. Black teachers' salaries and standards were usually far less than those of white teachers. Later in the twentieth century, Black youngsters (and sometimes whites as well) were bused—in some cases many miles away from home—so they could attend segregated schools. Much later in the 1970s, defenders of school busing to achieve integration pointed this out.

In 1910 the National Association for the Advancement of Colored People (NAACP) was founded. It, along with other African American organizations, was intent on overthrowing racial segregation. When this practice was in full force, there was little doubt among most Black people that it was horrible. Yet through phenomenal fortitude and perseverance, Blacks survived. Many talented, creative, and prominent Americans were a product of segregated schools: W. E. B. Du Bois, Paul Dunbar, Paul Robeson, Ralph Bunche, Martin Luther King, Thurgood Marshall, and countless others. For Black professionals, one of the few avenues of vertical mobility was in becoming a teacher. Although teachers' salaries were low, Blacks were able to achieve respect in the Black community and sometimes among whites as well.

Throughout the 1930s and 1940s the NAACP—especially its legal defense branch, which was headed by the young attorney Thurgood Marshall—zealously pursued the goal of eliminating legal racial segregation, especially in schools. Marshall's strategy was to whittle away at racial segregation. At first, segregation in southern law schools and other professional schools was overthrown through several brilliant court cases. Eventually, university segregation was overturned, and in 1954 the "big one" was finally fought out: *Brown v. Board of Education of Topeka, Kansas*. The justices ruled in that case that enforced racial segregation was liable "to do irreparable harm" to Black children. Although entrenched southern politicians and white racists began a campaign of "massive resistance" and other strategies, both peaceful and extremely violent, the writing was on the wall: victory had finally been achieved.

School desegregation, however, was never really achieved in most of the United States. Initially, after legal resistance had ended for the most part, white children were sent to private schools. This was quickly supplemented by massive "white flight" from America's cities. There is now far more racial segregation than there was in 1970.

In the recent past, even a hint of abandoning the goal of racial integration was anathama to traditional Black leaders. Indeed, the head of an NAACP chapter in North Carolina was instantly terminated when he called for a return to segregation. Naturally, there have always been Black leaders who objected to the goal of integration as demeaning for Blacks. However, until recently, most Blacks rejected segregation.

The current social, economic, political, and educational situations seem to demand an abandonment of the former goal. Note the many reasons that Paul Ruffins gives in the following selection for rejecting racial segregation. Consider if his delineation of what he considers to be three myths is accurate. Note the reasons why Glenn C. Loury defends segregation in the second selection.

Paul Ruffins  **YES**

Segregation Is a Sign of Failure

In recent years, America's public schools have become more, rather than less segregated. This has painfully frustrated those who fought segregation in the belief that integrated schools were the basis of a tolerant, multi-cultural society. Because integration has not been easy, even some African Americans now argue that civil rights organizations should abandon desegregation cases, and no longer advocate busing black children to better schools in white neighborhoods, or support constructing magnet programs to draw white students back into public schools. Instead, they argue, we should focus on the "real issue" of getting black children more resources. This thinking is based on erroneous myths about how social and educational integration actually works.

Myth One: It is possible to make separate equal.

There is no contradiction between fighting to improve schools that are predominantly black or Latino, and also striving for social and racial integration. However, there are just some things that can not be learned in segregated environments. One can teach basic math in an all-black setting. However, you can't give black or Latino students confidence that they can learn calculus as fast as Asian or Jewish kids if they have never tested their skills against kids from other backgrounds.

More importantly, it is naive to think that white, or even middle-class black citizens will be willing to provide a high level of resources to a school system where there are few if any white or middle class students. As Elaine Jones of the NAACP Legal Defense Fund Points out, "In Kansas City, Missouri, from almost the precise moment the school district became majority black, the majority white electorate consistently voted against bond issues and tax levies, precipitating a catastrophic decline in the capital and educational resources of the school district." This has happened again and again as conservatives move to reduce local property taxes.

According to Gary Orfield, who ran the Harvard Project on School Segregation, separate is unlikely to ever be equal because the most important predictors of academic achievement are not school-related variables, such as class size, but family, parental and student variables.

In schools with large concentrations of poor students, it is virtually impossible to supply small enough classes or good enough teachers to make up for the lack of educated parents or stable families. If majority-black cities like Detroit, Washington D.C. or Newark could have provided high enough levels of resources to make segregated, high-poverty schools work, they would have done so. One of the reasons they can't is because they lost their tax bases as the middle class fled to the suburbs.

This is why busing is an economically efficient tool for increasing the academic achievement of black students. For example, for the price of a bus ride a student can receive the invaluable experience of attending a school where most kids plan to attend college.

Myth Two: After the Supreme Court's Milliken vs Bradley *decision preventing city suburban busing, further integration is virtually impossible.*

This myth is based on several false assumptions. One is that the Supreme Court will never reverse itself and require busing across city lines. The *Brown* decision itself was a reversal of earlier thinking. The court can change its mind.

Another assumption is that the boundaries between city and suburban school districts are unchangeable. In some parts of the country, such as North Carolina and Tennessee, the trend is toward merging smaller districts into county-wide school systems to increase efficiency. Nearly 20 states have court cases calling for statewide funding, creating the real potential that city/suburban boundaries may be re-drawn.

The final false assumption is there can't be any meaningful progress on integration because white students are too small a percentage of the public school population. In Boston, white students may only be 18% of the public school students, but this does not mean they only make up 18% of the school-age children. If school reform succeeds, there are many non-racist parents who would prefer to bring their children and their energies back to public schools rather than pay to send their children to private schools.

Social integration is also not limited to black and white. The key may be to entice middle-class African-American, Asian and Hispanic parents to return to the public schools to restore family stability and cultural diversity.

Finally, there is value in holding on to federal desegregation orders, even in places like Prince George's County, Maryland, where the schools are now 75% African-American. Desegregation orders don't just mandate busing. They also help to prevent discrimination against black teachers and staff, and ensure equitable funding.

Myth Three: As long as it isn't forced, segregation doesn't really hurt anyone.

In virtually every case, increasing segregation has had a terrible effect on black students, leaving them more ghettoized and marginalized than ever before. However, recent ecological research is beginning to show that even "voluntary residential segregation" is having a terrible effect on white citizens and on the physical environment. Another word for white (and often black) flight out of the cities is suburban sprawl, which is paving over farms and woodlands as Americans try to run from, rather than solve, their urban and racial problems. Many families feel severe strain as a result of having to own, insure and maintain two or more cars, and drive several hours to work each day.

Segregation is a sign that Americans have failed to complete the hard work of creating a society where a diverse population can live comfortably side by side. If we don't face this problem soon, we'll run out of places to run to.

NO

Glenn C. Loury

Integration Is Yesterday's Struggle

A report of the Harvard Project on School Desegregation issued [recently] found that racial segregation in the nation's public schools has increased steadily over the last 15 years to a level greater than at any time since the 1971 Supreme Court decision in *Swann v. Charlotte-Mecklenburg Board of Education,* which authorized "forced busing" to achieve racial balance. This development has alarmed many in the civil rights community who worry that this increasing racial isolation portends disaster for the black community. I believe those concerns are misplaced.

This is not to say that all is well with the education of African American youngsters. For example, the National Assessment of Educational Progress, a comprehensive effort to test the knowledge of a representative national sample of primary and secondary school students, has revealed a widening gap between the educational achievements of white and black students over the past decade. But while great disparities do exist in the quality of public education—black and Latino students in central cities are especially poorly served—a renewed emphasis on racial integration is the wrong response. Achieving true equality of opportunity for the poorest public school students means securing for them better teachers, smaller class sizes, longer school hours and greater support services in the schools they attend. If these things can be achieved, our youngsters will do well, whatever the racial composition of their schools.

In any event, both the Supreme Court and the American people have shown little enthusiasm for open-ended judicial intervention aimed at securing racial balance. The Court's opinion in the 1995 case *Missouri v. Jenkins,* for example, reversed a lower court's order that Kansas City undertake an expensive plan to attract suburban whites to an increasingly black, inner-city district through specialized "magnet schools." Indeed, Federal courts around the country—especially in the South—have relaxed earlier decrees ordering school districts to promote integration, even though those districts have been moving toward resegregation.

I am not arguing that these cases were rightly decided in every instance. What is clear, however, is that it would be unwise to expect a revival of 1970s-style judicial activism on behalf of the cause of integration. Moreover, the flight of white middle-class families from urban districts subject to desegregation decrees has made it all but impossible to achieve anything beyond token integration in many places.

Thus, in 1972, before court-ordered busing began, 60 percent of Boston's public school students were white. Although the courts have been more flexible about integration efforts in recent years, only 18 percent of the students in this struggling school system now are white. Denver, Norfolk, Va., and Savannah, Ga., which were subject to mandatory busing, have also seen white enrollment decline, reflecting the decisions of white parents to live in suburban communities or to send their children to private schools. Such decisions are a stubborn reality, restricting the prospects that judicial mandates can much increase the extent of racial mixing in the schools. The Supreme Court's decision some twenty years ago in *Milliken v. Bradley,* put sharp limits on the ability of federal courts to use metropolitan-wide, cross-district busing plans to promote integration.

Of course, no public school district should discriminate on the basis of race, or actively promote racial segregation. But in the many districts where most students are non-white, it has long made more sense to address those students' educational needs directly, rather than to spend scarce resources trying to get white families to send their children to the same schools as minorities.

Many non-white parents are more concerned about the quality of their children's schools than about racial balance for its own sake. All parents want basically the same things from public schools: safety, order, and the teaching of solid academic skills. Regardless of racial composition, schools that deliver these things will be judged successful.

Also, a compulsive focus on racial integration can involve condescension (no doubt unintended) toward non-white students and their families. Justice Clarence Thomas put it well in his concurring opinion in *Missouri v. Jenkins:* "It never ceases to amaze me that the courts are so willing to assume that anything that is predominantly black must be inferior." The belief that "black students suffer an unspecified psychological harm from segregation that retards their mental and educational development," Justice Thomas said, rests on an assumption of black inferiority. This echoes something W.E.B. DuBois once wrote in the pages of *The Crisis* over a half-century ago: "Never in the world should our fight be against association with ourselves because by that very token we give up the whole argument that we are worth associating with."

To presume that blacks must have a sufficient quota of whites in the classroom in order to learn, is to presume that there is something inherently wrong with blacks. But while black kids may not need to have whites sitting nearby in order to master arithmetic, the most disadvantaged children do need better schools, with resources sufficient to compensate for the influences of poverty they bring to the classroom. Integrationists assume that the presence of whites is the only sure way to draw attention to this need. But that was yesterday's struggle.

Advocates of the interests of African-American youngsters should focus on achieving equal educational opportunity, but not by forced racial mixing. Instead, we must demand that students isolated in hard-pressed, big-city school districts receive the attention and resources which, as Americans, they so richly deserve.

POSTSCRIPT

Is Racial Segregation Necessarily Bad?

Ruffins contends that separate but equal is impossible because, among other reasons, whites will somehow shortchange Black schools as they have in the past. If economic equity could be rigorously maintained (equal budgets), would school segregation be desirable? Neither Ruffins nor Loury discuss schools that are both racially and gender-segregated, such as programs in which young Black males are taught only by Black male teachers. Are such programs a good idea? Do females, either Black or white, necessarily do a less effective job teaching Black males?

Ruffins bases much of his argument around school busing, which he feels is effective and should be resumed. He also argues for elimination of school boundaries between cities and counties. What objections might parents, either Black or white, have to these proposals? Both Loury and Ruffins seem critical of parents who flee the inner cities or place their children in private schools. However, should any society ever be expected to gamble with its children's lives in order to benefit one group or even future generations?

How might broader issues, such as the AIDS epidemic among Black Americans, the high rate of female-headed households, high rates of violent crime, high dropout rates, and high unemployment rates, be tied into the issue of school segregation? Do these and other conditions say more about American society than people may be willing to face? Could the school segregation issue be dismissed as a dangerous smoke screen to deflect public concerns away from the continued pervasiveness of racism and inequality?

Neither Ruffins nor Loury considers the widely discussed partial solution of school privatization or school vouchers. Both embrace the idea that pumping more dollars into needy schools will alleviate the problem. Is this accurate? Some Black parents are calling for a voucher system that would allow them to send their children to the schools of their choice. Is this a better idea than abandoning integration?

Three excellent works that provide useful background information are *Brown v. Board of Education: A Civil Rights Milestone and Its Troubled Legacy* by James T. Patterson (Oxford University Press, 2001); William H. Watkins, James H. Lewis, and Victoria Chou, *Race and Education: The Roles of History and Society in Educating African American Students* (Allyn & Bacon, 2001); and *The Unsteady March: The Rise and Decline of Racial Equality in America* by Philip A. Klinkner with Rogers M. Smith (University of Chicago Press, 1999). A broader global perspective on the effects of education on democracies is *Democracy, Authoritarianism and Education: A Cross-National Empirical Survey* by Russell F. Farner and Jos D. Meloen (St. Martin's Press, 2000).

Additional readings on the topic of segregation are NAACP head Kweisi Mfume's "We Demand a Fully Integrated Society," *Crisis* (October 1997); *Dismantling Desegregation: The Quiet Reversal of Brown v. Board of Education* by Gary Orfield, Susan E. Eaton, and the Harvard Project on School Desegregation (New Press, 1997); and C. Canady, "America's Struggle for Racial Equality," *Public Policy* (January/February 1999). An interesting case study of a specific school system's efforts to reverse the resegregation trend is "Remedies to De Facto School Segregation: The Case of Hartford," by Monte Piliawsky, *Black Scholar* (Summer 1998). Conservative M. Lind takes a liberal position in "Race and Reason: Moving Beyond Demagogues Toward a Color-Blind Society," *The Washington Monthly* (May 1998).

For a broad discussion of racial segregation, see former U.S. secretary of education Lamar Alexander's "Created Equal: The Principles of Racial Reconciliation," *Policy Review* (November/December 1998). Among the growing number of books written by and about successful Black families whose education enabled them to partially transcend racism is *Our Kind of People: Inside America's Black Upper Class* by Lawrence Graham (HarperCollins, 1999). For a discussion of continued segregation in colleges, see "Segregation Continues in Southern Colleges," *Society* (November/December 1998). A moving account of the courageous efforts to end segregation by Black leaders is *Walking With the Wind: A Memoir of the Movement* by John Lewis and Michael D'Orso (Simon & Schuster, 1998). An account of efforts to maintain segregation is Grace Elizabeth Hale's *Making Whiteness: The Culture of Segregation in the South, 1890–1940* (Pantheon, 1998).

Two controversial books that blame African American school problems on an alleged anti-intellectual subculture among many Black students and educators are John H. McWhorter, *Losing the Race: Self-Sabotage in Black America* (Free Press, 2000) and Larry Elder, *The Ten Things You Can't Say in America* (St. Martin's Press, 2000). An interesting gender-based discussion of segregation is *For Girls Only: Making a Case for Single-Sex Schooling* by Janice L. Streitmatter (State University of New York Press, 1999). A discussion of an innovative teaching tactic can be found in "Understanding Racial Inequality and Segregation Through a Virtual Laboratory," by M. Rich, *ASA Footnotes* (April 2001). A particularly contentious book is *By the Color of Our Skin: The Illusion of Integration and the Reality of Race* by Leonard Steinhorn and Barbara Diggs Brown (Dutton, 1999). Finally, see "Segregation Still Touches Minorities Where They Live," by H. Nasser, *The Washington Times* (April 4, 2001) and the November/December 1999 issue of *Poverty and Race,* which features several articles dealing with the topic "Is Integration Possible?"

ISSUE 12

Is Immigration a Problem
in the United States?

YES: Peter Brimelow, from *Alien Nation: Common Sense About America's Immigration Disaster* (Random House, 1995)

NO: David Cole, from "The New Know-Nothingism: Five Myths About Immigration," *The Nation* (October 17, 1994)

ISSUE SUMMARY

YES: Peter Brimelow, senior editor of *Forbes* and *National Review*, links the recent increase in immigration to many of America's major problems, including crises in health care, education, and pollution, and the potential loss of American identity.

NO: David Cole, a professor at the Georgetown University Law Center, maintains that, throughout history, immigrants to the United States have been poor, culturally different, and perceived as a threat by U.S. citizens and that these perceptions obscure reason and fairness. He refutes what he considers to be myths about immigrants to show that these people are beneficial to America.

It remains a paradox that both statistically and culturally, the United States is almost exclusively dominated by descendants of immigrants (most within the past 100 years) but that the country has always had significant problems accepting "outsiders." In the mid-1800s, for example, the Know-Nothing party, which was composed of Americans who felt that the influx of Germans and Irish was ruining the country's stock, emerged to fight for rigid restrictions on U.S. immigration laws. Established Americans despised these immigrants not only because they were foreign but also because their loyalty to Catholicism threatened the country's mostly Protestant ways. Prejudice toward these people was evident well into the twentieth century, as many factories announced that "Irish need not apply" in their help wanted advertisements and some rooming houses and restaurants refused service to Irish people.

Starting in the 1840s much of the worry was focused on the Chinese, whose opium dens, alleged low regard for human life, and general "mental and moral inferiority" were perceived as a threat to the United States. Many Asian immigrants in California and parts of the Southwest were beaten and lynched, often for no other reason than that they were different.

In spite of such ignorance and bigotry, many sociologists observe that during these times of immigration, *in general* America was a melting pot. Most ethnic groups eventually assimilated into the "American" way of life. Historically, this has been the avowed aim of most immigrants to the United States. Indeed, at least in terms of the Irish, the election of John F. Kennedy to the presidency in 1960 represented full inclusion into American society. By the 1960s scholars were predicting that it was just a matter of time before most, if not all, minorities would be accepted, at least symbolically.

The civil rights movement in the 1960s, through affirmative action, often emphasized group entitlements as much as individual rights. This, coupled with the dramatic drop in immigrants from Europe, led many commentators to conclude that pluralism, not assimilation, reflected changing immigration realities. Ideologically, these attitudes were reinforced by multiculturalists, who insisted that expecting others to "melt" into the majority culture was elitist and racist. These critics argued that all groups should maintain their own cultural identities and reside as "equals with differences." Current debates over bilingual education reflect the strength of this aspect of the controversy.

The complexion of U.S. immigrants is clearly changing. Between 1900 and 1920 Europeans constituted 85 percent of all newcomers. According to the U.S. Immigration and Naturalization Service, in the past 15 years 84 percent of new immigrants were Hispanics and Asians. The composition is changing in other ways too. In 1996, for example, more than 140,000 of the approximately 915,000 immigrants to the United States were political and humanitarian refugees. Recent court cases have allowed women from African and Muslim countries who were fleeing ritual female genital mutilation to obtain asylum. The United States receives about half of all immigrants to developed nations.

In the following selections, Peter Brimelow argues that trends in immigration pose a problem to the United States. He suggests that most Americans disagree with liberal immigration policies and that these policies must be radically revised to reduce the number of annual immigrants and to retain a distinctly American culture. David Cole asserts that the current negativity toward immigration is an instance of history repeating itself. He maintains that not only are liberal U.S. immigration policies just but they actually help the economy and reduce other problems.

As you compare these two points of view, consider what statistics both authors cite and what interpretations they make. What practical impacts would Brimelow's concept of a new, anti-immigration society have on the United States? Are the five myths of immigration that Cole repudiates relevant to the overall issue? Is immigration a problem in the United States? In what ways might it be hurting or helping America? In debating this issue, should all immigrants be considered the same? Or are some more helpful or harmful than others? Last, consider the drastically different emigration patterns that are rapidly unfolding in central Europe, the Middle East, and parts of Africa and Asia as a consequence of ethnic conflict or genocide. Are these problems similar to those addressed in this issue?

Peter Brimelow

 **YES**

Immigration: Dissolving the People

There is a sense in which current immigration policy is Adolf Hitler's posthumous revenge on America. The U.S. political elite emerged from the war passionately concerned to cleanse itself from all taints of racism or xenophobia. Eventually, it enacted the epochal Immigration Act (technically, the Immigration and Nationality Act Amendments) of 1965.

And this, quite accidentally, triggered a renewed mass immigration, so huge and so systematically different from anything that had gone before as to transform—and ultimately, perhaps, even to destroy—the one unquestioned victor of World War II: the American nation, as it had evolved by the middle of the 20th century.

Today, U.S. government policy is literally dissolving the people and electing a new one. You can be for this or you can be against it. But the fact is undeniable.

"Still," *Time* magazine wrote in its fall 1993 "Special Issue on Multiculturalism," "for the first time in its history, the U.S. has an immigration policy that, for better or worse, is truly democratic."

As an immigrant, albeit one who came here rather earlier than yesterday and is now an American citizen, I find myself asking with fascination: What can this possibly mean? American immigration policy has always been democratic, of course, in the sense that it has been made through democratic procedures. Right now, as a matter of fact, it's unusually undemocratic, in the sense that Americans have told pollsters long and loudly that they don't want any more immigration; but the politicians ignore them.

The mass immigration so thoughtlessly triggered in 1965 risks making America an alien nation—not merely in the sense that the numbers of aliens in the nation are rising to levels last seen in the 19th century; not merely in the sense that America will become a freak among the world's nations because of the unprecedented demographic mutation it is inflicting on itself; not merely in the sense that Americans themselves will become alien to each other, requiring an increasingly strained government to arbitrate between them; but, ultimately, in the sense that Americans will no longer share in common what Abraham Lincoln called in his first inaugural address "the mystic chords of memory, stretching from every battlefield and patriotic grave, to every living heart and hearth stone, all over this broad land."

Alexander James Frank Brimelow is an American, although I was still a British subject and his mother a Canadian when he shot into the New York delivery room, yelling indignantly, one summer dawn in 1991. This is because of the 14th Amendment to the U.S. Constitution. It states in part:

"All persons born or naturalized in the United States, and subject to the jurisdiction thereof, are citizens of the United States and of the State wherein they reside."

The 14th Amendment was passed after the Civil War in an attempt to stop Southern states denying their newly freed slaves the full rights of citizens. But the wording is general. So it has been interpreted to mean that any child born in the United States is automatically a citizen. Even if its mother is a foreigner. Even if she's just passing through.

I am delighted that Alexander is an American. However, I do feel slightly, well, guilty that his fellow Americans had so little choice in the matter.

But at least Maggy and I had applied for and been granted legal permission to live in the United States. There are currently an estimated 3.5 million to 4 million foreigners who have just arrived and settled here in defiance of American law. When these illegal immigrants have children in the United States, why, those children are automatically American citizens too.

And right now, two-thirds of births in Los Angeles County hospitals are to illegal-immigrant mothers.

All of which is just another example of one of my central themes:

The United States has lost control of its borders—in every sense. A series of institutional accidents, of which birthright citizenship is just one, has essentially robbed Americans of the power to determine who, and how many, can enter their national family, make claims on it—and exert power over it.

In 1991, the year of Alexander's birth, the Immigration and Naturalization Service reported a total of over 1.8 million legal immigrants. That was easily a record. It exceeded by almost a third the previous peak of almost 1.3 million, reached 84 years earlier at the height of the first great wave of immigration, which peaked just after the turn of the century.

The United States has been engulfed by what seems likely to be the greatest wave of immigration it has ever faced. The INS [Immigration and Naturalization Service] estimates that 12 million to 13 million legal and illegal immigrants will enter the United States during the 1990s. The Washington, D.C.-based Federation for American Immigration Reform (FAIR), among the most prominent of the groups critical of immigration policy, thinks the total will range between 10 million and 15 million.

It's not just illegal immigration that is out of control. So is legal immigration. U.S. law in effect treats immigration as a sort of imitation civil right, extended to an indefinite group of foreigners who have been selected arbitrarily and with no regard to American interests.

The American immigration debate has been a one-way street. Criticism of immigration, and news that might support it, just tends not to get through.

For example, the United States is in the midst of a serious crime epidemic. Yet almost no Americans are aware that aliens make up one-quarter of the prisoners in federal penitentiaries—almost three times their proportion in the population at large.

Indeed, many problems that currently preoccupy Americans have an unspoken immigration dimension.

Two further instances:

- The health care crisis. Americans have been told repeatedly that some 30 million to 40 million people in the country have no health insurance at any one point in time. Typically, nobody seems to know how many are immigrants. But immigrants certainly make up a disproportionate share—particularly of the real problem: the much smaller hard core, perhaps 6 million, that remains uninsured after two years.
- The education crisis. Americans are used to hearing that their schools don't seem to be providing the quality of education that foreigners get. Fewer of them know that the U.S. education system is also very expensive by international standards. Virtually none of them know anything about the impact of immigration on that education system.

Yet the impact of immigration is clearly serious. For example, in 1990 almost one child in every 20 enrolled in American public schools either could not speak English or spoke it so poorly as to need language-assistance programs. This number is increasing with striking speed: Only six years earlier, it had been one child in 31.

Current law is generally interpreted as requiring schools to educate such children in their native language. To do so, according to one California estimate, requires spending some 65 percent more per child than on an English-speaking child. And not merely money but, more importantly, teacher time and energy are inevitably being diverted from America's children.

My thesis is that the immigration resulting from current public policy:

- Is dramatically larger, less skilled and more divergent from the American majority than anything that was anticipated or desired.
- Is probably not beneficial economically—and is certainly not necessary.
- Is attended by a wide and increasing range of negative consequences, from the physical environment to the political
- Is bringing about an ethnic and racial transformation in America without precedent in the history of the world—an astonishing social experiment launched with no particular reason to expect success.

Some of my American readers will be stirring uneasily at this point. They have been trained to recoil from any explicit discussion of race.

Because the term "racist" is now so debased, I usually shrug off such smears by pointing to its new definition: anyone who is winning an argument with a liberal. Or, too often, a libertarian. And, on the immigration issue, even some confused conservatives.

This may sound facetious. But the double standards are irritating. Anyone who has got into an immigration debate with, for example, Hispanic activists must be instantly aware that some of them really are consumed by the most intense racial animosity—directed against whites. How come what's sauce for the goose is not sauce for the gander?

I have indeed duly examined my own motives. And I am happy to report that they are pure. I sincerely believe I am not prejudiced—in the sense of committing and stubbornly persisting in error about people, regardless of evidence —which appears to be to be the only rational definition of "racism." I am also, however, not blind.

Race and ethnicity are destiny in American politics. And, because of the rise of affirmative action quotas, for American individuals too.

My son, Alexander, is a white male with blue eyes and blond hair. He has never discriminated against anyone in his little life (except possibly young women visitors whom he suspects of being baby-sitters). The sheer size of the so-called "protected classes" that are now politically favored, such as Hispanics, will be a matter of vital importance as long as he lives. And their size is basically determined by immigration.

For Americans even to think about their immigration policy, given the political climate that has prevailed since the 1960s, involves a sort of psychological liberation movement. In Eugene McCarthy's terms, America would have to stop being a colony of the world. The implications are shocking, even frightening: that Americans, without feeling guilty, can and should seize control of their country's destiny.

If they did, what would a decolonized American immigration policy look like? The first step is absolutely clear:

The 1965 Immigration Act, and its amplifications in 1986 and 1990, have been a disaster and must be repealed.

It may be time for the United States to consider moving to a conception of itself more like that of Switzerland: tolerating a fairly large foreign presence that comes and goes, but rarely if ever naturalizes. It may be time to consider reviving a version of the bracero program, the agricultural guest-worker program that operated from the 1940s to the 1960s, allowing foreign workers to move in and out of the country in a controlled way, without permanently altering its demography and politics.

This new conception may be a shock to American sensibilities. Many Americans, like my students at the University of Cincinnati Law School, are under the charming impression that foreigners don't really exist. But they also tend to think that, if foreigners really do exist, they ought to become Americans as quickly as possible.

However, the fact is that we—foreigners—are, in some sense, all Americans now, just as Jefferson said everyone had two countries, his own and France, in the 18th century. That is why we are here, just as the entire world flocked to Imperial Rome. The trick the Americans face now is to be an empire in fact, while remaining a democratic republic in spirit. Avoiding the Romans' mistake of diluting their citizenship into insignificance may be the key.

The New Know-Nothingism:
Five Myths About Immigration

For a brief period in the mid-nineteenth century, a new political movement captured the passions of the American public. Fittingly labeled the "Know-Nothings," their unifying theme was nativism. They liked to call themselves "Native Americans," although they had no sympathy for people we call Native Americans today. And they pinned every problem in American society on immigrants. As one Know-Nothing wrote in 1856: "Four-fifths of the beggary and three-fifths of the crime spring from our foreign population; more than half the public charities, more than half the prisons and almshouses, more than half the police and the cost of administering criminal justice are for foreigners.

At the time, the greatest influx of immigrants was from Ireland, where the potato famine had struck, and Germany which was in political and economic turmoil. Anti-alien and anti-Catholic sentiments were the order of the day, especially in New York and Massachusetts, which received the brunt of the wave of immigrants, many of whom were dirt-poor and uneducated. Politicians were quick to exploit the sentiment: There's nothing like a scapegoat to forge an alliance.

I am especially sensitive to this history: My forebears were among those dirt-poor Irish Catholics who arrived in the 1860s. Fortunately for them, and me, the Know-Nothing movement fizzled within fifteen years. But its pilot light kept burning, and is turned up whenever the American public begins to feel vulnerable and in need of an enemy.

Although they go by different names today, the Know-Nothings have returned. As in the 1850s, the movement is strongest where immigrants are most concentrated: California and Florida. The objects of prejudice are of course no longer Irish Catholics and Germans; 140 years later, "they" have become "us." The new "they"—because it seems "we" must always have a "they"—are Latin Americans (most recently, Cubans), Haitians and Arab-Americans, among others.

But just as in the 1850s, passion, misinformation and shortsighted fear often substitute for reason, fairness and human dignity in today's immigration debates. In the interest of advancing beyond know-nothingism, let's look at five current myths that distort public debate and government policy relating to immigrants.

America is being overrun with immigrants.

In one sense, of course, this is true, but in that sense it has been true since Christopher Columbus arrived. Except for the real Native Americans, we are a nation of immigrants.

It is not true, however, that the first-generation immigrant share of our population is growing. As of 1990, foreign-born people made up only 8 percent of the population, as compared with a figure of about 15 percent from 1870 to 1920. Between 70 and 80 percent of those who immigrate every year are refugees or immediate relatives of U.S. citizens.

Much of the anti-immigrant fervor is directed against the undocumented, but they make up only 13 percent of all immigrants residing in the United States, and only 1 percent of the American population. Contrary to popular belief, most such aliens do not cross the border illegally but enter legally and remain after their student or visitor visa expires. Thus, building a wall at the border, no matter how high, will not solve the problem.

Immigrants take jobs from U.S. citizens.

There is virtually no evidence to support this view, probably the most widespread misunderstanding about immigrants. As documented by a 1994 A.C.L.U. Immigrants' Rights Project report, numerous studies have found that immigrants actually *create* more jobs than they fill. The jobs immigrants take are of course easier to see, but immigrants are often highly productive, run their own businesses and employ both immigrants and citizens. One study found that Mexican immigration to Los Angeles County between 1970 and 1980 was responsible for 78,000 new jobs. Governor Mario Cuomo reports that immigrants own more than 40,000 companies in New York, which provide thousands of jobs and $3.5 billion to the state's economy every year.

Immigrants are a drain on society's resources.

This claim fuels many of the recent efforts to cut off government benefits to immigrants. However, most studies have found that immigrants are a net benefit to the economy because, as a 1994 Urban Institute report concludes, "immigrants generate significantly more in taxes paid than they cost in services received." The Council of Economic Advisers similarly found in 1986 that "immigrants have a favorable effect on the overall standard of living."

Anti-immigrant advocates often cite studies purportedly showing the contrary, but these generally focus only on taxes and services at the local or state level. What they fail to explain is that because most taxes go to the federal government, such studies would also show a net loss when applied to U.S. citizens. At most, such figures suggest that some redistribution of federal and state monies may be appropriate; they say nothing unique about the costs of immigrants.

Some subgroups of immigrants plainly impose a net cost in the short run, principally those who have most recently arrived and have not yet "made it." California, for example, bears substantial costs for its disproportionately large undocumented population, largely because it has on average the poorest and least educated immigrants. But that has been true of every wave of immigrants that has ever reached our shores; it was as true of the Irish in the 1850s, for example, as it is of Salvadorans today. From a long-term perspective, the economic advantages of immigration are undeniable.

Some have suggested that we might save money and diminish incentives to immigrate illegally if we denied undocumented aliens public services. In fact, undocumented immigrants are already ineligible for most social programs, with the exception of education for schoolchildren, which is constitutionally required, and benefits directly related to health and safety, such as emergency medical care and nutritional assistance to poor women, infants and children. To deny such basic care to people in need, apart from being inhumanly callous, would probably cost us more in the long run by exacerbating health problems that we would eventually have to address.

Aliens refuse to assimilate, and are depriving us of our cultural and political unity.

This claim has been made about every new group of immigrants to arrive on U.S. shores. Supreme Court Justice Stephen Field wrote in 1884 that the Chinese "have remained among us as a separate people, retaining their original peculiarities of dress, manners, habits, and modes of living, which are as marked as their complexion and language." Five years later, he upheld the racially based exclusion of Chinese immigrants. Similar claims have been made over different periods of our history about Catholics, Jews, Italians, Eastern Europeans and Latin Americans.

In most instances, such claims are simply not true; "American culture" has been created, defined and revised by persons who for the most part are descended from immigrants once seen as anti-assimilationist. Descendants of the Irish Catholics, for example, a group once decried as separatist and alien, have become Presidents, senators and representatives (and all of these in one family, in the case of the Kennedys). Our society exerts tremendous pressure to conform, and cultural separatism rarely survives a generation. But more important, even if this claim were true, is this a legitimate rationale for limiting immigration in a society built on the values of pluralism and tolerance?

Noncitizen immigrants are not entitled to constitutional rights.

Our government has long declined to treat immigrants as full human beings, and nowhere is that more clear than in the realm of constitutional rights. Although the Constitution literally extends the fundamental protections in the

Bill of Rights to all people, limiting to citizens only the right to vote and run for federal office, the federal government acts as if this were not the case.

In 1893 the executive branch successfully defended a statute that required Chinese laborers to establish their prior residence here by the testimony of "at least one credible white witness." The Supreme Court ruled that this law was constitutional because it was reasonable for Congress to presume that nonwhite witnesses could not be trusted.

The federal government is not much more enlightened today. In a pending case I'm handling in the Court of Appeals for the Ninth Circuit, the Clinton Administration has argued that permanent resident aliens lawfully living here should be extended no more First Amendment rights than aliens applying for first-time admission from abroad—that is, none. Under this view, students at a public university who are citizens may express themselves freely, but students who are not citizens can be deported for saying exactly what their classmates are constitutionally entitled to say.

Growing up, I was always taught that we will be judged by how we treat others. If we are collectively judged by how we have treated immigrants—those who appear today to be "other" but will in a generation be "us"—we are not in very good shape.

POSTSCRIPT

Is Immigration a Problem in the United States?

Are immigrants to the United States a problem? National legislation since 1965 has clearly provided immigrants with group entitlements that were unheard of in the past. Is this necessarily bad? Should the fact that one out of every five school-aged children is foreign-born be viewed as a source of concern or as a healthy challenge to Americans to live up to their ideals?

Until recently, the population problem for most other countries, especially European ones, has been emigration; too many people were leaving. The main problem was the depletion of skilled laborers and other needed workers. Now, according to the U.N. Population Fund, there are over 100 million international migrants, most of whom migrate from poorer nations to wealthier ones. Many countries have mocked the perceived xenophobia (fear of foreigners) in the United States and prided themselves on their tolerant immigration policies and lack of ethnic and racial conflict. However, the United States has always contained far greater numbers of immigrants reflecting a far greater diversity than any other country in the world. Moreover, in the 1990s many nations that traditionally welcomed immigrants, especially those from former colonies, have passed laws sharply restricting immigration. Many have also experienced bitter ethnic conflicts.

Brimelow states that there are now more immigrants entering the United States than there were during the highest point of immigration between 1900 and 1910. Yet he does not mention that the *proportion* of immigrants either entering or currently residing in America is much lower than it was in the past. On the other hand, Cole does not seem to take into account that the origins of current immigrants to the United States are radically different than they were in the past or that other changes might impede comparing immigration today with immigration in the past. These changes include legislative changes that provide ethnic group entitlements (including education and social services), an increasingly militant faction of racial and ethnic leaders demanding preservation of immigrants' national identities and preferences, and the public denunciation by many intellectuals of American values and institutions.

Should major immigration policy changes be put into effect? Should the United States refuse to automatically grant citizenship to children born inside its borders? Should there be clearer demarcations between political refugees, temporary workers, permanent immigrants, and single immigrants versus those with families, as well as stricter enforcement against and more severe punishment for illegal immigrants? Should the United States simply shut down its borders and refuse to accept immigrants whose cultures, values, and appearances are vastly different from Americans'?

In addition to the rapidly changing international situation, relations with Mexico and other nations that are vital to U.S. interests are influenced by U.S. immigration policies. The federal government's actions since 1996 have been to give the Immigration and Naturalization Service increasing powers to deport immigrants or to block their entry. At the state level California's Proposition 187, which denies public support for illegal immigrants and which is currently being challenged in the courts, has wide public support. Meanwhile, debates rage over how immigrants do or do not contribute to the economy, whether or not they take jobs away from U.S. citizens, how much they add to the crime problem, and so on.

John J. Miller supports Brimelow's thinking in "The Politics of Permanent Immigration," *Reason* (October 1998). Linda Chavez, a conservative and the daughter of immigrants, shares her views in "Rising to Overcome Criticism," *The Washington Times* (March 19, 1999). A spirited attack on Chavez's ideas by several critics and her response can be found in "Immigration and Multiculturalism," *Commentary* (September 1998). Also contrast Samuel P. Huntington's *Clash of Civilizations and the Remaking of World Order* (Simon & Schuster, 1996), which offers a critical analysis of immigration, with Hans Vermeulen and Joel Perlmann, eds., *Immigrants, Schooling and Social Mobility: Does Culture Make a Difference?* (St. Martin's Press, 2000).

Support for Cole's position can be found in *In Defense of the Alien, vol. 20,* edited by L. Tomast (Center for Migration Studies, 1999) and "Land of Opportunity," by R. Brenner, *Forbes* (October 12, 1998). The "mend it, don't end it" position is reflected in M. Lind's "Hiring From Within," *Mother Jones* (July/ August 1998).

Two useful reports on legal changes are "In California, a Softer Stance on Immigrants?" by D. Wood, *Christian Science Monitor* (April 1, 1999) and M. Valburn's "Clamor for U.S. Citizenship Spurs Debate on Its Cause," *The Wall Street Journal* (February 25, 1999). Other research on the topic includes Nancy Foner, Ruben G. Rumbaut, and Steven J. Gold, eds., *Immigration Research for a New Century: Multidisciplinary Perspectives* (Russell Sage Foundation, 2000) and Stefano Luconi, *From Paesani to White Ethnics: The Italian Experience in Philadelphia* (State University of New York Press, 2001). Also useful is *Immigration and Race: New Challenges for American Democracy* by Gerald D. Jaynes (Yale University Press, 2000). A case study of skilled immigrants who are clearly making it is "The Indians of Silicon Valley," by M. Warner, *Fortune* (May 15, 2000). A much more typical tale is that of immigrant labor exploitation, one of which can be found in "Silence in the Fields," by B. Yeoman, *Mother Jones* (January/February 2001).

Among the proliferating literature on crime and immigrants is Tony Waters, *Crime and Immigrant Youth* (Sage Publications, 1999) and *The Russian Mafia in America: Immigration, Culture, and Crime* by James Finckenauer and Elin Waring (Northeastern University Press, 1998).

ISSUE 13

Does Environmental Racism Exist?

YES: Robert D. Bullard, from *Dumping in Dixie: Race, Class, and Environmental Quality*, 3rd ed. (Westview Press, 2000)

NO: David Friedman, from "The 'Environmental Racism' Hoax," *The American Enterprise* (November/December 1998)

ISSUE SUMMARY

YES: Professor of sociology Robert D. Bullard attacks corporations, politicians who allow corporations to pollute the environment, and their apologists, including scientists, arguing that their actions primarily harm Blacks and Hispanics and are therefore clearly racist.

NO: David Friedman, a writer and an international consultant, contends that charges of environmental racism are a hoax at best and, at worst, lies. He maintains that much of the current debate is spill-over from the many perceived irresponsibilities of the Clinton administration that aims to garner political support and to strengthen muddled agencies such as the Environmental Protection Agency.

Most religions of the Western world embrace the biblical injunction "Be fruitful and multiply," meaning that mankind's task is to rule the Earth. In contrast, the religious systems of the East, especially among the Buddhists and the Hindus (as well as many Native American tribes), seem to revere the Earth and all living (and inanimate) things far more. In many religious systems, the Earth is viewed as the mother of all things, the sustainer and nurturer of life, and as such, is venerated.

According to the German sociologist Max Weber (1864–1920), a major unanticipated consequence of the emergence of Protestantism in the sixteenth century was the development of capitalism. Weber, in *The Protestant Ethic and the Spirit of Capitalism* (1905), described this system as emphasizing acquisitiveness, hard work, diligence, thrift, and honesty. Such Puritan values functioned to greatly enrich Protestant farmers, merchants, and, later, businessmen as others came to trust them and as they, being thrifty, saved their earnings and invested in new machinery and land to increase future profits. Conspicuous consumption, the flaunting of material wealth, and so on were prohibited. The historical irony of this unanticipated consequence is that these thrifty individuals, primarily in England and the United States, initially, spawned the wealthiest and most wasteful nations in history by the late 1800s. For a contrast to Weber's views of capitalism in the 1700s, see Thorstein Veblen's *Theory of the Leisure Class* (1899).

The initial phase of conspicuous consumption—the vulgar flaunting of wealth, the acquisition of stables of homes and servants, the wasting of food and clothing, etc.—partially paralleled and then was overtaken by the destruction of forests; the pollution of streams, rivers, bays, and other waterways; the spewing of toxic substances in the air; and the utilization and wasting of a significant portion of the Earth's natural resources (as high as 70 percent of natural resources by a few industrial nations, according to some estimates). Since World War II, landfills and other trash problems have been compounded by the disposal of nuclear and highly toxic industrial waste at, beneath, and within many (usually, but not always, poor) communities.

There are many collateral issues that you might wish to consider as you read this debate. For example, many supporters of industrialization hold that the trade-off of pollution for unsurpassed wealth is worth it. According to this argument, in the industrialized West, especially in the United States, even the poor are better off than most people living elsewhere. With regard to the main issue, those who hold this position are likely to agree with David Friedman, who argues in the second of the following selections that whatever damages to the environment occur are about equally distributed: no class, ethnic, or racial categories of people have been unduly burdened with pollution. In addition, he asserts, claims of "environmental racism" are based on misuses of science, self-serving ideologues who are peddling their own agendas and who have little real compassion for the poor, and the failure to recognize the enormous benefits that industrialization provides for all.

The English economist John Maynard Keynes (1883–1946) once said, "In the end, we are all dead." Consider whether or not Robert D. Bullard's analysis in the first of the following selections is a similar warning that polluting the environment primarily to the detriment of Blacks and Hispanics is not only racial discrimination but a means of hastening the end of all of us. How do Bullard's and Friedman's discussions tie in to the remarkable about-face on almost all environmental issues of the current Bush administration? Also, Weber insisted that to be an effective scholar, one's terms must be continuously clarified. What is "environmental racism," according to the two authors? Is it a "hoax," as Friedman contends?

In addition to basic terms, consider Friedman's use of loaded, potentially inflammatory terms and labels, such as "interest group extortion." Do such terms add value to the discussion, or are they simply attempts by Friedman to score debater's points? Also notice Bullard's avowed contempt for the South. Can he be accused of "moral hypocrisy"; that is, of blaming the South for problems that exist throughout the United States and elsewhere?

Robert D. Bullard

**YES**

Dumping in Dixie

Blacks did not launch a frontal assault on environmental problems affecting their communities until these issues were couched in a civil rights context beginning in the early 1980s. They began to treat their struggle for environmental equity as a struggle against institutionalized racism and an extension of the quest for social justice. Just as black citizens fought for equal education, employment, and housing, they began to include the opportunity to live in a healthy environment as part of their basic rights. Moreover, they were convinced that disparate enforcement of environmental policies and regulations contributes to neighborhood decline much like housing discrimination, redlining practices, and residential segregation do.

Black resistance to environmental threats in the 1970s was confined to local issues and largely involved grassroots individuals. In the 1980s some changes occurred in the way black community groups and national advocacy groups dealt with the toxics issue. This new environmental activism among blacks did not materialize out of thin air nor was it an overnight phenomenon. It did, however, emerge out of the growing hostility to facility siting decisions that were seen as unfair, inequitable, and discriminatory toward poor people and people of color.

Toxic-waste disposal has generated demonstrations in many communities across the country. The first national protest by blacks on the hazardous-waste issue occurred in 1982. . . .

Environmental Racism Revisited . . .

The Role of Racism

Many of the differences in environmental quality between black and white communities result from institutional racism, which influences local land use, enforcement of environmental regulations, industrial facility siting, and the locations in which people of color live, work, and play. The roots of institutional racism are deep and have been difficult to eliminate. Discrimination is a manifestation of institutional racism and results in life being very different for whites and blacks. Historically, racism has been and continues to be a "conspicuous part of the American sociopolitical system, and as a result, black people in particular, and ethnic and racial minority groups of color, find themselves at a disadvantage in contemporary society."

Environmental racism is real; it is not merely an invention of wild-eyed sociologists or radical environmental justice activists. It is just as real as the racism found in the housing industry, educational institutions, the employment arena, and the judicial system. What is environmental racism, and how does one recognize it? *Environmental racism* refers to any policy, practice, or directive that differentially affects or disadvantages (whether intended or unintended) individuals, groups, or communities based on race or color. Environmental racism combines with public policies and industry practices to provide *benefits* for whites while shifting industry *costs* to people of color. It is reinforced by governmental, legal, economic, political, and military institutions. In a sense, "Every state institution is a racial institution."

Environmental decision making and policies often mirror the power arrangements of the dominant society and its institutions. A form of illegal "exaction" forces people of color to pay the costs of environmental benefits for the public at large. The question of who pays for and who benefits from the current environmental and industrial policies is central to this analysis of environmental racism and other systems of domination and exploitation.

Racism influences the likelihood of exposure to environmental and health risks as well as of less access to health care. Many U.S. environmental policies distribute the costs in a regressive pattern and provide disproportionate benefits for whites and individuals at the upper end of the education and income scales. Numerous studies, dating back to the 1970s, reveal that people-of-color communities have borne greater health and environmental risk burdens than the society at large.

Elevated public health risks are found in some populations even when social class is held constant. For example, race has been found to be independent of class in the distribution of air pollution, contaminated fish consumption, location of municipal landfills and incinerators, abandoned toxic-waste dumps, cleanup of Superfund sites, and lead poisoning in children.

Lead poisoning is a classic example of an environmental health problem that disproportionately affects African American children at every class level. Lead affects between 3 and 4 million children in the United States—most of whom are African Americans and Latinos who live in urban areas. Among children five years old and younger, the percentage of African American children who have excessive levels of lead in their blood far exceeds that of whites at all income levels.

The federal Agency for Toxic Substances and Disease Registry (ATSDR) found that in families earning less than six thousand dollars a year, 68 percent of African American children had lead poisoning, compared with 36 percent of white children. In families with an annual income exceeding fifteen thousand dollars, more than 38 percent of African American children suffered from lead poisoning, compared with 12 percent of whites. Even when income was held constant, African American children were two to three times more likely than their white counterparts to suffer from lead poisoning.

Virtually all of the studies of exposure to outdoor air pollution have found significant differences in exposure according to income and race. African Americans and Latinos are more likely than are whites to live in areas with reduced air quality. For example, National Argonne Laboratory researchers D. K. Wernette and L. A. Nieves found:

> In 1990, 437 of the 3,109 counties and independent cities failed to meet at least one of the EPA ambient air quality standards.... Fifty-seven percent of whites, 65 percent of African Americans, and 80 percent of Hispanics live in 437 counties with substandard air quality. Out of the whole population, a total of 33 percent of whites, 50 percent of African Americans, and 60 percent of Hispanics live in the 136 counties in which two or more air pollutants exceed standards. The percentages living in the 29 counties designated as nonattainment areas for three or more pollutants are 12 percent of whites, 20 percent of African Americans, and 31 percent of Hispanics.

The public health community has insufficient information to explain the magnitude of some of the air pollution–related health problems. However, we do know that persons suffering from asthma are particularly sensitive to the effects of carbon monoxide, sulfur dioxides, particulate matter, ozone, and nitrogen oxides. African Americans, for example, have a significantly higher prevalence of asthma than the general population. Environmental problems are endangering the health of communities all across the United States.

Unequal Protection

The nation's environmental laws, regulations, and policies are not applied uniformly; as a result, some individuals, neighborhoods, and communities are exposed to elevated health risks. A 1992 study by staff writers from the *National Law Journal* uncovered glaring inequities in the way the federal Environmental Protection Agency (EPA) enforces its laws:

> There is a racial divide in the way the U.S. government cleans up toxic waste sites and punishes polluters. White communities see faster action, better results and stiffer penalties than communities where blacks, Hispanics and other minorities live. This unequal protection often occurs whether the community is wealthy or poor.

In their study, these writers examined census records, civil court dockets, and the EPA's own record of performance at 1,177 Superfund toxic-waste sites. The report revealed the following:

1. Penalties imposed under hazardous-waste laws at sites having the greatest percentage of whites were 500 percent higher than penalties in areas with the greatest minority populations, averaging $335,556 for white areas compared to $55,318 for minority areas.

2. The disparity under the toxic-waste law occurred by race alone, not by income. The average penalty in areas with the lowest income levels was $113,491, 3 percent more than the average penalty in areas with the highest median income.

3. When all of the federal environmental laws aimed at protecting citizens from air, water, and waste pollution were considered, penalties imposed in white communities were 46 percent higher than those in minority communities.

4. Under the giant Superfund cleanup program, it took 20 percent longer to place hazardous-waste sites in minority areas on the national priority list than it took for those in white areas to be placed on the list.

5. In more than half of the ten autonomous regions that administer EPA programs around the country, action on cleanup at Superfund sites took from 12 to 42 percent longer to initiate at minority sites than at white sites.

6. At minority sites, the EPA chose "containment," the capping or walling off of a hazardous-waste dump site, 7 percent more frequently than the cleanup method preferred under the law: permanent "treatment" to eliminate the waste or rid it of its toxins. At white sites, the EPA ordered treatment 22 percent more often than it did containment.

These findings suggest that unequal protection is placing communities of color at special risk. The study also supplements the findings of earlier studies and reinforces what grassroots leaders have long been saying: Not only are people of color differentially affected by industrial pollution, but they can also expect different treatment from the government.

Environmental decision making operates at the juncture of science, economics, politics, special interests, and ethics. The current environmental model places communities of color at special risk. African American and other communities of color are often victims of land-use decision making that mirrors the power arrangements of the dominant society. Historically, exclusionary zoning (and rezoning) has been a subtle form of using government authority and power to foster and perpetuate discriminatory practices. Generally, planning and zoning commissions are not racially and ethnically diverse.

Exclusionary and restrictive practices that limit participation of African Americans and other people of color in decision-making boards, commissions, regulatory bodies, and management staff are all forms of environmental racism. The various governmental agencies charged with protecting the public are far from achieving a racially and ethnically diverse work force. The demonstration of a strong commitment to fostering diversity in the work force is essential to achieving the government's mission of protecting human health and the environment.

Limiting the access of African Americans, Latino Americans, Asian Americans, and native Americans to management positions has no doubt affected the outcomes of some important environmental decisions in at-risk communities. In order to get balanced and just decisions, the decision makers (managers) must reflect the diversity—cultural, racial, ethnic, and gender—of the United States.

At the federal EPA there are over eighteen thousand employees; one third are assigned to headquarters offices in the metropolitan Washington, D.C., area, and two thirds work in regional and laboratory offices scattered throughout the United States. The EPA work force is about evenly divided between men (51 percent) and women (49 percent), and just over one fourth (26 percent) are members of minority groups. However, women and minorities continue to be underrepresented in EPA's management staff. In 1992, women and minorities constituted 28 percent and 9.7 percent, respectively, of the management staff.

Data from a 1992 EPA report, *Women, Minorities and People with Disabilities,* show that the agency missed numerous opportunities to further diversify its work force. In fiscal year 1991, for example, a total of 412 management hires were made, with only 33 positions (8 percent) going to minorities and 142 (34 percent) going to white women. In fiscal year 1992, 354 management hires were made, with 42 positions (11.9 percent) going to minorities and 126 (35.6 percent) going to white women.

EPA's 1991 Equal Employment Opportunity Commission (EEOC) report reveals that the agency lagged behind many other federal agencies in hiring and promoting racial and ethnic minorities to professional positions. Of the fifty-six federal agencies that have five hundred or more employees, the EPA ranked thirty-fifth in the percentage of African Americans in professional positions, twenty-second in the percentage of Latino Americans in professional positions, and thirty-ninth in the number of native Americans in professional positions. Clearly, work force diversity is an essential component in any strategy to combat environmental racism.

Environmental Apartheid

Apartheid-type housing, development, and environmental policies limit mobility, reduce neighborhood options, diminish job opportunities, and decrease choices for millions of Americans. Race still plays a significant role in the distribution of public "benefits" and public "burdens" associated with economic growth. Why do some communities get dumped on and others do not? Why do some communities get cleaned up whereas others have to wait? Waste generation is directly correlated with per capita income; however, few waste facilities are proposed and actually built in the mostly white suburbs.

The Commission for Racial Justice's landmark study, *Toxic Wastes and Race,* found race to be the single most important factor (i.e., more important than income, the percentage of people who own their homes, and property values) in the location of abandoned toxic-waste sites. The study also found that (1) three of five African Americans live in communities with abandoned toxic-waste sites; (2) 60 percent (15 million) of African Americans live in communities with one or more abandoned toxic-waste sites; (3) three of the five largest commercial hazardous-waste landfills are located in predominately African American or Latino communities, accounting for 40 percent of the nation's total estimated landfill capacity; and (4) African Americans are heavily overrepresented in the population of cities with the largest number of abandoned toxic-waste sites, which include Memphis, St. Louis, Houston, Cleveland, Chicago, and Atlanta.

Communities with hazardous-waste incinerators generally have large minority populations, low incomes, and low property values. A 1990 Greenpeace report, *Playing with Fire,* found that (1) the minority portion of the population in communities with existing incinerators is 89 percent higher than the national average; (2) communities in which incinerators are proposed have ratios of minorities to whites that are 60 percent higher than the national average; (3) average annual income in communities with existing incinerators is 15 percent lower than the national average; (4) property values in communities that have incinerators are 38 percent lower than the national average; and (5) in communities in which incinerators are proposed, average property values are 35 percent lower than the national average.

Waste facility siting imbalances that were uncovered by the U.S. General Accounting Office (GAO) in 1983 have not disappeared. The GAO discovered that three-quarters of the offsite commercial hazardous-waste landfills in Region IV (Alabama, Florida, Georgia, Kentucky, Mississippi, North Carolina, South Carolina, and Tennessee) were located in predominately African American communities. A decade later, African Americans still made up about one fifth of the population in EPA Region IV. In 1993, all of the offsite commercial hazardous-waste landfills in the region were located in two mostly African American communities.

Some residents of the region suspect that their communities are rapidly becoming "sacrifice zones" because of the placement there of garbage dumps, landfills, incinerators, and petrochemical plants. Nowhere is this more apparent than in southeast Louisiana, where unincorporated African American communities are especially vulnerable to industrial pollution....

Clearly, the time is long overdue for the United States to provide equal protection for all of its people—in their homes, workplaces, and playgrounds—and places (e.g., rural, urban, suburban, reservations, and similar locales). Environmental justice and pollution prevention must become overarching principles of environmental protection if we are to eliminate existing inequities.

David Friedman  **NO**

The "Environmental Racism" Hoax

When the U.S. Environmental Protection Agency (EPA) unveiled its heavily criticized environmental justice "guidance" [in 1998], it crowned years of maneuvering to redress an "outrage" that doesn't exist. The agency claims that state and local policies deliberately cluster hazardous economic activities in politically powerless "communities of color." The reality is that the EPA, by exploiting every possible legal ambiguity, skillfully limiting debate, and ignoring even its own science, has enshrined some of the worst excesses of racialist rhetoric and environmental advocacy into federal law.

"Environmental justice" entered the activist playbook after a failed 1982 effort to block a hazardous-waste landfill in a predominantly black North Carolina county. One of the protesters was the District of Columbia's congressional representative, who returned to Washington and prodded the General Accounting Office (GAO) to investigate whether noxious environmental risks were disproportionately sited in minority communities.

A year later, the GAO said that they were. Superfund and similar toxic dumps, it appeared, were disproportionately located in non-white neighborhoods. The well-heeled, overwhelmingly white environmentalist lobby christened this alleged phenomenon "environmental racism," and ethnic advocates like Ben Chavis and Robert Bullard built a grievance over the next decade.

Few of the relevant studies were peer-reviewed; all made critical errors. Properly analyzed, the data revealed that waste sites are just as likely to be located in white neighborhoods, or in areas where minorities moved only after permits were granted. Despite sensational charges of racial "genocide" in industrial districts and ghastly "cancer alleys," health data don't show minorities being poisoned by toxic sites. "Though activists have a hard time accepting it," notes Brookings fellow Christopher H. Foreman, Jr., a self-described black liberal Democrat, "racism simply doesn't appear to be a significant factor in our national environmental decision-making."

٭

This reality, and the fact that the most ethnically diverse urban regions were desperately trying to *attract* employers, not sue them, constrained the environmental racism movement for a while. In 1992, a Democrat-controlled Congress

From David Friedman, "The 'Environmental Racism' Hoax," *The American Enterprise*, vol. 9, no. 6 (November/December 1998). Copyright © 1998 by David Friedman. Reprinted by permission of *The American Enterprise*.

ignored environmental justice legislation introduced by then-Senator Al Gore. Toxic racism made headlines, but not policy.

All of that changed with the Clinton-Gore victory. Vice President Gore got his former staffer Carol Browner appointed head of the EPA and brought Chavis, Bullard, and other activists into the transition government. The administration touted environmental justice as one of the symbols of its new approach.

Even so, it faced enormous political and legal hurdles. Legislative options, never promising in the first place, evaporated with the 1994 Republican takeover in Congress. Supreme Court decisions did not favor the movement.

So the Clinton administration decided to bypass the legislative and judicial branches entirely. In 1994, it issued an executive order—ironically cast as part of Gore's "reinventing government" initiative to streamline bureaucracy—which directed that every federal agency "make achieving environmental justice part of its mission."

At the same time, executive branch lawyers generated a spate of legal memoranda that ingeniously used a poorly defined section of the Civil Rights Act of 1964 as authority for environmental justice programs. Badly split, confusing Supreme Court decisions seemed to construe the 1964 Act's "nondiscrimination" clause (prohibiting federal funds for states that discriminate racially) in such a way as to allow federal intervention wherever a state policy ended up having "disparate effects" on different ethnic groups.

Even better for the activists, the Civil Rights Act was said to authorize private civil rights lawsuits against state and local officials on the basis of disparate impacts. This was a valuable tool for environmental and race activists, who are experienced at using litigation to achieve their ends.

Its legal game plan in place, the EPA then convened an advocate-laden National Environmental Justice Advisory Council (NEJAC), and seeded activist groups (to the tune of $3 million in 1995 alone) to promote its policies. Its efforts paid off. From 1993, the agency backlogged over 50 complaints, and environmental justice rhetoric seeped into state and federal land-use decisions.

❧

Congress, industry, and state and local officials were largely unaware of these developments because, as subsequent news reports and congressional hearings established, they were deliberately excluded from much of the agency's planning process. Contrary perspectives, including EPA-commissioned studies highly critical of the research cited by the agency to justify its environmental justice initiative in the first place, were ignored or suppressed.

The EPA began to address a wider audience in September 1997. It issued an "interim final guidance" (bureaucratese for regulation-like rules that agencies can claim are not "final" so as to avoid legal challenge) which mandated that environmental justice be incorporated into all projects that file federal environmental impact statements. The guidance directed that applicants pay particular attention to potential "disparate impacts" in areas where minorities live in "meaningfully greater"numbers than surrounding regions.

The new rules provoked surprisingly little comment. Many just "saw the guidance as creating yet another section to add to an impact statement," explains Jennifer Hernandez, a San Francisco environmental attorney. In response, companies wanting to build new plants had to start "negotiating with community advocates and federal agencies, offering new computers, job training, school or library improvements, and the like" to grease their projects through.

In December 1997, the Third Circuit Court of Appeals handed the EPA a breathtaking legal victory. It overturned a lower court decision against a group of activists who sued the state of Pennsylvania for granting industrial permits in a town called Chester, and in doing so the appeals court affirmed the EPA's extension of Civil Rights Act enforcement mechanisms to environmental issues.

(When Pennsylvania later appealed, and the Supreme Court agreed to hear the case, the activists suddenly argued the matter was moot, in order to avoid the Supreme Court's handing down an adverse precedent.... [T]he Court agreed, but sent the case back to the Third Circuit with orders to dismiss the ruling. While activists may have dodged a decisive legal bullet, they also wiped from the books the only legal precedent squarely in their favor.)

Two months after the Third Circuit's decision, the EPA issued a second "interim guidance" detailing, for the first time, the formal procedures to be used in environmental justice complaints. To the horror of urban development, business, labor, state, local, and even academic observers, the guidance allows the federal agency to intervene at any time up to six months (subject to extension) after any land-use or environmental permit is issued, modified, or renewed anywhere in the United States. All that's required is a simple allegation that the permit in question was "an act of intentional discrimination or has the effect of discriminating on the basis of race, creed, or national origin."

The EPA will investigate such claims by considering "multiple, cumulative, and synergistic risks." In other words, an individual or company might not itself be in violation, but if, combined with previous (also legal) land-use decisions, the "cumulative impact" on a minority community is "disparate," this could suddenly constitute a federal civil rights offense. The guidance leaves important concepts like "community" and "disparate impact" undefined, leaving them to "case by case" determination. "Mitigations" to appease critics will likewise be negotiated with the EPA case by case.

This "guidance" subjects virtually any state or local land-use decision—made by duly elected or appointed officials scrupulously following validly enacted laws and regulations—to limitless ad hoc federal review, any time there is the barest allegation of racial grievance. Marrying the most capricious elements of wetlands, endangered species, and similar environmental regulations with the interest-group extortion that so profoundly mars urban ethnic politics, the guidance transforms the EPA into the nation's supreme land-use regulator.

✦

Reaction to the Clinton administration's gambit was swift. A coalition of groups usually receptive to federal interventions, including the U.S. Conference of Mayors, the National Association of Counties, and the National Association of Black County Officials, demanded that the EPA withdraw the guidance. The House amended an appropriations bill to cut off environmental justice enforcement until the guidance was revised. This August, EPA officials were grilled in congressional hearings led by Democratic stalwarts like Michigan's John Dingell.

Of greatest concern is the likelihood the guidance will dramatically increase already-crippling regulatory uncertainties in urban areas where ethnic populations predominate. Rather than risk endless delay and EPA-brokered activist shakedowns, businesses will tacitly "redline" minority communities and shift operations to white, politically conservative, less-developed locations.

Stunningly, this possibility doesn't bother the EPA and its environmentalist allies. "I've heard senior agency officials just dismiss the possibility that their policies might adversely affect urban development," says lawyer Hernandez. Dingell, a champion of Michigan's industrial revival, was stunned when Ann Goode, the EPA's civil rights director, said her agency never considered the guidance's adverse economic and social effects. "As director of the Office of Civil Rights," she lectured House lawmakers, "local economic development is not something I can help with."

Perhaps it should be. Since 1980, the economies of America's major urban regions, including Cleveland, Chicago, Milwaukee, Detroit, Pittsburgh, New Orleans, San Francisco, Newark, Los Angeles, New York City, Baltimore, and Philadelphia, grew at only one-third the rate of the overall American economy. As the economies of the nation's older cities slumped, 11 million new jobs were created in whiter areas.

Pushing away good industrial jobs hurts the pocketbook of urban minorities, and, ironically, harms their health in the process. In a 1991 *Health Physics* article, University of Pittsburgh physicist Bernard L. Cohen extensively analyzed mortality data and found that while hazardous waste and air pollution exposure takes from three to 40 days off a lifespan, poverty reduces a person's life expectancy by an average of 10 *years*. Separating minorities from industrial plants is thus not only bad economics, but bad health and welfare policy as well.

❧

Such realities matter little to environmental justice advocates, who are really more interested in radical politics than improving lives. "Most Americans would be horrified if they saw NEJAC [the EPA's environmental justice advisory council] in action," says Brookings's Foreman, who recalls a council meeting derailed by two Native Americans seeking freedom for an Indian activist incarcerated for killing two FBI officers. "Because the movement's main thrust is toward ... 'empowerment' ..., scientific findings that blunt or conflict with that goal are ignored or ridiculed."

Yet it's far from clear that the Clinton administration's environmental justice genie can be put back in the bottle. Though the Supreme Court's dismissal of the Chester case eliminated much of the EPA's legal argument for the new rules, it's likely that more lawsuits and bureaucratic rulemaking will keep the program alive. The success of the environmental justice movement over the last six years shows just how much a handful of ideological, motivated bureaucrats and their activist allies can achieve in contemporary America unfettered by fact, consequence, or accountability, if they've got a President on their side.

POSTSCRIPT

Does Environmental Racism Exist?

Although Friedman makes the case that the Environmental Protection Agency and many other agencies are using the issue of environmental racism to garner more bureaucratic power, does he refute Bullard's evidence that a significantly disproportionate number of Black and Hispanic children have lead poisoning and other medical problems? Are his proposals for continuing local regulations realistic?

If Bullard's charges are accurate, then should those who are guilty of environmental destruction—the polluters as well as the politicians, law enforcement officials, and others who allow them to continue polluting—be charged with murder, or at least assault? Is it fair to worry about minorities being harmed when the whole issue may be one of socioeconomic class? That is, poor people everywhere, including poor white people, are being harmed. Is the focus in certain areas solely on Blacks and Hispanics divisive?

Friedman argues that the poor and local politicians alike favor industrialization because it produces employment and other opportunities that benefit minorities and others. Is Friedman correct when he suggests that environmentalists are Luddites who fear modernization and who are deploying the race card to enhance their own agenda? Is it possible for everyone to have jobs and economic progress as well as clean air, clean water, and a safe environment?

A good overview that identifies several perspectives on the class-versus-race controversy and the notion of equity in waste distribution is "Local Risks, States' Rights, and Federal Mandates: Remedying Environmental Inequities in the U.S. Federal System," by E. Ringquist and D. Clark, *Publicus* (Spring 1999). Additional views on the race/class controversy are L. Downey, "Environmental Injustice: Is Race or Income a Better Predictor?" *Social Science Quarterly* (December 1998) and H. White, "Race, Class, and Environmental Hazard," in David E. Cuesta-Camacho, ed., *Environmental Injustices, Political Struggles: Race, Class, and the Environment* (Duke University Press, 1998).

Among the many articles that deal with empirical cases of communities' fighting for environmental justice is "Seeking Justice in Roads and Runways," by M. Murray, *National Journal* (March 4, 2000). Shepard Krech III debunks the commonly accepted notion that Native Americans were necessarily conservationists in *The Ecological Indian: Myth and History* (W. W. Norton, 1999). Two books that look at the issue as it has arisen in countries outside of the United States are Xiaoying Ma and Leonard Ortolano, *Environmental Regulation in China: Institutions, Enforcement, and Compliance* (Rowman & Littlefield, 2000) and Rosaleen Duffy, *Killing for Conservation: Wildlife Policy in Zimbabwe* (Indiana University Press, 2000).

ISSUE 14

Are Black Leaders Part of the Problem?

YES: Eugene F. Rivers III, from "Beyond the Nationalism of Fools: Toward an Agenda for Black Intellectuals," *Boston Review* (Summer 1995)

NO: Edmund W. Gordon and Maitrayee Bhattacharyya, from "Have African Americans Failed to Take Responsibility for Their Own Advancement?" *Long Term View* (Fall 1994)

ISSUE SUMMARY

YES: Eugene F. Rivers III, founder and pastor of the Azusa Christian Community, notes the many social and economic problems of Black youth in the United States and argues that three types of Black leaders—celebrity intellectuals, detached scholars, and rabble-rousers—have contributed to the problems rather than the solutions.

NO: Emeritus professor of psychology Edmund W. Gordon and researcher Maitrayee Bhattacharyya maintain that neither Blacks nor their leaders are responsible for the poor state of Black development. The problem, they argue, is intentional neglect and racism by all of society.

It has been said that among any great people, there are often bitter controversies reflecting profound disagreements. Indeed, some attribute greatness, as well as survival, to a group's *not* walking in lockstep to the beat of a single drummer.

Blacks in the United States have never been a unified, homogeneous entity or of a single mind. For generations there have been rifts, controversies, and conflicts of a stimulating yet divisive nature. One of the most noteworthy schisms crystallized at the start of the twentieth century: the profound disagreement between Booker T. Washington (1856–1915), the conservative Black leader and founder of the Tuskegee Institute, and prominent Black intellectual W. E. B. Du Bois (1868–1963). Du Bois, a Harvard Ph.D., spent many years debating Washington's call for Black self-help. Du Bois demanded that Blacks organize and fight for equal rights, and he rejected the idea that Blacks, through hard work, thrift, and good habits, had to first demonstrate that they "deserved" the rights that whites already enjoyed as citizens.

The role of leaders among any group of people is always problematic at best. Among marginalized, exploited, subjugated people, it is even more difficult. In the past, the only way leaders of acutely oppressed minorities could obtain benefits from the dominant group was by being servile or at least by seeming to pose no threat. After the 1960s, however, Black leaders who worked this way were openly disdained as "Uncle Toms." Washington's policy of self-help was either ridiculed or forgotten by the Black community. By the 1970s even Dr. Martin Luther King, Jr's dream of men and women being judged not "by the color of their skin, but by the content of their character" was ignored as unrealistic. The feeling was that Blacks had been and continued to be so overcome and victimized by racism that it was impossible and unfair to judge them by their character.

In the following selections, Eugene F. Rivers III states that a new breed of Black leader—ranging from intellectuals and politicians to talk-show celebrities —is promoting the image of Blacks as helpless victims who are not responsible for their own actions or destinies. He argues that these leaders must stand up and lead their communities in finding solutions to the Black problem. Edmund W. Gordon and Maitrayee Bhattacharyya contend that Black leaders cannot be blamed for the problems of Black people. The blame, they argue, resides with all of society and the forces within that prevent Blacks and other minorities from successfully developing.

The 2000 election to determine who would succeed President Bill Clinton—a president whom some Black leaders openly called America's "first Black president" due to his perceived strong support of minorities—resulted in added leadership controversies. Specifically, some national Black leaders, such as Julian Bond, chairman of the National Association for the Advancement of Colored People (NAACP), have accused President George W. Bush of encouraging murder because of his opposition to hate crime legislation. Other leaders counter that such assertions are demagogic, splitting both Blacks from other Blacks and Blacks from whites.

To many, the recent revelation that Reverend Jesse Jackson fathered a child with a woman who is not his wife is just business as usual among powerful, energetic leaders of any racial or ethnic background. However, significant controversies surround his alleged fabrications over the incident. In addition, Jackson and other minority leaders are now being accused of shaking down large companies for profits by threatening to picket them. A recent spate of books and articles by prominent African American scholars and writers assert that many Black leaders have become "program pimps" and "race hustlers" and that they are turning Dr. King's legacy into a self-serving racket. Some say that new terms are needed for these new types of leaders to separate them from the vast majority of dedicated, selfless leaders who are working to benefit the race.

As you read this debate, consider each selection's emphasis on individual actions or group actions. How does Rivers classify Black leaders? What heuristic value does this classification have? From Gordon and Bhattacharyya's point of view, what should white capitalists do or stop doing to help Blacks? Which modern Black leaders would you say are contributing to the problems of the inner city? Which ones are contributing to the solutions?

Eugene F. Rivers III  **YES**

Beyond the Nationalism of Fools: Toward an Agenda for Black Intellectuals

Each day 1,118 Black teenagers are victims of violent crime, 1,451 Black children are arrested, and 907 Black teenage girls get pregnant. A generation of Black males is drowning in its own blood in the prison camps that we euphemistically call "inner cities." And things are likely to get much worse. Some 40 years after the beginning of the Civil Rights movement, younger Black Americans are now growing up unqualified even for slavery. The result is a state of civil war, with children in violent revolt against the failed secular and religious leadership of the Black community.

Consider the dimensions of this failure. A Black boy has a 1-in-3,700 chance of getting a PhD in mathematics, engineering, or the physical sciences; a 1-in-766 chance of becoming a lawyer; a 1-in-395 chance of becoming a physician; a 1-in-195 chance of becoming a teacher. But his chances are 1-in-2 of never attending college, even if he graduates high school; 1-in-9 of using cocaine; 1-in-12 of having gonorrhea; and 1-in-20 of being imprisoned while in his 20s. Only the details are different for his sister.

What is the responsibility of Black intellectuals in the face of this nightmare? I raised this question three years ago in an open letter to the *Boston Review* (September/October, 1992). My point of departure was the stunning disparity between the grim state of Black America and the recent successes of the Black intelligentsia. My aim was to encourage Black intellectuals to use their now-considerable prestige and resources to improve the lives of Black Americans. The letter provoked wide-ranging discussion—forums at Harvard and MIT, attended by 1,500 people, with participation by bell hooks, Margaret Burnham, Henry Louis Gates, Jr., Cornel West, Glenn Loury, Regina Austin, Selwyn Cudjoe, K. Anthony Appiah, and Randall Kennedy; a series of letters and short essays in *Boston Review* by, among others, Eugene Genovese, Eric Foner, Farah Griffin, and john powell; debates on NPR and public television. Although the discussion did not have clear practical consequences, much of it was constructive.

Recently, a number of less constructive articles on Black intellectuals have appeared in the *New Yorker, Atlantic, New Republic, Village Voice, Los Angeles Times*, and *New York Times Book Review*. Those articles fall into two categories.

First, there are what Northwestern University political scientist Adolph Reed rightly described as "press releases." Articles by Michael Bérubé in the *New Yorker* (January 9, 1995) and Robert Boynton in the *Atlantic* (March, 1995), for example, applauded the achievements of a celebrity intelligentsia, but failed to ask any hard questions: for example, what have we learned from the recent work of leading Black intellectuals?

Then we have the more provocative, "you dumb and yo-mamma's ugly" perspective. This second approach was pioneered by Leon Wieseltier in a *New Republic* attack on Cornel West (March 6, 1995), and perfected by Adolph Reed in his *Village Voice* "I-hate-you-because-you're-famous-and-I'm-not" attack on West, Michael Dyson, bell hooks, Robin Kelley, and Skip Gates for being little more than the academic wing of the entertainment industry—a collection of mutual back-slapping, verbally adept "minstrels" (April 11, 1995).

Reed did score some important points. For many Black intellectuals, fame and fortune appear to be ends in themselves. Displays of erudition and post-modern fashion masquerade as intellectual contribution: no new ideas, just expensive theater. But Professor Reed is hardly the one to be leveling these charges. He has devoted himself to criticizing Jesse Jackson and Cornel West, and presenting himself as the only smart native in the jungle, not to advancing an alternative political, theoretical, or policy project.

The debate about responsibility has degenerated into star-worship and name-calling, the stuff of television talk shows. The issues are too serious for that. It is time to get back on track. The Black community is in a state of emergency; Black intellectuals have acquired unprecedented power and prestige. So let's quit the topic of salaries and lecture fees, leave the fine points about Gramsci on hegemony to the journals, and have a serious discussion of how intellectuals can better mobilize their resources to meet the emergency.

An historical model provides useful instruction. W.E.B. Du Bois was asked by Atlanta University President Horace Bumstead to head an annual conference series to produce "the first... thoroughly scientific study of the conditions of Negro life, covering all its most important phases,... resulting in a score of annual Atlanta University publications." The studies, Bumstead hoped, would result in an authoritative statement about the lives of Black Americans. According to Du Bois, the work at Atlanta University from 1897 to 1910 developed "a program of study on the problems affecting American Negroes, covering a progressively widening and deepening effort, designed to stretch over the span of a century."

The first Atlanta Conference, held in 1896, focused principally on the health problems of the Black community. "For 13 years," Du Bois wrote in his autobiography, "we poured forth a series of studies; limited, incomplete, only partially conclusive, and yet so much better done than any other attempt of the sort." The studies were published as Proceedings of the Annual Conferences on the Negro Problem, and included: *Social and Physical Condition in Cities* (1897); *The Negro in Business* (1899); *the Negro Common School* (1901); *The Negro Artisan*

(1902); *The Negro Church* (1903); *Some Notes on Negro Crime* (1904); *The Health and Physique of the Negro American* (1906); *Negro American Family* (1908); *Efforts for Social Betterment Among Negro Americans* (1910); and *Morals and Manners Among Negro Americans* (1915).

So nearly 100 years ago, a Black intelligentsia—endowed with few resources, facing every imaginable form of racial disenfranchisement, living in a world of routine racist lynchings—conducted an intellectually serious program of cooperative and engaged research, focused on the basic life conditions of Black Americans.

Concerns about these conditions remain as urgent today as they were then. And with the maturation of African-American studies as an academic field, vastly greater resources are now available for pursuing an Atlanta-type project that would explore the life conditions of Black Americans, and evaluate strategies for improving those conditions. But no comparable project is now in evidence.

In Greater New England, we have Harvard's Du Bois Institute and the University of Massachusetts' William Monroe Trotter Institute, and at least 25 academic departments, committees, subcommittees, or museums devoted to African or African-American Studies. Consider the distinguished roster of African-American intellectuals in the region: Henry Louis Gates, Jr., Cornel West, Evelyn Brooks-Higginbotham, Orlando Patterson, James Jennings, Hubert Jones, K. Anthony Appiah, James Blackwell, Willard Johnson, Theresa Perry, Marilyn Richardson, John Bracey, Michael Thelwell, Constance Williams, Stephen Carter, Charles Ogletree. How have these institutions and scholars failed—despite their incomparably superior information, financial and institutional support, and comparative wealth, freedom, and safety—to produce a coherent and coordinated research agenda addressing the contemporary devastation of the Black community? Why has this generation's peculiar collective genius been to product to little from so much?

✧

This question is of interest in its own right, and will make a good research topic for some future historian. Of more immediate concern is how we might start to change directions. In a constructive spirit, I will make some suggestions about two sorts of challenges we need to address.

The first challenges are conceptual—matters of political philosophy. Developing a rational vision of and for the Black community will require ridding ourselves of obsolete and malign intellectual categories. That means a new, anti-antisemitic Black intellectual movement, aimed at resurrecting a vision of hope and faith in the face of the spiritual nihilism and material decay in our inner cities. More specifically, we need to reassess our understanding of social and political equality; reconsider the meaning of freedom in a post–Civil Rights era; examine the implications of secularization for Black culture, politics, and social thought; come to terms with the intimate connections between rights and responsibilities; and show the central role of theological ideas in moral doctrine and ethical life.

These are all large issues, and I cannot develop any of them in detail here. But I will offer two illustrations of the kind of philosophical discussion that we need.

Consider first the issue of equality. After the Supreme Court announced its 1954 decision in *Brown v. Board of Education*, Thurgood Marshall told the *New York Times* that, as a result of the decision, school segregation would be stamped out within five years, and all segregation within seven. Marshall's views were utopian, but not unrepresentative of the middle-class leadership of the period. That leadership assumed—despite much counter-evidence—that the US political system was racially inclusionary and politically capable of fully integrating the Black Americans into national life. The assumption reflected and reinforced an *integrationist* conception of racial equality. The integrationist idea was that the American racial caste system would be replaced with civil and political equality only through racial integration of schools, neighborhoods, and businesses, rather than—as a competing *nationalist* conception argued—through a strategy focused at least initially on building strong, autonomous Black institutions.

For more than 40 years, the integrationist conception of racial equality has dominated the nationalist alternative. But skin color determines life-chances; millions of Blacks continue to be excluded from American life: segregated residentially, educationally, and politically. Moreover, racial barriers show no signs of falling, and affirmative action is all but dead. Committed to racial equality, but faced with a segregated existence, we need to rethink our identification of racial equality with integration, and reopen debate about a sensible nationalist conception of racial equality. As historian Eugene Genovese said in his reply to my open letter: "The Black experience in this country has been a phenomenon without analog." Blacks constitute a "nation-within-a-nation, no matter how anti-separatist their rhetoric or pro-integrationist their genuine aspirations" (*Boston Review*, October/November 1993). What are the political implications of this distinctive history?

Before addressing this question, I need to eliminate a common confusion about Black nationalism. Leonard Jeffries and Louis Farrakhan are widely regarded, even by such experts as Cornel West, as representatives of the Black nationalist perspective. This is a serious misconception. Jeffries and Farrakhan, along with Tony Martin, Khalid Muhammad, and Frances Cress Welsing, represent the *nationalism of fools*. They are cynically antisemitic, mean-spirited, and simply incompetent. Their trains, unlike Mussolini's, do not run on time; in fact, they do not run at all. They are all demagoguery, uniforms, bow ties, and theater. Because they lack programmatic and policy substance, Jeffries and company are not really Black nationalists at all, but ambitious competitors on the game-show circuit posing in nationalist red, black, and green. Their public prominence reflects the leadership vacuum created by a cosmopolitan intelligentsia lacking any pedagogical relationship to poor, inner-city Blacks—the natural outcome of a bankrupt integrationist project.

This nationalism of fools should not be confused with the serious Black nationalist tradition, which has claimed among its adherents such extraordinary 19th century figures as Robert Alexander Young, Henry Highland Garnet, Martin R. Delaney, Henry McNeill Turner, Henry Bibb, and Mary Ann Shadd, and in the 20th century W.E.B. Du Bois, Paul Robeson, Albert Cleage, Harold Cruse, Sterling Stuckey, Joyce Ladner, Nathan Hare, and John H. Bracey, Jr. (Along with such international allies as Frantz Fanon, Aimé Césaire, Walter Rodney, C.I.R. James, and George Beckford).

Endorsing this serious nationalist project does not mean adopting an essentialist or biological conception of racial difference; Black nationalism is rooted in politics, culture, and history, not biology. Nor does it mean, as Genovese puts it, "a separatist repudiation of the American nationality;" Black Americans are part of the American nation, and should start being treated as such. Nor certainly does it mean that we should return to forced racial segregation, which violates basic human rights.

A sensible nationalist strategy, while taking individual rights seriously, is principally about advancing the interests of a community—a "nation-within-a-nation." Its account of that nation starts from the central role of slavery in the formation of Black identity, emphasizes the subsequent experience of racial subordination, and highlights the special importance of religion in the evolution of the Black nation. As Genovese has argued: "[b]lack religion [was] more than slave religion... because many of its most articulate and sophisticated spokesmen were Southern free Negroes and Northerners who lived outside slave society, but because of the racial basis of slavery laid the foundation for a black identity that crossed class lines and demanded protonational identification. The horror of American racism... forced them out of themselves—forced them to glimpse the possibilities of nationality rather than class." Drawing on this distinctive experience, and its religio-cultural expression, the nationalist project aims to improve the lives of Black Americans by concentrating the scarce resources of time, money, and political will on addressing the grave deficiencies of, for example, Black churches, Black schools, Black neighborhoods—on reconstructing the institutions of Black civil society. Moreover, this project of improvement and reconstruction—unlike the nationalism of fools—has a deeply universalistic core. Once more, Genovese has formulated the point with particular power: "the black variant of Christianity laid the foundations of protonational consciousness and a the same time stretched a universalist offer of forgiveness and ultimate reconciliation to white America."

Despite their universalism, nationalists always rejected the integrationist project as impractical. The integrationist idea, as Richard Cloward and Frances Fox Piven described it in 1967, was that Blacks and Whites "ought to reside in the same neighborhoods, go to the same schools, work together and play together without regard to race and, for that matter, without regard to religion, ethnicity, or class." To the Black middle class, this dream has had a measure of reality. For the Black poor in northern cities, integration was always hopelessly irrelevant. Nationalist critics understood that irrelevance; they predicted that the project would fail because of intense White resistance. They turned out to be right.

But even if it could have worked at the time, its time has passed. The Civil Rights movement assumed the health of Black communities and churches, and the integrationist approach to racial equality built upon them (and upon a widespread commitment to an activist national government). But we can no longer make that assumption (nor is there the commitment to activist national government). Given current conditions in inner cities, a strategy for ending a racial caste system in which color fixes life-chances now needs to focus on rebuilding Black institutions: this should be acknowledged by all, whatever their ultimate ideals. Such rebuilding may, of course, involve strategic alliances with other organizations and communities—joining, for example, with largely White unions and environmental groups in efforts to rebuild metropolitan economies. But those alliances will deliver benefits to the inner-city core of those economies only if we also build our own organizational capacities.

Consider next the issue of freedom. What does freedom mean when, 30 years after the passage of the Voting Rights Act, Black Americans lock themselves in their homes and apartments to avoid being caught in urban cross-fire? What does freedom mean for a people psychologically debased by its own internalized racism? What does freedom mean for a people enslaved by the spiritual and political blindness of its own leadership? What does freedom mean for a generation of young people who buy what they want and beg for what they need?

For the Civil Rights movement, freedom was principally a matter of rights. That idea contains a truth of fundamental importance: in our relations with other citizens and the state, rights are essential. They express our standing as moral equals, and as equal citizens.

But a new vision of freedom cannot simply address relations of Black citizens to the broader political community and the state. As American politics devolves and inner-city life degenerates, our vision must also be about the relations within our communities: about Black families and the importance of parental responsibilities to the health of those families, the evil of Black-on-Black violence, the stupidity of defining Black culture around antisemitism of other forms of racial and ethnic hatred, the value of education and intellectual achievement, the importance of mutual commitment and cooperative effort, and the essential role of personal morality and of religious conviction in defining that morality.

❧

The second set of challenges is more programmatic. Suppose we agree to stop the name-calling and back-slapping long enough to have a serious discussion about a common research agenda to improve the current state of Black America. What might such a discussion look like? What follows is a sketch of an answer. In essence, my proposal is that we follow the Atlanta project model, and convene a multi-year *Conference on Black America:* a coordinated research effort, based in current African American studies programs, focused on basic life conditions of Black Americans, issuing in a series of publications backed by the authority of the convening institutions, and developing new strategies to address the state of emergency in Black communities.

- **Convene Annual Meetings:** Major institutes of African American studies—for example, the Du Bois and Trotter Institutes—should jointly commit to convening a series of annual meetings, each of which would be thematically defined, and devoted to examining some fundamental aspect of Black American life.

- **Begin with Economics and Politics:** Early meetings should explore two themes:

  > *Urban Economies:*   The economic fate of Black Americans continues to be tied to inner cities, which are economic basket cases. Are there promising strategies of economic development—for example, metropolitan strategies—that would deliver new employment opportunities in inner cities?
  >
  > *Blacks and Democrats:*   Black support for the Democratic Party is rooted in the post–New Deal nationalization of American politics, the role of the Democrats as the party of national government, and the importance of national government in ensuring civil rights. What are the implications of the denationalization of American politics and a post–civil rights Black political agenda for this political alliance?

- **Stay With Fundamentals:** Topics for subsequent meetings might include: Black-on-Black violence; the state of Black families; equalizing employment opportunities for Black women; the narcotics industry and its role in Black communities; and the current state of mathematical, computer, and scientific literacy among Black youth.

- **Publish the Results:** Each meeting would result in a published volume. These volumes should not simply collect the separate contributions of participants, but provide—where possible—a consensus statement of problems, diagnoses, and directions of potential response.

- **Focus on Policy:** Above all, the Conference should produce practical policy recommendations. And those recommendations will need to be addressed to different actors: the Black community, faith communities, state and federal government, the private sector, and foundations.

- **Measure the Effects:** How will we know if we are doing anything to address the current crisis in Black America? We should measure the health of a community by the conditions of its least advantaged members. So part of the work of the Conference on Black America should be to monitor those conditions, and to assess the effects of its own work on improving them.

No series of analyses, papers, discussions, and books will stop the slaughter in our streets, or children from having children, or men from beating up women. The role of intellectuals is limited; excessive expectations will only produce disappointment. But that limited role is crucial, and fears of disappointment should not serve as an excuse for continuing along the current course. The fate of Black America is in the balance: or, if that description of the stakes seems too collective, then think of the fates of the millions of Black Americans whose lives are now at risk.

**Edmund W. Gordon and
Maitrayee Bhattacharyya**

 **NO**

Have African Americans Failed to Take Responsibility for Their Own Advancement?

The question is not whether African Americans have failed to take responsibility for their own development. Rather, the more correct question is whether the forces that have frustrated the development of African Americans and other minority groups in the United States have been sufficiently identified and addressed.... All of us must become more aware that the problems of poor people and low status minorities in this country are the result of intentional neglect and systemic design which serve the surplus profit-making motives of a few.

The assertion that Black people fail to work toward their own self-development is obviously fallacious and may be a deliberate misrepresentation or obfuscation, advanced by the forces in our society which stand to benefit from such distortion and fiction. Subordinated minorities, such as African Americans in the United States, who have been pushed into surplus labor pools, disenfranchised groups, and dysfunctional underclasses, have extremely limited opportunities to determine their own development. To speak of the relative absence of a minority group's assumption of responsibility for its own development in a heterogenous capitalist society like ours, where one group has achieved hegemony at the cost of the subjugation of others, is ludicrous and borders on being immoral.

This does not mean that we wish to assert that marginalized people have no responsibility for participating in their own development. In fact, these are the very people who must assume responsibility, since oppressors cannot be expected to support the liberation of the oppressed. It is remarkable that persons of African descent have wrested as much as they have from systems of political-economic relations that have been designed to enslave, exploit, and contain Blacks rather than enable them and facilitate their development.

The initiative of Black folks throughout the history of the African diaspora in the United States is evidence enough that this lesson was learned. Despite enormous odds against success, Blacks resisted their enslavement; some fled from their masters, others learned to read and write, and most importantly, Blacks created a unique culture that retained elements of their African heritage and gave them a measure of independence even during the worst days of slavery.

In the period of the Reconstruction, and even after its betrayal, Blacks joined with disenfranchised Whites to assert political power, to advance public responsibility for education, to develop the economic infrastructures of African American communities, and to establish stable families.

The reactions of the dominant social forces interrupted these developments. Nevertheless, at a later period, when Blacks relocated en masse to the urban and industrial centers of the nation, strong Black cultural and economic networks again developed. Black families restabilized. Religious, economic, cultural and social groups flourished. Black people sought education and many became as well educated as they could in schools that were not meant to educate them well or equally. And let us not forget the leadership role that Blacks took more recently during the Civil Rights movement, a movement that benefited Blacks and non-Blacks alike.

Despite these achievements, African American progress has been challenged, frustrated, and disrupted repeatedly. The African American community has never gained nor been able to even initiate invulnerable or sustained development. Time and time again, advancement has been brought to a screeching halt by the forces of external circumstances.

Today, the issues of African American self-determination and responsibility for advancement are complicated by the declining economic health of this country. At the very time that African Americans had developed enough social capital to support accelerated group development, the United States entered a period of economic stagnation and dislocation. In this advanced stage of capitalism, the United States has experienced the exportation of its industrial capacity and its job opportunities. Businesses have searched elsewhere for a cheaper and more docile labor force than the one that has developed in the United States, where employees have organized to demand proper benefits, work conditions, and wages. These economic conditions have thrown all of society into a state of social disorder, political turmoil, and economic chaos. As significant members of the surplus labor pool, many African Americans now face some of the most imposing obstacles to success as a result of the current societal decay.

There is no question that in comparison with other minority groups in the United States, with the exception of ethnically identifiable Native Americans, fewer African Americans have attained economic, academic, and professional successes and stability. African Americans even appear to have developed less productive self-help groups, and many communities that are primarily African American appear self-destructive. "Black-on-Black" violence has been increasingly featured in the media, prompting greater worry about the psychosocial development of African Americans, especially adolescent males. As we focus on the unfortunate fact that many African Americans live in communities where violence, drugs, and crime abound, there are those who reason that African Americans have brought this condition upon themselves.

But the question is not whether African Americans have failed to take responsibility for their own development. Rather, the more correct question is whether the forces that have frustrated the development of African Americans and other minority groups in the United States have been sufficiently identified and addressed. Scholars who have sought to explain these differences in group development call attention to the ubiquitous problem of racism, the caste status of Blacks in the United States, the absence of Blacks' access to capital, and the changes in the political economy that miserably coincided with the very time that Blacks had developed enough social capital to support accelerated group development. But none of these explanations seem to quiet the pervasive and widespread impression that Blacks are inherently incapable of taking full advantage of the opportunities available in the latter 20th century U.S.A.

⋯⊙⋯

Questions concerning Blacks' failures to take responsibility for their own development have possibly arisen because of the disproportionate number of African Americans who are poverty stricken, who are characterized as socially dysfunctional, and who must depend on the nation's welfare system for support. While poverty, dysfunctionality, and dependency reduce the capacity for autonomous behavior, for a segment of the African American community these ailments are due to the devastating breakdown in the economic infrastructure and social networks which are necessary for group development. In James Weldon Johnson's words, "hope unborn had died" in too many instances. Thus, we do see evidence in many of our people of learned helplessness and resignation—in part as a function of an inept system of welfare support, in part also as a result of a tradition of alienation and exclusion from the society, and in part as a function of a degree of depression and lethargy that leaves no energy for self-development. The society which has created this social pathology is doubly culpable when it then blames the victims for their failure to correct their oppression and underdevelopment.

We can not end on this point, however. As pessimistic as we may be in light of the current state of the Black community and the country, it should be obvious that Black people have and will continue to try to overcome the barriers to opportunity and advancement that they face. Perhaps an unprecedentedly large part of the community has given up hope, but it is too soon to dismiss the possibility that the community will stabilize once again and gather momentum as a whole. While members of the Black community face uncertain, precarious development, there are persons who have made it against the odds and even more who are trying. Effective Black families *do* exist, and in countless small communities across this country tiny groups of Black people struggle daily to make better lives for themselves and their children. Individuals and groups from the Black community *have* made important contributions to society at large, and they are usually the products of Black communities which provided the only support for their development. Nor can we can ignore the several national organizations which year after year advocate, organize, demonstrate, provide services, and raise money in support of the development of Black people.

These successful Blacks and their life strategies should not be forgotten, but neither should their example be held against those who have not made it as proof of a culpability that lies with those who are underachieving or less fortunate. It is a mistake to view the problem of Black underdevelopment through the narrow lens of our least developed members. The success of a handful must not blind us to the problems of racism that face all African Americans.

❧

Could it be that we ask whether the victims are responsible for their misery so we will worry more about responsibility for the self and less about society's collective responsibility for all? National values which favor collective responsibility just might require radical redistribution of our nation's resources and access to power for all people. As long as we believe that poor people are responsible for their poverty, that African Americans and other low status peoples are caught up in abusive, drug related, and violent behaviors of their own choosing, and that African Americans do not want to end their marginalization, the privileged and those who are simply more fortunate can look the other way and do nothing.

All of us must become more aware that the problems of poor people and low status minorities in this country are the result of intentional neglect and systemic design which serve the surplus profit-making motives of a few. The present challenge is not so much the determination of responsibility as it is the creation of a greater sense of national community, which would enable all segments of society to assume responsibility and engage in corrective action. The nation can not survive the current economic, political, and social problems without eliminating the tremendous gap between the "haves" and the "have nots." A sense of national community demands collective action to facilitate the development of both the self and others. Those who continue to enjoy privilege must realize that while it is "them" who are marginalized today, it may be "us" tomorrow.

POSTSCRIPT

Are Black Leaders Part of the Problem?

Many people in America today are fed up with affirmative action and criminal rehabilitation programs that do not seem to be effective. In light of this, will Gordon and Bhattacharyya's demand for even more inner-city support likely be heeded? What (if anything) do you think prominent Black leaders of the past, such as W. E. B. Du Bois, Martin Luther King, Jr., Booker T. Washington, Ella Baker, and Fannie Jackson Coppin, would be able to do to solve the problem of Black poverty, crime, drugs, and demoralization today? Which modern leaders, both Black and white, seem to be working for Blacks? Which ones seem to be taking advantage of the Black situation?

Several articles that debate this issue can be found in the Fall 1994 issue of *Long Term View*, from which the selection by Gordon and Bhattacharyya was taken. John Leland, in "Savior of the Streets," *Newsweek* (June 1, 1998), provides an update on Gene Rivers, who, unlike many leaders, white or Black, is living what he preaches in that he resides in an impoverished, drug-infested ghetto in Boston, Massachusetts.

For a bitter attack on Black leadership, see "Racial Divide," by Center for Equal Opportunity counsel Roger Clegg, *Legal Times* (November 20, 2000), followed by NAACP chairman Julian Bond's response in the December 4 issue and Clegg's rebuttal in the December 18 issue. Additional attacks can be found in "Self-Sabotage a Major Problem for African-Americans," by W. Williams, *Annapolis Gazette* (November 15, 2000); "Liberals Lead Blacks Down Road to Nowhere," by G. Kane, *The Baltimore Sun* (December 2, 2000); and "Do Black Americans Still Need Black Leaders?" by J. Riley, *The Wall Street Journal* (April 10, 2001). For attacks on Reverend Jesse Jackson, see "Jesse Came to Do Good and Did Well," by P. Flaherty, *The Baltimore Sun* (March 18, 2001).

For more balanced accounts of Black leaders, see *Black Leadership for Social Change* by Jacob U. Gordon (Greenwood, 2000) and Ronald W. Walters and Cedric Johnson, *Bibliography of African American Leadership: An Annotated Guide* (Greenwood Press, 2000). A perspective that is in opposition to that of Rivers is reflected in Margaret L. Anderson and Patricia Hill Collins, eds., *Race, Class, and Gender: An Anthology,* 4th ed. (Wadsworth, 2001). An interesting article that is laudatory of Historically Black Colleges and Universities (HBCUs) nonetheless suggests that administrators of HBCUs often use tactics close to those of street thugs. See J. Basinger, "A Savvy and Demanding President," *Chronicle of Higher Education* (March 17, 2000).

On the Internet ...

Council of the Great City Schools

The Council of the Great City Schools is an organization of the largest urban public school systems in the United States, advocating K–12 education in inner-city schools and governed by superintendents and board of education members from 58 cities across the nation.

http://www.cgcs.org

The Affirmative Action and Diversity Project: A Web Page for Research

This site presents diverse opinions regarding affirmative action topics. Rather than taking a singular pro or con position, it is designed to help lend many different voices to the debates surrounding the issues of affirmative action.

http://aad.english.ucsb.edu

PART 4

Negotiating Social Justice and Hierarchies

*T*he United States and other modern nations have been entering a new phase in terms of minority-majority relations. Creating a level playing field, where all groups have an equal chance at competing, is not considered enough by many people today. Some insist that to compensate for past injustices, many active, positive things must be done to assist less-privileged racial and ethnic citizens. Only by doing more, this argument goes, can the existing hierarchies be erased and social justice for all be achieved. However, what is social justice? Can it ever be negotiated or politically campaigned for? Which hierarchies need to be smashed? How can the emergence of alternative, possibly more dysfunctional hierarchies be prevented? What about hierarchies that exist within minority groups? Should they be reduced or eliminated as well?

- Should Standardized Tests Be Eliminated From Applicant Processes?

- Should Inner-City Blacks and Hispanics Be Relocated?

- Should Race Be a Consideration in College Admissions?

ISSUE 15

Should Standardized Tests Be Eliminated From Applicant Processes?

YES: Susan Sturm and Lani Guinier, from "The Future of Affirmative Action," *Boston Review* (December 2000/January 2001)

NO: Stephen Steinberg, from "Mending Affirmative Action," *Boston Review* (December 2000/January 2001)

ISSUE SUMMARY

YES: Law professors Susan Sturm and Lani Guinier reject the idea that affirmative action is doing enough to reduce injustices and social hierarchies. They argue that testing candidates either for jobs or for educational slots is inherently unfair and dysfunctional, especially for women and people of color.

NO: Sociologist Stephen Steinberg, an internationally renowned authority on race and ethnicity in the United States, questions Sturm and Guinier's contention that hiring, training, and promoting employees on the basis of job performance eliminates possible discrimination and unfairness. He maintains that affirmative action in employment and education should be amended, not eliminated.

In the following selection, Susan Sturm and Lani Guinier contend that not enough has been done to erase unfair hierarchies that continue to systematically exclude many females and African Americans from jobs, higher education, and equal participation in society. They argue that despite affirmative action, civil rights gains, and a raising of the cultural conscience about the many injustices in the United States and other countries, much more needs to be done.

One of the continuing barriers to social justice, Sturm and Guinier maintain, is pen-and-paper tests that are used to hire and promote employees, admit students to colleges, and allow others into different spheres of public life. To them, most, if not all, of these tests privilege economically secure white males, who are encouraged early in life to compete with others via test-taking and the demonstration of personal merit. Not only do these white males' advantaged backgrounds enable them to perform better, but the tests themselves often have built-in biases, with examples, concepts, and assumptions drawn from middle-class subcultural experiences. Survival problems, vocabulary, and the general worldview of minorities and the poor are almost never part of standardized tests. Hence, say Sturm and Guinier, the "intelligence" and abilities of many Americans are not legitimately reflected on such tests.

As you read Sturm and Guinier's selection, consider their presuppositions about social, economic, and political life. In what ways do they present a radical alternative to traditional individualism that, at least in rhetoric, has characterized attitudes toward social justice? As you consider their assertion that eliminating standardized tests would have positive consequences that are both functional (e.g., a much larger pool of excellent workers would become available) and related to social justice (e.g., existing unfairness would be minimized), think about their image of the workplace. That is, in what ways do they assume that a collectivized workforce is needed and could be created and maintained? What kinds of changes do they call for?

Stephen Steinberg, who also favors social justice and the reduction of unfair hierarchies, challenges Sturm and Guinier on many fronts in the second selection. He contends that affirmative action has achieved many of its goals and should not be rejected. He also worries that Sturm and Guinier support opponents of affirmative action who attack affirmative action and other programs for very different reasons. Steinberg raises important questions about the alternative strategies that Sturm and Guinier recommend for hiring employees and admitting students other than written tests.

As you read this debate, consider the broad philosophical and ethical background out of which it has emerged. Over 30 years ago sociologists T. H. Marshall and Talcott Parsons identified three decisive stages that are necessary for one to achieve full citizenship inclusion in modern societies. The first two, civil and political, have to do with legal and political justice—citizens need protections under the law, the right to vote, freedom to speak out, and so forth. Such dimensions of justice are so basic that few Americans today even realize how hard-earned they are, how unique they are historically, and how rare they are in many contemporary societies. Although violations still occur, Americans tend to assume that they have the right to political and criminal justice.

The third stage of citizenship inclusion, however, is far more problematic. It has to do with social justice, which includes the freedom from want and the right to food, shelter, employment, a solid education, medical services, and so on. Much of the civil rights legislation that has been passed since 1964 and many state and federal court cases have attempted to provide minorities—especially African Americans and females—protection from job, housing, and educational discrimination. Efforts have also been made to redress former injustices: schools and employers, for example, have been encouraged to recruit minorities. Affirmative action in its various forms is a major indicator of such government actions. The fact that affirmative action has been a bumpy road and that many recent court and legislative actions have gone against the practice is another issue. The *concept* of leveling the playing field so that all can participate remains intact, as does legal, political, and often social intolerance of discrimination based on race, ethnicity, and gender.

The Future of Affirmative Action

For more than two decades, affirmative action has been under sustained assault. In courts, legislatures, and the media, opponents have condemned it as an unprincipled program of racial and gender preferences that threatens fundamental American values of fairness, equality, and democratic opportunity. Such preferences, they say, are extraordinary departures from prevailing "meritocratic" modes of selection, which they present as both fair and functional: fair, because they treat all candidates as equals; functional, because they are well suited to picking the best candidates.

This challenge to affirmative action has met with concerted response. Defenders argue that affirmative action is still needed to rectify continued exclusion and marginalization. And they marshal considerable evidence showing that conventional standards of selection exclude women and people of color, and that people who were excluded in the past do not yet operate on a level playing field. But this response has largely been reactive. Proponents typically treat affirmative action as a crucial but peripheral supplement to an essentially sound framework of selection for jobs and schools.

We think it is time to shift the terrain of debate. We need to situate the conversation about race, gender, and affirmative action in a wider account of democratic opportunity by refocusing attention from the contested periphery of the system of selection to its settled core. The present system measures merit through scores on paper-and-pencil tests. But this measure is fundamentally unfair. In the educational setting, it restricts opportunities for many poor and working-class Americans of all colors and genders who could otherwise obtain a better education. In the employment setting, it restricts access based on inadequate predictors of job performance. In short, it is neither fair nor functional in its distribution of opportunities for admission to higher education, entry-level hiring, and job promotion.

To be sure, the exclusion experienced by women and people of color is especially revealing of larger patterns. The race- and gender-based exclusions that are the target of current affirmative action policies remain the most visible examples of bias in ostensibly neutral selection processes. Objectionable in themselves, these exclusions also signal the inadequacy of traditional methods of selection for everyone, and the need to rethink how we allocate educational and employment opportunities. And that rethinking is crucial to our capacity to develop productive, fair, and efficient institutions that can meet the challenges of a rapidly changing and increasingly complex marketplace. By using the experience of those on the margin to rethink the whole, we may forge a new, progressive vision of cross-racial collaboration, functional diversity, and genuinely democratic opportunity.

Affirmative Action Narratives

Competing narratives drive the affirmative action debate. The stock story told by critics in the context of employment concerns the white civil servant—say a police officer or firefighter—John Doe. (Similar stories abound in the educational setting.) Doe scores several points higher on the civil service exam and interview rating process, but loses out to a woman or person of color who did not score as high on those selection criteria.[1]

Doe and others in similar circumstances advance two basic claims: first, that they have more merit than beneficiaries of affirmative action; and second, that as a matter of fairness they are entitled to the position for which they applied. Consider these claims in turn.

The idea of merit can be interpreted in a variety of ways: for example, as a matter of desert (because they were next in line, based on established criteria of selection, they deserve the position), or as earned recognition ("when an individual has worked hard and succeeded, she deserves recognition, praise and/or reward"[2]). But, most fundamentally, arguments about merit are functional: a person merits a job if he or she has, to an especially high degree, the qualities needed to perform well in that job. Many critics of affirmative action equate merit, functionally understood, with a numerical ranking on standard paper-and-pencil tests. Those with higher scores are presumed to be most qualified, and therefore most deserving.

Fairness, like merit, is a concept with varying definitions. The stock story defines fairness formally. Fairness, it assumes, requires treating everyone the same: allowing everyone to enter the competition for a position, and evaluating each person's results the same way. If everyone takes the same test, and every applicant's test is evaluated in the same manner, then the assessment is fair. So affirmative action is unfair because it takes race and gender into account, and thus evaluates some test results differently. A crucial premise of this fairness challenge to affirmative action is the assumption that tests afford equal opportunity to demonstrate individual merit, and therefore are not biased.

Underlying the standard claims about merit and fairness, then, is the idea that we have an objective yardstick for measuring qualification. Institutions are assumed to know what they are looking for (to continue the yardstick analogy, length), how to measure it (yards, meters), how to replicate the measurement process (using the ruler), and how to rank people accordingly (by height). Both critics and proponents of affirmative action typically assume that objective tests for particular attributes of merit—perhaps supplemented by subjective methods such as unstructured interviews and reference checks—can be justified as predictive of performance, and as the most efficient method of selection.

Merit, Fairness, and Testocracy

The basic premise of the stock narrative is that the selection criteria and processes used to rank applicants for jobs and admission to schools are fair and valid tests of merit. This premise is flawed. The conventional system of selection does not give everyone an equal opportunity to compete. Not everyone who could do the job, or could bring new insights about how to do the job even better, is given an opportunity to perform or succeed. The yardstick metaphor simply does not withstand scrutiny.

Fictive Merit

For present purposes, we accept the idea that capacity to perform—functional merit—is a legitimate consideration in distributing jobs and educational opportunities. But we dispute the notion that merit is identical to performance on standardized tests. Such tests do not fulfill their stated function. They do not reliably identify those applicants who will succeed in college or later in life, nor do they consistently predict those who are most likely to perform well in the jobs they will occupy. Particularly when used alone or to rank-order candidates, timed paper-and-pencil tests screen out applicants who could nevertheless do the job.

Those who use standardized tests need to be able to identify and measure successful performance in the job or at school. In both contexts, however, those who use tests lack meaningful measures of successful performance. In the employment area, many employers have not attempted to correlate test performance with worker productivity or pay. In the educational context, researchers have attempted to correlate standardized tests with first-year performance in college or post-graduate education.[3] But this measure does not reflect successful overall academic achievement or performance in other areas valued by the educational institution.

Moreover, "successful performance" needs to be interpreted broadly. A study of three classes of Harvard alumni over three decades, for example, found a high correlation between "success"—defined by income, community involvement, and professional satisfaction—and two criteria that might not ordinarily be associated with Harvard freshmen: low SAT scores and a blue-collar background.[4] When asked what predicts *life success,* college admissions officers at elite universities report that, above a minimum level of competence, "initiative" or "drive" are the best predictors.[5]

By contrast, the conventional measures attempt to predict successful performance, narrowly defined, in the short-run. They focus on immediate success in school and a short time-frame between taking the test and demonstrating success. Those who excel based on those short-term measures, however, may not in fact excel over the long-run in areas that are equally or more important. For example, a study of graduates of the University of Michigan Law School found a negative relationship between high LSAT scores and subsequent community leadership or community service.[6]

Those with higher LSAT scores are less likely, as a general matter, to serve their community or do pro bono service as a lawyer. In addition, the study found that admission indexes—including the LSAT—fail to correlate with other accomplishments after law school, including income levels and career satisfaction.

Standardized tests may thus compromise an institution's capacity to search for what it really values in selection. Privileging the aspects of performance measured by standardized tests may well screen out the contributions of people who would bring important and different skills to the workplace or educational institution. It may reward passive learning styles that mimic established strategies rather than creative, critical, or innovative thinking.

Finally, individuals often perform better in both workplace and school when challenged by competing perspectives or when given the opportunity to develop in conjunction with the different approaches or skills of others.

The problem of using standardized tests to predict performance is particularly acute in the context of employment. Standardized tests may reward qualities such as willingness to guess, conformity, and docility. If they do, then test performance may not relate significantly to the capacity to function well in jobs that require creativity, judgment, and leadership. In a service economy, creativity and interpersonal skills are important, though hard to measure. In the stock scenario of civil service exams for police and fire departments, traits such as honesty, perseverance, courage, and ability to manage anger are left out. In other words, people who rely heavily on numbers to make employment decisions may be looking in the wrong place. While John Doe scored higher on the civil service exam, he may not perform better as a police officer.

Fictive Fairness

Scores on standardized tests are, then, inadequate measures of merit. But are the conventional methods of selecting candidates for high-stakes positions fair? The stock affirmative action narrative implicitly embraces the idea that fairness consists in sameness of treatment. But this conception of fairness assumes a level playing field—that if everyone plays by the same rules, the game does not favor or disadvantage anyone.

An alternative conception of fairness—we call it "fairness as equal access and opportunity"—rejects the automatic equation of sameness with fairness. It focuses on providing members of various races and genders with opportunities to demonstrate their capacities and recognizes that formal sameness can camouflage actual difference and apparently neutral screening devices can be exclusionary. The central idea is that the standards governing the process must not *arbitrarily advantage* members of one group over another. It is not "fair," in this sense, to use entry-level credentials that appear to treat everyone the same, but in effect deny women and people of color a genuine opportunity to demonstrate their capacities.

On this conception, the "testocracy" fails to provide a fair playing field for candidates. Many standardized tests assume that there is a single way to complete a job, and assess applicants solely on the basis of this uniform style. In this way, the testing process arbitrarily excludes individuals who may perform equally effectively, but with different approaches.

❧❦❧

For example, in many police departments, strength, military experience, and speed weigh heavily in the decision to hire police officers. These characteristics relate to a particular mode of policing focusing on "command presence" and control through authority and force.[7]

If the job of policing is defined as subduing dangerous suspects, then it makes sense to favor the strongest, fastest, and most disciplined candidates. But not every situation calls for quick reaction time. Indeed, in some situations, responding quickly gets police officers and whole departments in trouble.

This speed-and-strength standard normalizes a particular type of officer: tough, brawny, and macho. But other modes of policing—dispute resolution, persuasion, counseling, and community involvement—are also critical, and sometimes superior, approaches to policing. One study of the Los Angeles Police Department, conducted in the wake of the Rodney King trials, recommended that the department increase the number of women on the police force as part of a strategy to reduce police brutality and improve community relations. The study found that women often display a more interactive and engaged approach to policing.[8]

Similarly, an informal survey of police work in some New York City Housing Authority projects found that many women housing authority officers, because they could not rely on their brawn to intimidate potential offenders, developed a mentoring style with young adolescent males.[9] The women, many of whom came from the community they were patrolling, increased public safety because they did not approach the young men in a confrontational way. Their authority was respected because they offered respect.

The retention and success of new entrants to institutions often depend on expanding measures of successful performance. But because conventional measures camouflage their bias, one-size-fits-all testocracies invite people to believe that they have earned their status because of a test score, and invite beneficiaries of affirmative action to believe exactly the opposite—that they did not earn their opportunity. By allowing partial and underinclusive selection standards to proceed without criticism, affirmative action perpetuates an asymmetrical approach to evaluation.

In addition to arbitrarily favoring certain standards of performance, conventional selection methods advantage candidates from higher socioeconomic backgrounds and disproportionately screen out women and people of color, as well as those in lower income brackets. When combined with other unstructured screening practices, such as personal connections and alumni preferences, standardized testing creates an arbitrary barrier for many otherwise-qualified candidates.

❧✦❧

The evidence that the testocracy is skewed in favor of wealthy contestants is consistent and striking. Consider the linkage between test performance and parental income. Average family income rises with each 100-point increase in SAT scores, except for the highest SAT category, where the number of cases is small. Within each racial and ethnic group, SAT scores increase with income.

Reliance on high school rank alone excludes fewer people from lower socioeconomic backgrounds. When the SAT is used in conjunction with high school rank to select college applicants, the number of applicants admitted from lower-income families decreases. This is because the SAT is more strongly correlated with every measure of socioeconomic background than is high school rank.[10]

Existing methods of selection, both objective and subjective, also exclude people based on their race and gender. For example, although women as a group perform worse than males on the SAT, they equal or outperform men in grade point average during the first year of college, the most common measure of successful performance. Similar patterns have been detected in the results of the ACT and other standardized college selection tests.[11]

Supplementing class rank with the SAT also decreases black acceptances and black enrollments.[12] Studies show that the group of black applicants rejected based on their SAT scores includes both those who would likely have failed and those who would likely have succeeded, and that these groups offset each other. Consequently, the rejection of more blacks as a result of using SAT scores "does not translate into improved admissions outcomes. The SAT does not improve colleges' ability to admit successful blacks and reject potentially unsuccessful ones."[13]

Thus, it is incontestable that the existing meritocracy disproportionately includes wealthy white men. Is this highly unequal outcome fair? Even if the "meritocracy" screens out women, people of color, and those of lower socioeconomic status, it could be argued that those screens are fair if they serve an important function. But the testocracy fails even on this measure; it does not reliably distinguish successful future performers from unsuccessful ones, even when supplemented by additional subjective criteria. Therefore, racial, gender, and socioeconomic exclusion cannot legitimately be justified in the name of a flawed system of selection.

A New Approach

We have seen how the stock affirmative action narrative normalizes and legitimates selection practices that are neither functional nor fair. Now it is time to use these criticisms as an occasion to move from affirmative action as an add-on to affirmative action as an occasion to rethink the organizing framework for selection generally.

Such rethinking should begin by reconsidering the connection between predetermined qualifications and future performance. The standard approach proceeds as if selection were a fine-tuned matching process that measures the capacity to perform according to some predetermined criteria of performance. This assumes that the capacity to perform—functional merit—exists in people apart from their opportunity to work on the job. It further assumes that institutions know in advance what they are looking for, and that these functions will remain constant across a wide range of work sites and over time.

But neither candidates nor positions remain fixed. Often people who have been given an opportunity to do a job perform well because they learn the job by doing it. Moreover, on-the-job learning has assumed even greater significance in the current economy, in which unstable markets, technological advances, and shorter product cycles have created pressures for businesses to increase the flexibility and problem-solving capacity of workers. Under these circumstances, access to on-the-job training opportunities will contribute to functional merit—the opportunity to perform will precede the capacity.

The concept of selection as a matching process also presumes that institutions have a clear idea of what they value, and of the relationship of particular jobs to their institutional goals. Even in a relatively stable economic and technological environment, institutions rarely attempt to articulate goals, much less develop a basis for measuring successful achievement of those goals. But without a definition of successful performance, it is difficult to develop fair and valid selection criteria and processes.

Defining successful performance has also become more complicated in the current economic and political environment. Traditional measures of success, such as short-term profitability, do not fully define success, and may in fact distort the capacity to evaluate and monitor employee performance. In addition, standards must increasingly change to adapt to technological developments and shifting consumer demand. Students of economic organization and human resources now emphasize the importance of developing complex, interactive, and holistic approaches to measuring both institutional and individual performance.[14] Conventional matching approaches to selection do not easily accommodate this move toward more dynamic and interrelated assessments of successful performance.

Current selection approaches also focus on the decontextualized individual, who is assumed to possess merit in the abstract and to demonstrate it through a test or interview. Social science evidence shows that the testing environment can selectively depress the test performance of highly qualified individuals.[15] And individual performance does not take into account how an applicant functions as part of a group. Increasingly, work requires the capacity to interact effectively with others, and the demands of the economy are moving in the direction of more interactive, team-oriented production. The capacity to adapt to rapid changes in technology, shifts in consumer preferences, and fluid markets for goods requires greater collaboration at every level.[16] Paper-and-pencil tests do not measure or predict an individual's capacity for creativity and collaboration.

⁕

Assessment through opportunity to perform often works better than testing for performance. Various studies have shown that "experts often fail on 'formal' measures of their calculating or reasoning capacities but can be shown to exhibit precisely those same skills in the course of their ordinary work."[17] Those who assess individuals in situations that more closely resemble actual working conditions make better predictions about those individuals' ultimate performance. Particularly when those assessments are integrated into day-to-day work over a period of time, they have the potential to produce better information about workers and better workers.

Moreover, many of those who are given an opportunity to perform, even when their basic preparation is weaker, catch up if they are motivated to achieve. Indeed, a recent study of a 25-year policy of open admissions at the City University of New York found that the school was one of the largest sources in the United States of undergraduate students going on to earn doctorates, even though many of its undergraduates come from relatively poor backgrounds and take twice as long to complete their bachelor's degree.[18]

Reclaiming Merit and Fairness

Critics of affirmative action defend prevailing selection practices in the name of meritocracy and democracy. We have argued that those practices put democratic opportunity fundamentally at risk. Even when they are modified by a commitment to affirmative action, current modes of selection jeopardize democratic values of inclusiveness (no one is arbitrarily shut out or excluded); transparency (the processes employed are open and are functionally linked to the public character or public mission of the institution); and accountability (the choice of beneficiaries is directly linked to a public good). The failure of existing practice to achieve inclusiveness is perhaps the most telling. Although some people will lose as a result of any sorting and ranking, a democratic system needs to give those losers a sense of hope in the future, not divide us into classes of permanent losers and permanent winners. But that is precisely what happens when we make opportunity dependent on past success.

How, then, can we develop a model of selection that expresses a more inclusive, transparent, and accountable vision of democratic opportunity—an approach to selection that will benefit everyone, and advance racial and gender justice?

An Emerging Model

Because of the importance in a democracy of ensuring opportunities to perform, we can start by shifting the model of selection from prediction to performance. This model builds on the insight that the opportunity to participate helps to create the capacity to perform, and that actual performance offers the best evidence of capacity to perform. So instead of making opportunity depend on a strong prior showing of qualification, we should expand opportunities as a way of building the relevant qualifications.

To follow this model, organizations need to build assessment into their activities, integrate considerations of inclusion and diversity into the process of selection, and develop mechanisms of evaluation that are accountable to those considerations. The result would be a dynamic process of selection, with feedback integrated into productivity. At the level of individual performance assessment, it would mean less reliance on one-shot predictive tests and more on performance-based evaluation.

One fundamental change resulting from our framework would be a shift away from reliance on tests as a means of distinguishing among candidates. Tests would be limited to screening out individuals who could not learn to perform competently with adequate training and mentoring, or be simply discontinued as a part of the selection process. Of course, decreasing reliance on tests to rank candidates would create the need to develop other ways of distinguishing among applicants. There is no single, uniform solution to this problem. One approach would be a lottery system that would distribute opportunity to participate among relatively indistinguishable candidates by chance. Concerns about a lottery's insensitivity to particular institutional needs or values could be addressed by increasing the selection prospects of applicants with skills, abilities, or backgrounds that are particularly valued by the institution. A weighted lottery may be the fairest and most functional approach for some institutions. Particularly in the education arena, where opportunity lies at the core of the institution's mission, a lottery may be an important advance. Above that test-determined floor, applicants could be chosen by several alternatives, including portfolio-based assessment or a more structured and participatory decision-making process.[19]

A more institutionally grounded approach might work in non-educational contexts. In some jobs, for example, decision-makers would assume responsibility for constructing a dynamic and interactive process of selection that is integrated into the day-to-day functioning of the organization. Recent developments in the assessment area, such as portfolio-based and authentic assessment, move in this direction. These might build on the tradition and virtues of apprenticeship, and indeed might "more closely resemble traditional apprenticeship measures than formal testing."[20] They would build from and acknowledge the effects of context on performance and the importance of measuring performance in relation to context.

To take the next step in developing an experience-based approach to opportunity and assessment, it would be necessary to consider the needs, interests, and possibilities of the particular institutional setting. The central challenge is to develop systems of accountable decision-making that minimize the expression of bias, and structure judgment around identified, although not static, norms. For each assessment, decision-makers would articulate criteria of successful performance, document activities and tasks relevant to the judgment, assess candidates in relation to those criteria, and offer sufficient information about the candidates' performance to enable others to exercise independent judgment.

For this model to work, institutions would also need to change the relationship between race, gender, and other categories of exclusion to the overall decision-making process. Institutions would continue to assess the impact of various selection processes on traditionally excluded groups. But institutions would use that information in different ways. Rather than operating as an add-on, after-the-fact response to failures of the overall process, race and gender would serve as both a signal of organizational failure and a catalyst of organizational innovation. We will return to this issue later, but let's first try to imagine what this more integrated approach would look like.

꩜

Consider the case of Bernice, now the general counsel of a major financial institution. Initially, she was hired as local general counsel to a bank, after having previously been partner in a prestigious law firm. (She left the firm after reaching the glass ceiling, unable to bring in enough new clients to progress further.)

Bernice ultimately became general counsel to a major national corporation that previously had no women in high-level management positions. Her promotion resulted from the opportunities presented in an interactive and extended selection process. Her local bank merged with a larger company. In part to create the appearance of including women, she was permitted to compete for the job of general counsel for the new entity. Three lawyers shared the position for nine months. She initially did not view herself as in the running for the final cut.

During this time period, Bernice had a series of contacts with high-level corporate officials, contacts she never would have had without this probationary team approach. As it turned out, Bernice was able to deal unusually well with a series of crises. If standard criteria, such as recommendations and interpersonal contacts, had been used to select a candidate, it is doubtful Bernice would have been picked. But teamwork, decentralized management, and collaborative and flexible working relationships allowed her to develop the contacts and experiences that trained her. The opportunity to interact over a period of time allowed her to demonstrate her strengths to those who made promotion decisions. Bernice did not know she had those strengths until she took the job.[21]

Now, as general counsel, she is positioned to expand opportunities for women, and corporate culture in general. She can structure the same kind of collaborative decision-making in selection that provided her the opportunity to work her way into the job. She determines who is promoted within the legal department, and who is hired as outside counsel. She is also in a position to influence how women are assessed as managers within the company.

This story illustrates the potential for integrating concerns about diversity into the process of recruitment and selection. It also shows the value of using performance to assess performance. At the core of this integrative move is a functional theory of diversity animated both by principles of justice and fairness (the inclusion of marginalized groups and the minimization of bias) and by strategic concerns (improving productivity). It is crucial to this integration that decision-makers and advocates understand and embrace a conception of diversity that comprises normative and instrumental elements. In public discourse, diversity has become a catchall phrase or cliché, used to substitute for a variety of goals, or a numerical concept that is equated with proportional representation.[22] Too often, the different strands of diversity remain separate, with those concerned about justice emphasizing racial and gender diversity as a project of remediation, and those concerned about productivity emphasizing differences in background and skills. Without an articulated theory that links diversity to the goals of particular enterprises and to the project of racial justice, public discussion and public policy-making around race and gender issues is more complicated.

Selection and Productivity

One argument for more closely integrating selection and performance is that doing so has the potential to improve institutions' capacity to select productive workers, pursue innovative performance, and adapt quickly to the demands of a changing economic environment. The conventional top-down approach short-circuits the capacity of selection to serve as a mechanism for feedback about an institution's performance and its need to adapt to changing conditions. It also keeps institutions from developing more responsive, integrated, and dynamically efficient selection processes.

Instead of relying on standardized tests, the system of performance-based selection would focus decision-makers' attention on creating suitable scenarios for making informed judgments about performance. This would improve the capacity of institutions to find people who are creative, adaptive, reliable, and committed, rather than just good test-takers. In some instances, these structured opportunities could directly contribute to the productivity of the organization.

A more interactive process of selection also provides an ongoing opportunity to assess and monitor organizational performance and to perceive and react to the changing character and needs of clients and employees. It provides information learned through the process of selection to the rest of the organization. In the process of redefining the standards for recruitment, the organization also redefines how those already in the institution should function. Selection operates at the boundaries of the organization. It exposes decision-makers to the environment they operate in, provides access to information about the world in which the organization operates, and forces choices about its relationship with that environment. The process of defining the standards for positions also reflects and reinscribes the organization's priorities and direction. Emphasizing one set of skills over another in the selection process communicates to employees and students how the organization defines good work. Thus, the selection process provides the opportunity and challenge of continually redefining standards in relation to stakeholders, both inside and outside of the organization.

The Benefits of Diversity

More open-ended processes of selection also embrace and harness difference. And the resulting diversity—in particular, an interactive dynamic among individuals with different vantage points, skills, or values—appears to help generate creative solutions to problems.

Studies have shown that work-team heterogeneity promotes more critical strategic analysis, creativity, innovation, and high-quality decisions. Analyses of group decision-making suggest that participation of groups with different prior beliefs or predispositions in decision making improves the quality of the decision for everyone. Studies of jury deliberations support the contention that diversity of participants contributes to improved deliberation. A jury consisting of people from diverse backgrounds has more accurate recall and "more nuanced understanding of the behavior of the parties than [a more homogeneous jury]."[23]

Diversity in culture, style, and background also enhances the knowledge base and repertoire of skills and responses available to a particular group or institution, which can enhance institutions' capacity to perform and innovate. Again, the example of the Los Angeles Police Department illustrates this theory. The benefits of racial and gender diversity may be most obvious in the educational and human services areas, where customers, clients, and perspectives may themselves be identified by race and gender.

Racial and cultural diversity in a workforce can also provide opportunities for companies marketing products that serve racially and culturally diverse client groups. As David Thomas and Robin Ely have documented, customers and clients from different racial, ethnic, and cultural communities constitute distinctive market niches that companies have sought to address by diversifying their workforces.

Inside an organization, the experience of those who have been excluded or marginalized often signals more general or systemic problems that affect a much larger group and may hurt the organization's overall productivity. Race and gender complaints may be symptomatic of more general management problems, such as poor organization or arbitrary treatment of workers. For example, recent studies documenting that many women find law school silencing and exclusionary reveal patterns of problems that many men experience as well.[24]

Similarly, sexual harassment of graduate students sometimes reveals a more general institutional inadequacy that would otherwise remain hidden. Faculty and students frequently lack shared understandings about fair, respectful, non-exploitative supervisory relationships between students and their faculty advisors. Addressing sexual harassment—a problem ordinarily associated with women—can prompt a conversation on ways to promote productive and successful working relationships in general.

⌘

These observations answer a large question about the status of affirmative action in the performance-based model: Once we use the lens of the margins to rethink the whole, why do group status and performance continue to be crucial in assessing the adequacy of selection criteria? If we are successful in transforming the discourse and practice of merit and selection for everyone, why are race, gender, and other categories of exclusion still relevant to the discussion?

In responding to this question, we take the world as it currently exists. The workforce is becoming increasingly diverse: almost two-thirds of entrants to the civilian workforce in the period between 1992 and 2005 are projected to be women and racial minorities. Women and people of color have long been excluded and marginalized, and continue to experience exclusion in many institutional settings. Race continues to be a divisive issue for many Americans, one that prompts skepticism and mistrust. Our continued focus on race and gender moves forward from the current legal and organizational landscape. In many institutions, particularly those that are private and non-union, categories such as race and gender offer the only avenue for challenging decisions and practices.

Under these conditions, race- and gender-based inquiries continue to form the cornerstone of an integrated approach to a progressive economic agenda. Many members of marginalized groups predicate their willingness to participate in collaborative conversation on the majority's recognition of the ongoing significance of group-based exclusion. For members of historically excluded groups, a meaningful program of inclusion is a prerequisite to participating in ventures that benefit the whole community. Affirmative action has become a symbol of society's recognition of its responsibility for its history of legal disenfranchisement, and of the equal citizenship and respect of those who have historically been excluded. History shapes the perception and experience of those who have experienced formal exclusion, and this historic pattern of racial inequality will continue to be experienced unless it is affirmatively acknowledged and altered.

Without the cooperation of those concerned with race and gender justice in building this new progressive agenda, the dialogue will continue to be polarized, divisive, and adversarial. Unless we can build the concerns of racial and gender inclusion into the process of collaboration, these issues will continue to be addressed in settings that undermine the capacity of institutions to adapt to changing conditions.

In addition, research consistently shows that ignoring patterns of racial and gender exclusion causes these patterns to recur. A proven method of minimizing the expression of bias in decision-making consists of reminding decision-makers of the risk of bias or exclusion and requiring them be fair and unbiased. Unless we continue to pay attention to the impact of our decisions on members of groups that are the target of subtle bias and exclusion, those group members will continue to be marginalized.

Fairness

Using the margins to rethink the whole—by using performance to develop opportunity—will help with fairness as well as functionality. The functional approach to selection reduces the importance of criteria that have excluded women and people of color and favored wealthier applicants. It enables previously excluded people to "show their stuff." Moreover, by rethinking the standards of selection for everyone, this approach destabilizes the idea that the existing meritocracy is fair. Embedding the role of diversity enables other people to see how benefiting women and people of color benefits them. In addition, the functional approach has the potential to create a participatory and accountable selection process, which can enhance individuals' autonomy and institutions' legitimacy.

Finally, conditions for sustained contact, genuine collaboration, and fair assessment provide outsiders with a meaningful opportunity to learn, perform, and succeed. Studies of multi-racial teamwork suggest that the opportunity to work as relative co-equals in interdependent, cooperative teams may also reduce bias.[25] Indeed, carefully structured, accountable, and participatory work groups may replicate the conditions most likely to reduce bias and permit genuine participation by women and people of color.

To be sure, these more interactive and informal forms of selection and management rely explicitly on discretion and subjectivity. Preconceptions and biases will likely affect evaluations of performance in ways that often exclude women and people of color. And unstructured discretion exercised without accountability or participation by diverse decision-makers will likely reproduce biased and exclusionary results. But these biases have not been eliminated by formal selection practices and paper-and-pencil tests. More importantly, the model of formal fairness that is outcome-driven, rule-bound, and centralized will not reach many of the places where women and people of color seek to enter.[26] If the economy is moving in the direction of creating and restructuring work along more team-oriented, participatory lines, we need approaches to selection and performance that permit women and people of color to participate fairly and to succeed in this changing environment. Otherwise, women and people of color will remain on the margins of the new economy. Moreover, as business entities become more fluid and rely more on subcontracting and temporary work, we must devise new and more interactive strategies for inclusion and empowerment that embrace a workforce existing in the margins of traditional legal categories. The exercise of discretion cannot and should not be eliminated. Instead, discretionary decision making must become the subject and site of participation, accountability, and creative problem-solving.

A Democratic Imperative

Access to work and education is a fundamental attribute of modern citizenship. Work provides an identity that is valued by others. Work organizes and shapes the citizen's sense of self. Virtually every aspect of citizenship is channeled through participation in the workplace. For most people, medical care, pensions, and social insurance are linked to workplace participation. In these ways, work has become a proxy for citizenship.

Increasingly, the opportunity to work in a non-contingent, full-time position that provides these benefits of citizenship depends on access to higher education. People who are not educated do not get jobs, and thus cannot participate in the responsibilities and benefits of citizenship. Moreover, those without the benefits of higher education increasingly work in shifting, temporary, and task-centered jobs. Such individuals may fail to develop a sense of personal worth, institutional or communal loyalty, or positive agency, all attributes essential to functioning as citizens.

In addition, voting—the process that has traditionally served to permit participation and influence public decision-making—does not afford individuals the capacity to deliberate and exercise much influence over the conditions of day-to-day life. Without the opportunity to participate in intermediate institutions, such as places of work and schools, many citizens have no sense that their voices are being heard.[27]

If, as we believe, work and education are basic components of citizenship, screens or barriers to participation should be drawn in the least exclusive manner consistent with the institution's mission. Access and opportunity to participate is critical to equipping citizens to fulfill their responsibilities, to respecting their status and autonomy as individuals, and to legitimating society's decisions as reflecting the participation of the community. People who feel they have a voice in the decision-making process are more likely to accept the ultimate decision as legitimate, even if it is different from the one they initially supported.

Through the first two centuries of our nation's history, restrictions on voting based on race, gender, and wealth were gradually lifted "only after wide public debate" about "the very nature of the type of society in which Americans wished to live."[28] These barriers were invalidated because they came to be seen as unduly burdening access to this fundamental aspect of citizenship. Courts also recognized that these burdens, through the exercise of selective discretion by local officials, fell disproportionately on disempowered groups such as African Americans.[29]

We believe a national debate on the terms of participation in equivalent forms of citizenship is long overdue. Just as "history has seen a continuing expansion of the scope of the right of suffrage in this country,"[30] so we would argue that 21st-century democracy will depend on a commensurate expansion of the scope of access to higher education and opportunities for on-the-job training. Even if there are justifications for requirements relating to the capacity to exercise citizenship responsibilities effectively, these requirements must be drawn in the most narrow way possible because of the importance of assuring democratic access and legitimacy in the distribution of citizenship opportunities and responsibilities. A performance-based framework of selection is the equivalent, in employment and education, to the elimination of poll taxes and restrictive registration laws in the arena of voting.

We seek to open up a conversation about issues that many people treat as resolved. Our institutions do not currently function as fair and functional meritocracies. Only by rethinking our assumptions about the current system and future possibilities can we move toward the ideals that so many Americans share. This enterprise offers the possibility of bringing together many who are adversaries in the current affirmative action debate but share an interest in forging fairer, more inclusive, and more democratic institutions. It reconnects affirmative action to the innovative ideal. In this way, affirmative action can reclaim the historic relationship between racial justice and the revitalization of institutions to the benefit of everyone.

Notes

1. See *Johnson v. Transportation Agency,* 480 US 616 (1987); *Wygant v. Jackson Board of Education,* 476 US 267 (1986). The most politicized version of the anti-affirmative action narrative is typified by the campaign strategy used by Sen. Jesse Helms, the white incumbent, against Harvey Gantt, his black challenger in 1990. The Helms campaign commercial displayed a white working class man tearing up a rejection letter while the voice-over said, "You needed that job, and you were the best qualified.... But it had to go to a minority because of a racial quota." See Andrew Hacker, *Two Nations: Black and White, Separate, Hostile, Unequal* (New York: Scribner, 1992), p. 202.

2. Laura K. Bass, "Affirmative Action: Reframing the Discourse" (unpublished manuscript, December 4, 1995).

3. No tester claims that the LSAT or SAT, which is designed to predict academic performance, has ever been validated to predict job performance or pay. One study by Christopher Jencks finds that people who had higher paying jobs also had higher test scores. One problem with this conclusion is that higher test scores were used to screen out applicants from earlier, formative opportunities. Another study, by David Chambers, et al., of graduates of the University of Michigan Law School finds no correlation between LSAT and either job satisfaction or pay.

4. See David K. Shipler, "My Equal Opportunity, Your Free Lunch," *New York Times,* 5 March 1995.

5. As Walter Willingham, an industrial psychologist who consults with the Educational Testing Service (the organization that prepares and administers the SAT), points out, leadership in an extracurricular activity for two or more years is also a good proxy for academic performance, future leadership, and professional satisfaction.

6. "In all decades, those with higher index scores tend to make fewer social contributions ... than those with lower index scores." See Richard O. Lempert, David L. Chambers, and Terry K. Adams, "The River Runs Through Law School," *Journal of Law and Social Inquiry* 25 (2000): 468. See also, William G. Bowen and Derek Bok, *The Shape of the River: Long-Term Consequences of Considering Race in College and University Admissions* (Princeton, N.J.: Princeton University Press, 1998).

7. See Mary Anne C. Case, "Disaggregating Gender from Sex and Sexual Orientation: The Effeminate Man in the Law and Feminist Jurisprudence," *Yale Law Journal* 105 (1995): 88–89.

8. See the *Report of the Independent Commission on the Los Angeles Police Department,* pp. 83–84. "Female LAPD officers are involved in excessive use of force at rates substantially below those of male officers.... The statistics indicate that female officers are not reluctant to use force, but they are not nearly as likely to be involved in use of excessive force," due to female officers' perceived ability to be "more communicative, more skillful at de-escalating potentially violent situations and less confrontational."

9. J. Phillip Thompson, director of management and operations for the New York City Housing Authority from 1992–93, told us that an internal evaluation conducted by the Housing Authority revealed that women housing authority officers were policing in a different, but successful, way. As a result of this evaluation, the authority sought to recruit new cops based on their ability to relate to young people, their knowledge of the community, their willingness to live in the housing projects, and their interest in police work. They also offered free housing to any successful recruit willing to live in the projects.

10. See James Crouse and Dale Trusheim, *The Case Against the SAT* (Chicago: University of Chicago Press, 1988), p. 128.

11. See Phyllis Rosser, *The SAT Gender Gap: Identifying the Causes* (Washington, D.C.: Center for Women's Policy Studies, 1989), p. 4. Also, "ETS Developing 'New' GRE," *FairTest Examiner,* Fall/Winter 1995–96, p. 11. "Research... shows the GRE underpredicts the success of minority students. And an ETS Study concluded the GRE particularly under-predicts for women over 25, who represent more than half of female test-takers."

12. Crouse and Trusheim, p. 103.

13. Crouse and Trusheim, pp. 107–08.

14. See John G. Belcher, "Gainsharing and Variable Pay: The State of the Art," *Compensation & Benefits Review* 26 (May–June 1994): 50–51. Belcher advocates the use of a family of measures approach, which "utilizes multiple, independent measures to quantify performance improvement."

15. See, for example, Claude M. Steele and Joshua Aronson, "Stereotype Threat and the Intellectual Test Performance of African Americans," *Journal of Personality and Social Psychology* 69 (1995): 797–811.

16. Although there is debate about the degree of fundamental change in approaches to management, a significant portion of private businesses have adopted some form of collaborative or team-oriented production. See Edward E. Lawler III et al., *Employee Involvement and Total Quality Management: Practices and Results in Fortune 1000 Companies* (1992), which analyzes the employee-involvement programs many corporations have adopted; Paul Osterman, "How Common is Workplace Transformation and Who Adopts It?" *Industrial & Labor Relations Review* 47 (1994): 173, 176–78, which finds that over 50 percent of firms surveyed had introduced at least one innovation such as quality circles and work teams, and that 36.6 percent have at least two practices in place with at least 50 percent of employees involved in each.

17. Howard Gardner, *Multiple Intelligences: The Theory in Practice* (New York: Basic Books, 1993), p. 172.

18. See Karen W. Arenson, "Study Details Success Stories in Open Admissions at CUNY," *New York Times,* 7 May 1996. A study of open-admissions policy at City University of New York (CUNY) found more than half of the students eventually graduated, even though it took many as long as ten years to do so. Many of these students had to work full time while they attended college. According to Professor David Lavin, one of the co-authors of the CUNY study, open admissions "provided opportunities that students used well, and that translated into direct benefits in the job market and clearly augmented the economic base." Similarly, at Haverford College, professors of biology, chemistry, and mathematics told one of us in interviews that many students of color with weak preparation in the natural sciences took two years to catch up with their better prepared peers. However, by junior year, those same students managed to excel, having overcome their initial disadvantages.

19. When one of us was on the admissions committee in the early 1990s at the University of Pennsylvania Law School, the process of admitting people who had some

"special" quality to be considered—which included being a poor, white chicken farmer from Alabama—was an openly deliberative process. It included students who knew more about the specific localities in which many of the applicants resided. The applications were redacted to eliminate personal identifying information but were otherwise available to the entire committee. The recommendations were read and considered (by contrast to the 50 percent of the class who were admitted solely on a mathematical equation based on their LSAT scores, their college rank, and the "quality" of their college as determined by the median LSAT score of its graduating class). In this process, the committee of both faculty, students and admissions personnel had a sense we were admitting a "class" of students, not just random individuals. Thus, we might give weight to some factors over others, depending upon the "needs" of the institution to have racial and demographic diversity, but also upon our commitment to fulfilling the needs of the profession to serve the entire public and to train private and public problem-solvers who would become the next generation of leaders. Thus, not all students were admitted primarily because of their academic talents. We considered those who might be better oral advocates and eventual litigators. Others were already accomplished negotiators or future practitioners of alternative dispute-resolution practices. None of these students were admitted if we felt they were unqualified to do the work demanded of them at the institution.

20. Gardner, *Multiple Intelligences,* pp. 171–73.

21. She learned that she was proficient in skills that she did not previously identify as related to lawyering: problem solving, thinking about the public-relations management of crises, strategic planning, and dealing with internal disruption stemming from crisis and change.

22. For example, the court in *Hopwood v. Texas* rejected the concept of diversity as a basis for using affirmative action. The opinion lacked almost any reflection on the functional role diversity plays in higher education. It simply asserted that "the use of race, in and of itself, to choose students simply achieves a student body that looks different." 78 F.3d 932, 945 (Fifth Circuit, 1996), cert. denied, 116 S. Ct. 2582 (1996).

23. Jonathan D. Casper, "Restructuring the Traditional Civil Jury: The Effects of Changes in Composition and Procedures," in *Verdict: Assessing the Civil Jury System,* ed. Robert E. Litan (Washington, D.C.: Brookings Institution Press, 1993), p. 420.

24. See Susan P. Sturm, "From Gladiators to Problem Solvers: Women, the Academy, and the Legal Profession," *Duke Journal of Gender Law & Policy* (1996).

25. See Samuel L. Gaertner et al., "The Contact Hypothesis: The Role of a Common Ingroup Identity on Reducing Intergroup Bias," *Small Group Research* 25 (1994): 224, 226; Samuel L. Gaertner et al., "How Does Cooperation Reduce Intergroup Bias?" *Journal of Personality & Social Psychology* 59 (1990): 692.

26. See Elizabeth Bartholet, "Application of Title VII to Jobs in High Places," *Harvard Law Review* 95 (1982): 947, 967–78, which discusses courts' reluctance to scrutinize high-level employment decisions; Deborah L. Rhode, "Perspectives on Professional Women," *Stanford Law Review* 40 (1988): 1163, 1193–94 notes courts' deference to employers' judgments.

27. This is a complex argument that requires more elaboration than the limits of this article permit. Suffice it to state the obvious: we are experiencing a retreat from public life on many levels, evidenced by, among other factors, declining voter turnout. See also Lani Guinier, "More Democracy," *University of Chicago Legal Forum* (1995): 16–22.

28. *Harper v. Virginia Board of Elections,* 383 US 684 (1966) (Harlan, J., dissenting).

29. See *United States v. Louisiana,* 225 F. Supp. 353, 355–56 (E.D. La. 1963). The decision found that the interpretation test as a prerequisite for registration "has been the highest, best-guarded, most effective barrier to Negro voting in Louisiana," and that the test "has no rational relation to measuring the ability of an elector to read and write," aff'd., 380 US 145 (1965).

30. *Reynolds v. Sims,* 377 US 533, 544 (1964).

NO

Stephen Steinberg

Mending Affirmative Action

The purpose of affirmative action is to break down the wall of occupational segregation that excluded racial minorities and women from entire occupational sectors throughout American history. Whatever else one might want to say about affirmative action, it has achieved its policy objective: substantial desegregation of the American workplace, for women and minorities alike. This is true not only in the professions and in corporate management, but also in major blue-collar industries and in the public sector, where nearly one out of every three black workers is employed. If logic and principle had prevailed, we would now be exploring ways to expand affirmative action to industries and job sectors that have been immune to change.

The problem is that "for more than two decades, affirmative action has been under sustained assault," as [Susan] Sturm and [Lani] Guinier write in their opening sentence. Though they do not say so explicitly, they seem resigned to the fact that the Supreme Court, which has already eviscerated affirmative action through a series of decisions, is now poised to deliver the *coup de grace*. Against this background, Sturm and Guinier declare that "it is time to shift the terrain of debate." The entire thrust of their argument is to explore alternatives to affirmative action that will broaden access of minorities and women to jobs and universities.

At first blush, this strategy may appear to be a sensible concession to political reality. However, two troubling questions arise. First, are Sturm and Guinier capitulating to the anti-affirmative action backlash and prematurely throwing in the towel for the sake of an illusory consensus? Second, would their proposed reforms of the selection process, even if enacted, provide the access to jobs and opportunities that are today secured by affirmative action?

The logic of Sturm and Guinier's brief can be stated as follows:

1. Affirmative action is assailed by critics as violating cherished principles of "merit."
2. On closer examination, the "testocracy" that is used to assess merit is neither fair nor functional.

3. Therefore—alas, here the syllogism runs into trouble. Sturm and Guinier could have concluded that the case against affirmative action is specious and therefore affirmative action should be upheld. As the saying goes, "if it ain't broke, don't fix it."

Instead Sturm and Guinier make a case for overhauling the selection process that evaluates candidates for jobs and college admissions. To be sure, there are compelling arguments for abandoning standardized tests that favor privileged groups who, aside from the advantages that derive from better schooling, have the resources to pay for expensive prep courses. Sturm and Guinier also make a compelling case that it would be fairer and more productive to judge applicants on the basis of performance criteria, rather than scores on "paper-and-pencil" tests. The problem, though, is that they implicitly advocate these reforms as a surrogate for affirmative action policy. They may tell themselves that they are driven by *realpolitik,* but they end up acquiescing to the reversal of hard-won gains and falling back on reforms that are unlikely to be enacted in the foreseeable future. Their ideological enemies will revel in this retreat to a second line of defense by two law professors who are identified with the cause of affirmative action. Nor will Sturm and Guinier get the concessions they are bargaining for. Is this not the lesson of Bill Clinton's ill-fated proposal to "end welfare as we know it"?

❧

What evidence is there that overhauling the selection criteria would open up avenues for women and minorities? In most large-scale organizations—corporations and universities alike—employees are routinely evaluated by superiors on an array of performance criteria. Is so-and-so a "team player"? Does she do her job well? Does he have good communication skills? Does she make the tough decisions? Does he demonstrate leadership? Such judgments are easily tainted by personal prejudices, especially when the people doing the evaluations are white and male and the people being evaluated belong to stigmatized groups. Indeed, studies have consistently found that performance appraisal ratings of women and people of color are prone to bias.

A second problem with the "performance-based model" advocated by Sturm and Guinier is that the benefits would be diffused to many groups, and could easily miss African Americans, who were the original targets of affirmative action policy. Besides, how do people demonstrate "performance" when they cannot get their foot in the door?

Finally, Sturm and Guinier place emphasis on jobs "where customers, clients, and perspectives may themselves be identified by race and gender." Granted, corporations need black managers to interface with the black consumer market, and police departments need women to deal with domestic violence. But women and minorities deserve equal access to *all* jobs in the workforce. Though Sturm and Guinier endorse this principle, their proposal runs the risk of typing jobs by gender and race, thereby validating the patterns of internal segregation that exist within many job structures.

The lesson of history is that the only mechanism that has ever worked to counteract occupational segregation is affirmative action, and that even good-faith efforts were ineffectual until they were backed up with specific goals and timetables. Too much is at stake to retreat to a second line of defense, especially one so fraught with difficulty. The crusade against affirmative action may well be on the verge of achieving its nefarious objective. But this is all the more reason to remain steadfast in defense of a policy that has not only advanced the cause of justice for women and minorities, but in doing so, has enhanced American democracy. Instead of venturing into the realm of personnel relations and testing, it would have been far better had Sturm and Guinier used their talents as legal scholars to plead the case for affirmative action. As we know it.

POSTSCRIPT

Should Standardized Tests Be Eliminated From Applicant Processes?

The late criminologist Edward Sagarin once called for "outrageous proposals" for conference papers. He felt that the discipline needed fresh, contentious ideas. However, much of U.S. society is overtly contemptuous toward intellectuals, who are often seen as people who "talk to hear their heads roar."

Are Sturm and Guinier "talking to hear their heads roar"? While much of their discussion relates to employment in service areas, some of it clearly has to do with hiring and retaining minorities in professional jobs. However, would these authors want hospitals and law firms to hire physicians and lawyers who were not minimally competent, as measured by standardized tests, in order to become more diversified? Some people maintain that even in the service area (e.g., fast-food chains), where little testing is done, customers and managers are not satisfied with underqualified employees. When pre-employment tests are waived or minimized, customers are forced to wait while slow food servers, cashiers, gas pump attendants, and so on are trained on the job.

Neither side considers the question of whether or not it is fair to expect private industries of any kind to absorb the high costs likely to be needed to provide extra training to those who need it simply because they are a gender or racial minority. Moreover, as Steinberg points out, problems with Sturm and Guinier's proposal include the addition of another layer of bureaucratic fat to oversee the process. In addition, on-the-job decisions to retain or promote employees are potentially discriminatory.

This issue might become moot as courts strike down affirmative action rulings, which they are doing with increasing frequency. Should efforts be made to fight the trend toward eliminating affirmative action? Should Sturm and Guinier's proposals be supported as necessary for achieving social justice in lieu of affirmative action failures? Or should affirmative action be scrapped altogether?

Guinier, whom President Bill Clinton nominated for assistant attorney general for civil rights but who was rejected by the U.S. Senate in 1993, has authored many articles and books on racial injustice, including *The Tyranny of the Majority: Fundamental Fairness in Representative Democracy* (Free Press, 1995). Steinberg's publications include *Turning Back: The Retreat From Racial Justice in American Thought and Policy,* 3rd ed. (Beacon Press, 2001). Eight commentators, including Howard Gardner and Ward Connerly, attack and defend Sturm and Guinier, who also respond, in the December 2000/January 2001 issue of the *Boston Review.* A helpful reader on hierarchies and social justice is Barbara A. Arrighi's edited book *Understanding Inequality: The Intersection of*

Race, Ethnicity, Class and Gender (Rowman & Littlefield, 2001). A study that shares Sturm and Guinier's pessimism is *The Color of Opportunity: Pathways to Family, Welfare, and Work* by Haya Stier and Marta Tienda (University of Chicago Press, 2001). One account of on-the-job discrimination that supports some of Steinberg's concerns is "The Secret Service in Black and White," by P. Perl, *The Washington Post Magazine* (January 7, 2001). A different issue not addressed by either Sturm/Guinier or Steinberg is touched upon in "Colleges Struggle to Maintain a Balance Between Their Male and Female Students," *The Wall Street Journal* (February 20, 2001).

A classic study of social justice is John Rawls's *Theory of Justice* (Harvard University Press, 1971). An interesting account that blends the sociological and the biological (which was considered heresy less than 20 years ago) is "Evolutionary Psychology and the Origins of Justice," by A. Walsh, *Justice Quarterly* (December 2000). Among the emerging literature dealing with minorities and job entrance and training are *Stories Employers Tell: Race, Skill and Hiring in America* by Philip Moss and Chris Tilly (Russell Sage Foundation, 2001) and "The Brave New World of Corporate Education," by J. Meister, *Chronicle of Higher Education* (February 9, 2001). Finally, two recent books that attack liberal scholarly work are *The Burden of Bad Ideas: How Modern Intellectuals Misshape Our Society* by Heather MacDonald (Ivan R. Dee, 2001) and *Incorrect Thoughts: Notes on Our Wayward Culture* by John Leo (Transaction, 2001).

ISSUE 16

Should Inner-City Blacks and Hispanics Be Relocated?

YES: Owen Fiss, from "What Should Be Done for Those Who Have Been Left Behind?" *Boston Review* (Summer 2000)

NO: J. Phillip Thompson, from "Beyond Moralizing," *Boston Review* (Summer 2000)

ISSUE SUMMARY

YES: Professor of law Owen Fiss contends that the government has historically carried out the wishes of society to discriminate against and mistreat minorities, resulting in many of them being stuck in the modern wasteland of America's inner cities. He argues that justice will be served only when minorities are moved out of the cities and into middle- and upper-middle-class communities.

NO: Political scientist J. Phillip Thompson asserts that Fiss's ideas are liable to do more harm than good. In particular, he is bothered by "pretensions of white middle-class moral superiority" that would destroy the African American churches, families, friendships, and neighborhoods.

In all societies, some people are "more equal" than others. However, the basis and the range of inequality vary sharply. Historically, social hierarchies have been based on ascribed status or birth: a few were born to nobility and riches, while most were born poor serfs, peasants, slaves, and so on. For thousands of years such inequities were seen as the natural order of things—hardly indicators of injustice. Often, the poor existed in hovels, sleeping and eating with animals, having no running water or indoor toilets, and using the crudest forms of clothing, furniture, and eating utensils. Life in many poorer, more isolated sections of war-torn Europe, Africa, and Asia remains "short, nasty, and brutish." Physicians, medical supplies, electricity, transportation, modern forms of communication, and schooling are frequently nonexistent in these areas.

In the United States social hierarchies are based primarily on class, or socioeconomic status, along with race, gender, ethnicity, and (to a lesser extent) age, religion, and level of education. These variables are often interrelated; however, they may also go in opposite directions. For example, while poorer African Americans are often at the bottom of poverty measurements, African American females have demonstrated some of the most significant gains in vertical mobility (movement up the social ladder).

Although many Mexican Americans and Latinos are near the bottom of the ladder, Cuban Americans in Miami, Florida, and other areas are frequently found in solid middle- and upper-class areas. Many recent Asian immigrants remain at the poverty level, while other Asian immigrants have achieved economic and political successes for generations. Moreover, although gender discrimination still exists in the workplace, white, Black, and Hispanic women are achieving great success on this traditionally male turf.

After World War II sociologists theorized that the traditional immigrant "success story"—landing in a U.S. city, living for a generation or two in poorer, urban areas, and then moving into the middle-class suburbs—had come to an end. The influx of Puerto Ricans into New York City and other areas was cited as an example showing that this historical immigrant pattern had ended. Experts said that the changing job structure in the United States, the lack of skills among many Hispanic immigrants, and the language barrier accentuated by the industrialization of the U.S. economy all led to the demise of the immigrant success story. However, by the 1960s research showed that Puerto Ricans and other immigrants were indeed "making it" in the United States.

In contrast, research indicated that many Blacks—sometimes going back four or more generations—remained trapped in hopeless poverty in the inner cities. However, beginning with the civil rights movement in the 1950s and 1960s, when Blacks could no longer *legally* be kept out of middle-class neighborhoods, many Blacks purchased homes outside of the cities and made the transition that so many others before them had made. Yet this exodus of successful African Americans from the inner cities only compounded the problem for the many Blacks who were left behind. Furthermore, the disappearance of industry from the inner cities combined with other factors to prevent these residents from pulling themselves out of poverty.

Comparatively speaking, even inner-city residents in the United States are "well off" in terms of the recent past (the last 40 years or so) and in terms of living conditions in other countries. Most American homes today feature VCRs, telephones, indoor plumbing, heat, refrigerators, furniture, and even air conditioning. Likewise, most inner-city residents have access to at least some medical care as well as to public education. However, most Americans still see inner-city communities as severely problematic, and many feel that they are a blatant indicator of social injustice and of the unfairness of the hierarchy in U.S. society.

What should be done? In the following selection, Owen Fiss calls for moving inner-city residents on a voluntary basis to middle- and upper-middle-class neighborhoods, despite possible objections by those neighborhoods' residents to what might be seen as an "invasion" of their community. In the second selection, J. Phillip Thompson acknowledges that something needs to be done for inner-city minorities, but he rejects Fiss's solution.

What Should Be Done for Those Who Have Been Left Behind?

The gods have been good to America. The political system has remained stable, and the country is prospering economically. More and more Americans are enjoying a standard of living that is the envy of all the world. Improvements in our economic well-being have brought with them the sense of freedom and fulfillment that comes from being able to enjoy the things that money can buy —travel, leisure, cars, and beautiful homes.

In the midst of plenty, however, problems persist. Perhaps the most glaring is the presence in our urban centers of communities known as ghettos. The persons living in the typical ghetto are black, but even more significantly poor. Many are on welfare, and even those who work tend to receive salaries that place them beneath the poverty line. As a consequence, the housing stock is old and dilapidated, retail establishments scarce, crime rates high, gangs rampant, drugs in surplus, and jobs in short supply.

Living under such adverse conditions tests the human spirit. It demands resiliency and ingenuity, and a fair measure of faith. The survivors are strong and determined individuals, who through hard work and the elemental bonds of love and friendship have made a life in the inner city for themselves and their families. The ghetto is their home. It has also been home for some of America's most talented writers and artists. Yet alongside these individual truths is a collective one, vividly and poignantly described by James Baldwin almost forty years ago in *A Letter from a Region of My Mind*. The ghettos of America were produced by the most blatant racial exclusionary practices. They isolate and concentrate the most disadvantaged, and through this very isolation and concentration perpetuate and magnify that disadvantage.

Since Baldwin first wrote, many blacks have prospered and left the ghetto. Some have made their homes in racially integrated neighborhoods; others, perhaps the bulk, have settled in what have become black middle-class neighborhoods. This exodus, and the emergence of the black middle class, is among the great achievements of our recent history. At the same time, however, the departure of these families from the ghetto has left behind a community that is even more impoverished than before simply because those with the economic means fled. On top of that, manufacturing jobs, one of the traditional sources of employment in the ghetto, have moved to the suburbs or to developing countries. As a result, the destructive dynamics of ghetto life that Baldwin so powerfully depicted in 1962 have become only more intense. As the institution that isolates and concentrates the most destitute, the urban ghettos of America have created and promise to perpetuate a sector of the black community known as the underclass.

Many remedies for this betrayal of our egalitarian ideals have been proposed, some even tried. All are imperfect. The disparity between the magnitude of the problems and the modesty of proposed remedies is simply overwhelming. The only remedy that has any meaningful chance of success recognizes the ghetto itself as a structure of subordination and seeks to provide those who live within its walls what earlier generations secured for themselves—an opportunity to leave. Pursuing this remedy requires that resources be provided to allow individual families to leave the ghetto and to move to better neighborhoods if they so choose. Such voluntary relocation strategies have been tried with success in the very recent past, though only as pilot programs and only on a limited basis. I believe that we must expand these programs and recognize that they are founded on the most elemental sentiments of justice. They must be seen as a remedy for the role society in general and its agent, the state, have played in constructing these ghettos in the first place.

Providing these resources will have vast economic consequences for the country; it will also impose great human costs. Means might be devised to facilitate moving, and to lessen the disruption of a move. But no matter what, those who take advantage of the option to leave will face substantial hardships in adjusting to new communities, and lose the comfort and support of neighbors they have known over the years. Those wishing to stay may find that choice effectively removed if many leave. Communities may be broken up, and receiving communities themselves will need to undergo long processes of adjustment. These consequences, like the results of earlier efforts at school desegregation, are disturbing, very disturbing. But they seem inescapable. The only alternative to a program that seeks to expand choice is to condemn a sector of the black community to suffer in perpetuity from the devastating effects of our racial history.

Changes in the Ghetto

Our ghettos were never surrounded by the physical walls that often marked the European ones, but even as late as the 1960s a blend of economics and racial practices produced the same sense of confinement. Few blacks could afford to live anywhere other than densely populated urban neighborhoods with poor housing stock. Public housing projects tended to be located only in black neighborhoods. Those blacks who were better off found it difficult, if not impossible, to move out of these areas because property owners in the more affluent neighborhoods, invariably white, were unwilling to rent or sell to them. Usually the state acquiesced in these exclusionary practices, and sometimes it actively supported them. As late as 1964, the voters of California approved an initiative, the notorious Proposition 14, that reaffirmed the right of property owners to sell or rent to whomever they wished, a measure that was later described by the Supreme Court as a thinly veiled attempt to encourage racial discrimination.

In April 1968, in the immediate wake of the assassination of Martin Luther King Jr., Congress passed a federal fair-housing law. That law opened opportunities for those who had the economic means to move out of the ghettos into more affluent, typically white neighborhoods. Admittedly, blacks seeking to move had to cope with resistance to that law and considerable informal hostility, brutally portrayed only a decade earlier by Lorraine Hansberry in *A Raisin in the Sun.* Still, the 1968 law made exodus or movement easier and thus began to chip away at one important source of confinement.

When the fair housing act was initially passed, only a few blacks were able, as a practical matter, to take advantage of their newly expanded freedom. Yet over the next thirty years things began to change. The number of blacks financially able to leave the ghettos increased significantly, thanks to the general growth of the economy and, perhaps even more importantly, to a number of civil rights strategies.

One such strategy consisted of efforts to enlarge educational opportunities. Resources were spread more equitably among schools, and black Americans gained access to some of the better elementary and secondary schools and colleges. The 1954 decision of the Supreme Court in *Brown v. Board of Education* decreed as much, but it was not until the late-1960s that open resistance to that decision subsided and practical steps, usually under court order, were taken to implement it. The emergence of the black middle class can also be traced to a federal law prohibiting racial discrimination in employment. That law was first enacted in 1964, and full enforcement began in 1968. Affirmative action programs appeared at about the same time. They gave preferential treatment to blacks in employment and also in certain educational sectors that controlled access to the professions and other high-paying careers. As a result of these policies, plus a growing economy, a sector of the black community emerged with the economic means to exercise the freedom conferred under the 1968 fair housing law.

Moving to a better neighborhood is part of the American dream. It is hard to leave friends and familiar surroundings, but everyone recognizes that the quality of life—vulnerability to crime, the friends and classmates of one's kids, the quality of stores and housing—depends in good part on one's neighborhood. Many people move (provided, of course, they have the economic means to do so), and the new black middle class was no exception to this rule. Most moved to what were then white, middle-class neighborhoods. Some of these stabilized as integrated neighborhoods; others experienced so-called "white flight" and emerged, as I said before, as middle-class black neighborhoods.

Although moving out of the ghetto presumably improved the quality of life of those who moved, it had an unfortunate effect on the economic and social profile of the community they left. It turned the black ghetto into a community of the most disadvantaged. Surely, some of those who remained might have valued their established relationships above all else and stayed for that very reason; others may have remained for religious or political reasons. My own sense, however, is that, generally speaking, those who stayed were the least mobile. They were the ones who had benefited least from the general growth of the economy or the more specific civil rights policies such as fair employment or affirmative action—the ones who suffered the deepest effects of our long history of racial oppression.

Along with the departure of the black middle class from the ghettos, these communities also suffered an exodus of jobs. Some plants once located in the inner city fell to global competition and closed altogether. Others moved outside the inner city to suburban communities to take advantage of cheaper land, proximity to airports, lower crime rates, and perhaps a workforce that appeared to be better educated or more able. Racial assumptions about the ability of the workforce no doubt played a role in these employer calculations. But given the manifest economic considerations involved, it is hard to believe that race was the only, or even primary factor. In any event, the result was that jobs were leaving just as the most successful in the neighborhood were also leaving. This made the plight of those left behind even worse.

Like the propensity of the upwardly mobile to move to better neighborhoods, commuting to work is a familiar American tradition. The hour commute from Stamford, Connecticut, to New York's financial district is familiar. Those who remained in the ghetto were not, however, readily able to adapt to the relocation of jobs by this means. Some jobs left the country altogether, and commuting to the suburbs was difficult, in some cases impossible. The distances were long, the pay was insufficient to cover the costs of whatever transportation might exist, and working outside one's immediate neighborhood was especially difficult for parents of small children. They wanted to be available for calls from schools and daycare providers.

Ghetto residents also faced a skills mismatch. The economic plight of the inner-city neighborhood parallels that of the United States over the last thirty years—the decline of manufacturing jobs. For America in general, the void has been filled by a growing service sector, which takes the Stamford commuter to Manhattan. But most of these new jobs were unavailable to those left behind in the ghetto, for, almost by definition, they had the lowest educational achievements and little work experience. They were not in position to compete for high-paying jobs in finance or communications. True, entry-level jobs in retail establishments, hotels, and other such service providers remained within reach, but there were few such jobs in their immediate neighborhoods because the residents were poor. One study reported that the ratio of applicants to those hired at fast-food restaurants in Harlem was fourteen-to-one.

◄◙►

We thus confront the fact that over the last thirty years—just as the black middle class has left the ghettos—joblessness in those communities has risen. In the 1980s, William Julius Wilson called attention to the emergence of the black middle class. In 1996, Wilson began his new book, *When Work Disappears,* with this startling observation: "For the first time in the twentieth century, most adults in many inner-city ghetto neighborhoods are not working in a typical week." To be sure, many of these adults have child-care responsibilities, which is work but which Wilson excluded from his calculus. Also, some account needs to be taken of those who cannot work because of age or disability. Still, the fact that a very large number of the adults in certain urban neighborhoods are jobless is astonishing. It well warrants the stir that Wilson's book caused.

Joblessness means no income, and it accounts for poverty and dependence on the welfare system, with all the stigmatization and loss of self-esteem such dependence entails. The human impact of joblessness goes even deeper. Drawing on the work of Pierre Bourdieu and, before it, the famed study of Marienthal by Marie Jahoda, Paul Lazarsfeld, and Hans Zeisel, Wilson explained how joblessness deprives people of the patterned set of expectations that teaches discipline, instills our activities with meaning, and provides a framework for daily life. Individuals without jobs are not only poor; they are less able to cope with life's challenges and, also, probably pretty bored. Sustained joblessness can lead to activities that are self-destructive and a threat to others, most often neighbors. It might lead individuals to seek such palliatives as drugs and alcohol; or it might lead them to join gangs, which import a structure to ordinary life but pursue antisocial ends.

The contemporary urban ghetto, then, can be seen as the home of the black underclass, a group that suffers from a multitude of disadvantages—above all, joblessness and poverty—that relegate its members to the lowest stratum in society and lock them into it. The concentration of this social group in one relatively compact geographic area intensifies both the deprivation and the barriers to upward mobility. It turns the group upon itself, exposing those in the ghetto to a heightened risk of crime and violence, which impairs the quality of life in the community and creates further incentives for those who are able —both individual families and local businesses—to flee. The sense of isolation increases as the quality of life spirals downward.

Social Resources

Ghettos are not entirely without social resources—from the family to churches and schools—that might counter these dynamics. But these resources all seem too meager given the magnitude of the problem. Indeed, two changes in family structure exacerbate the downward spiral and may well entrench the underclass even more deeply. One is the prevalence in the ghetto of single-parent families; the other is the extreme youth of many of the mothers. Barely able to fend for themselves, teenage mothers are called upon to perform one of the most taxing responsibilities imaginable—instilling their children with socially constructive norms and values, teaching them social skills, and helping them set goals and aspirations. Even parents in more traditional family structures face severe obstacles. Sustained joblessness impairs one's capacity not only to make material provisions for one's family but, perhaps even more significantly, to socialize and help in the education of one's children.

Everyone turns outside the immediate family for help in raising children, and this practice exists in the ghetto. Sometimes the surrogate parent is a grandparent, uncle, or aunt; often it is a neighbor. But the problems of the immediate family—sustained joblessness, or single-parent households, or teenage parents—are often replicated in the extended family. Sometimes these problems are compounded by the scars of the most blatant forms of racism. A grandfather who has been without meaningful work for decades is not likely to be an ideal care provider, let alone a role model, for the child of his sixteen-year-old granddaughter. An aunt who was herself an unmarried mother at age fifteen, and who spent the last decade in a state of dependency, is not an ideal surrogate parent for her newborn nephew. Nor are the immediate neighbors, many of whom—in part thanks to the black-middle-class exodus—are poor, jobless, or young single parents.

Local churches can occasionally help. They stand between the family and the state and often serve a crucial role supplying discipline and structure to children otherwise lacking direction. As James Baldwin explained, surely this must be one great source of the appeal of the evangelical churches and the Nation of Islam. Yet these institutions cannot fully compensate for the limits of the family as a socializing institution because membership or participation is typically within the control of a parent, who, for various reasons, including the problems induced by a life of joblessness, might be reluctant or even unable to cede control to another institution. At fourteen, Baldwin joined the church, but only over the strong objection of his father. Account must be taken of the increasing secularization of American culture, as prevalent in the ghettos as in the large cities of which they are part. Moreover, we must confront the possibility that certain less constructive characteristics of ghetto life might be replicated in the local churches—which, to some extent, reflect the culture of the neighborhood of which they are a part.

Access to a number of intermediate organizations is not controlled by parents, and, accordingly, these organizations might have greater potential than do churches to serve as parents' surrogates. But because they too are neighborhood-based and thus fully dominated by youngsters who must grow up with insufficient family support or control, they can hardly fill the void. Local gangs teach discipline, but most often in service of criminal ends. The public schools stand ready to socialize the children who are entrusted to their care and to fill whatever parental void might exist, but because enrollment is normally determined on the basis of residence, elementary and secondary schools in a ghetto contain a heavy concentration of those children who have insufficient family support. As a result, such schools are likely to fail, not just in fulfilling their academic mission—teaching cognitive skills and knowledge of the wider world—but also in their even less well-defined socialization function: imposing discipline, building confidence, heightening aspirations, and instilling the values needed for personal success and a well-functioning society. Public schools in other communities are important sources of opportunity for social mobility, but not those in the typical urban ghetto. The challenge they confront is simply overwhelming.

The Failure of Familiar Remedies

Governments have tried a wide variety of public policy remedies to address this self-reinforcing system of disadvantage. The 1996 federal welfare reforms were designed to create incentives or pressure for welfare recipients to find work. A lifetime limit of five years was imposed on the receipt of welfare. Implicit in this measure was a recognition of the destructiveness of joblessness and the importance of work—even low-paid work—for the self-esteem it engenders and the structure it gives to day-to-day existence. The fear was also present that the availability of welfare for families with dependent children might encourage women to have children regardless of their economic ability to provide for them. In fact, the 1996 welfare reform measure was often presented as a strategy to combat teenage pregnancy and single-parent families.

In the long term, the 1996 welfare reforms might have the desired effect —though the available evidence indicates that the number of people who are able to move from welfare to work is smaller than many people imagine. In the immediate future, however, it is likely to have disastrously counterproductive effects on the capacity of parents to assist in the socialization process. The bulk of federal welfare recipients are single mothers, and though the 1996 law pressures them to look for work, it makes no provision to pay for child-care services. As a result, the social processes that entrench the underclass across generations are only strengthened.

Tougher and more aggressive police tactics—proposed by some to end what they consider to be the under-enforcement of the criminal law in the ghetto—entails a similar dynamic. The hope is that by reducing criminal activity in the inner city, we will curtail the victimization of those who happen to live there and, at the same time, reduce the exodus of jobs and people attributable to high crime rates. It is doubtful that these new police tactics—for example, blanket searches of public housing projects in pursuit of illegal arms— can actually reduce the level of crime in the short run, but more fundamentally, a question can be raised about the impact these tactics will have on the life of the community in general. The level of crime might be reduced but only by ushering in the most strict police regime. The oppressiveness of such a regime is of concern to everyone, but particularly to ghetto residents who remember all too well the racial practices of the city police. Moreover, some of the proposed new enforcement strategies—for instance, enhancing sentences for drug-related crimes—may well increase the number of young males from the ghetto who will spend a good chunk of their lives in prison. Not only would this impoverish the ghetto community further, but it would also exacerbate the dynamics responsible for the prevalence in the community of single-parent families.

Other governmental interventions may have greater short-run chances of success. One is Head Start, which has its roots in the civil rights era and, more specifically, in the War on Poverty. It is based on a recognition that the family is sometimes an inadequate socializing agency, and reaches children at an early age, even before elementary school begins. Most Head Start programs are based in the ghetto. The burden these programs take on is immense, given their neighborhood-centered quality and the backgrounds of the children they receive.

Head Start can succeed only through enormous investments, and even then the benefits might well be overrun by the hours spent back on the streets. We can also expect the lessons Head Start teaches to be unlearned once the child reaches a certain age, leaves the program, and enters the public schools, where resources, student/teacher ratios, the length of the school day, and the school year are likely to be set on a city-wide basis, without consideration given to the special needs of inner-city communities. Programs such as Head Start will make a difference in the lives of a few—who are likely to exit the ghetto—and for that reason must be continued as long as the ghetto exists. But they will not have a broad enough impact to break the ghetto's overall confining grip.

꿏

The most promising economic remedies are those that seek to deal with the spatial mismatch between workers and jobs, the fact that jobs have moved to the suburbs while the workers remain in the inner city. One strategy—the creation of enterprise zones in the inner city—provides economic incentives for businesses to relocate or simply remain there. Such incentives would have to compensate for higher land costs, increased security needs, and perhaps even lack of skills in the ghetto workforce due to sustained joblessness and inadequate social institutions. The economic logic behind the move of businesses to the suburbs seems so compelling, however, that there is reason to doubt the efficacy of such proposals.

William Julius Wilson, also concerned with the spatial mismatch, fully understands the difficulties of bringing business back to the ghetto and as a result has thrown his support behind another strategy for bringing jobs there: a neo-WPA [Work Projects Administration] program. Government would hire the unemployed, much as it did during the New Deal, to do jobs that improve the quality of life in the ghetto. These workers could repair the streets, clean the parks, construct new playgrounds, and perhaps even run various social programs.

Wilson's proposal does not have much chance of working. Certainly, government can create jobs and open them to everyone. But what jobs will they be? How much will they pay? And what will be the chances of advancement? In essence, Wilson responds to these worries in a single, succinct sentence: "Most workers in the inner city are ready, willing, able, and anxious to hold a steady job." Notice that Wilson refers to "workers," not the "jobless," which he told us was the norm in the ghetto, and fails to give any specific content to the phrase "steady job." In truth, Wilson's rejoinder is at odds with the governing sociological insight of his book: that sustained joblessness not only produces poverty, but also undermines character. Joblessness removes structure from individuals' lives, and it tends to cause people to be decidedly not "willing, able, and anxious" to take the government jobs Wilson envisions.

A large number of ghetto residents may have flocked to the new McDonald's in search of work, but there is reason to doubt that they will pursue

Wilson's neo-WPA jobs with such intensity. Such jobs contain few opportunities for advancement and would be tinged with the stigma that in our society is associated with any government handout. They are likely to be viewed as make-work. Wilson contemplates that the wages of the new government jobs would be slightly below minimum wage, but even if they were above the minimum they would not be sufficient—absent some further welfare program, say an expanded Earned Income Tax Credit—to lift the employee above the official poverty line.

More fundamentally, Wilson's proposal, or for that matter, any program to end the spatial mismatch by bringing the jobs to the ghetto, is doomed to failure. It overlooks the structural dimension of the problem—specifically, that the jobless individual is situated in a neighborhood with lots of other jobless individuals and that over the years this neighborhood has been racked by a host of destructive forces. Job creation in the ghetto must not only overcome the reluctance of any particular individual to accept a menial job, but also must reckon with the fact that this individual is a member of a group or community of similarly situated individuals. Together, these individuals exert pressure on one another and produce a culture in the ghetto that makes it most unlikely for a job creation strategy such as the one Wilson proposes to work.

An Alternative

Any ameliorative strategy must confront the fact that the ghetto is not just the place where the underclass happens to live, but also, because it concentrates and isolates the most disadvantaged and creates its own distinctive culture, a social structure that entrenches the underclass. More than a location, it is a means by which a group is prevented from sharing in society's successes and kept far beneath others in terms of wealth, power, and living standards. This structure must be dismantled. The walls that confine those who live within the ghetto must be torn down. To speak less metaphorically, we must provide those who now live there with the economic means to move into middle- or upper-class neighborhoods.

Such a voluntary relocation strategy would: eliminate the spatial mismatch between jobs and residence, by allowing the jobless to move closer to where the jobs exist; break up the concentration of impoverished, single-parent households, by enabling ghetto residents to move to safer neighborhoods where there is more of a mix of economic classes and family structures; and enhance access to intermediate institutions, such as schools and churches, that are not so heavily burdened as those of the ghetto and that might have more of a chance of succeeding.

This strategy would improve the lives of the dispersed adults by situating them in communities where jobs exist—environments conducive to reshaping one's life into something more fulfilling and productive. It would also break the entrenchment of the underclass across generations, because children in the families that relocated themselves would be raised in safer, more positive surroundings and would reap the benefits of those surroundings. Of course middle- and upper-class neighborhoods, both black and white, have their own dysfunctions. Still, they have advantages over the ghetto in terms of safety, social services, education, and employment opportunities. Dispersal would capitalize on those advantages.

⋅◦⟨◉⟩◦⋅

The strategic advantage of choosing racially integrated or predominantly white middle- and upper-class neighborhoods as the receiving communities of those who relocate should not be overlooked. Tying the fate of blacks to that of whites, which would be accomplished by such residential integration, may be the most reliable means of securing equal protection for the minority, because only then will every gain enjoyed by whites in social services or neighborhood improvements redound to the benefit of blacks. The integrative ideal affirmed by *Brown v. Board of Education* in part rested on the feat that the majority would always shortchange the schools attended only by the minority.

Although gains might be achieved if families relocate to racially integrated or predominantly white middle- and upper-class neighborhoods, the receiving communities need be defined only by class, which will by itself mean enhanced access to jobs, better schools and social services, nicer housing, and higher-quality retail establishments. A black middle-class community created over the last thirty years as a result of antidiscrimination laws in housing and employment could thus be a suitable receiving community for some of the residents moving from the ghetto, as would an upscale racially integrated or predominantly white community. Sometimes the search for such neighborhoods might take us beyond the city limits, sometimes not.

Those who decide to move must not, however, be regrouped into another ghetto. The very purpose of this program is to allow people to leave the ghetto, under the theory that it is a structure of subordination, so care must be taken not to create another concentration of poor, jobless, single-parent families headed by teenagers. To achieve this objective, an agency needs to be created that would seek out the opportunities for such a move and allocate those being sent among the various middle- and upper-class communities. This agency would also need to assist in the relocation process itself. Every move is difficult, but the challenges of moving out of a poor, ghetto neighborhood and into one considerably more upscale and possibly predominantly white would be extreme. The tasks that burden every move—trips to the hardware store for light bulbs, meeting the new neighbors, signing the children up for schools, knowing what social services are available—are intensified when the racial or class makeup of the new neighborhood is different from that of the old one.

Charitable organizations might be able to help in this relocation process, but given the magnitude of the endeavor, it will be necessary to rely on the government and its unique powers to raise and distribute funds. The relocation agency will need to be state-funded. In addition, state funds will be necessary to enable people who were living below the poverty level to afford the rents in the receiving neighborhoods. The rent of those moving would be subsidized, though the subsidies may go directly to those providing the housing. One method of implementing this plan would be to issue rent vouchers and to require that realtors and landlords in the specially designated receiving communities accept these vouchers. Such a requirement would be only one small part of the effort needed to render it impossible for receiving communities to thwart the purpose of the relocation program, which is to create class, and maybe racial, integration. Tough enforcement of existing antidiscrimination laws and perhaps the fashioning of new ones would also be necessary.

⚜

Any program seeking to end the dynamics responsible for the entrenchment of the underclass will require enormous dollar investment. The relocation program I have outlined is no exception to this rule, though in no way should these costs be assumed to be prohibitive. The magnitude of these costs can be gauged by considering a 1994 effort by the Department of Housing and Urban Development (HUD) to institute an analogous, but smaller, relocation program. This program, called "Moving to Opportunity," offered aid to families who had children and were living in public housing in high-poverty census tracts within Baltimore, Boston, Chicago, Los Angeles, and New York. (A high-poverty census tract is one in which more than 40 percent of the residents have incomes below the poverty level.) Those who applied and were selected were given Section 8 rent vouchers that could be used only in census tracts that had under a ten percent poverty rate. Local non-profit organizations played a crucial role, supplying each moving family with a counselor who actively helped the family to find an apartment and to overcome the obstacles associated with the move. The cost of moving 6,200 families was $234 million over two years.

These figures need to be adjusted to account for the scale of the program I am proposing, which would not be confined to persons living in public housing in five cities, but rather be nationwide in scope and available to all people living in areas marked by the high concentration of extremely poor black families. It is hard to estimate the total number of families in such areas, but a 1990 survey estimates that there are six million American blacks living in the inner-city ghettos or high-poverty tracts. Obviously, the number of families is less than six million, but using that figure for lack of a better one, we can estimate the total cost of the relocation program at $100 billion per year if every ghetto resident chose to move. The actual net cost should be substantially less because money that might otherwise have been spent on community development programs, public housing, and perhaps even general antipoverty and welfare programs would be saved. Regardless, in light of the $792 billion tax cut passed recently by both houses of Congress, the cost of dismantling the ghettos of America is surely within our reach.

Money is not everything. To assess fully the impact of this relocation plan, account must also be taken of the human costs arising from moving and even more from the disruption of communal ties in inner-city neighborhoods. In doing so, however, care must be taken not to romanticize the familiar. Some might recognize the reality of ghetto life and how it deteriorated over the last thirty years, and yet still hope that it is possible to keep the communities intact while transforming them into safe, flourishing environments with good jobs, attractive housing, safe streets, easy access to stores, strong schools, and all of the other characteristics of thriving neighborhoods. This honorable hope cannot be attained. Putting an end to the social dynamics that have transformed some particular black ghetto into a structure of subordination would require so many deep interventions into the life of that community as to disrupt, if not actually destroy, all preexisting communal ties. The geography would remain the same but the community would be different. The program I envision openly acknowledges the threat to community but allows the residents of the ghetto to weigh the benefit of the preexisting communal ties against what might be a better life for themselves and their children. Integration, in any form, has never been a picnic, but neither is staying put. Here the choice is vested where it belongs: in the individual family.

Admittedly, the choices of those most anxious to leave will affect the options of those inclined to stay since the option of staying appears less appealing when so many of one's neighbors have left. But such decisional interdependence is inescapable and it is not clear why the balance should be cast in favor of the status quo. My sense is that most in the ghetto would jump at the offer of a subsidized move to a better neighborhood. Experience confirms this assumption. In the 1980s, HUD instituted another such relocation program, then in the context of a lawsuit, and the number of applications greatly exceeded the available subsidies. During one call-in application period lasting only a few days, 15,000 applicants called in pursuit of 250 places. With the prospect of a subsidy, most will leave, and that will be enough to break the concentration of destructive forces—poverty, joblessness, crime, children without adequate supervision, poorly functioning social institutions—that turns the ghetto into a mechanism for perpetuating the subordination of those who find themselves living there. The physical space that once belonged to the ghetto will quickly be claimed by developers for gentrification and for transformation into a new, up-and-coming neighborhood in the city.

Justice

To put the human and financial costs in perspective, we must come to understand that relocation is required not only as good social policy, but also as a matter of justice. The costs entailed in such programs are indeed great, as would be the costs of any program that seeks to tackle the problem of the underclass, but they are comparable to those entailed in implementing *Brown* and are justified by an analogous theory of equal protection. The dual school system of Jim Crow was condemned because it tended to perpetuate the caste structure of slavery; the inner-city ghetto today has a similar effect, though the subjugated group is not defined, as under slavery or Jim Crow, in purely racial terms—race must be supplemented by economic and social coordinates. The subjugated group is not blacks in general, but the black underclass. The inner-city ghetto stands before us as the instrument responsible for the maintenance of that form of subjugation and thus represents the most visible and perhaps most pernicious vestige of racial injustice in the United States—the successor to slavery and Jim Crow.

Presently the state is not by statutes or regulations confining people to the ghetto. To the contrary, through antidiscrimination laws and affirmative action programs touching employment, education, and housing, the state has helped to create the black middle class and thereby enabled some to leave. But the state, as the representative of the larger society, also played an important role in the very creation of the ghetto, and is thus duty-bound to use its powers to remedy the present-day consequences of that action. In the historic decision that provided the foundation of the Voting Rights Act of 1965, Justice Hugo Black emphasized that any court had "not merely the power but the duty to render a decree which will as far as possible eliminate the discriminatory effects of the past as well as bar like discrimination in the future." He was referring to the judiciary, for the duties of that institution were being contested, but the obligation he spoke of extends to all branches of government.

State complicity in the creation of the ghetto took various forms. Some of the state's responsibility derives from the failure, for most of our history, to prevent acts of discrimination and violence aimed at keeping blacks out of white neighborhoods. In other instances the state played a more active role, for example by enforcing racially restrictive covenants. Though this practice was outlawed in 1948, it played a crucial role in the formation of the black ghetto for a good part of our history. Later it was supplemented by more subtle, but equally pernicious practices, such as California's Proposition 14. Restrictions on loan guarantee programs and on the location of public housing projects had a similar effect. The means by which residential segregation has been established and maintained in the United States—detailed in Douglas S. Massey and Nancy A. Denton's important 1993 book *American Apartheid*—are as sinister, and their effects as lasting, as Jim Crow segregation in the South, especially when coupled with this country's traditional economic and social policies.

⚜

The foundation, perhaps the inspiration, for a voluntary relocation program along the lines I envision can be traced to the 1976 Supreme Court decision in *Hills v. Gautreaux*. The case involved the Chicago Housing Authority (CHA)—the agency specifically charged with the construction and management of public housing projects in Chicago—and arose from the Authority's practice of giving the local city council members the power to prevent the construction of such projects in their wards. It was understood that the residents of such projects would be largely or predominantly black, and council members from white wards used their power to prevent the construction of public housing projects in their wards. As a result, for years all public housing projects in Chicago were located only in black neighborhoods and thus helped constitute the urban ghettos of that city. By way of remedy, the Supreme Court sustained an order of a lower court requiring HUD to provide funds to disperse these concentrations of poor black families.

The relocation program upheld in *Gautreaux* was more focused than the one I am arguing for here. The moving subsidies went only to the residents of public housing projects, whereas I contemplate their being made available to all the residents of the ghetto, defined in terms of the high concentration of extremely poor black families. Moreover, because of this focus, the *Gautreaux* subsidies could be conceptualized as a form of compensation for a highly discrete act of racial discrimination, namely, the decision to locate the public housing projects only in black neighborhoods. Such a reading of *Gautreaux* would limit its scope and reduce it to a public housing precedent, but I see lurking beneath its surface a far more powerful principle: an obligation on the part of the state to eliminate the social dynamics responsible for the perpetuation of the black underclass.

For one thing, it must be stressed that the remedial obligation imposed in *Gautreaux*—funding the relocation agency and providing the subsidies—was placed on HUD, the federal agency, not the CHA or the Chicago City Council. HUD did not play any role in choosing the site of the public housing projects. At most, it could be accused only of funding public housing projects with the knowledge that they were being built only in black wards. This conduct might be described as a means of supporting or acquiescing in the acts of discrimination, so as to bring it within the ambit of both Title VI of the Civil Rights Act of 1964 and the Constitution's equal protection guarantee. But the involvement of federal and state governments in creating urban ghettos may be similarly characterized. So may the government's role in the dynamics responsible for joblessness and poverty in the ghetto, low levels of income, and the inferior quality of schools and social services available there.

Account must also be taken of the fact that the *Gautreaux* remedy required HUD to provide subsidies that would enable the public housing residents to move to predominantly white suburbs and to do so in a scattered fashion. A remedy conceived in purely individualistic terms—as a corrective for the race-based decision as to where to build public housing projects—could not possibly have that reach. At best, such a remedy would mandate the construction of public housing projects in white parts of the city—the relocation of the Robert Taylor Homes, for example, in a predominantly white ward with comparable land value or a similar socio-economic profile. Yet the remedy approved in *Gautreaux* sought a class transformation: moving the public housing residents, all of whom were black, into middle- or upper-class neighborhoods of the suburbs and scattering them so as to avoid any concentration of lower-class families that had lived in the public housing projects.

In purely personal terms, the *Gautreaux* remedy succeeded admirably. The employment opportunities and educational achievements of those who moved increased significantly. According to studies first published in 1991 by James Rosenbaum, among adults who had never previously held a job, those moving to the suburbs were over 50 percent more likely to become employed than those who stayed in the city. Among those who were children at the time of the move, 75 percent of those who moved to the suburbs were employed seven years after the move, compared with 41 percent of those who stayed; 21 percent in the suburbs had jobs paying more than $6.50 per hour, compared with 5 percent of those who remained in the city; 54 percent in the suburbs went to college, compared with 21 percent in the city; and 27 percent of those moving to the suburbs attended four-year colleges, compared with 4 percent of those who stayed in the city.

Even more remarkable, I believe, is the fact that *Gautreaux* marked the beginning of the process of dismantling the massive public housing projects in Chicago, such as the Robert Taylor Homes, and thus represents the first decisive step toward the dissolution of the ghetto. In this respect the *Gautreaux* remedy should be seen not as a compensation for a discrete act of discrimination—as an attempt to put certain persons in the position they would have been in but for a particular act of discrimination—but as a broader remedy designed to eliminate a structure of subordination. *Gautreaux* was premised on an understanding of how massive public housing projects—with their concentration of poor, jobless families, often unable to assist significantly in the socialization process, all sending their children to the same local school, victimized by crime and gangs—have become a mechanism for both creating and entrenching the black underclass across generations. It also constitutes a recognition of government's responsibility for dismantling that mechanism.

Although the *Gautreaux* remedy had grandiose ambitions, it was rather limited in its numbers. Only 7,100 families received subsidies. This, I believe, was a function of the fact that the precise number of families receiving subsidies was set in a consent decree or bargained-for agreement between HUD and the plaintiffs. The number was not dictated by considerations of justice, which is, after all, the only metric for a court or any other institution bold enough to provide equal protection. Every affirmative remedy poses the question of precise limits: How much must be spent to do justice? How much is enough? No detailed response can be given to these questions at this stage other than to say that the subsidies must be large enough to move out all residents of the ghettos who choose to move—large enough to bring an end to this social mechanism that is entrenching the black underclass. Anything short of that would allow to remain in place an instrument perpetuating a hierarchical structure that is at odds with the egalitarian aspirations of the Constitution.

In an attempt to minimize or trivialize dispersal remedies, and thus to highlight his neo-WPA program and the effort to bring the jobs to the ghetto, William Julius Wilson reminds his readers of the conditions of acceptability: "The success of this program," he writes of *Gautreaux*, "is partly a function of its relatively small size. Since only a few families are relocated to other housing sites each year, they remain relatively invisible and do not present the threat of a mass invasion." It is not at all clear what Wilson means by a "mass invasion," or whether that would ever be present given policies that are designed to avoid the creation of a new ghetto in a previously upper-middle-class neighborhood. The approach I envision entails moving few enough ghetto residents into each middle- or upper-class neighborhood that the prior residents remain. The more fundamental point, however, is to recognize that whatever hostility this relocation program engenders—either from whites or from blacks who pride themselves on having escaped the ghetto—it cannot be a basis for limiting the program or, even worse, turning one's back upon it. Justice permits of no such compromise. It requires instead that the state undertake all action necessary to end "lock, stock, and barrel"—as Judge John Minor Wisdom once put it in talking of the remedies for school segregation—the social processes that continue to perpetuate the near-caste structure of American society.

J. Phillip Thompson

 **NO**

Beyond Moralizing

Owen Fiss argues that the contemporary black ghetto is a product of jobs "leaving just as the most successful in the neighborhood were also leaving." With a high concentration of jobless individuals concentrated in inner-city communities, a "culture in the ghetto," is produced that "makes it most unlikely for a job creation strategy such as the one [William Julius] Wilson proposes to work." In his analysis of what created the ghetto, Fiss says that, "given the manifest economic considerations involved, it is hard to believe that race was the only or even primary factor." Fiss's strategy is to break apart black ghettos once and for all and to disperse ghetto residents into resource-rich middle- and upper-class white neighborhoods.

I disagree with Fiss's description of how the ghetto emerged and his proposal about how it might be eradicated. I think the best place to begin this critique is with Fiss's characterization of what created the ghetto of the "underclass." Fiss argues that economics, not race, was the primary factor in making the ghetto. He points to Wilson's observations that jobs did in fact leave cities and that the black middle class left certain black neighborhoods as well. Fiss does not discuss at all the history of political debate surrounding these issues over the last thirty years. His account makes it seem as though the ghetto is just a big accident that well-intentioned Americans created unknowingly. I find this hard to swallow. The civil rights movement made full employment a key issue after its legal victories over Jim Crow in 1964 and 1965. After waves of black congressmen were elected on the heels of the Voting Rights Act, they too focused on jobs. They linked the necessity for full employment to the need to repair the damage done by three hundred-plus years of slavery and segregation. And they warned as well that a failure to act would entrench segments of the black community into perpetual poverty and despair. They demanded, thirty years ago, that African Americans not be forced to pay the price (in the form of persistent unemployment) for federal anti-inflation monetary policies. Congress mostly ignored them. The response of the American public was to elect a series of Republican presidents (with the exception of Democrat Jimmy Carter) who decimated support for cities between 1968 and 1992. Carter, it must be noted, was conservative on urban issues as well. Clinton, despite the best economy in memory, did virtually nothing to change the urban policy course put in place by Reagan. Perhaps as a former governor, Clinton was aware of how the Republican party exploited anti-urban (read: anti-minority) attitudes to win control of nearly two-thirds of the gubernatorial seats in the country. Another factor in the rise of conservatism in national politics was intense local opposition to forced school integration *in the North* as well as the South. Overall, efforts to integrate schools failed miserably. Black middle-class parents seeking quality schools for their children had few options other than leaving inner-city black neighborhoods.

It is important to remember these points because neither the exodus of jobs from cities nor the departure of the black middle class from the ghetto happened in a political and social vacuum. By separating race and economics, as Fiss does in saying that "manifest economic considerations" obviate race as a cause of the ghetto, Fiss implicitly makes the two assumptions. He assumes that political decisions made by government officials had no impact on economic decisions by firms on where to locate and who to hire. Second, he assumes that race did not affect these fundamental political decisions. Both assumptions are invalid. The US "free" market economy is no less a state product than the former Soviet economy. The US markets are no less "structured" than were Soviet five-year plans; the difference lies in how they are structured. The federal government's decision *not* to ensure full employment in response to black demands, or *not* to put limits on firms' mobility despite devastating regional impacts on the rustbelt, were political decisions.

Race has everything to do with the politics. Nixon's appeal to the "silent majority," Reagan's visit during the 1980 presidential campaign to Philadelphia, Miss. (site of the murder of three civil rights workers in the 1960s), Bush Sr.'s use of Willie Horton, Bush Jr.'s and McCain's deference to state's rights on the issue of South Carolina's adoption of the Confederate flag—all of these are important symbolic reminders of how consistently Republicans have played the race card. Much more debilitating to African Americans, and more bipartisan, have been the attacks on "big government" and the "War on Drugs."

Exactly what is "big" government? It does not mean the military, or social security, or tax deductions for suburban homeowners. It means programs designed to help the undeserving poor (read: minorities). Tax cuts and spending limits brought about through the revolution against big government have severely undermined the capacity of city governments to do much about poverty. Big government does not include prisons, which are a booming public/private industry. African American and Latino youth are being incarcerated *en masse.* Even though illegal drug usage is roughly evenly distributed across race and ethnic groups in the United States, close to 90 percent of those jailed for drug offenses are black and Latino. In some cities, more than a third of all young black men are in jail, awaiting trial, or on probation. The vast majority are incarcerated for non-violent drug and property offenses. Those convicted of drug crimes frequently serve long sentences. Under the mandatory sentencing guidelines of the Rockefeller drug laws in New York State, for example, an offender convicted of possessing two ounces of marijuana is required to serve fifteen years to life. The California legislature passed more than 1,000 new criminal justice statutes in the late 1980s and early 1990s alone. These statistics represent a massive deployment of aggressive policing and punishment directed at black youth. Virtually no black person is immune to it because police tactics initially employed in the ghettos, what is called racial profiling, are now employed on the nation's highways and downtown areas.

Even more alarming than the climate of terror produced by over-zealous policing and the criminalization of huge numbers of non-violent and poor black youth has been the public's acceptance of it. Since the victory of civil rights advocates in winning formal legal protection of African American citizens in the 1960s, a more effective and defensible form of racial subordination has set in—namely, racial subordination brought about through the normal mechanisms of democracy and government bureaucracy. It is not necessary for white Americans to be intense about their opposition to programs aimed at helping African Americans (or Latinos). Whites do not need demonstrations or protest movements. Since they are a strong voting majority in the nation and in nearly every state, they only need to vote. Voting is low-intensity politics. So long as white Americans are willing to tolerate a few middle-class blacks in their midst, they can absolve themselves of charges of racism. They can justify spending more on prisons than education (already a fact in some states) as giving minority youth what they deserve based on their bad behavior. It is argued by some that this is American egalitarianism at work. This is a lie. If bureaucratic enforcement were egalitarian, 70 percent of those jailed for drug possession would be white, and the sheer numbers involved would ruin the economy and turn the nation into a complete police state. I seriously doubt that lawmakers intend to do this, or that white Americans want aggressive policing targeted against *their* neighborhoods. Arrest statistics indicate clearly that white drug users are being exempted from targeting. There seems to be an unspoken assumption that the War on Drugs is not supposed to attack the white middle class. The white public expects this double-standard *in practice,* in the selective enforcement of drug laws. This expectation of favorable treatment by government, where equal treatment with blacks and Latinos would be unthinkable, constitutes corruption of the body politic—and it is a powerful form of racism built into the normal workings of majoritarian democracy and government bureaucracy. What is most dangerous about it is precisely its normality—it does not require an abandonment of egalitarian rhetoric, nor does it require much political mobilization. Blacks are being terrorized and incarcerated *en masse* in a climate of public indifference.

To return to Fiss's article. I want to suggest that there are two cultural problems involved in the ghetto, not just one. There is a problem of ghetto sub-cultures organized around gangs and prison life that is threatening to most people who live in the ghetto and harmful to the participants themselves. The second problem is the corruption of broad sections of the white public that stems from their social privileges and basic control of public institutions. It is the latter that has created and maintained the ghetto. And it is the latter that blames the fruits of its creation solely on its victims. Fiss wants to disrupt the comfort and disinterest of white suburbia. I applaud this intent. But his proposal to integrate white suburbs is far removed from political reality. White suburbia has already shown *in practice* where it stands on racial integration and poverty deconcentration. With so many of those Fiss wants to move into white suburbia coming out of prison today, it would be harder than ever to convince white communities to accept them. Trying to legally force white Americans to integrate against their will, in a country where they are a voting majority, has not worked and it will not. In this context, *in place* strategies such as Wilson's public works jobs proposal are a lot more politically realistic than housing and school integration.

To tackle the larger issue of continuing segregation, I think that more micro strategies are needed that engage whites on racial issues beyond moralizing arguments appealing to some fictional commitment to actual equality. One might want to figure out which predominantly white institutions or movements are disposed to want to fight against housing and school segregation, or the mass criminalization of African Americans and Latinos, and help them forge ties with groups concerned about urban poverty. Labor unions are targeting low-income minorities in organizing drives these days, and they are good institutions for engaging the race issue. It could be suggested to labor unions, for example, that building schools instead of prisons will create a lot more jobs and union members in the long and short run. Environmental groups are another potential source of support for eradicating inner-city ghettos. It might be suggested to environmentalists that the best cure for urban sprawl—air pollution and degradation of open spaces—would be to build livable dense cities, and the key to that is eradicating concentrated poverty. There is potential for real coalition building on urban issues that address group's self-interest but also move them beyond narrow definitions of their selves to a bigger "We."

Finally, I hope that instead of telling poor blacks that they cannot afford to live with each other (as Fiss does), some kind of democratic and empowering process can be envisioned in which African Americans might be able to utilize their churches, clubs, community organizations, and other social networks to promote their own vision of how they want to live with other Americans. Fiss's proposal would all but eliminate the black urban church, and would do deep damage to black political efficacy. I think this would be dangerous for African Americans. Fiss does not seem to understand this at all. He characterizes churches together with schools as "intermediate institutions," that in the suburbs, "are not so heavily burdened as those of the ghetto and that might have more of a chance of succeeding." He seems to think that churches are like public corporations where goods can be shipped around according to capacity and output can be ranked on an economic performance sheet. That is not what black churches are. They are voluntary associations consisting of dense social networks that frequently span generations. It takes a long time to build a sense of trust, caring, and community within a church. Some churches never achieve it, and those are the failures. The success of a church is not measured by how well established its members are in the economy, or by how many of its youth go to college. A successful church may produce these results, but it does not follow that an unsuccessful church cannot produce these results.

Fiss suggests that entrenched poverty has corrupted the black church, and that "we must confront the possibility that certain less constructive characteristics of ghetto life might be replicated in the local churches, which, to some extent, reflect the culture of the neighborhood of which they are a part." Fiss does not give any examples or explain exactly what "less constructive" characteristics he has in mind. I can only conclude that his economic and spatial determinism has led him to indict black churches by association with ghetto poverty. I am tempted to say that, no, white churches are the corrupt failures because their entrenched wealth and privilege silenced them through centuries of brutal racial oppression. I have seen too many caring white churches, however, to warrant such a simplistic indictment by association. I will say, however, that I have not found that "ghetto" churches are lacking in moral fabric as compared to their counterparts in rich neighborhoods. I bet Fiss has not either. Maybe a good place to begin a discussion of how to eradicate ghetto poverty would be to put a hold on pretensions of white middle-class moral superiority.

POSTSCRIPT

Should Inner-City Blacks and Hispanics Be Relocated?

One criticism of the social sciences (especially sociology) is that human beings are viewed as mere puppets, with no volition, choice, or control over their own lives. Dennis Wong once called this tendency the "oversocialized" conception of human behavior. Fiss says that inner-city residents should be free to decide whether or not they want to leave the cities, but he does not seem to credit them with the ability to make such a decision. That is, he considers several policy recommendations, such as providing jobs and other opportunities within the communities, but he rejects them, maintaining that the poor have been rendered too helpless by poverty, racism, and inequality to do anything other than be physically removed to a white community.

Neither Fiss nor Thompson pays much attention to the toll that drugs have taken on poor as well as middle-class communities, a problem that probably should be reckoned with. The issue of democracy is also overlooked in this discussion. That is, the vast majority of middle-class communities, both white and Black, do not want to be hosts for transferred inner-city residents. But Fiss dismisses this view, suggesting that relocating the poor to middle-class communities is simply retribution for the injustices done to the poor in the past. Is this justice?

In addition to the articles by Fiss and Thompson, the Summer 2000 issue of *Boston Review* features six additional responses to Fiss's arguments. Among the helpful books on this controversy are *Prismatic Metropolis: Inequality in Los Angeles* edited by Lawrence Bobo et al. (Russell Sage Foundation, 2000); *Urban Planning in a Multicultural Society* edited by Michael A. Burayidi (Greenwood, 2000); and *The Public Assault on America's Children* edited by Valerie Polakow (Teachers College Press, 2000), which captures some of the horrors of inner cities. An interesting account of the ties to the community that Thompson alludes to is "A Housing Project Falls, but the Poor Resist Orders to Move Out," by J. Eig, *The Wall Street Journal* (December 19, 2000). E. J. Dionne, Jr., expresses concern with the conservative backlash in "The Overreaching Court," *The Washington Post* (February 23, 2001), while sources that defend a cautious approach to economic repairs include T. Sowell, *Basic Economics* (Basic Books, 2001) and "Inequality Isn't Poverty," *Barron's* (May 15, 2000). A possible lesson can be found in *Moving Nearer to Heaven: The Illusions and Disillusions of Migrants to Scenic Rural Places* by Patrick C. Jobes (Greenwood, 2000). Finally, a scathing attack on some of the programs cited by Fiss is N. Thompson's "HUD Audit Fails City's Section 8: Rent Program to Have Misspent, Forfeited Missions —Not Serving the People," *The Baltimore Sun* (March 31, 2001).

ISSUE 17

Should Race Be a Consideration in College Admissions?

YES: William G. Bowen and Derek Bok, from "Get In, Get Ahead: Here's Why," *The Washington Post* (September 20, 1998)

NO: Dinesh D'Souza, from "A World Without Racial Preferences," *The Weekly Standard* (November 30/December 7, 1998)

ISSUE SUMMARY

YES: William G. Bowen, president of the Andrew W. Mellon Foundation, and Derek Bok, former president of Harvard University, contend that the high rate of success of the Black college graduates that they studied would not have happened if they had attended lesser schools. Because admission to the elite schools for many of these students resulted from affirmative action, Bowen and Bok argue that the policy of considering race should be continued.

NO: Dinesh D'Souza, the John M. Olin Scholar at the American Enterprise Institute, dismisses the conclusions of Bowen and Bok and asserts that admission to any organization should always be based on merit, not preferential treatment. He maintains that judging people by the color of their skin, which he sees affirmative action as doing, is an insult to the memory of Dr. Martin Luther King, Jr., and may be largely a strategy used by white and Black elites to advance their own agendas at the expense of common sense and morality.

$\mathbf{B}$enjamin Disraeli (1804–1881), a writer who later became England's prime minister, wrote in his acclaimed novel *Sybil* in the 1840s that England had become two countries consisting of the rich and the poor. Following riots in the 1960s, the Kerner Report concluded that the United States consisted of two societies that were drifting apart. More recently, writers on race relations have lamented the "two nations, separate and unequal" theme.

Paradoxically, many African Americans' lives have improved significantly within the past 30 years. There is a rapidly expanding Black middle class; several thousand elected officials, including mayors of many cities, are Black; Black females, especially professionals, are reflecting gains well above those of both male and female whites; and almost 8 percent of all lawyers and doctors in the United States are Black, compared with less than 2 percent in the 1960s. However, many aspects of Black culture and their problems pervade the mass media: Black illegitimacy, Black leadership, Black artistic accomplishments, Black illnesses, Black language, Blacks in sports, Blacks and AIDS, Afrocentrism in schools and universities, continued racism, Black entertainers, and Black criminals are frequent topics of America's news stories. The Black racial minority arguably dominates America more than all other ethnic, religious, and racial minorities combined. Judging from the media accounts, the political debates, and the educational and social agendas, both white and Black Americans are fascinated with Blacks.

Yet America remains for many (at least) two nations. There are now more Blacks under the umbrella of America's justice system (i.e., in prison, on parole or probation, or in jail awaiting trial) than at any other time in U.S. history. A young Black male, reports say, has a greater chance of being killed in the streets by other Blacks or being arrested than of going to college. The sheer despair and ugliness of America's inner cities, which are now spreading to small towns and suburbs as "mini-ghettoes," provide ample evidence that while many Blacks are succeeding, for a significant number of Blacks something is terribly wrong. Or, as William G. Bowen and Derek Bok imply in the following selection, the continued wretchedness of the existence of many Black Americans shows that something is not right with U.S. society.

In addition to hard work and perseverance, the traditional road to success in the United States has been education. Yet it has always been known that life's opportunities are stacked clearly in favor of wealthy children, males, whites, and Protestants, as well as those born in affluent urban areas. More recently, many Americans have come to the conclusion that an oppressive, exploitive, racist system has handicapped Blacks in the United States. For years some had assumed that since discrimination in hiring practices had been legally prohibited, Black nuclear physicists, for example, could apply for a good job and be hired. Quickly it became apparent that due to years of discrimination, very few Blacks were trained in nuclear physics (or many other professions). One easy remedy would be to monitor all schools—especially the elite colleges—to ensure that qualified Blacks could get in. However, as Bowen and Bok point out, unless race is taken into account along with other standard criteria, many Blacks simply would not be admitted to elite colleges. This, in turn, would deny the Black community of vital civic leadership and of Black doctors, lawyers, and businesspeople.

In the second selection, Dinesh D'Souza argues that even if Bowen and Bok's contention were true, both Blacks and the nation as a whole would be better off living up to the original dream of achieving a color-free society.

Should race be a consideration in college admission? What are the possible negative and positive consequences thus far of this policy?

William G. Bowen and Derek Bok  **YES**

Get In, Get Ahead: Here's Why

In his classic 1969 study of Wall Street lawyers, Erwin Smigel reported that: "I only heard of three Negroes who had been hired by large law firms. Two of these were women who did not meet the client." Smigel's statement should not surprise us. In the 1960s, barely 2 percent of America's doctors and lawyers were black, and only 280 blacks held elected office of any kind. At that time, few leading professional schools and nationally prominent colleges and universities enrolled more than a handful of blacks. Late in the decade, however, selective institutions set about to change these statistics, not by establishing quotas, but by considering race, along with many other factors, in deciding whom to admit.

This policy was adopted because of a widely shared conviction that it was simply wrong for overwhelming numbers of blacks to continue to hold routine jobs while the more influential positions were almost always held by whites. In a nation becoming more racially and ethnically diverse, these educators also considered it vital to create a learning environment that would prepare students of all races to live and work together effectively.

In recent years, the use of race in college admissions has been vigorously contested in several states and in the courts. In 1996, a federal appeals court in New Orleans, deciding the Hopwood case, declared such a race-sensitive policy unconstitutional when its primary aim is not to remedy some specific wrong from the past. Californians have voted to ban all consideration of race in admitting students to public universities. Surprisingly, however, amid much passionate debate, there has been little hard evidence of how these policies work and what their consequences have been.

To remedy this deficiency, we examined the college and later-life experiences of more than 35,000 students—almost 3,000 of whom were black—who had entered 28 selective colleges and universities in the fall of 1976 and the fall of 1989. This massive database, built jointly by the schools and the Andrew W. Mellon Foundation, for the first time links information such as SAT scores and college majors to experiences after college, including graduate and professional degrees, earnings and civic involvement. Most of our study focused on African Americans and whites, because the Latino population at these schools was too small to permit the same sort of analysis. What did we discover?

Compared with their extremely high-achieving white classmates, black students in general received somewhat lower college grades and graduated at moderately lower rates. The reasons for these disparities are not fully understood, and selective institutions need to be more creative in helping improve black performance, as a few universities already have succeeded in doing. Still, 75 percent graduated within six years, a figure well above the 40 percent of blacks and 59 percent of whites who graduated nationwide from the 305 universities tracked by the National Collegiate Athletic Association. Moreover, blacks did not earn degrees from these selective schools by majoring in easy subjects. They chose substantially the same concentrations as whites and were just as likely to have difficult majors, such as those in the sciences.

⚬⚬⚬

Although over half of the black students attending these schools would have been rejected under a race-neutral admissions regime—that is, if only high school grades and test scores had been counted—they have done exceedingly well after college. Fifty-six percent of the black graduates who had entered these selective schools in 1976 went on to earn advanced degrees. A remarkable 40 percent received either PhDs or professional degrees in the most sought-after fields of law, business and medicine, a figure slightly higher than that for their white classmates and five times higher than that for blacks with bachelor's degrees nationwide. (As a measure of change, it is worth noting that by 1995, 7.5 percent of all law students in the United States were black, up from barely 1 percent in 1960; and 8.1 percent of medical school students were black, compared with 2.2 percent in the mid-1960s. Black elected officials now number more than 8,600.)

By the time of our survey, black male graduates who had entered selective schools in 1976 were earning an average of $85,000 a year, 82 percent more than other black male college graduates nationwide. Their black female classmates earned 73 percent more than all black women with bachelor's degrees. Not only has the marketplace valued the work of these graduates highly, but the premium associated with attending one of these selective institutions was substantial. Overall, we found that among blacks with similar test scores, the more selective the college they attended, the more likely they were to graduate, earn advanced degrees and receive high salaries. This was generally true for whites as well.

Despite their high salaries, the blacks in our study were not just concerned with their own advancement. In virtually every type of civic activity, from social service organizations to parent-teacher associations, black men were more likely than their white classmates to hold leadership positions. Much the same pattern holds for women. These findings should reassure black intellectuals who have worried that blacks—especially black men—would ignore their social responsibilities once they achieved financial success.

Were black students demoralized by having to compete with whites with higher high school grades and test scores? Is it true, as Dinesh D'Souza asserts in his book "Illiberal Education," that "American universities are quite willing to sacrifice the future happiness of many young blacks and Hispanics to achieve diversity, proportional representation, and what they consider to be multicultural progress"? The facts are very clear on this point. Far from being demoralized, blacks from the most competitive schools are the most satisfied with their college experience. More than 90 percent of both blacks and whites in our survey said they were satisfied or very satisfied with their college experience, and blacks were even more inclined than whites to credit their undergraduate experience with helping them learn crucial skills. We found no evidence that significant numbers of blacks felt stigmatized by race-sensitive policies. Only 7 percent of black graduates said they would not attend the same selective college if they had to choose again.

Former students of all races reported feeling that learning to live and work effectively with members of other races is important. Large majorities also believed that their college experience contributed a lot in this respect. Consequently, almost 80 percent of the white graduates favored either retaining the current emphasis on enrolling a diverse class or emphasizing it more. Their minority classmates supported these policies even more strongly.

Some critics allege that race-sensitive admissions policies aggravate racial tensions by creating resentment among white and Asian students rejected by colleges they hoped to attend. Although we could not test this possibility definitively, we did examine the feelings of white students in our sample who had been rejected by their first-choice school. Significantly, they said they supported an emphasis on diversity just as strongly as students who got into their first-choice schools.

Our findings also clarify the much misunderstood concept of merit in college admission. Many people suppose that all students with especially high grades and test scores "deserve" to be admitted and that it is unfair to reject them in favor of minority applicants with lower grades and test scores. But selective colleges do not automatically offer admission as a reward for past performance to anyone. Nor should they. For any institution, choosing fairly, "on the merits," means selecting applicants by criteria that are reasonably related to the purposes of the organization. For colleges and universities, this means choosing academically qualified applicants who not only give promise of earning high grades but who also can enlarge the understanding of other students and contribute after graduation to their professions and communities. Though clearly relevant, grades and test scores are by no means all that matter.

Because other factors are important—including hard-to-quantify attributes such as determination, motivation, creativity and character—many talented students, white and black, are rejected even though they finished in the top 5 percent of their high school class. The applicants selected are students who were also above a high academic threshold but who seemed to have a greater chance of enhancing the education of their classmates and making a substantial contribution to their professions and society. Seen from the perspective of how well they served the missions of these educational institutions, the students admitted were surely "meritorious."

Could the values of diversity be achieved equally well without considering race explicitly? The Texas legislature has tried to do so by guaranteeing admission to the state's public universities for all students who finish in the top 10 percent of their high school class. Others have suggested using income rather than race to achieve diversity. Our analysis indicates that neither alternative is likely to be as effective as race-sensitive admissions in enrolling an academically well prepared and diverse student body. The Texas approach would admit some students from weaker high schools while turning down better-prepared applicants who happen not to finish in the top tenth of their class in academically stronger schools. Income-based strategies are unlikely to be good substitutes for race-sensitive admissions policies because there are simply too few blacks and Latinos from poor families who have strong enough academic records to qualify for admission to highly selective institutions.

What would happen if universities were flatly prohibited from considering race in admissions? Our findings suggest that over half of the black students in selective colleges today would have been rejected. We can estimate what would be lost as a result:

- Of the more than 700 black students who would have been rejected in 1976 under a race-neutral standard, more than 225 went on to earn doctorates or degrees in law, medicine or business. Approximately 70 are now doctors and roughly 60 are lawyers. Almost 125 are business executives. The average earnings of all 700 exceeds $71,000, and well over 300 are leaders of civic organizations.
- The impact of race-neutral admissions would be especially drastic in admission to professional schools. The proportion of black students in the Top Ten law, business and medical schools would probably decline to less than 1 percent. These are the main professional schools from which most leading hospitals, law firms and corporations recruit. The result of race-neutral admissions, therefore, would be to damage severely the prospects for developing a larger minority presence in the corporate and professional leadership of America.

The ultimate issue in considering race-sensitive admissions policies is how the country can best prepare itself for a society in which one-third of the population will be black and Latino by the time today's college students are at the height of their careers. With that in mind, would it be wise to reduce substantially the number of well-prepared blacks and Latinos graduating from many of our leading colleges and professional schools? Considering students' own views about what they have gained from living and learning with classmates from different backgrounds and races, and the demonstrated success of black graduates in the workplace and the community, we do not think so.

Dinesh D'Souza

 **NO**

A World Without Racial Preferences

If color-blind admissions policies are put into effect," I was warned at a recent debate on the topic, "the number of black students at the most selective colleges and universities would plummet to around 2 percent. Should we as a society be willing to live with such an outcome?"

I hesitated, and in that moment of hesitation, my interlocutor saw his opportunity. "Well, should we?" he pressed.

The answer, it turns out, is yes. But it is an answer that supporters of the current system consider outrageous. They take for granted that the only possible response is "Of course not." So, for example, two pillars of the education establishment, former Princeton president William Bowen and former Harvard president Derek Bok, have just published a widely reviewed defense of affirmative action, *The Shape of the River: Long-Term Consequences of Considering Race in College and University Admissions.* They insist that some form of preferential recruitment is inevitable to avoid the unthinkable outcome of very few African Americans at top-ranked universities. "The adoption of a strict race-neutral standard would reduce black enrollment at . . . academically selective colleges and universities by between 50 and 70 percent," Bowen and Bok observe. "The most selective colleges would experience the largest drops in black enrollment."

These numbers are more or less correct. But what they actually illustrate is not the unacceptable future but the unconscionable present: the magnitude of racial preferences currently in effect. Affirmative action in practice does not mean—as its supporters claim—considering two equally qualified applicants and giving the minority candidate the nod. It has instead come to mean admitting Hispanic and African-American students with grade-point averages of 3.2 and SAT scores of 1100, while turning away white and Asian-American applicants with GPAs of 4.0 and SAT scores of 1300. Far from waging a war against discrimination, advocates such as Bowen and Bok find themselves waging a war against merit. And far from vindicating idealism and promoting social justice, they find themselves cynically subverting the principle of equal rights under the law to the detriment of society as a whole.

એ©ે

Before we can decide whether it is simply too embarrassing to permit elite institutions to enroll a very small percentage of blacks or other minorities, we must first ask the question of what produces the racial disparities that so unsettle us and that seem to require affirmative action to counteract. Consider the example of the National Basketball Association. It is no secret that the NBA does not "look like America": African Americans, who are 12 percent of the population, make up 79 percent of the players, while Jews and Asian Americans are conspicuously scarce.

Of course, one never hears demands that the NBA establish a preferential recruitment program for Jews or Asians. But before the notion is dismissed as simply silly, it is instructive to ask why. The answer is presumably that it is merit and not discrimination that produces the racial imbalance on the basketball court. If the coaches hire the best passers and shooters, we tend to think, it shouldn't matter if some ethnic groups dominate and others are hardly represented.

The lesson to be drawn from this example is that inequalities in racial outcomes that are produced by merit are far more defensible than inequalities produced by favoritism or discrimination. And when we turn from the NBA to America's elite colleges and universities, we discover a similar result: Ethnic inequalities are the result not of biased selection procedures but of unequal performance on the part of different groups.

Affirmative action has traditionally been defended as necessary to fight discrimination. But has anyone demonstrated that the blacks and Hispanics preferentially admitted to the best universities were in fact victims of discrimination? Has anyone uncovered at Berkeley or Princeton bigoted admissions officers seeking to exclude minorities? And is there any evidence that the white and Asian-American students refused admission were discriminating against anyone? The answer to these questions is no, no, and no. No one has even alleged unfairness of this sort.

There was, at one time, an attempt by advocates of affirmative action to argue for racial and cultural bias in the SAT and other standardized tests that most elite universities require their applicants to take. This argument, however, has collapsed in recent years, and even Bowen and Bok admit that it is no longer possible to claim that the SAT discriminates against blacks or other minorities. In *The Shape of the River,* they try to confuse the issue by insisting on the obvious point that standardized-test scores "do not predict who will be a civic leader or how satisfied individuals will be with their college experience or with life." But they are at last forced to the chagrined confession: "Almost all colleges have found that when they compare black and white undergraduates who enter with the same SAT scores, blacks earn *lower* grades than whites, not just in their first year but throughout their college careers.... Tests like the SAT do not suffer from prediction bias."

This is not to say that the test describes genetic or biological ability. It merely measures differences in academic preparation, and Bowen and Bok acknowledge that the low black enrollments at elite universities that affirmative-action policies seek to remedy are primarily produced by "continuing disparities in pre-collegiate academic achievements of black and white students." On those measures of merit that selective colleges use to decide who gets in, not all groups perform equally.

For the civil-rights leadership, these results have come as a nasty surprise. The movement led by Martin Luther King Jr. originally placed itself on the side of merit in opposition to racial nepotism. If laws and public policies were allowed to judge solely on the basis of individual merit, King repeatedly promised, we would see social rewards in America widely dispersed among groups.

In the generation since King's death, it is this premise—that equality of rights for individuals would invariably produce equality of results for groups—that has proved false. The dismaying truth is that even merit sometimes produces ethnic inequality. Consequently it is hardly surprising that some who manned the barricades alongside King now insist that merit is the new guise in which the old racism manifests itself. It is now fashionable for advocates of affirmative action to place the term "merit" in quotation marks or to speak sarcastically of "so-called merit." Their main objection is that merit selection is not producing the outcomes they desire, and their enthusiasm for affirmative action can be attributed to their rediscovery of the blessings of nepotism.

***

Meanwhile, behind the scenes, there has been underway a fascinating debate about why merit produces such ethnic inequality. Two views have dominated the debate. The first is the "bell-curve" position, put forward most publicly in recent years by Charles Murray and Richard Herrnstein, which implies that there may be natural or biological differences between groups that would account for their unequal performance on indices of merit. The second is the traditionally liberal position, which insists that when group differences in academic achievement and economic performance exist, they have been artificially created by social deprivation and racism.

***

These two views have functioned like a see-saw: When one goes up, the other goes down. In the early part of this century, most people took for granted that there were natural differences between the races and that these accounted for why some groups were advanced and others relatively backward. This view was fiercely attacked in the middle of this century by liberals who argued that it was unreasonable and unconscionable to contend that natural deficiencies were the cause of blacks' doing poorly when blacks were subjected to so much legal and systematic discrimination, especially in the South.

The liberal view was entirely plausible, which is why the biological explanation was largely discarded. But the liberal view has begun to collapse in recent years, precisely as it proved unable to explain the world that resulted from its triumph. Consider a single statistic: Data from the college board show that, year after year, whites and Asian Americans who come from families earning less than $15,000 a year score higher on both the verbal and math sections of the SAT than African Americans from families earning more than $60,000 a year.

This stunning statistic, whose accuracy is unquestioned by anyone in this debate, is sufficient by itself to destroy the argument of those who have repeated for years that the SAT is a mere calibration of socioeconomic privilege. But it is equally devastating to the liberal attribution of black disadvantage to racial discrimination. Even if discrimination were widespread, how could it operate in such a way as to make poor whites and Asians perform better on math tests than upper-middle-class blacks?

On this question, most advocates of affirmative action do not know how to react. Some simply refuse to discuss the implications of the evidence. Others, like Nathan Glazer, seem to adopt a private conviction of the veracity of the bell-curve explanation. A few years ago, in a review of Murray and Herrnstein in the *New Republic*, Glazer seemed to accept the existence of intrinsic differences in intelligence between the races—while objecting to any mention of the fact in public.

In more recent articles, Glazer has reversed his longtime criticism of affirmative action and said he is now willing to bend admissions standards to avoid the distressing outcome of very few blacks in the best universities. Glazer's second thoughts about affirmative action point to something often missed in such debates, for if the bell-curve thesis is correct, then it in fact constitutes the strongest possible argument *in favor* of affirmative action.

If there are natural differences in ability between ethnic groups that cannot easily be eradicated, then it makes sense for those of us who do not want America to be a racial caste society to support preferential programs that would prevent the consolidation of enduring group hierarchies. Forced, by the collapse of the liberal view, to accept natural inequality, Glazer unsurprisingly now treats blacks as a handicapped population that cannot be expected to compete against other groups.

⁓⟨◉⟩⁓

But there is, in fact, a third possible view of racial inequality—a view advanced by Thomas Sowell and me and others who find profoundly condescending and degrading the notion that blacks require a "special Olympics" of their own. Basically, we contend that there are cultural or behavioral differences between groups. These differences can be observed in everyday life, measured by the techniques of social science, and directly correlated with academic achievement and economic performance. Even *The Black-White Test Score Gap*, a recent study by two noted liberal scholars, Christopher Jencks and Meredith Phillips, proves upon careful reading to implicitly endorse this cultural view. Jencks and Phillips make all the appropriate genuflections to racial pieties, but they are courageously seeking to make the cultural argument more palatable to liberals.

A few years ago, a Stanford sociologist named Sanford Dornbusch was puzzled at claims that Asian Americans do especially well in math because of some presumed genetic advantage in visual and spatial ability. Dornbusch did a comparative study of white, black, Hispanic, and Asian-American students in San Francisco and concluded that there was a far more obvious reason for the superior performance of Asian Americans: They study harder. Asian Americans simply spend a lot more time doing homework than their peers.

⋅⟨◉⟩⋅

Of course, this sort of finding leaves unanswered the question of why they study harder. The causes are no doubt complex, but one important factor seems to be family structure. It is obvious that a two-parent family has more time and re-sources to invest in disciplining children and supervising their study than does a single-parent family. For Asian Americans, the illegitimacy rate in this country is approximately 2 percent. For African Americans, it's nearly 70 percent.

Such a huge difference cannot easily be corrected. Indeed, in a free soci-ety, public policy is limited in its ability to transform behavior in the private sphere. Still, while not reverting to the discredited liberal position, the cultural view of racial inequality is at least more hopeful than the bell-curve acceptance of ineradicable difference: We cannot change our genes, but we can change our behavior.

One thing is clear: Racism is no longer the main problem facing blacks or any other group in America today. Even if racism were to disappear overnight, this would do nothing to improve black test scores, increase black entrepreneur-ship, strengthen black families, or reduce black-on-black crime. These problems have taken on a cultural existence of their own and need to be confronted in their own terms.

The difficult task is rebuilding the cultural capital of the black commu-nity, and the role of black scholars, black teachers, black parents, and black entrepreneurs is crucial. The rest of us cannot be leaders, but we can be cheer-leaders. Rather than try to rig the numbers to make everyone feel better, we are better off focusing our collective attention on developing the skills of young African Americans at an early age so that they can compete effectively with others in later life.

⋅⟨◉⟩⋅

So why doesn't this obvious solution win broad support? In his new book, *A Dream Deferred: The Second Betrayal of Black Freedom in America,* Shelby Steele argues that affirmative action is popular with black and white elites because it serves the purposes of both groups. White elites get to feel morally superior, thus recovering the ethical high ground lost by the sins of the past, and black elites enjoy unearned privileges that they understandably convince themselves they fully deserve. (In *The Shape of the River,* Bowen and Bok devote several chapters to proving the obvious point that blacks who go to Ivy League schools derive financial benefits in later life as a result and are generally satisfied with attending Yale instead of a community college.)

Steele's book bristles with the psychological insights that are his distinctive contribution to the race debate. White liberals, Steele argues (and he might as well be speaking directly of Bowen and Bok), are quite willing to assume general blame for a racist society causing black failures—so long as it's the careers of other people, all the qualified Asian-American and white students rejected from Harvard and Princeton, that are sacrificed in order to confer benefits on blacks and win for liberals recognition as the white saviors of the black race.

❦

What Steele is doing—and it has drawn considerable criticism from reviewers—is something that advocates of affirmative action have always done: questioning the motives of the other side. For years, conservatives have treated liberals as well meaning in their goals though mistaken in their means. And during that same period, liberals have treated conservatives as greedy, uncaring racists. By asking advocates of preferences what's in it for them, Steele unmasks the self-interest that frequently hides behind the banners of equality, diversity, and social uplift.

Steele's main objective is to show that neither the black nor the white elites have an interest in asking fundamental questions: Isn't color-blindness the only principle that is consistent with the fundamental principles of American society? Isn't equality of rights under the law the only workable basis for a multiracial society? Is the black community well served in the long term by a public policy that treats them as an inferior people incapable of competing with others?

Advocates of racial preferences "offer whites moral absolution for their sins and blacks concrete benefits that are hard to turn down," Steele observed to me a few weeks before the recent electoral victory of a referendum abolishing affirmative action in Washington state. "I think we are going to lose because our side has only one thing to offer, and that is moral principle." I ruefully agreed that the scales were tipped in precisely that way. But the astonishing triumph of the referendum in Washington by a comfortable majority—like the triumph of a similar measure two years ago in California—shows that we should not underestimate the power of moral principle in American politics.

When the issue is posed in the basic vocabulary of right and wrong—a lexicon that is utterly incomprehensible to Bowen and Bok—the tortured rationalizations of affirmative-action advocates collapse and the common-sense moral instinct of the American people tends to prevail. There is no cause for conservatives to lose their nerve. The election in 2000 could be the moment when color-blindness is at last the issue on the ballot in many states and at the center of the Republican party's agenda.

POSTSCRIPT

Should Race Be a Consideration in College Admissions?

In several states over the past four years, voters and courts have decided to reject preferences based on race for college admissions (as well as other areas involving recruitment). While Americans are supportive of "fair play" and of compensating victims of past injustice, they have consistently opposed a quota system based on race in hiring or college admissions. For some ethnic and religious minorities, opposition is partially based on their groups' members sometimes being denied college admission because of preferential treatment programs for Blacks and partially on the fact that in the past, quotas were used to keep many of them *out* of elite universities. For instance, Harvard University and other colleges apparently limited the number of Jews they would allow to attend any given class.

Yet there has always been some form of a preferential quota system in operation. The children of alumni, star athletes, wealthy donors, and others have traditionally been favorites for admission. There have also been subtle biases in favor of wealthy, male, Protestant students for generations, as well as prohibitions against the admission of Blacks and others (e.g., females in law or medical schools). Has the system ever been fair in this matter?

Neither Bowen and Bok nor D'Souza address the issue that research seems to show that the best predictor of college success is high school curriculum quality. The more academic and better the curriculum is, the greater likelihood of college success. One question that has been asked is, would the 28 elite schools studied by Bowen and Bok be willing to send their faculties on a grand scale into inner-city schools to strengthen the schools' curricula? Also, would they be willing to triple or even just double their class sizes in order to admit two or three times more academically needy racial minority students?

Another concern that applies to many related ethnic-racial minority debates is that of class. Some ask, shouldn't preferences, if they are to exist at all, be based on wealth and income, not race? On many university campuses there is a high number of poor whites and poor Asians, both in terms of percentages and gross numbers. Indeed, critics such as D'Souza maintain that many preferentially admitted Black students are of solid middle-class or higher backgrounds. Should these Blacks be given special consideration? Doesn't this put middle-class whites and others in direct conflict over scarce educational resources with the Black middle class?

Another related issue is, what good have the impressive accomplishments of many of the Black alumni from the elite schools been for the majority of Blacks who are poor? How much of these Black physicians' and lawyers' time is spent, professionally or socially, with needy Blacks and other poor people? Does Bowen and Bok's research necessarily show anything other than that graduates of elite schools, white or Black, are successful and generally do all the ritualistic things that are expected of them (including earning huge salaries) while leaving the system intact?

At another level, are D'Souza's insinuations that liberals who support affirmative action are self-serving hypocrites fair? If nothing else, haven't preferences demonstrated at least symbolically that many Americans, including members of the judicial system, are making a good-faith effort to better minorities' social status? Finally, although initial studies showed immediate sharp declines in minority enrollments in top universities in states banning admission based on race, subsequent research reveals that less prestigious but otherwise excellent schools are "catching" many of these students. Doesn't it make more sense for racial minorities to attend colleges for which, based on traditional standards, they technically qualify?

For their original research, see Bowen and Bok's *Shape of the River: Long-Term Consequences of Considering Race in College and University Admissions* (Princeton University Press, 1998). A good overview of the debate arising out of California's ban of race consideration for public university applicants is "What Has Happened to Faculty Diversity in California?" by A. Schneider, *Chronicle of Higher Education* (November 20, 1998). Reflecting America's confusion over the issue is "Racial Preferences Are Outdated," by W. Terry, *Parade Magazine* (May 31, 1998) and "Affirmative Action Debate Rages On," *Parade Magazine* (April 4, 1999). A look at the defense of using preferences to maintain campus diversity is "Back to Square One," by Adam Cohen, *Time* (April 20, 1998). For an interesting reversal of himself, see Nathan Glazer's "In Defense of Preference," *The New Republic* (April 6, 1998). Glazer's sometimes rival has a different argument in "How to Mend Affirmative Action," by Glenn Loury, *The Public Interest* (Spring 1997). A different perspective is "Beyond Quotas," by Roger Clegg, *Policy Review* (May/June 1998).

Among those who partially defend D'Souza's position are M. Rees, "Still Counting by Race," *The Weekly Standard* (April 27, 1998); R. Worth, "Beyond Racial Preferences," *The Washington Monthly* (March 1998); and Stephan Thernstrom and Abigail Thernstrom, *America in Black and White: One Nation, Indivisible* (Simon & Schuster, 1997). For a broader, more liberal view, see Farai Chideya's *The Color of Our Future* (William Morrow, 1999). A helpful set of debates can be found in Faye J. Crosby and Cheryl VanDeVeer, eds., *Sex, Race, and Merit: Debating Affirmative Action in Education and Employment* (University of Michigan Press, 2001) and in *Beyond Affirmative Action: Reframing the Context of Higher Education* by Robert A. Ibarra (University of Wisconsin Press, 2001). Finally, a sad discussion of a Black lawyer who thought he had it all only to be dashed in midcareer by racism is *The Good Black* by Paul M. Barrett (Dutton, 1999).

On the Internet ...

Reparations for Slavery: Newer News and Links

This Adversity.Net, Inc., Web site offers several recent news stories on reparations for slavery as well as additional links to older news stories and background
information.

http://www.adversity.net/reparations/news1.htm

Israeli-Palestinian Conflict 2000–2001: What's *Really* Going On?

This page is intended as an attempt to get a clear picture of the current situation in Israel/Palestine. The site provides an abbreviated history of the conflict,
media representation of the conflict, and a variety of links with opinions representing both sides.

http://www.mtholyoke.edu/~amgreer/worldpol/

AfricaAIDS.org

This site supports a research forum opening up the debate on HIV issues as
they are seen in Africa and the West, often from very differing viewpoints.

http://www.africanaids.org

DRCNet: The Drug Reform Coordination Network

The Drug Reform Coordination Network is a national network of nearly
20,000 activists and concerned citizens, including parents, educators, students, lawyers, health care professionals, academics, and others, working for
drug policy reform from a variety of perspectives. This site features weekly
articles, archives of past articles, drug war facts and statistics, discussion lists,
and useful links for research and activism.

http://www.drcnet.org

PART 5

Future Policies and Global Issues

*O*ne central question for social scientists is the how and why of social order. How do societies "hang together"? Is it a matter of shared values? Or does the threat of social coercion by the powerful bond societies together? A related concern is the functions of social conflict. Does conflict bring about needed change for minorities, or is it more often disruptive and counterproductive? For example, does offering monetary reparations to African Americans whose ancestors may have been slaves strengthen social order by forging bonds of trust and forgiveness for past wrongs, or does it generate increased contempt in the majority, many of whom feel that minorities have "already been given too much"? Another issue is the use of military force to keep minorities in check in their own country. Can Palestine and Israel be held together by Israeli aggression? Also, are the actions of African leaders in trying to maintain control in a society that is overrun with AIDS always for the benefit of the nation? Lastly, is the international drug war really a war against minorities in the United States? Is U.S. social order kept together by the waging of a battle against the country's minorities?

- Are Reparations a Good Idea?

- Is Israel the Aggressor in the Israeli-Palestinian Conflict?

- Are African Leaders Misguided in Their Fight Against AIDS?

- Is the Drug War Harming Blacks?

ISSUE 18

Are Reparations a Good Idea?

YES: Victoria Barnett, from "Payback," *The Christian Century* (October 25, 2000)

NO: John V. Brain, from "About Atonement and Reparations," *The Sentinel* (November 2000)

ISSUE SUMMARY

YES: Historian Victoria Barnett contends that paying back African Americans for the horror that many of their ancestors experienced as slaves is both a moral and a possible thing to do, and she cites numerous examples indicating that there is a precedent for reparations.

NO: Journalist John V. Brain rejects arguments for reparations because it would be unjust to many Americans whose ancestors did not participate in slavery as well as to the millions of Americans and their descendants who came to the United States after slavery had ended. He maintains that atonement, not reparations, is the sensible action.

In the late 1940s the Nuremberg Trials were held, during which World War II German Nazi leaders were charged with war crimes. These trials established the legal precedent that politicians and soldiers can be held liable for participating in "crimes against humanity." Some of the more terrible acts resulted in execution for a relatively few German leaders.

Among the ancients, including the Greeks, elaborate funeral ceremonies were held and the dead were buried largely to bring symbolic closure to the lives of the dead. In almost all societies, ritualistic grieving times are allocated for survivors to come to terms with the death of a loved one, a friend, or a revered political leader.

Historically, when individual or numerous members of a family, tribe, religious group, political circle, or other group were murdered, demands for vengeance were forthcoming. In such situations, reaching closure through grieving, burial or cremation of the dead, or mourning was impossible until the death or deaths were avenged. Unlike in the past, however, in modern times individuals are not allowed to seek vengeance or justice on their own. The state is entrusted with that responsibility.

Following civil wars or intense periods of racial, ethnic, or religious strife, such governmental bodies as war tribunals, council commissions, and courts often have to perform elaborate rituals to reduce the likelihood that conflict will continue. These rituals may include publicizing trials on television, reassuring victims or survivors that justice will be done, and convincing those who are associated indirectly with or who played minor roles in claimed atrocities that only the directly guilty will be prosecuted and punished. Fears of land confiscation, exile, or mass retaliation must be assuaged; otherwise, the conflict will not end.

Following his victorious revolution in Cuba in 1959, Fidel Castro televised the trials of dictator Fulgencio y Zaldivar Batista's henchmen, who were accused of murdering many Cubans. When they were found guilty of serious human rights violations, hundreds of Batista's men were shot. The public cried out for even more executions. Many North Americans were outraged by Castro's behavior. However, those who were knowledgeable about Cuba realized that such seemingly extreme actions probably saved thousands of lives because before Castro took action, the Cuban people were preparing to personally extract vengeance from those who they believed killed their loved ones. For similar reasons, war crime tribunals in Central Europe and Africa today scrupulously mete out justice to the more blatant violators while assuring their followers that massive punishments will not happen.

The issue of reparations for Blacks in the United States to compensate for the wrongs of slavery, which legally ended over 135 years ago, is far trickier. For example, compensation is currently being paid out to victims of the Holocaust (1932–1945) and their immediate survivors. However, no U.S. slaves and few of their children are still alive today. Some victims and survivors of race riots and family members of Blacks who were lynched during the twentieth century are still alive, but not many. Some towns have nevertheless taken action to compensate them. Victims of the carnage in Central Europe and Africa are being financially compensated piecemeal. Yet the argument for paying reparations for all African Americans is quite different from those supporting reparations to those suffering from atrocities today, largely due to the temporal distance. Other confounding factors include the fact that most Americans' ancestors did not own slaves, the question of how to set a price on something that happened long ago, the issue of how much compensation is due (if any), and the possibility that many Blacks living today have the blood of slave owners in their veins. On the other hand, it is clear that whites, including those who immigrated to the United States only a few years ago, are at least indirect beneficiaries of Black labor and that many African Americans continue to be victimized—in the forms of poverty and racism—by the existence of slavery, regardless of how many years ago it existed.

The issue of reparations is taken up in the following selections, with Victoria Barnett arguing in favor of reparations and John V. Brain arguing against them. As you wrestle with this difficult issue, consider the possible negative consequences of reparations, such as significant resentment and anger by non-African Americans—particularly other minorities, such as Asians and Hispanics—and by poor whites.

Victoria Barnett

 **YES**

Payback

In 1969, I dropped out of college, moved to Racine, Wisconsin, and worked for a community action program and then for a welfare rights organization. The focus of my work was tenants' rights—helping tenants negotiate with landlords over things like rent and housing violations. Among my many indelible memories from that year was the situation of a family with six children. A large part of their welfare check paid for the worst housing conditions I had ever seen. The stucco house looked reasonably sound on the outside; inside, however, parts of the floor were rotten, pipes and wires were exposed, and the infestation of roaches was so great that there was literally a moving carpet of them on the floor. The landlord said that "these people" were "animals," and that fixing the house up would be a waste of time and money. The landlord was white; the family was African-American.

When I went to Racine, I idealistically thought of myself as color-blind.... The first day I worked for the welfare rights organization I was told by its director, a black ex-welfare mother, that I might as well know that I was in a foreign country. She was right. Although I didn't like to think about it, I came from the same country—the white middle class—as the slum landlord.

After leaving Racine I returned to college and to that country.... In 1985 I drove back to Racine and found the neighborhoods where I had worked looked exactly as I remembered. The stucco house was still there, and there were still people living in it.

I think about that house in Racine when I listen to discussions these days about granting reparations to African Americans. The call for reparations is not new; it began as soon as slavery ended. But it has gained steam in recent years, fueled by growing historical scholarship about the details of slavery, an increased worldwide readiness to call societies to account for their pasts, and an eloquent and passionate debate within the African-American community. In 1993 the Organization of African Unity called for some form of restitution from the U.S. and from those European countries that were involved in the slave trade....

Some precedents already exist. In 1994 Florida paid $2.1 million to descendants of the African-American victims of the 1923 Rosewood massacre.

Earlier this year, the Tulsa Race Riot Commission recommended that reparations be paid to the survivors of the 1921 race riot in that city, in which as many as 300 African-Americans were killed. The issue is relevant for other groups as well. The 1988 Civil Liberties Act, for example, paid $20,000 to each Japanese-American who was incarcerated during World War II. State and federal courts and mediators are dealing with hundreds of Native American land claims, and indigenous tribes in the U.S. and Canada have filed suits demanding reparations for various crimes, such as the abuse of students in parochial and government-run schools.

Reparations are a form of compensation for past injuries. Yet, particularly with respect to the African-American and Native American populations, we are not just looking at past injuries, because the original injustices have been compounded by decades of discrimination. For that reason, discussion of reparations for slavery touches on a number of deeper issues. Proponents contend that the destructive legacy of slavery continues to hinder many African-Americans from achieving equal status in this society. In measurable ways—infant mortality rates, unemployment, incarceration rates, etc.—African-Americans are at a disadvantage. Racism remains an ugly reality in our society....

Proponents of reparations point to this reality and say that the descendants of slaves are owed some form of monetary settlement. [O]thers contend that reparations are not the solution. Glenn Loury of the Institute on Race and Social Division at Boston University argued in the *New York Times* that money wouldn't solve the problem: "We need some reckoning with the racist past, but reparations encourage the wrong kind of reckoning." ... While some proponents advocate a flat monetary settlement to every descendant of a slave, others seek a social or political settlement—a percentage of the U.S. budget that would be allotted to improving schools with large minority populations, for example, or set aside for job training programs. Indeed, many whites and blacks view existing social programs and political attempts to redress past injustices, including programs like affirmative action, as a form of reparations.

... Some people think that social or political solutions to these issues are impossible, and that the change of heart necessary for a real end to racism will not come about through legislation.

⟡

When I was growing up, it was often said with reference to civil rights: "You can't legislate morality." On one level, this is true. It may be one reason why the so-called Great Society programs and other social programs did not go to the heart of the problem....

Slavery was not perpetrated just by traders and slaveholders. It created patterns of complicity that extended throughout U.S. society and still affect each one of us. Complicity in such cases does not consist of a singular sin; it becomes an ongoing pattern of individual behavior that is interwoven with predominant social patterns. In the long term, complicity is about the continued social effects of individual and communal misdeeds.

It is this ongoing aspect of complicity that makes reparations (and all attempts at apology, restitution, reconciliation or forgiveness) so complex and controversial. When injustice is perpetrated against an entire group, when it persists over a long period and its effects permeate society, no one is untouched. The dividing lines that result—religious, ethnic or economic—warp public and private relationships. The longer such dividing lines exist, the more difficult it is to have genuine and honest dialogue between those on opposite sides. Even the best-intended attempts to change the situation remain part of a much greater process that steadily undermines them. The ensuing moral paralysis, rationalization and defensiveness hinder us from getting further. This is why individual attempts to address the racial divide in this country so often hit a stone wall. We are confronting a social sin, and the problem and its possible solutions cannot be addressed apart from the larger issues.

⊷⊶⊷

Recent history has included a number of such attempts, not all of which entail actual reparations; the post-World War II response by Germany to the Holocaust is only the most prominent example. South Africa, Chile, Argentina, Brazil, Northern Ireland, Cambodia and Rwanda have attempted to deal with issues of individual and collective complicity. These are new and hopeful developments in human history. It is a sign of progress that history now includes the victims' voices. We recognize now that "settling" matters without doing justice or paying attention to the victims doesn't settle them at all.

Addressing this task in a politically viable way, however, raises difficult questions. Can individuals be held accountable for political and social injustice that occurs on a massive scale? Are later generations accountable for the sins of their forebears; if so, how can this be instituted effectively? In addressing past injustice and its legacy, how do we create a different foundation for the future? What factors give such attempts the legitimacy and fairness that are crucial if they are to be accepted by individual citizens with differing political viewpoints? Most important, how do victims, bystanders and perpetrators—or their descendants—speak to one another about these questions?

The complexity of these questions becomes clear when we consider what can and cannot be dealt with by a court of law. Legal redress for those who suffered injury and are still living (Holocaust survivors, Japanese-Americans imprisoned during World War II, African-Americans who are not hired or cannot obtain housing due to their race) is a difficult and politicized process, but as long as the plaintiffs and defendants are still living it is somewhat straightforward. It is possible to put war criminals on trial, demand that Swiss banks return money to Holocaust survivors or their descendants, and require corporations that profited directly from Nazi forced labor camps to pay compensation for that injustice.

Even in these cases, however, "justice" will seem incomplete, and the amount of monetary compensation will be symbolic. What amount of money could ever "compensate" victims who have been tortured, lost family members, or been forcibly deprived of their homes and livelihoods? These limitations are magnified in dealing with an issue like slavery. What kind of compensation is due and who, precisely, is liable? We confront these issues several generations after the original crime. It is no longer possible to bring the slave owners and traders to justice—yet the legacy of their crimes continues to benefit those who inherited the power and privileges that emerged from that injustice.

❧◈❧

Thus, while proponents of reparations present their case in the clear-cut language of a legal claim for damages, the issue is really political and moral, and this sets certain limitations. As Martha Minow writes in *Beyond Vengeance and Forgiveness* (Beacon Press, 1998), reparations do not offer "tidy endings." They are not a way out or a means of settling accounts. They can't enact the kind of justice that many people would like to have. The key to understanding their potential is the root word *reparare*—to repair something, which in this case is the political body and society as a whole.

Restitution and reparations are primarily symbolic acts that serve as catalysts for a very different—and much longer—political process. The demand for reparations calls us to think in a different way about the enduring legacy of racism and to articulate possible solutions in ways that are both relevant and reasonable to individual citizens. Where successful, this process can create a foundation for reconciliation. Part of this process is ongoing reflection about the moral nature of how we confront the past. As the work of the Truth and Reconciliation Commission in South Africa illustrated, religious people can raise such questions in the public sphere in a particular way.

This task may seem obvious, but experience shows that such questioning is precisely the work that often falls by the wayside. The tendency of many religious groups is to take sides and clear stands. While such moral leadership is crucial, especially in acute situations marked by violence, deeper theological and ethical reflection on these issues is just as crucial for the long term. In particular, there are two ways in which churches can serve to expand on the more traditional roles of mediator or advocate.

The first is that religious communities can help their members talk about the truth. If this is to be recognized as a truth that shapes our present reality, it must include the voices of as many groups as possible. The real test in our society will be whether these voices can be brought into a genuine conversation with one another, a conversation that moves beyond political posturing. Because the topics of reparations and racism are connected, ethical and religious perspectives could be brought into the public discourse on how prejudice functions, and how racism and injustice reflect different levels of complicity. We need to understand the history of slavery as a very central part of our history and our consciousness as a nation; tourists who visit the White House or the U.S. Capitol building in Washington, D.C., for example, should know that those buildings were constructed, in part, with slave labor.

Second, we need to confront this history in its entirety. Historical denial takes many forms. One form is the denial of the injustice, the silencing of the victims' voices, the refusal to acknowledge that our ancestors played a role in the original oppression. Another form of denial is ignorance about past attempts to address the issues we wrestle with today. Part of any conversation about race includes the history of the civil rights movement and the various interracial and interfaith attempts to do things differently. These efforts, even where incomplete and unsuccessful, are also part of our common history. Because the religious community has been a central part of this history (and because so many leading activists are still among us), it has a special contribution to make here.

There are very pragmatic reasons why we should confront this matter with more honesty and long-term commitment than we've done in the past, but the main reason goes beyond self-interest. It has to do with the fabric of our society, with who we are as individuals in our private and public lives, with the mental and moral compromises that enable us to tolerate the intolerable. Visitors to the Holocaust Museum in Washington often come (and leave) with the question: how could people let this happen? But the human capacity to disclaim responsibility for the suffering of those who are not "like us" shouldn't be that hard for anyone in this society to understand.

I saw things in Racine years ago that continue to haunt me, for they were outrageous, and showed that many people in our democracy are viewed and treated as less than human. As citizens, we need to figure out how to change such things in a public way, precisely because our involvement as individuals has to be part of any social solution. Germans, South Africans and others throughout the world have learned that dealing with the past is the only means toward creating a different kind of future. If we want a different relationship among races in this country, we will have to find some way of addressing our past. And that means talking about reparations.

NO

John V. Brain

About Atonement and Reparations

Arguments are again surfacing that African Americans should be compensated for the exploitation of their slave ancestors. On his African tour the President spoke movingly of feeling the pain of Africa: a nice gesture. But apologies are easy; reparations difficult.

Making reparations is a concept accepted in law, when it relates to individuals who have been wronged or have wronged others. But for entire classes of individuals to owe a debt of restitution to another is on shakier ground. Is every individual equally culpable or equally deserving?

Apportioning Blame Difficult

Before emancipation, some American states were slave-owning and some free. Do the descendants of those who opposed slavery owe reparations equal to those who defended it? And what of the majority of modern Americans who came to these shores long after slavery was abolished? Shall a recent immigrant be burdened with the guilt and obligations of those descended from the founders? Or shall we return to the mathematics of the slave era and apportion blame according to the proportion of guilty blood?

Slavery in History

Slavery has been practiced for most of history. Wars produced prisoners, and prisoners—if not killed outright—became slaves. Slaves ran the Roman Empire. Rowed the galleys. Built the roads. Wrote books. Taught philosophy. Their treatment varied, from the absolute right of owners to do as they wished with their property, to legal restrictions on terms of service and punishment. Serfdom survived in Russia into modern times, and in many countries today women are still virtual slaves.

The great British social reformer Robert Owen, who labored to improve the lot of cotton mill workers in the early years of the industrial revolution, wrote after a visit to America in the 1830s that the working conditions in British cotton mills were far worse than any he had seen among slaves in the South.

From John V. Brain, "About Atonement and Reparations," *The Sentinel,* vol. 12, no. 2 (November 2000). Copyright © 2000 by John V. Brain. Reprinted by permission of Publishers' Marketing Service and the author.

In the cotton mills five-year-old children worked 12 hours a day under appalling conditions, and few survived to adulthood. If any reparations are in order, surely those exploited by capitalism must be near the front of the line?

Then there are the inhabitants of conquered countries, the innumerable victims of war and colonial empire-building who were forced to pay tribute, the native races of India, Africa, the Americas. Humans have exploited other humans throughout history. The Viking system was simplest: send out raiding parties to attack, kill, rape, pillage, carry off anything of value, burn, and move on. These were the fierce people who came from Scandinavia and settled in northeast England, the Angles and the Danes. Today they are inextricably mixed with the older inhabitants, the Scots, Picts, Celts, and those latecomers from the North, the Normans. History is the story of injustice, and thank God most of the old wounds have healed as the races intermingled.

Different Cultures, Religions Fuel Longest Grudges

But where races and ethnic groups remained separated by culture and religion, memories are long and grudges nurtured and horribly avenged. Hutus and Tutsis, Serbs and Croats, Hindus and Moslems nurse their resentments and, exploited by political opportunists, engage in pogroms and genocide.

But the history of reparations is also not a happy one. After World War I the Allies demanded punitive reparations of conquered Germany that further devastated a proud people and led to the resurgence of aggressive nationalism in the Nazi era. The Second World War was the outcome. By contrast, the magnanimity of the Allies, and especially of the United States' Marshall Plan after World War II, laid the foundation for the rebuilding of shattered Europe and a lasting peace.

Few modern peoples would seem to be more deserving of reparations than the Jews of Europe, decimated by Hitler's policy of extermination. Today, their survivors are having difficulty reclaiming funds stashed by the Nazis in Swiss banks, and I have heard of no initiative to compensate the Jewish people as a whole for the crimes against them. Not a few of those who survive today enjoy above-average good fortune, and it would seem unfair to reward them when so many others are in need.

For African Americans the road up from slavery has been long and hard. Emancipation did not bring equality or empowerment, and not until another hundred years had passed did the real struggle for civil rights begin. But the last half century has seen significant gains, evidenced by the end of legal segregation and the rise of black leaders and a substantial black middle class. Even so, many African Americans remain as an economic underclass trapped in ghettoes where gangs, crime, drugs, and hopelessness prevail.

Adding Another Hurt to a Wound That Hasn't Healed

So how shall we respond to the demand for compensation for slavery? Only that it adds another hurt to an old wound that prevents natural healing and results in further alienation. The great majority of Americans today feel they had no part in slavery and that yet another exploitative group is out to get them, branding them as oppressors and casting themselves as victims.

The great American educator Booker T. Washington had little time for whiners. He believed that America would reward initiative and study and hard work, and that the lot of his people would henceforth be primarily in their own hands. Though rosy, his philosophy of self-reliance has merit. His advice was, Be useful: your worth will be recognized. By contrast, he might have added, if you are lazy, dependent, irresponsible, not only will you fail personally, but you will contribute to the perception of your people as being a burden on society.

We Are All Inheritors of the Crimes of History

Those who are repelled by the demand for reparations from all the survivors of groups victimized by history may be more inclined to the religious concept of atonement.

Atonement in theology is the recognition that man is sinful, though capable of redemption, and accepts a responsibility to make amends. Stripped of its more grotesque breast-beating, it is a salutary reflection. It makes us aware that we are all inheritors of the crimes of history, and that as survivors we owe others a vague obligation of remorse.

Who but we are the beneficiaries? Whom but to others can we make amends? The outcome is the opposite of festering resentment, of the "you owe me" attitude, and a new openness to offering and accepting the helping hand, not as a monetary payoff, but as a sincere personal gesture. If one day a year were to be dedicated to the memory of all who have suffered injustice, and if this sense of collective and universal obligation could be channeled into helping those who today need help, that would be a form of reparation we could all subscribe to.

And, business owners—remember the exploited children!

POSTSCRIPT

Are Reparations a Good Idea?

Former president Bill Clinton supports reparations, as do many African American leaders and citizens. Many college students support it as well, so much so in some cases that when David Horowitz, a critic of reparations for African Americans, ran a newspaper ad entitled "Ten Reasons Why Reparations for Slavery Is a Bad Idea," students at Brown University broke into the newspaper office and stole all the papers containing the ad.

One related issue not addressed by either Barnett or Brain is the possibility that if reparations are paid out to African Americans, the sheer number of even vaguely identifiable African Americans might double or even triple. For instance, a few years after government subsidies were set aside for Native Americans, their count increased by thousands as greedy people discovered (or constructed) their Native American ancestry. Another concern is that the money that would be used to pay out reparations might be better spent on poor children in need of education and other services. Many conservative African American intellectuals oppose reparations because they feel that a monetary amount would cheapen the horrors experienced by slaves. Others contend that Blacks should be *glad* that their ancestors were brought to the United States in the first place, even as slaves, because Blacks are better off in America today than they would be anywhere else.

A variety of Americans, both Black and white, point out that large sections of entire cities and even of some suburbs are perceived as too dangerous for many people to enter at night. Indeed, some assert that many areas that were once wonderful places to live or visit are now too horrible or dangerous to drive through even in the daytime. Conditions of crime, decay, and waste are often unfairly linked to a large minority population. The existence of these conditions are sometimes taken as indicators that perhaps Blacks "owe" something to the rest of the United States.

In a highly industrialized, capitalist society, the idea of reparations—or money being spent largely for symbolic reasons—is widely viewed with suspicion and anger. Yet can the United States afford not to admit to the fact of slavery and its continuing negative consequences into the twenty-first century? Wouldn't the costs be reasonable if healing is accomplished? On the other hand, are the costs worth it in terms of working out paybacks, acquiring the money, generating resentment from majority members who feel no guilt for an activity that their ancestors may or may not have engaged in, and angering other minority groups who feel that they are suffering even more than African Americans are?

Among the many works that support Barnett's viewpoint is Manning Marable's "Along the Color Line: Escaping From Blackness: Racial Identity and Public Policy," `http://www.jacksonprogressive.com/issues/civilliberties/marable/blackness.html`. For an update on the negative reactions to Horowitz's attack on reparations, see his articles "Racial McCarthyism," *The Wall Street Journal* (March 20, 2001) and "No Comparison With David Duke," *The Washington Times* (April 4, 2001). Those who would support Brain's thinking include Larry Elder, in *The Ten Things You Can't Say in America* (St. Martin's Press, 2000), and W. Williams, in "Self-Sabotage a Major Problem for African-Americans," *The Washington Post* (November 15, 2000).

Strong support for reparations can be found in John Conyers et al., "The Case for Reparations: Why? How Much? When?" *Ebony* (August 2000) and "Blacks' Call for U.S. Slavery Reparations Gains Strength," *The Washington Post* (December 26, 2000). Opposing reparations is S. Crouch, in "Money Isn't Cure for Blacks' Problems," *The Baltimore Sun* (February 27, 2001). Some excellent philosophical aspects of justice and equality can be found in Ronald Dworkin's *Sovereign Virtue: The Theory and Practice of Equality* (Harvard University Press, 2000) and *Political Forgiveness* by Peter Digeser (Cornell University Press, 2001). Finally, a thoughtful article on reparations in countries outside the United States is J. Murphy's "S. Africa Bitterly Debates Reparations for Apartheid," *The Baltimore Sun* (February 20, 2001).

ISSUE 19

Is Israel the Aggressor in the Israeli-Palestinian Conflict?

YES: James Ron, from "Jewish Liberals and Voices of Reason," *The Baltimore Sun* (November 10, 2000)

NO: Kenneth Lasson, from "Israel's Voice Muffled Amid Hail of Stones," *The Baltimore Sun* (December 3, 2000)

ISSUE SUMMARY

YES: Sociologist James Ron, a former Israeli soldier, asserts that Israel is violating treaties, waging an unfair and bloody war against Palestinians, and inaccurately characterizing Muslims as murderers and Jews as victims.

NO: Professor of law Kenneth Lasson presents an interview with a colonel in the Israel Defense Forces, who relates several accounts of Palestinians' deliberately having their own children attack Israeli soldiers. The media, Lasson asserts, overlook the aggressiveness of the Arabs, preferring instead to cast the Israelis as the bad guys.

T he issue of Israeli-Palestinian conflict is infused with ethnic, racial, and religious connotations, some of which run both deep and long. For over 2,000 years Jews have looked at the city of Jerusalem as their holy city and have longed for it to be returned to the Jews. They saw the land that has been referred to as Palestine in recent times as part of the land of the Jews—the homeland. Muslims who have lived in Jerusalem and in what has been the Jewish state of Israel since 1948 believe that the area belongs to them. In east Jerusalem, the Temple Mount has two core Muslim religious sites. The Western Wall for Jews is said to be their most revered area. Christians also revere these areas.

When the state of Israel was created in 1948, some 750,000 Palestinians were expelled or left to settle in nearby Lebanon, Jordan, and other Muslim nations. Compensation for the Palestinians and their desire to return to the area have been contentious political issues for generations. Israelis contend that they could not possibly absorb the large number of Palestinians who wish to return to the area. They also argue that the Palestinians have lived elsewhere for years and do not really want to return anyway. Various Muslim governments and organizations maintain the opposite. Others feel that the refugee issue is being stoked simply to embarrass Israel.

In 1967 Israel was unexpectedly invaded by surrounding Arabic countries that wished to drive the Jews from the area. The remarkable Israeli army responded and, in six days, crushed and expelled the invaders. However, after the Six Day War, Israel expanded its territory allegedly to protect its borders from future attacks. That is, Israel occupied the West Bank and the Gaza Strip (a slice of land 30 miles long and 10 miles wide lying slightly east of Egypt). The Israelis also took control of east Jerusalem.

Muslim Palestinians were enraged by Israel's expansion, especially after Israeli settlers streamed into Gaza and the West Bank. Israel's prime minister at the time, Ariel Sharon, coordinated the settlements, and in 1982, when Muslims led attacks on Israel from Lebanon, Sharon allegedly attacked the militants' villages, killing both soldiers and civilians.

Currently, the West Bank has approximately 190,000 Israeli settlers and 2 million Palestinians. In the Gaza Strip there are about 6,500 Israeli settlers and 1.2 million Palestinians. Although the Israelis make up less than 1 percent of those populations, many of the settlers are militants who view Arabs with contempt. Some are quite bellicose, and Israeli soldiers are often needed to protect them. Throughout the Muslim world, the continued presence of Israeli soldiers and settlers in the occupied territories is viewed with horror and anger. Meanwhile, Jews from around the world ask themselves how they can claim to occupy a higher moral ground and maintain pride in Judaism's rich history of humanitarianism and tolerance if the Israelis are subjugating other people. Hard-liners, such as Sharon, argue that they have protected others' religious shrines and have tried to be fair and that it is the Palestinian Authority (ruling party) under Yasser Arafat that provokes turmoil. Muslims respond that blame lies with the Israeli soldiers, who are shooting Palestinian children and teenagers.

The *intifada* (uprising) that has occurred since September 2000 has resulted in at least 450 deaths, most of which were Palestinians, and 12,000 injured Palestinians, as compared to 780 Israelis. During the same period, footage of Israeli soldiers being lynched by Palestinians was aired on television. In return, Muslims produced hundreds of pictures of civilians, including children, who were maimed or killed allegedly by Israeli fire.

Is Israel the aggressor in this conflict? In the following selections, James Ron argues that it is, while Kenneth Lasson places blame on the Muslims. As you read this debate, keep in mind that both writers have deep ties to Israel and that both have served in the Israeli army and therefore have first-hand knowledge. Also keep in mind that for both sides the stakes are high. Many Israelis feel that their country's very existence, if not the existence of Jewish people everywhere, depends on their soldiers' taking whatever actions are needed when they are provoked. For Palestinians, their survival is threatened by Israelis who they feel want to drive them from their homes and to steal their honor. As you read, also think about solutions to the conflict that might be formulated based on experiences with other conflicts, such as Black-white conflicts in the United States or the Serbian-Croation conflict in central Europe.

James Ron

 **YES**

Jewish Liberals and Voices of Reason

Adisturbing byproduct of recent Middle Eastern violence is the decline in critical thinking among Jews. Even political liberals are being swept up in a tribal "us-against-them" mentality, viewing Palestinians as aggressors and Jews as victims.

But in doing so, they ignore an uncomfortable reality: It is Israel that threatens the Palestinian state to be, not the other way around.

The Palestinian predicament is often obscured by Israel's popular media, which focus largely on the experiences of Jewish soldiers and settlers, rather than on Palestinians under Jewish control. Although reporters have covered Jewish casualties in great depth, they have not afforded Palestinians equal respect.

In the United States, Jewish leaders are closing ranks behind the Israeli government, believing Israel is, once again, under mortal threat. Like many diasporas located far from the conflict, however, American Jews are often more hard-line than their Israeli co-nationals.

As a result, few Jewish commentators here or in Israel are dispassionately examining the roots of Palestinian frustration, resorting instead to the stereotypes of Arab murderers and Jewish victims.

Although this reflex is understandable given Jewish history, it makes little sense in the context of today's Middle East. Palestinians are doing most of the dying, not Jews, and it is Ramallah that is besieged by tanks, not Tel Aviv. The West Bank and Gaza are vigorously patrolled by occupation troops, not Israel, and it is the Palestinian economy that is in tatters. Although terrorists have killed Jews, it is Palestine's national security, for the most part, that is under systematic threat.

Imagine that Palestinian and Israeli positions were reversed: Palestinian helicopter gun ships overflying Haifa, Palestinian tanks firing into Ramat Gan and Palestinian generals, backed by the United States, threatening to retaliate against Netanya if Jewish gunmen keep firing. Rather than engaging in such mental exercises, most Jewish commentators dwell on the irrationality and ill-will of Palestinian leaders.

Instead, it might be more useful to dispassionately consider Palestinian grievances. Although Jews are not obliged to accept all of the Palestinian claims, they should try to understand their opponents' views.

Genuine curiosity might reveal that, for Palestinians, the Israeli occupation has become more painful in recent years. Successive Israeli governments, including that of Prime Minister Ehud Barak, have continued to encourage Jewish settlement in the West Bank, slicing the area into non-contiguous Palestinian enclaves. Palestinians feel that military checkpoints have made life impossible in the occupied zone, destroying normal public and economic life.

More important, perhaps, the final-status deal offered at Camp David... did not address Palestinian concerns, failing to offer meaningful control over Arab East Jerusalem or Palestinian borders, and annexing lands around Jerusalem and elsewhere. The outcome was seen as a patchwork of semi-autonomous islands within an Israeli sea, not as a state worth living in.

Jews often complain that Arabs do not acknowledge the pernicious legacy of global anti-Semitism. They believe that Palestinians would accept Israeli concerns if they would understand Jewish suffering. But have Israelis ever really tried to imagine the Palestinian experience?

Growing up in Israel, I was never encouraged to consider Palestinian life under military occupation and was not told that during the 1948 war of Israeli independence, many of the 750,000 Palestinian refugees were forced out by Jewish troops. Revealingly, I was never asked to consider why Palestinians opposed Zionism in the first place. Arab opposition was explained as anti-Semitism, not as a response to displacement.

This education continued during my military service, when the talk was always of "terrorists," never of human beings. Although armies are not famed for critical thinking, militarized worldviews should not penetrate into civilian life. Since most Israeli Jews are conscripted for three years and serve regularly in the reserves, their views are heavily shaped by that experience.

After the 1993 Oslo peace accord, a growing number of Jews gradually began to develop a more nuanced vision of politics. Although most still prioritized the needs of their own "tribe" over others, that black-and-white world was increasingly shaded with gray.

These gains are now being rolled back, however, and even liberals are slipping into the seductive embrace of nationalism. Here, the parallels to the former Yugoslavia are unnerving. In the late 1980s, observers warned that Serbian intellectuals in Belgrade, once the most free-thinking city in all of Eastern Europe, were becoming increasingly close-minded, carrying their people with them.

If the Middle East is to avoid a similar tragedy, Jewish liberals must develop their own critical voice, now.

Kenneth Lasson

 **NO**

Israel's Voice Muffled Amid Hail of Stones

W hy," I ask my colleague, a visiting law professor from the University of Haifa and a ranking colonel in the Israel Defense Forces. "Why must Israel confront stone-throwing children with tanks and live ammunition?"

"You don't understand," replies Emanuel Gross, who is at the University of Baltimore School of Law . . . teaching courses in Constitutional Victims' Rights and Comparative Criminal Process.

"Please educate me," I say.

"It is very complicated. This is not a situation such as in Lebanon, where there is a discreet border that can be defended," he says. "Here the Army is defending Jewish settlements within the West Bank and Gaza and Israel itself. There is no way to retreat, no place to go, no way to let the rock-throwers simply have their way."

Moreover, Gross continues, the demonstrators are not just a group of children hurling pebbles.

They are organized in waves. On the front line are young Palestinians, throwing stones by the hundreds. Behind them are masked teenagers slinging rocks, some of which are large and lethal. Behind them are those with Molotov cocktails and other explosive devices.

And behind them are those shooting pistols, rifles, and machine guns with, of course, live ammunition.

It is the rear lines that attack Israeli soldiers with explosives and bullets, he says. "And although the army uses great restraint—more than most other countries would, even when we fire back in self-defense—there are sometimes tragedies and the world sees children being killed. But they have been put there by their own people to mobilize the world's outrage.

"It reminds us that, during the gulf war, the Iraqis placed their Scud missile launchers next to a hospital, and when the Americans bombed the military installation, the outcry was that they were bombing a hospital. The same mentality motivates the Palestinians. The other day an ambulance came into one of our settlements in the territories, but there were no injured people inside. Instead, it was filled with explosives sent by Israeli Arabs.

"In short, our citizens and our soldiers are being threatened, and not just with stones but with live ammunition. The army does not have a slingshot corps to fight back, and there is no place to retreat. What are we to do?"

If that is the case, I ask, why hasn't Israel been able to convey a more accurate picture of that version of events?

"I don't know," responds Gross, with more than a little frustration.

"I am in the U.S. until February. A few weeks ago, I went to our embassy in Washington and offered to speak on Israel's behalf, to present the true story of what's going on, to counter the very effective job being done by the Palestinians of making it appear as if they are Davids fighting Goliath, and we are not getting the truth out. But the people at the embassy just shrugged."

I understand the Israeli shrug. It is a combination of apathy and arrogance and resignation. We have always been under siege by those around us, it says, and we will always be blamed, so it is a waste of time and effort to court world opinion.

I show Gross a letter, forwarded to me by e-mail, from an American woman who lives in Haifa with her Israeli husband:

"The past month has been one of stress, tension, and worry. We are comparatively lucky here in Haifa. It has always been a city where Arabs and Jews have gotten along. But suddenly, as a result of the violence and the call to arms by the Arabs in Gaza and the Palestinian-controlled territories, the Israeli Arabs have also been involved in violent acts, and that is a development that we never expected.

"Suddenly we have a fifth column. Arab citizens are driving just a few miles outside their villages to attack Israeli civilians on our streets and cars on our highways. Now we are viewing our Israeli Arabs with suspicion and resentment. People here have agreed upon a boycott, although we personally support those Arabs who have shown moderation.

"What I am writing about, you will not have seen or read in any reports of the violence of the past two weeks. Did you know that several days before Ariel Sharon and a group of Knesset members visited the Temple Mount, a convoy of Israeli military trucks was blown up by mines that had been put on the road shortly before they passed through, killing and injuring many of our soldiers?

"What distresses us most of all is that there is no one here who presents to the world the truth of what is going on, no one who sets straight the Palestinian propaganda and distortions."

She mentions a Knesset member who just returned from the United States, dismayed at how the American media has bought into Arab propaganda. She had asked the Israeli ambassador in Washington how it could be that no spokesman presented the Israeli position, and was told that that was the function of the consulate in New York. She contacted the consul himself. She found that he could hardly speak English.

"Had I written this letter the day of the Sharm-el Sheik agreement," concluded the woman from Haifa, "I would have told you that a great weight was suddenly lifted from our shoulders.

"But right now, we do not expect the agreement to last. We are preparing for war. It is a dreadful prospect but a reality that we must face. At dinner last night, I was astonished when my sister-in-law said, 'The sooner we have the war, the better it will be, especially CNN, rather than to let the violence escalate.'

"My husband and I don't share these sentiments, but they may represent the overwhelming feelings in the country right now. And that leaves us with a heavy heart. Say a prayer for us...?"

Gross reads the letter, shakes his head, and once again says he doesn't understand why Israel cannot speak better for itself.

What he does know are the facts on the ground and in the history books, and he can tick them off in logical and chronological order.

He knows that Israel became a nation at least 1,800 years before the rise of Islam, and that Jews have had a continuous presence in the land for the past 3,300 years.

He knows that Jerusalem was founded by King David and has been the Jewish capital for over three millennia, but never has it been the capital of any Arab or Muslim entity, not even when the Jordanians occupied the city.

He knows that Jerusalem is mentioned more than 700 times in Jewish Holy Scriptures but not once in the Koran.

He knows that in 1948 some 630,000 Arab refugees were encouraged to leave Israel by their leaders, who promised to purge the land of Jews. Instead, they became the only refugee group in the world that has never been absorbed into their own peoples' countries.

He knows that the Arabs are represented by eight nations—not including the Palestinians—that initiated five wars against Israel and lost each time.

He knows that the Palestine Liberation Organization's charter still calls for the destruction of the state of Israel, which has given the Palestinians most of the West Bank land and autonomy under the Palestinian Authority.

And finally, he knows that the United Nations has passed hundreds of resolutions directed solely against Israel, but was utterly silent while, between 1948 and 1967, over 50 Jerusalem synagogues and an ancient Jewish cemetery on the Mount of Olives were destroyed and desecrated by the Arabs, who also prevented Jews from visiting their holy shrines.

In contrast, under Israeli rule, all Muslim and Christian sites have been preserved and made accessible to people of all faiths.

Why, I ask once again, hasn't Israel been able to convey these facts to the world?

Gross, neither apathetic nor arrogant nor resigned, turns, looks me in the eye, and shrugs.

POSTSCRIPT

Is Israel the Aggressor in the Israeli-Palestinian Conflict?

Neither Ron nor Lasson discuss in-depth the significant factions within both sides. For instance, the Palestinian Authority has been under bitter attack by its own people for not compromising. As a result, Palestinians find themselves broke, unemployed, and at times without food or shelter. Moreover, some Palestinians are especially angry over Arafat's alleged censorship.

Among the Israelis, there are terrible splits between the ultra-Orthodox Jews, who reject even the principal of statehood, and religious nationalist extremists who want even more Jews in the settlements. The long-term ethnic division between the Ashkenazi (European founders and their descendants) and the Sephardic immigrants (largely from North Africa and Muslim countries) is intensified by the rapid emergence of the Sephardic Shas (extreme theological conservatives who oppose the secular Ashkenazi).

At the international level, Israel's strongest support continues to come from the United States. Yet both U.S. government officials and American Jews may be tiring of the Middle Eastern conflict. Both sides of the conflict continue to malign each other in popular music, school textbooks, and political speeches. Although the hard-liner Sharon won an unprecedented 62 percent of the vote in the February 2001 election for prime minister of Israel, many point out that voter turnout was extremely low. This too probably reflects a desire for some solution beyond continued violence.

Among the many books on the Middle Eastern conflict is *From Herzl to Rabin: The Changing Image of Zionism* by Amnon Rubinstein (Holmes & Meier, 2001). A broader discussion of global ethnic conflicts is *Ethnopolitical Warfare: Causes, Consequences, and Possible Solutions* edited by Daniel Chirot and Martin E. Seligman (American Psychological Association, 2001). The Marxist-humanist publication *News & Letters* assigns blame to both sides but generally attacks the Israelis more than the Palestinians. See "Sharon's Election, Bush's Bombs Deepen Crisis in Middle East" in the March 2001 issue.

For a bitter attack on the allegedly pro-Israeli media, see the media advisory by Fairness & Accuracy in Reporting (FAIR) entitled "Muffled Coverage of U.N. Vote: Media Ignores Broad Mideast Consensus" (October 16, 2000), which can be found on the Internet at http://www.fair.org/reports/israel-un-advisory.html. For an attack on the press from the other side, see "The 'Washington Post' vs. Israel," by A. Levin, *Commentary* (November 1997). Finally, for a discussion of the conflict between Israeli academicians and conservatives, see "Conservative Think Tanks Take on Israeli Academics," by H. Watzman, *Chronicle of Higher Education* (February 23, 2001).

ISSUE 20

Are African Leaders Misguided in Their Fight Against AIDS?

YES: James A. Harmon, from "It's Not Direct Aid, But It's What a Bank Can Offer," *The Washington Post* (September 17, 2000)

NO: Kalumbi Shangula, from "We Can't Shoulder More Debt to Treat an Incurable Disease," *The Washington Post* (September 17, 2000)

ISSUE SUMMARY

YES: James A. Harmon, chairman of the Export-Import Bank, contends that the "HIV/AIDS pandemic" in sub-Saharan Africa is a moral issue that the rest of the world must address and that humanitarian assistance and loans are needed to fight the problem. He maintains that the Export-Import Bank is trying to do its part by offering extended loan terms and keeping in mind potential debt forgiveness and that such aid will not add to the region's economic woes.

NO: Nambian official Kalumbi Shangula, while acknowledging the seriousness of the HIV and AIDS problem in sub-Saharan Africa, rejects the "noble impulse" of the Export-Import Bank and other organizations to loan money to help control it. He argues that antiretroviral drugs only serve to prolong the lives (and expenses) of victims, not cure them; that the drugs are too expensive; and that repayment in most African countries is impossible.

Few other controversial issues are undergoing as rapid a metamorphosis as the HIV situation in sub-Saharan Africa. On the surface, the issue should be clear-cut: globally, there are at least 36 million known cases of HIV and AIDS, with some 25 million being in Africa. The simple question is, How do we get medicine to them to help? In reality, the issue is far more complicated. In addition to the social, political, economic, and psychological aspects that surround the controversy, there are huge scientific and medical disagreements. How can *any* medicine be imported, even for free, to countries in which there are few medical infrastructures, such as sufficient hospitals, trained personnel, distribution centers that are relatively free of corruption, mechanisms for providing basic information, and so on?

One medical concern is the way in which HIV and AIDS are transmitted in Africa. In the United States and other countries, the most common mode of transmitting HIV is through intravenous drug use and homosexual contact. In contrast, the vast majority of cases in Africa are transmitted through heterosexual contact. About 0.6 percent of North Americans between ages 15 and 49 (high-risk population) have HIV or AIDS; about 20 percent of those are female. In sub-Saharan Africa females compose over 55 percent of HIV and AIDS cases, and just under 10 percent of the total population is affected.

The social, economic, political, and racial aspects of this issue are equally contentious, as is partially reflected in the debate between James A. Harmon and Kalumbi Shangula that follows. The issue's major antagonists include five major U.S. drug companies whose initial charges for various pharmaceutical help ranged from $12,000 to $15,000 per year. This is far higher than most family incomes in African nations. In fact, the average per capita incomes of many African countries are well below $1,000 per year, and some are under $100 per year. However, several factors have resulted in greatly reduced costs (down to $1 per day per patient) for drugs to fight HIV. One is drug companies' deeply entrenched determination to retain patent rights to their pharmaceuticals. However, since 1997 South Africa has had a law that gives the country the right to compulsory licensing. This means that South African companies can ignore manufacturers' patents and make less expensive variants of drugs. South Africa also allows parallel importing, which is the buying of drugs from manufacturers that have not been approved by the patent holders.

Because drug companies in South Africa and elsewhere, especially in the United States, greatly fear these practices, they are now offering HIV and AIDS drugs approximately at cost. In addition, world opinion has shifted dramatically, with massive protests being waged against the World Trade Organization, drug companies, and others. Protesters are successfully linking the AIDS plague with corporate greed and selfishness. Many respected private organizations, such as Doctors Without Borders, question how those who possess medical supplies that could help millions of AIDS victims can ignore their plight.

Different issues are raised by influential Africans such as Shangula. They question the wisdom of buying drugs that they cannot possibly afford on credit. Even with the 80–90 percent reductions in prices, most sub-Saharan African countries cannot afford them. Also, prolonging the lives of HIV and AIDS victims with drugs increases both the misery of the high costs of keeping those patients alive and the likelihood of their passing the disease on to others.

In the following selection, Harmon acknowledges that far more needs to be done than the $1 billion annual loan from his bank. He feels that many private organizations that are devoted to charity also need to help. In the second selection, Shangula maintains that Harmon's seemingly humanitarian position may not help African countries achieve the necessary medical help and social justice. He contends that funds are better spent to fight tuberculosis, malaria, cholera, and sexually transmitted diseases other than HIV.

James A. Harmon  **YES**

It's Not Direct Aid, But It's What a Bank Can Offer

Who would not be horrified by the statistics coming out of sub-Saharan Africa? The HIV/AIDS pandemic threatens to bring decades of slow, hard-won progress to an abrupt end. It is a catastrophe that can only be reversed by a massive influx of resources—a staggering need that far outruns available humanitarian aid.

The U.S. Export-Import Bank is not an aid agency. We cannot donate assistance. By law, we are a trade agency. Our authority is limited by Congress to providing credit, primarily to the developing world, to purchase U.S. goods and services. But we felt a need to join Africa's war on HIV/AIDS. So we asked ourselves a simple question: How can we help?

After some soul-searching, we found a way to offer assistance that is both constructive and consistent with our mission, and with our traditional role of financing the buildup of infrastructure in the developing world. In the old economy, "infrastructure" meant pipelines and roads. But in the 21st century economy, it also means telecommunications and health care.

Among the $17 billion in exports the Bank financed last year were hospitals, medical equipment and pharmaceuticals. In Africa, this clearly is where the bank can add value. The historic Durban conference, which last month drew the international spotlight to Africa's HIV/AIDS struggle, identified longer credit terms and sustainable resources as an essential part of a broader solution. Accordingly, we decided to offer $1 billion a year in financing to the region to build a sustainable, effective infrastructure of health care across sub-Saharan Africa.

This offer has been incompletely described as a loan program for African governments to purchase antiretroviral drugs to treat HIV-infected patients. In reality, it offers countries the opportunity to purchase whatever is needed— from medical equipment to adviser services to hospitals, as well as pharmaceuticals. It also fills in a vital resource gap by extending financing not only to governments in the region, but also to private hospitals and clinics.

Health care is an essential building block of a strong nation. Stable public health is a prerequisite to a stable economy. Yet in many parts of sub-Saharan Africa, we essentially need to start from scratch in building a medical delivery system that can ensure that treatments and services reach those who need them. Today, too many supplies are stranded on the docks or lost to the underground market because this infrastructure does not exist. The Ex-Im Bank can help change that and establish a key beachhead that is essential to winning this war.

I am frequently asked: Why add to the region's debt? Without a doubt, the international donor community should do more. But in reality, there remains a significant gap between existing need and available aid. The Joint United Nations Program on HIV/AIDS (UNAIDS) estimates that more than $2 billion in annual global investment is necessary. Yet only $300 million has been invested in the effort [in 2000]. Bluntly put, today's resource levels are inadequate.

By providing substantial, consistently available credit, the Ex-Im Bank can help ensure that adequate resources are available when needed, not solely when donated. And our program is not inconsistent with potential debt forgiveness in the region. Debt forgiveness wipes the slate clean so that countries can then better direct resources to their most pressing priorities.

The Ex-Im Bank will do what it can to ease the strain on countries that accept credit. For example, we will extend financing for up to five years, rather than the traditional six-month term for medicines. Without question, however, the success of our program hinges on American companies' significantly reducing their prices to put vital medicines and supplies within economic reach. We currently are in discussions with pharmaceutical companies to achieve this result. Clearly, the humanitarian need challenges all of us to set aside business as usual. I do believe that private-sector companies will step forward and act for the broader good in the face of this crisis.

With these talks in motion, the Ex-Im Bank has begun negotiations with several African countries that are interested in using this program. We are working closely with the United Nations, the World Bank and a host of U.S. agencies. We also hope that our move triggers other export credit agencies in Europe and Japan to make even more resources available.

Clearly, the Ex-Im Bank is only one piece of a broader solution. Debt forgiveness can give countries more freedom to acquire what they need—be it medical equipment or goods to build their economy. The international community should give more direct aid. But the need of others to do more does not negate the moral obligation of all parties to find a way to help.

Too many in the Western world have learned to steel themselves to the hardships in sub-Saharan Africa. It's a habit we should abandon in the 21st century. For Africa to win this war, it will take all of us tackling this vast humanitarian crisis, and doing what is in our power to make a difference.

We Can't Shoulder More Debt to Treat an Incurable Disease

T here is no question that HIV/AIDS is a serious public health problem. AIDS causes slow and agonizing death, leaves family members, relatives and friends of victims traumatized, and creates an army of orphans. It has a negative impact on the economy and the demographic structure of a nation. No one knows this better than the governments of southern Africa.

Sub-Saharan Africa, with only 10 percent of the world's population, is home to 71 percent of the world's cases of HIV/AIDS. More than 24.5 million of our people are infected with the HIV virus, and this number continues to grow.

In my country, current estimates place the number of those infected at about 160,000, representing 9.5 percent of our population of 1.8 million. Among pregnant women, the percentage is even higher; surveys taken in 1998 showed an infection rate of 17.4 percent. In 1993, we had 92 recorded deaths from AIDS. By 1999, that number had risen steeply to 2,823.

In the face of such numbers, of which our government and all the governments in the region are acutely aware, it is baffling that some in the West accuse us of practicing denial about the AIDS epidemic and of lacking the political commitment to battle it. In fact, the governments of sub-Saharan Africa have fully recognized the extent of the problem. It dominates discussions at all national, regional and international forums. The Southern Africa Development Community (SADC), chaired by Namibian President Sam Nujoma, has declared HIV/AIDS a top priority and has approved an essential package of HIV/AIDS-related interventions, including joint programs for prevention, education, and patient care and support.

Yet the charge that we are not moving aggressively to deal with AIDS has once again been raised. This time it is because of the decision by Namibia and at least three other African nations not to accept an offer from the U.S. Export-Import Bank to provide loans to buy antiretroviral drugs to treat HIV infection.

The bank's $1 billion lending program is offered in conjunction with the decision in May [2000] by five major pharmaceutical companies to reduce the prices of antiretroviral drugs for developing countries. We recognize that the bank's proposal, like the pharmceuticals' offer, was made from a noble impulse to help out in a case of need, and from the realization that a significant proportion of the world population faces a huge catastrophe if the developing countries take no action.

But our decision not to accept the offer was based on the conviction that the risks our country faced in taking on the burden of a loan outweighed the benefits we would receive from the drugs.

The tragic truth of AIDS is that it is a long, drawn-out disease, lasting 10 years or more from first infection. Antiretroviral drugs prevent early onset of opportunistic infections and improve the quality of life, but they are not a cure. Once a person is HIV-positive, he cannot be made HIV-negative. The people who would be treated with HIV drugs will almost certainly die of AIDS in any case. In some instances, there are indications that they might even die faster with the drugs, depending upon the stage the disease has reached by the time intervention is begun.

If HIV drugs were a cure, many African countries would consider accepting the Ex-Im Bank offer. But given the duration of treatment required and the increasing number of AIDS patients, assuming a loan to purchase antiretroviral drugs does not make sense for developing countries, many of which are already burdened by foreign indebtedness. It does not make sense for Namibia. It would mean plunging ourselves into perpetual debt from which we would not be able to extricate ourselves. If we do not have the money to buy antiretroviral drugs directly, where will we get the money to pay back this loan plus interest? This is a trap into which we cannot afford to fall.

HIV/AIDS is not the only major public health problem in sub-Saharan Africa. Tuberculosis affects millions, as does malaria, which kills more children under the age of 5 than any other disease in the world. From our point of view, it is wiser, with limited resources, to invest in antimalarial drugs that will save thousands of lives than in HIV drugs that may not save any. It is wiser to invest in drugs that treat the conditions that are caused by AIDS, to alleviate suffering to the extent that we can.

A fundamental problem for the developing countries is that all drugs, not just antiretrovirals, cost too much. For a number of years, African governments have been exploring options for obtaining drugs for a variety of diseases, from TB and malaria to sexually transmitted infections, at affordable prices. These options include bulk purchasing of drugs, and those arrangements for purchasing drugs manufactured at lower cost by non-patent-holding companies, as allowed in cases of demonstrated public health need under the World Trade Organization's agreement on Trade Related Property Rights. Thus, we do not say that we will never purchase antiretroviral drugs. When the drugs are affordable, we will buy them.

Health is a fundamental right enshrined in the Namibian constitution. The Namibian government accepts full responsibility for ensuring that our people enjoy the highest possible standard of health and social well-being. To this end, we have adopted a health care system that emphasizes prevention and education. We have put in place programs to prevent occurrence of diseases and to mitigate the effects of those diseases that are not amenable to prevention. At least 15 percent of the Namibian budget is dedicated annually to health care.

Our National AIDS Committee, established by President Nujoma in March 1999, is well aware that prevention is the only weapon that will effectively halt the HIV/AIDS epidemic. Our chief aim now is to reduce the rate of new infections through a multifaceted approach of education, condom promotion, treatment of sexually transmitted diseases and raising public awareness.

Every sector of the Namibian government, as well as the majority of private sector and nongovernmental organizations, is involved in the fight against HIV/AIDS. Every ministry is responsible for specific activities aimed at AIDS prevention and makes provisions in its annual budget for them.

Meanwhile, we are extensively treating the people in our country who suffer from AIDS. We give supportive treatment for opportunistic infections. We counsel patients on their illness and families on how to care for the sick.

The accusation that we are not doing enough is not only baseless, but unfair. It is born of ignorance of what is happening here on the ground where the epidemic rages. The daily effort being made to control AIDS is not a sensational story, so it is difficult to sell in the West. But we cannot waste much time worrying about that. We have too much hard work to do.

POSTSCRIPT

Are African Leaders Misguided
in Their Fight Against AIDS?

Are African leaders who reject Western loans for medicines to fight AIDS simply holding out until they can get the drugs for free? Are they deliberately trying to make large U.S. corporations appear responsible for the terrible suffering in their countries?

Neither Harmon nor Shangula discusses the practical issue of distribution. In nations where the largest employer is the government, corruption is often widespread. How should medications be distributed to minimize their being stolen? Who should be provided with the drugs? Single, unemployed males? Mothers? Spouses who are both affected? Only the male spouse or only the female spouse? Neonates? The middle-aged? The issue of distribution is crucial because in many countries only a few thousand among a million or more HIV and AIDS victims are currently being treated. Should sex workers and males, who are generally more likely to have frequent sexual contacts, be treated before members of lower-risk populations are treated? Is it just for the United States to extend aid to other countries when its own HIV and AIDS problem is not yet solved? Are African leaders' resistance to such efforts misguided?

An excellent analysis of the medical and social implications of the issue can be found in "The AIDS Questions That Linger," by L. K. Altman, *The New York Times* (January 30, 2001). An insightful delineation of the legal issues from the corporations' perspective is "Drug Makers' Battle Is One Over Ideas," by A. Murray, *The Wall Street Journal* (March 19, 2001). J. Murphy, in "Abortion Policy in a Time of AIDS," *The Baltimore Sun* (February 28, 2001), asserts that President George W. Bush's decision to cut off funding to agencies in Africa that support abortions is detrimental to the fight against AIDS. For an analysis of the usefulness of AIDS drugs, see "Kenyan Orphanage Takes Initiative on AIDS Drugs," by K. Vick, *The Washington Post* (February 22, 2001). S. Sternberg discusses the high costs of drugs in "AIDS Drug Costs Hurt Africa," *USA Today* (March 15, 2001). Broader historical considerations of illness and different societies' responses can be found in Peter Lewis Allen's *Wages of Sin: Sex and Disease, Past and Present* (University of Chicago Press, 2000) and Edward O. Laumann and Robert T. Michael, eds., *Sex, Love, and Health in America: Private Choices and Public Policies* (University of Chicago Press, 2000).

ISSUE 21

Is the Drug War Harming Blacks?

YES: Thomas Szasz, from *Our Right to Drugs: The Case for a Free Market* (Praeger, 1992)

NO: James A. Inciardi, from "Against Legalization of Drugs," in Arnold S. Trebach and James A. Inciardi, *Legalize It? Debating American Drug Policy* (American University Press, 1993)

ISSUE SUMMARY

YES: Psychiatrist and psychoanalyst Thomas Szasz maintains that the current drug war harms almost all people, especially Blacks, and that its main function is to increase the power of the medical and criminal justice establishments.

NO: James A. Inciardi, director of the Center for Drug and Alcohol Studies at the University of Delaware, surveys several arguments supporting the legalization of drugs and rejects them all, insisting that Blacks and others would be hurt by legalization.

T hroughout the twentieth century, America's problems have often been traced to dubious origins that have served primarily as scapegoats. The shifting nature of the American family; the changing behavioral patterns of the young; the broadening of opportunities for Blacks, women, and other minority groups; and increasing political disenchantment—which were all partially the result of increasing modernization, an unpopular war, and other specific structural precipitants—were variously blamed on the movie industry, comic books, bolshevism, gambling, alcohol, organized crime, and, now and then, the devil himself. Currently, the continued concern with the changing nature of the American family, the increasing fear of crime, and the widening generation gap are linked with drug use. If only we could get the dealers off the streets or at least get the kids to say no to drugs, then we could restore our family system. If only we could arrest everyone who takes drugs, then we could eliminate crime, since it is drugs that cause most people to commit crimes. If only the students in our junior high schools, high schools, and colleges were not taking drugs, then they would not only do better on their academic achievement tests but once again love and obey their parents.

The entire criminal justice system, it seems, has been marshalled to fight in the war on drugs. A 1998 report by the National Center on Addiction and Substance Abuse indicates that the tripling of the prison population from 500,000 in 1980 to 1.7 million in 1997 is largely attributable to drug dealing, drug abuse, and drug- and alcohol-related felonies. One of every 14 Black males is behind bars (compared with one of every 144 U.S. citizens). In some urban areas, one of every four Black males is under the auspices of the criminal justice system, many because of drug crimes. A young Black male has a higher chance of being incarcerated than being in college.

The costs of fighting the drug war are enormous, and greater expenditures for police, prisons, and drug control continue with no end in sight. The drug war is seen by critics as demoralizing entire communities, especially the poor. Paradoxically, far more whites use drugs than Blacks, but the war is clearly pitched at inner-city dwellers.

Opinions on this issue are divided. On the one hand, politicians frequently attack anyone who is seen as "soft" on drugs. On the other hand, many visible problems related to drug control grow. These include sharp criticisms by scholars that crime is not decreasing, minorities are becoming increasingly estranged from the police, and the costs are escalating. In addition, cases of police abuse are often uncovered, ranging from harassment of minorities to police themselves being arrested for trafficking in drugs.

Defenders of current drug policies counter that without the drug war (i.e., if drugs were decriminalized), crime, poverty, hopelessness, demoralization, and loss of direction, especially among the young and minorities, would be far worse than it is now. If we let up on fighting drugs, they assert, crime would skyrocket. For many, even the idea of providing clean needles to heroin addicts is offensive.

This debate is crucial for criminal justice and minority relations. Specifically, some feel that the handling of crimes that are largely blamed on minorities through the powerful legal system is a good measure of society's commitment to fairness and justice, as opposed to discrimination and racism. As you read the following selections, you will notice that it differs from most standard discussions of the issue: it puts up front the effects of the drug war on those who are most directly and frequently affected.

Thomas Szasz, emphasizing individual liberty, chides both the medical establishment, for usurping American's right to select drugs, and the criminal justice system, for defining drug use (and sales) as a crime. Szasz also ridicules many Black leaders for waging the drug war, claiming genocide and enslavement, and bootlegging victimhood as rational talk. James A. Inciardi, in response, itemizes specific types of drugs and their respective harms. As you read his ideas, consider how he debates and rejects legalizers' perspectives.

As you wrestle with this debate, consider what is meant by "harm." Think about who, if anyone, is currently being harmed the most, and how, by the war. Who might be harmed if drugs are allowed to be sold openly and legally? Would Blacks and other minorities be helped if the drug war were ended?

Thomas Szasz  **YES**

Blacks and Drugs: Crack as Genocide

Crack is genocide, 1990's style.

— Cecil Williams

No one can deny that, in the tragicomedy we call the War on Drugs, blacks and Hispanics at home and Latin Americans abroad play leading roles: They are (or are perceived to be) our principal drug abusers, drug addicts, drug traffickers, drug counselors, drug-busting policemen, convicts confined for drug offenses, and narco-terrorists. In short, blacks and Hispanics dominate the drug abuse market, both as producers and as products.

I am neither black nor Hispanic and do not pretend to speak for either group or any of its members. There is, however, no shortage of people, black and white, who are eager to speak for them. Which raises an important question, namely: Who speaks for black or Hispanic Americans? Those persons, black or white, who identify drugs—especially crack—as the enemy of blacks? Or those, who cast the American state—especially its War on Drugs—in that role? Or neither, because the claims of both are absurd oversimplifications and because black Americans—like white Americans—are not a homogeneous group but a collection of individuals, each of whom is individually responsible for his own behavior and can speak for himself?

Black Leaders on Drugs

For the mainline black drug warrior, illegal drugs represent a temptation that African-Americans are morally too enfeebled to resist. This is what makes those who expose them to such temptation similar to slaveholders depriving their victims of liberty. After years of sloganeering by anti-drug agitators, the claim that crack enslaves blacks has become a cliché, prompting the sloganeers to escalate their rhetoric and contend that it is genocide.

Crack as Genocide, Crack as Slavery

The assertion that crack is genocide is a powerful and timely metaphor we ought to clarify, lest we get ourselves entangled in it. Slavery and genocide are the manifestations and the results of the use of force by some people against some other people. Drugs, however, are inert substances unless and until they are taken into the body; and, not being persons, they cannot literally force anyone to do anything. Nevertheless, the claim that black persons are "poisoned" and "enslaved" by drugs put at their disposal by a hostile white society is now the politically correct rhetoric among black racists and white liberals alike. For example, *New York Times* columnist A. M. Rosenthal "denounces even the slightest show of tolerance toward illegal drugs as an act of iniquity deserving comparison to the defense of slavery." Of course, people who want to deny the role of personal agency and responsibility often make use of the metaphor of slavery, generating images of people being enslaved not only by drugs but also by cults, gambling, poverty, pornography, rock music, or mental illness. Persons who use drugs may, figuratively speaking, be said to be the "victims" of temptation, which is as far as one can reasonably carry the rhetoric of victimology. However, this does not prevent Cecil Williams, a black minister in San Francisco, from claiming,

> The crack epidemic in the United States amounts to genocide.... The primary intent of 200 years of slavery was to break the spirit and culture of our people.... Now, in the 1990's, I see substantial similarities between the cocaine epidemic and slavery.... Cocaine is foreign to African-American culture. We did not create it; we did not produce it; we did not ask for it.

If a white person made these assertions, his remarks could easily be interpreted as slandering black people. Being enslaved is something done to a person against his will, while consuming cocaine is something a person does willingly; equating the two denigrates blacks by implying that they are, en masse, so childish or weak that they cannot help but "enslave" themselves to cocaine. Williams's remark that cocaine is foreign to black culture and hence destructive compounds his calumny. Rembrandt's art, Beethoven's music, and Newton's physics are also foreign to black culture. Does that make them all evils similar to slavery?

Another black minister, the Reverend Cecil L. Murray of Los Angeles, repeats the same theme but uses different similes. He refers to drugs as if they were persons and asserts that "drugs are *literally* killing our people." Like other anti-drug agitators, Murray is short on facts and reasoning, and long on bombast and scapegoating. He excoriates proposals to legalize drugs, declaring, "This is a foul breach of everything we hold sacred. To legalize it, to condone it, to market it—that is to put a healthy brand on strychnine.... [W]e cannot make poison the norm."

By now, everyone knows that cigarettes kill more people than illegal drugs. But the point needs to be made again here. "Cigarette smoking," writes Kenneth Warner, a health care economist, "causes more premature deaths than do all of the following together: acquired immunodeficiency syndrome, heroin, alcohol, fire, automobile accidents, homicide, and suicide." Many of the conditions Warner lists affect blacks especially adversely. Both smoking and obesity are unhealthy ("poisonous") but "legal" (not prohibited by the criminal law), yet neither is regarded as the "norm."

Up With Hope, Down With Dope

The Reverend Jesse Jackson is not only a permanent presidential candidate, but is also A. M. Rosenthal's favorite drug warrior. Jackson's trademark incantation goes like this: "Up with hope, down with dope." Better at rhyming than reasoning, Jackson flatly asserts—no metaphor here, at least none that he acknowledges—that "drugs are poison. Taking drugs is a sin. Drug use is morally debased and sick." Poison. Sin. Sickness. Jackson the base rhetorician refuses to be outdone and keeps piling it on: "Since the flow of drugs into the U.S. is an act of terrorism, antiterrorist policies must be applied. . . . If someone is transmitting the death agent to Americans, that person should face wartime consequences. The line must be drawn."

It certainly must. The question, however, is this: Where should we draw it? I believe we ought to draw it by categorizing free trade in agricultural products (including coca, marijuana, and tobacco) as good, and dumping toxic wastes on unsuspecting people in underdeveloped countries as bad; by recognizing the provision of access to accurate pharmacological information as liberating drug education, and rejecting mendacious religiomedical bombast as lamentable political and racial demagogy.

Mayor Marion Barry as Drug Hero

In former days, moral crusaders—especially men of the cloth—thundered brimstone and hellfire at those who succumbed to temptation, typically of the flesh. Why? Because in those benighted pre-Freudian days, moral authorities held people responsible for their behavior. Not any more. And certainly not Jesse Jackson vis-à-vis prominent blacks who use illegal drugs. Foreign drug traffickers are responsible for selling cocaine. Washington, D.C., Mayor Marion Barry is not responsible for buying and smoking it. After the mayor was properly entrapped into buying cocaine and was videotaped smoking it, Jackson pontificated, "Now all of America can learn from the mayor's problems and his long journey back to health." A remarkable disease, this illegal drug use, U.S.A, anno Domini 1990: Caused by being arrested by agents of the state; cured by a "program" provided by agents of the state; its course a "journey"; its prognosis—known with confidence even by priest-politicians without any medical expertise—a return "back to health."

Shamelessly, Jackson used Barry's arrest as an occasion not only for sanctifying the defendant (as if he were accused of a civil rights violation) but also for promoting his own political agenda. A priori, the defendant was a good and great man, "entering the Super Bowl of his career." His accuser—the U.S. government—was, a priori, an evil "political system that can only be described as neocolonial." While thus politicizing drugs, Jackson impudently inveighs against his own practice. "Circumstances like these," he babbles, "remind us that the war on drugs . . . should not be politicized. It is primarily a moral crusade, about values and about health and sickness." Having unburdened himself of his pearls of wisdom about politics, moral values, and sickness and health, Jackson comes to his main point: "Behind these gruesome statistics lies the powerlessness of the people who live in the shadow of a national government from which they are structurally excluded. Now more than ever, it is time to escalate the effort to gain statehood and self-government for the district"—and elect Jesse Jackson senator-for-life-or-until-elected-president. Should we not expect political self-government to be preceded by personal self-government, as it normally is in progressing from disfranchised childhood to enfranchised adulthood? Jackson's envy of and thirst for the power of whites is clear enough. His contention that blacks in Washington, D.C., sell, buy, and use illegal drugs because they are "powerless" is thus but another instance of a drug warrior's fingering a scapegoat in the guise of offering an explanation.

Is Jackson, one of our most prominent anti-drug agitators, trying to protect black Americans from drugs or is he trying to promote his own career? Unlike the Black Muslims committed to an ideology of self-help, self-reliance, and radical separatism, Jackson is playing on the white man's turf, trying to gain power by the "enemy's" methods and rules. The War on Drugs presents him, as it presents his white counterparts, with the perfect social problem: Here is an issue on which Jesse Jackson can join—on common ground, shoulder to shoulder—not only such eminent white liberal-democrats as Mario Cuomo and Kitty Dukakis, but also such eminent white conservative-Republicans as Nancy Reagan and William Bennett. Indeed, on what other issue besides drugs could Jesse Jackson and Nancy Reagan—one a black militant struggling up the social ladder, the other a white conservative standing on its top rung—agree? As pharmacological agents, dangerous drugs may indeed be toxic for the body anatomic of the individuals who use them; but as a propaganda tool, dangerous drugs are therapeutic for the body politic of the nation, welding our heterogeneous society together into one country and one people, engaged in an uplifting, self-purifying, moral crusade.

The War on Drugs: A War on Blacks

A Martian who came to earth and read only what the newspaper headlines say about drugs would never discover an interesting and important feature of America's latest moral crusade, namely, that its principal victims are black or Hispanic. (I must add here that when I use the word *victim* in connection with the word *drug,* I do not refer to a person who chooses to use a drug and thus subjects himself to its effects, for good or ill. Being his own poisoner—assuming the drug has an ill effect on him—such a person is a victim in a metaphoric sense only. In the conventional use of the term, to which I adhere, a literal or real victim is a person unjustly or tragically deprived of his life, liberty, or property, typically by other people—in our case, as a result of the criminalization of the free market in drugs.)

However, were the Martian to turn on the television to watch the evening news, or look at a copy of *Time* or *Newsweek,* he would see images of drug busts and read stories about drug addicts and drug treatment programs in which virtually all of the characters are black or Hispanic. Occasionally, some of the drug-busting policemen are white. But the drug traffickers, drug addicts, and drug counselors are virtually all black or Hispanic.

Carl Rowan, a syndicated columnist who is black, finally spoke up. "Racist stereotypes," he correctly pointed out, "have crippled the minds of millions of white Americans." Then, rather selectively, Rowan emphasized that "white prejudice on this point has produced a terrible injustice," but chose to remain discreetly silent about the fact that black leaders are the shock troops in this anti-black drug war. "Blacks," complained Rowan, "are being arrested in USA's drug wars at a rate far out of proportion to their drug use." According to a study conducted by *USA Today,* blacks comprise 12.7 percent of the population and make up 12 percent of those who "regularly use illegal drugs"; but of those arrested on drug charges in 1988, 38 percent were blacks.

Other studies indicate that blacks represent an even larger proportion of drug law violators/victims. For example, according to the National Institute on Drug Abuse (NIDA, the leading federal agency on drug abuse research), "Although only about 12% of those using illegal drugs are black, 44% of those who are arrested for simple possession and 57% of those arrested for sales are black." Another study, conducted by the Washington-based Sentencing Project, found that while almost one in four black men of age 20–29 were in jail or on parole, only one in sixteen white men of the same age group were. Clarence Page dramatized the significance of these figures by pointing out that while 610,000 black men in their twenties are in jail or under the supervision of the criminal justice system, only 436,000 are in college. "Just as no one is born a college student," commented Page, "no one is born a criminal. Either way, you have to be carefully taught."

Page does not say who is teaching blacks to be criminals, but I will: The economic incentives intrinsic to our drug laws. After all, although black Americans today are often maltreated by whites, and are in the main poorer than whites, they were *more maltreated and were even poorer* fifty or a hundred years ago, yet fewer young black males chose a criminal career then than do now. This development is far more dangerous for all of us, black and white, than all the cocaine in Columbia. "Under the nation's current approach," a feature report in the *Los Angeles Times* acknowledges, "black America is being criminalized at an astounding rate." Nevertheless, the black community enthusiastically supports the War on Drugs. George Napper, director of public safety in Atlanta, attributes this attitude to "black people ... being more conservative than other people. They say: 'To hell with rights. Just kick ass and take names.'" Father George Clements, a Catholic priest who has long been in the forefront of the struggle against drugs in Chicago's black communities, exemplifies this posture: "I'm all for whatever tactics have to be used. If that means they are trampling on civil liberties, so be it." The black leadership's seemingly increasing contempt for civil liberties is just one of the disastrous consequences of drug prohibition. The drug war's impact on poor and poorly educated blacks is equally alarming and tragic. Instead of looking to the free market and the rule of law for self-advancement, the War on Drugs encourages them to look to a race war—or a lottery ticket—as a way out of their misfortune.

Drug Prohibition: Pouring Fuel on the Fire of Racial Antagonism

Clearly, one of the unintended consequences of drug prohibition—far more dangerous to American society than drugs—has been that it has fueled the fires of racial division and antagonism. Many American blacks (whose views white psychiatrists would love to dismiss as paranoid if they could, but happily no longer can) believe that the government is "out to get them" and the War on Drugs is one of its tools: A "popular theory [among blacks] is that white government leaders play a pivotal role in the drug crisis by deliberately making drugs easily available in black neighborhoods." Another consequence of our drug laws (less unintended perhaps) has been that while it is no longer officially permissible to persecute blacks qua blacks, it is permissible to persecute them qua drug law violators. Under the pretext of protecting people—especially "kids"—from dangerous drugs, America's young black males are stigmatized en masse as drug addicts and drug criminals. The possibility that black youths may be more endangered by society's drug laws than by the temptation of drugs surely cannot be dismissed out of hand. It is an idea, however, that only those black leaders who have shaken off the shackles of trying to please their degraders dare to entertain. Thus we now find the Black Muslim minister Louis Farrakhan articulating such a view, much as the martyred Malcolm X did a quarter of a century ago. "There is," says Farrakhan, "a war being planned against black youth by the government of the United States under the guise of a war against drugs." I suspect few educated white persons really listen to or hear this message, just as few listened to or heard what Malcolm X said. And of those who hear it, most dismiss it as paranoid. But paranoids too can have real enemies.

The U.S. Customs Service acknowledges that, to facilitate its work in spotting drug smugglers, the service uses "drug courier" and "drug swallower" profiles developed in the 1970s. Critics have charged that "one characteristic that most of those detained have in common is their race. 'The darker your skin, the better your chances,' said Gary Trichter, a Houston defense lawyer who specializes in such cases." In a ruling handed down on April 3, 1989, the Supreme Court endorsed the government's use of drug profiles for detaining and questioning airline passengers. Although the Court's ruling addressed only airports, the profiles are also used on highways, on interstate buses, and in train stations. In addition, the Customs Service is authorized to request the traveler, under penalty of being detained or not allowed to enter the country, to submit to an X-ray examination to determine if he has swallowed a condom containing drugs. "In Miami, of 101 X-rays, 67 found drugs. In New York, of 187 X-rays, 90 yielded drugs. In Houston... 60 people were X-rayed [and] just 4 were found to be carrying drugs." Although the profiles have proved to be of some value, this does not justify their use unless one believes that the government's interest in finding and punishing people with illegal drugs in their possession deserves more protection than the individual's right to his own body.

What do the statistics about the people stopped and searched on the basis of drug profiles tell us? They reveal, for example, that in December 1989 in

Biloxi, Mississippi, of fifty-seven stops on Interstate 10, fifty-five involved Hispanic or black people. On a stretch of the New Jersey Turnpike where less than 5 percent of the traffic involved cars with out-of-state license plates driven by black males, 80 percent of the arrests fitted that description. Topping the record for racially discriminatory drug arrests is the drug-interdiction program at the New York Port Authority Bus Terminal, where 208 out of 210 persons arrested in 1989 were black or Hispanic. Still, the anti-drug bureaucrats insist that "the ratio of arrests reflected a 'reality of the streets,' rather than a policy of racial discrimination."

However, in January 1991 Pamela Alexander, a black judge in Minnesota, ruled that the state's anti-crack law—which "calls for a jail term for first-time offenders convicted of possessing three grams of crack, but only probation for defendants convicted of possessing the same amount of powdered cocaine" —discriminated against blacks and was therefore unconstitutional. Her ruling focuses on the fact that crack cocaine and powdered cocaine are merely two different forms of cocaine, and that blacks tend to use the former, and whites the latter. The law thus addresses a difference in customs, not a difference in drug effects. "Drug policy," Judge Alexander concluded, "should not be set according to anything less than scientific evidence." Unfortunately, this is a very naive statement. There is no scientific basis for any of our "drug policies"—a term that, in this context, is a euphemism for prohibiting pharmaceutical and recreational drugs. Warning people about the risks a particular drug poses is the most that science can be made to justify.

In any case, science has nothing to do with the matter at hand, as the contention of the drug enforcers illustrates. Their rejoinder to Judge Alexander's ruling is that "crack is different." In what way? "The stuff is cheap and . . . affordable to kids in the school yard who can't afford similar amounts of powdered cocaine." Behind this pathetic argument stand some elementary facts unfamiliar to the public and denied by the drug warriors. Simply put, crack is to powdered cocaine as cigarettes are to chewing tobacco. Smoking introduces drugs into the body via the lungs; snorting and chewing, via the nasal and buccal mucosae. Different classes tend to display different preferences for different drugs. Educated persons (used to) smoke cigarettes and snort cocaine; uneducated persons chew tobacco and smoke crack. (This generalization is rapidly becoming obsolete. In the United States, though much less in Europe, Asia, and Latin America, smoking cigarettes is becoming a lower-class habit.) These facts make a mockery of the Minnesota legislators' disingenuous denunciation of Judge Alexander's decision: "The one thing we never contemplated was targeting members of any single minority group." It remains to be seen whether the Minnesota Supreme Court, to which the case was appealed, will uphold punishing crack smokers more severely than cocaine snorters.

The enforcement of our drug laws with respect to another special population—namely, pregnant women—is also shamefully racist. Many state laws now regard the pregnant woman who uses an illegal drug as a criminal—not because she possesses or sells or uses a drug, but because she "delivers" it to her fetus via the umbilical cord. Ostensibly aimed at protecting the fetus, the actual enforcement of these laws lends further support to the assumption that their real target is the unwed, inner-city, black mother. Although, according to experts, drug use in pregnancy is equally prevalent in white middle-class women, most women prosecuted for using illegal drugs while pregnant have been poor members of racial minorities. "Researchers found that about 15 percent of both the white and the black women used drugs... but that the black women were 10 times as likely as whites to be reported to the authorities."

Drugs and Racism

How do the drug warriors rationalize the racism of the War on Drugs? Partly by ignoring the evidence that the enforcement of drug laws victimizes blacks disproportionately compared to whites; and partly by falling back on a time-honored technique of forestalling the charge by appointing a respected member of the victimized group to a high position in the machinery charged with enforcing the persecutory practice. This is what former drug czar William Bennett did when he picked Reuben Greenberg, a black Jew, as his favorite drug cop. What has Greenberg done to deserve this honor? He chose to prosecute as drug offenders the most defenseless members of the black community. "The tactics Greenberg developed in Charleston [South Carolina]," explained *Time* magazine, "are targeted on the poorest of the poor—the residents of public-housing projects and their neighbors.... The projects were 'the easiest place to start, because that's where the victims are.'" Perhaps so. But, then, it must be safer—especially for a black Jewish policeman in South Carolina—to go after blacks in inner-city housing projects than after whites in suburban mansions.

The evidence supports the suspicion that the professional pushers of drug programs pander precisely to such racial prejudices, with spectacularly hypocritical results. Consider the latest fad in addictionology: a racially segregated drug treatment program for blacks. Because the program is owned by blacks, is operated by blacks for blacks, and offers a service called "drug treatment," its owner-operators have been able to pass it off as a fresh "culturally specific" form of therapy. If whites were to try to do this sort of thing to blacks, it would be decried as racist segregation. When black "former drug abusers" do it to fellow blacks, the insurance money pours in: Soon after opening, the clinic called Coalesce was handling three hundred patients at $13,000 a head per month—not bad pay for treating a nonexisting illness with a nonexisting treatment.

Black Muslims on Drugs

Mainstream American blacks are Christians, who look for leadership to Protestant priest-politicians and blame black drug use on rich whites, capitalism, and South American drug lords. Sidestream American blacks are Muslims, who look for leadership to Islamic priest-politicians and maintain that drug use is a matter of personal choice and self-discipline.

The Black Muslim supporters of a free market in drugs (though they do not describe their position in these terms) arrive at their conclusion not from studying the writings of Adam Smith or Ludwig von Mises, but from their direct experience with the American therapeutic state and its punitive agents decked out as doctors and social workers. As a result, the Black Muslims regard statist-therapeutic meddling as diminishing the person targeted as needing help, robbing him of his status as a responsible moral agent, and therefore fundamentally degrading; and they see the medicalization of the drug problem—the hypocritical defining of illegal drug use as both a crime and a disease, the capricious law enforcement, the economic incentives to transgress the drug laws, and the pseudotherapeutic drug programs—as a wicked method for encouraging drug use, crime, economic dependency, personal demoralization, and familial breakdown. I have reviewed the enduring Black Muslim principles and policies on drugs, as developed by Malcolm X, elsewhere. Here I shall summarize only what is necessary to round out the theme I developed in this [selection].

Black Muslims demand, on moral and religious grounds, that their adherents abstain from all self-indulgent pleasures, including drugs. Accordingly, it would be misleading to speak of a Black Muslim approach to the "treatment of drug addiction." If a person is a faithful Black Muslim he cannot be an addict, just as if he is an Orthodox Jew he cannot be a pork eater. It is as simple as that. The Muslim perspective on drug use and drug avoidance is—like mine—moral and ceremonial, not medical and therapeutic. Of course, this does not mean that we come to all the same conclusions.

Malcolm X: Triumph Through Resisting Temptation

Malcolm X's passion for honesty and truth led him to some remarkable drug demythologizings, that is, assertions that seemingly fly in the face of current medical dogmas about hard drugs and their addictive powers. "Some prospective Muslims," wrote Malcolm, "found it more difficult to quit tobacco than others found quitting the dope habit." As I noted, for Muslims it makes no difference whether a man smokes tobacco or marijuana; what counts is the habit of self-indulgence, not the pharmacomythology of highs or kicks. Evidently, one good mythology per capita is enough: If a person truly believes in the mythology of Black Muslimism—or Judaism, or Christianity—then he does not need the ersatz mythology of medicalism and therapeutism.

The Muslims emphasize not only that addiction is evil, but also that it is deliberately imposed on the black man by the white man. "The Muslim program began with recognizing that color and addiction have a distinct connection. It is no accident that in the entire Western Hemisphere, the greatest localized concentration of addicts is in Harlem." The monkey on the addict's back is not the abstraction of drug addiction as a disease, but the concrete reality of Whitey. "Most black junkies," explains Malcolm, "really are trying to narcotize themselves against being a black man in the white man's America." By politicizing personal problems (defining self-medication with narcotics as political oppression), the Muslims neatly reverse the psychiatric tactic of personalizing political problems (defining psychiatric incarceration as hospitalization).

Because for Muslims drug use—legal or illegal—is not a disease, they have no use for pretentious drug treatment programs, especially if they consist of substituting one narcotic drug for another (methadone for heroin). Instead, they rely on breaking the drug habit by expecting the drug user to quit "cold turkey." The ordeal this entails helps to dramatize and ritualize the addict's liberation from Whitey. "When the addict's withdrawal sets in," explains Malcolm, "and he is screaming, cursing and begging, 'Just one shot, man!' the Muslims are right there talking junkie jargon to him, 'Baby, knock that monkey off your back! ... Kick Whitey off your back!' " Ironically, what Black Muslims tell their adherents is not very different from what white doctors told each other at the beginning of this century. In 1921, writing in the *Journal of the American Medical Association,* Alfred C. Prentice, M. D.—a member of the Committee on Narcotic Drugs of the American Medical Association—rejected "the shallow pretense that drug addiction is a 'disease' ... [a falsehood that] has been asserted and urged in volumes of 'literature' by self-styled 'specialists.' "

Malcolm X wore his hair crew-cut, dressed with the severe simplicity and elegance of a successful Wall Street lawyer, and was polite and punctual. Alex Haley describes the Muslims as having "manners and miens [that] reflected the Spartan personal discipline the organization demanded." While Malcolm hated the white man—whom he regarded as the "devil"—he despised the black man who refused the effort to better himself: "The black man in the ghettoes ... has to start self-correcting his own material, moral, and spiritual defects and evils. The black man needs to start his own program to get rid of drunkenness, drug addiction, prostitution."

This is dangerous talk. Liberals and psychiatrists need the weak-willed and the mentally sick to have someone to disdain, care for, and control. If Malcolm had his way, such existential cannibals masquerading as do-gooders would be unemployed, or worse. Here, then, is the basic conflict and contradiction between the Muslim and methadone: By making the Negro self-responsible and self-reliant, Muslimism eliminates the problem and with it the need for the white man and the medicine man; whereas by making the white man and the doctor indispensable for the Negro as permanent social cripple and lifelong patient, medicalism aggravates and perpetuates the problem.

Malcolm understood and asserted—as few black or white men could understand or dared to assert—that white men want blacks to be on drugs, and that most black men who are on drugs want to be on them rather than off them. Freedom and self-determination are not only precious, but arduous. If people are not taught and nurtured to appreciate these values, they are likely to want to have nothing to do with them. Malcolm X and Edmund Burke shared a profound discernment of the painful truth that the state wants men to be weak and timid, not strong and proud. Indeed, perhaps the only thing Malcolm failed to see was that, by articulating his views as he did, he was in fact launching a religious war against greatly superior forces. I do not mean a religious war against Christianity. The religious war Malcolm launched was a war against the religion of Medicine—a faith other black leaders blindly worship. After all, blacks and whites alike now believe, as an article of faith, that drug abuse is an illness. That is why they demand and demonstrate for "free" detoxification programs and embrace methadone addiction as a cure for the heroin habit. Malcolm saw this, but I am not sure he grasped the enormity of it all. Or perhaps he did and that is why in the end, not long before he was killed, he rejected the Black Muslims as well—to whom, only a short while before, he gave all the credit for his resurrection from the gutter. He converted, one more time, to Orthodox Islam. Then he was murdered.

Do Drug Prohibitionists Protect Blacks?

Not surprisingly, drug prohibitionists systematically ignore the Black Muslim position on drugs. Neither bureaucratic drug criminalizers nor academic drug legalizers ever mention Malcolm X's name, much less cite his writings on drugs. The fact that Louis Farrakhan, the present leader of the Nation of Islam, continues to support Malcolm X's position on drugs does not help to make that position more acceptable to the white establishment. In characteristically statist fashion, instead of seeing drug laws as racist, the drug prohibitionists see the absence of drug laws as racist. If "the legalizers prevail"—James Q. Wilson, a professor of management and public policy at UCLA, ominously predicts—

> then we will have consigned hundreds of thousands of infants and hundreds of neighborhoods to a life of oblivion and disease. To the lives and families destroyed by alcohol we will have added countless more destroyed by cocaine, heroin, PCP, and whatever else a basement scientist can invent. Human character is formed by society.... [G]ood character is less likely in a bad society.

Virtually everything Wilson asserts here is false. Liberty is the choice to do right or wrong, to act prudently or imprudently, to protect oneself or injure oneself. Wilson is disingenuous in selecting alcohol and drugs as the "destroyers" of people. And as for his implying that our present prohibitionist mode of managing drugs has promoted the formation of "good character"—the less said, the better.

Wilson's argument brings us back full circle to the genocidal image of drugs, suggested here by a prominent white academic rather than a black priest-politician. As I observed before, this view casts the individual in a passive role, as victim. But if there are injured victims, there must be injuring victimizers. Wilson knows who they are: us. But he is wrong. Opportunity, choice, temptation do not constitute victimization. Wilson affronts the supporters of liberty by so categorizing them.

Finally, Wilson's explanation leaves no room for why some blacks succeed in not being consigned to what he revealingly calls "a life of oblivion and disease." Nor does Wilson consider the dark possibility that there might, especially for white Americans, be a fate worse than a few thousand blacks selling and using drugs. Suppose every black man, woman, and child in America rejected drugs, chose to emulate Malcolm X, and became a militant black separationist. Would that be better for American whites, or for the United States as a nation?

NO

James A. Inciardi

Against Legalization of Drugs

The Pro-Legalization Issues and Contenders

The drug legalization debate emerged in both generic and specific configurations. In its most generic adaptation, it went something like this. First, the drug laws have created evils far worse than the drugs themselves—corruption, violence, street crime, and disrespect for the law. Second, legislation passed to control drugs has failed to reduce demand. Third, you should not prohibit that which a major segment of the population is committed to doing; that is, you simply cannot arrest, prosecute, and punish such large numbers of people, particularly in a democracy. And specifically in this behalf, in a liberal democracy the government must not interfere with personal behavior if liberty is to be maintained....

Thomas S. Szasz and the control of conduct   Thomas S. Szasz is a Hungarian-born psychiatrist who emigrated to the United States in 1938 and studied medicine at the University of Cincinnati. Trained in psychiatry at the University of Chicago, he became a well-known critic of his profession. Szasz has written that "mental illness" is a mythological concept used by the state to control deviants and thereby limit freedom in American society. In his view, the conditions comprising mental illness are social and moral problems, not medical ones. He repeatedly warns against replacing a theological worldview with a therapeutic one. Moreover, he is an uncompromising libertarian and humanist who has argued against involuntary psychiatric examination and hospitalization, and who believes that the psychoanalytic relationship should be free of coercion and control....

During the 1970s, relying on the postulates and assertions that he had applied to mental illness, Szasz became the most outspoken critic of the medical or "disease" model of addiction. His primary concern with the disease model is that it diminishes an individual's responsibility for his or her dysfunctional or antisocial behavior. He also argues that the concept of addiction as a disease places undue emphasis on medical authority in determining how society should manage what is actually an individual violation of legal and social norms.

On the matter of whether society should attempt to control, and hence "prohibit" the use of certain substances, he offers the following:

> The plain historical facts are that before 1914 there was no "drug problem" in the United States; nor did we have a name for it. Today there is an immense drug problem in the United States, and we have lots of names for it. Which came first: "the problem of drug abuse" or its name?... My point is simply that our drug abuse experts, legislators, psychiatrists, and other professional guardians of our medical morals have been operating chicken hatcheries; they continue—partly by means of certain characteristic tactical abuses of our language—to manufacture and maintain the "drug problem" they ostensibly try to solve (Szasz 1974).

What he was suggesting is something that nominalists have been saying for centuries: that a thing does not exist until it is imagined and given a name. For Szasz, a hopeless believer in this position, the "drug problem" in the United States did not exist before the passage of the Harrison Act in 1914, but became a reality when the behavior under consideration was *labeled* as a problem. Stated differently, he argues that the drug problem in America was created in great part by the very policies designed to control it.

For Szasz, the solution to the drug problem is simple. Ignore it, and it will no longer be a problem. After all, he maintained, there is precedent for it:

> ... Our present attitudes toward the whole subject of drug use, drug abuse, and drug control are nothing but the reflections, in the mirror of "social reality," of our own expectations toward drugs and toward those who use them; and that our ideas about and interventions in drug-taking behavior have only the most tenuous connection with the actual pharmacological properties of "dangerous drugs." The "danger" of masturbation disappeared when we ceased to believe in it: when we ceased to attribute danger to the practice and to its practitioners; and ceased to call it "self-abuse" (Szasz 1974).

What Szasz seems to be suggesting is that heroin, cocaine, and other "dangerous drugs" be legalized; hence, the problems associated with their use would disappear. And this is where he runs into difficulty, for his argument is so riddled with faulty scholarship and flagrant errors of fact that he lost credibility with those familiar with the history of the American drug scene.

Szasz's libertarian-laissez-faire position has continued into the 1990s. He perseveres in his argument that people should be allowed to ingest, inhale, or inject whatever substances they wish. And it would appear from his comments that he is opposed to drug regulation of any type, even by prescription....

Arnold S. Trebach and harm reduction   Perhaps most respected in the field of drug-policy reform is Arnold S. Trebach....

Briefly, his proposals for drug-policy are the following:

1. Reverse drug-policy funding priorities....

2. Curtail AIDS: Make clean needles available to intravenous drug addicts....

3. Develop a plan for drug treatment on demand, allow Medicaid to pay for the poor, and expand the variety of treatment options available....

4. Stop prosecutions of pregnant drug users....

5. Make medical marijuana available to the seriously ill....

6. Appoint a commission to seriously examine alternatives to prohibition....

Although my objections and alternatives are discussed later, let me just say that Trebach has experienced a "conversion" of sorts in recent years. There was a time when he denied endorsing the legalization of drugs....

The Debate's Supporting Cast and Bit Players

An aspect of the drug-policy debates of the second half of the 1980s was a forum awash with self-defined experts from many walks of life.

The bit players   The "bit players" were the many who had a lot to say on the debate, but from what I feel were not particularly informed positions. They wrote books, or they published papers, but they remained on the sidelines because either no one took them seriously, their work was carelessly done, or their arguments were just not persuasive....

A rather pathetically hatched entry to the debate was Richard Lawrence Miller's book, *The Case for Legalizing Drugs* (1991).... Perhaps most misleading in the book is the list of "benefits" of using illicit drugs. I'll cite but one example to provide a glimpse of the author's approach:

> Heroin can calm rowdy teenagers—reducing aggression, sexual drive, fertility, and teen pregnancy—helping adolescents through that time of life (Miller 1991, 153).

I have a teenage daughter, so I guess I'll have to remember that if she ever gets rowdy. Enough!

Cameos and comic relief   ... Such well-known personages as conservative pundit William F. Buckley, Jr., Nobel laureate economist Milton Friedman, former Secretary of State George P. Shultz, journalist Anthony Lewis, *Harper's* editor Lewis H. Lapham, and even Washington, D. C., Mayor Marion Barry came forward to endorse legalization. The "legalizers" viewed the support of these notables as a legitimation of their argument, but all had entered the debate from disturbingly uninformed positions. With the exception of Marion Barry, and I say this facetiously, none had any first-hand experience with the issues....

Arguing Against Legalization

... While there are numerous arguments *for* legalization, there are likely an equal or greater number *against*.

Some Public Health Considerations

Tomorrow, like every other average day in the United States, about 11,449.3 babies will be born, 90 acres of pizza will be ordered, almost 600,000 M&M candies will be eaten, and some 95 holes-in-one will be claimed. At the same time, 171 million bottles of beer will be consumed, and almost 1.5 billion cigarettes will be smoked (Ruth 1992). In 1965, the annual death toll from smoking-related diseases was estimated at 188,000. By the close of the 1980s that figure had more than doubled, to 434,000, and it is expected to increase throughout the 1990s (Centers for Disease Control 1990, 1991b). And these figures do not include the almost 40,000 nonsmokers who die each year from ailments associated with the inhalation of passive smoke.

... [I]t is estimated that there are 10.5 million alcoholics in the United States, and that a total of 73 million adults have been touched by alcoholism (*Alcoholism and Drug Abuse Weekly,* 9 October 1991, 1). Each year there are some 45,000 alcohol-related traffic fatalities in the United States (Centers for Disease Control 1991a), and thousands of women who drink during pregnancy bear children with irreversible alcohol-related defects (Steinmetz 1992). Alcohol use in the past year was reported by 54 percent of the nation's eighth graders, 72 percent of tenth graders, and 78 percent of twelfth graders, and almost a third of high school seniors in 1991 reported "binge drinking." ... [T]he cost of alcohol abuse in the United States for 1990 has been estimated at $136.31 billion (*Substance Abuse Report,* 15 June 1991, 3).

Sophism, legalization, and illicit drug use   Keep the above data in mind, and consider that they relate to only two of the *legal* drugs. Now for some reason, numerous members of the pro-legalization lobby argue that if drugs were to be legalized, usage would likely not increase very much, if at all. The reasons, they state, are that "drugs are everywhere," and that everyone who wants to use them already does. But the data beg to differ. For example, ... 56 percent of high school seniors in 1991 had never used an illicit drug in their lifetimes, and 73 percent had never used an illicit drug other than marijuana in their lifetimes.... [T]he absolute numbers in these age cohorts who have never even *tried* any illicit drugs are in the tens of millions. And most significantly for the argument that "drugs are everywhere," half of all high school students do not feel that drugs are easy to obtain.

Going further, ... most people in the general population do not use drugs. Granted, these data are limited to the "general population," which excludes such hard-to-reach populations as members of deviant and exotic subcultures, the homeless, and others living "on the streets," and particularly those in which drug use rates are highest. However, the data do document that the overwhelming majority of Americans do not use illicit drugs. This suggests two things: that the drug prohibitions may be working quite well; and that there is a large population who might, and I emphasize might, use drugs if they were legal and readily available....

An interesting variety of sophist reasoning pervades segments of the pro-legalization thesis. It is argued over and over that drugs should be legalized because they don't really do that much harm.... The legalizers use ... data to demonstrate that not too many people actually have adverse encounters with heroin, cocaine, and other illicit drugs, as compared with the hundreds of thousands of deaths each year linked to alcohol and tobacco use.... But interestingly, it is never stated that proportionately few people actually use illicit drugs, and that the segment of the population "at risk" for overdose or other physical complications from illegal drug use is but an insignificant fraction of that at risk for disease and death from alcohol and tobacco use.

The problems with illegal drugs Considerable evidence exists to suggest that the legalization of drugs could create behavioral and public health problems that would far outweigh the current consequences of drug prohibition. There are some excellent reasons why marijuana, cocaine, heroin, and other drugs are now controlled, and why they ought to remain so....

Marijuana. There is considerable misinformation about marijuana. To the millions of adolescents and young adults who were introduced to the drug during the social revolution of the 1960s and early 1970s, marijuana was a harmless herb of ecstasy. As the "new social drug" and a "natural organic product," it was deemed to be far less harmful than either alcohol or tobacco (see Grinspoon 1971; Smith 1970; Sloman 1979). More recent research suggests, however, that marijuana smoking is a practice that combines the hazardous features of both tobacco and alcohol with a number of pitfalls of its own. Moreover, there are many disturbing questions about marijuana's effect on the vital systems of the body, on the brain and mind, on immunity and resistance, and on sex and reproduction (Jones and Lovinger 1985).

One of the more serious difficulties with marijuana use relates to lung damage.... Researchers at the University of California at Los Angeles reported ... in 1988 that the respiratory burden in smoke particulates and absorption of carbon monoxide from smoking just one marijuana "joint" is some *four times greater* than from smoking a single tobacco cigarette.... [M]arijuana deposits four times more tar in the throat and lungs and increases carbon monoxide levels in the blood fourfold to fivefold.

... [A]side from the health consequences of marijuana use, recent research on the behavioral aspects of the drug suggests that it severely affects the social perceptions of heavy users. Findings from the Center for Psychological Studies in New York City, for example, report that adults who smoked marijuana daily believed the drug helped them to function better—improving their self-awareness and relationships with others (Hendin et al. 1987). In reality, however, marijuana had acted as a "buffer," enabling users to tolerate problems rather than face them and make changes that might increase the quality of their social functioning and satisfaction with life. The study found that the research subjects used marijuana to avoid dealing with their difficulties, and the avoidance inevitably made their problems worse, on the job, at home, and in family and sexual relationships.

... [W]hat has been said about cocaine also applies to crack, and perhaps more so. Crack's low price (as little as $2 per rock in some locales) has made it an attractive drug of abuse for those with limited funds. Its rapid absorption brings on a faster onset of dependence than is typical with other forms of cocaine, resulting in higher rates of addiction, binge use, and psychoses. The consequences include higher levels of cocaine-related violence and all the same manifestations of personal, familial, and occupational neglect that are associated with other forms of drug dependence....

Heroin. A derivative of morphine, heroin is a highly addictive narcotic, and is the drug historically associated with addiction and street crime. Although heroin overdose is not uncommon, unlike alcohol, cocaine, tobacco, and many prescription drugs, the direct physiological damage caused by heroin use tends to be minimal. And it is for this reason that the protagonists of drug legalization include heroin in their arguments. By making heroin readily available to users, they argue, many problems could be sharply reduced if not totally eliminated, including: the crime associated with supporting a heroin habit; the overdoses resulting from unknown levels of heroin purity and potency; the HIV and hepatitis infections brought about by needle-sharing; and the personal, social, and occupational dislocations resulting from the drug-induced criminal lifestyle.

The belief that the legalization of heroin would eliminate crime, overdose, infections, and life dislocations for its users is for the most part delusional. Instead, it is likely that the heroin-use lifestyle would change little for most addicts regardless of the legal status of the drug, an argument supported by ample evidence in the biographies and autobiographies of narcotics addicts, the clinical assessments of heroin addiction, and the drug abuse treatment literature. And to this can be added the many thousands of conversations I have had over the past 30 years with heroin users and members of their families.

The point is this. Heroin is a highly addicting drug. For the addict, it becomes life-consuming: it becomes mother, father, spouse, lover, counselor, and confessor. Because heroin is a short-acting drug, with its effects lasting at best four to six hours, it must be taken regularly and repeatedly. Because there is a more rapid onset when taken intravenously, most heroin users inject the drug. Because heroin has depressant effects, a portion of the user's day is spent in a semi-stupefied state. Collectively, these attributes result in a user more concerned with drug-taking and drug-seeking than health, family, work, relationships, responsibility, or anything else.

The pursuit of pleasure and escape ... [R]esearch by professors Michael D. Newcomb and Peter M. Bentler of the University of California at Los Angeles has documented the long-term behavioral effects of drug use on teenagers (Newcomb and Bentler 1988). Beginning in 1976, a total of 654 Los Angeles County youths were tracked for a period of eight years. Most of these youths were only occasional users of drugs, using drugs and alcohol moderately at social gatherings, whereas upwards of 10 percent were frequent, committed users. The impact of drugs on these frequent users was considerable. As teenagers, drug use tended to intensify the typical adolescent problems with family and school. In addition, drugs contributed to such psychological difficulties as loneliness, bizarre and disorganized thinking, and suicidal thoughts. Moreover, frequent drug users left school earlier, started jobs earlier, and formed families earlier, and as such, they moved into adult roles with the maturity levels of adolescents. The consequences of this pattern included rapid family break-ups, job instability, serious crime, and ineffective personal relationships. In short, frequent drug use prevented the acquisition of the coping mechanisms that are part of maturing; it blocked teenagers' learning of interpersonal skills and general emotional development.

... [A]lthough we have no explicit data on whether the numbers of addicts and associated problems would increase if drugs were legalized, there are reasons to believe that they would, and rather dramatically. First, the number of people who actually use drugs is proportionately small. Second, the great majority of people in the United States have never used illicit drugs, and hence, have never been "at risk" for addiction. Third, because of the drug prohibition, illicit drugs are *not* "everywhere," and as a result, most people have not had the opportunity to even experiment with them. Fourth, alcohol *is* readily available, and the numbers of people who have been touched by alcoholism are in the dozens of millions.

Given this, let's take the argument one step further. There is extensive physiological, neurological, and anthropological evidence to suggest that we are members of a species that has been honed for pleasure. Nearly all people want and enjoy pleasure, and the pursuit of drugs—whether caffeine, nicotine, alcohol, opium, heroin, marijuana, or cocaine—seems to be universal and inescapable. It is found across time and across cultures (and species). The process of evolution has for whatever reasons resulted in a human neurophysiology that responds both vividly and avidly to a variety of common substances. The brain has pleasure centers—receptor sites and cortical cells—that react to "rewarding" dosages of many substances....

If the legalization model were of value, then ... the narcotic would just be there—attracting little attention. There would be minimal use, addiction, and the attendant social and public health problems—as long as the drug's availability was not restricted and legislated against.

... [C]onsider Poland. For generations, Poles have cultivated home-grown poppies for the use of their seeds as flavoring in breads, stews, pretzel sticks, cookies, cakes, and chocolates. During the early 1970s, many Polish farmers began transforming their poppy straw into what has become known as *jam, compote,* or "Polish heroin." Then, many Poles began using heroin, but the practice was for the most part ignored. By the end of the 1970s heroin use in Poland had escalated significantly, but still the situation was ignored. By late 1985, at a time when the number of heroin users was estimated at 600,000 and the number of heroin-dependent persons was fixed at 200,000, the Polish government could no longer ignore what was happening. The number of overdose deaths was mounting, and the range of psychosocial and public health problems associated with heroin use was beginning to affect the structure of the already troubled country. By 1986, feeling that heroin use had gotten out of hand, the Communist government in Poland placed controls on the cultivation of poppy seeds, and the transformation of poppy straw into heroin was outlawed....

Although the events in Poland have not been systematically studied, what is known of the experience suggests that introducing potent intoxicants to a population can have problematic consequences. Moreover, the notion that "availability creates demand" has been found in numerous other parts of the world, particularly with cocaine in the Andean regions of South America (see Inciardi 1992, 222).

The Legacy of Crack Cocaine

The great drug wars in the United States have endured now for generations, although the drug legalization debates have less of a history—on again, off again since the 1930s, with a sudden burst of energy at the close of the 1980s. But as the wars linger on and the debates abide, a coda must be added to both of these politically charged topics. It concerns crack cocaine, a drug that has brought about a level of human suffering heretofore unknown in the American drug scene. The problem with crack is not that it is prohibited, but rather, the fact that it exists at all.... The chemistry and psychopharmacology of crack, combined with the tangle of socioeconomic and psychocultural strains that exist in those communities where the drug is concentrated, warrant some consideration of whether further discussion of its legality or illegality serves any purpose. Focusing on crack as an example, my intent here is to argue that both the "drug wars" and "harm reduction effort" are better served by a shifting away from the drug legalization debate.

Crack cocaine in the United States   ... For the inner cities across America, the introduction of crack couldn't have happened at a worse time. The economic base of the working poor had been shrinking for years, the result of a number of factors, including the loss of many skilled and unskilled jobs to cheaper labor markets, the movement of many businesses to the suburbs and the Sun Belt, and competition from foreign manufacturers. Standards of living, health, and overall quality of life were also in a downward direction, as consequences of suburbanization and the shrinking tax bases of central cities, combined with changing economic policies at the federal level that shifted the responsibility for many social supports to the local and private sectors. Without question, by the early to mid–1980s there was a growing and pervasive climate of hopelessness in ghetto America. And at the same time, as HIV and AIDS began to spread through inner-city populations of injectable drug users and their sex partners and as funding for drug abuse treatment declined, the production of coca and cocaine in South America reached an all-time high, resulting in high-purity cocaine at a low price on the streets of urban America. As I said, crack couldn't have come to the inner city at a worse time....

I've been doing street studies in Miami, Florida, for more years than I care to remember, and during that time I've had many an experience in the shooting galleries, base houses, and open-air drug and prostitution markets that populate the local drug scene. None of these prepared me, however, with what I was to encounter in the crack houses. As part of a federally funded street survey and ethnography of cocaine and crack use, my first trip to a crack house came in 1988. I had gained entrée through a local drug dealer who had been a key informant of mine for almost a decade. He introduced me to the crack house "door man" as someone "straight but OK." After the door man checked us for weapons, my guide proceeded to show me around.

Upon entering a room in the rear of the crack house (what I later learned was called a "freak room"), I observed what appeared to be the forcible gang-rape of an unconscious child. Emaciated, seemingly comatose, and likely no older than 14 years of age, she was lying spread-eagled on a filthy mattress while four men in succession had vaginal intercourse with her. Despite what was happening, I was urged not to interfere. After they had finished and left the room, another man came in, and they engaged in oral sex.

Upon leaving the crack house sometime later, the dealer/informant explained that she was a "house girl"—a person in the employ of the crack house owner. He gave her food, a place to sleep, some cigarettes and cheap wine, and all the crack she wanted in return for her providing sex—any type and amount of sex—to his crack house customers.

That was my first trip to a crack house. During subsequent trips to this and other crack houses, there were other scenes: a woman purchasing crack, with an infant tucked under her arm—so neglected that she had maggots crawling out of her diaper; a man "skin-popping" his toddler with a small dose of heroin, so the child would remain quietly sedated and not interrupt a crack-smoking session; people in various states of excitement and paranoia, crouching in the corners of smoking rooms inhaling from "the devil's dick" (the stem of the crack pipe); arguments, fist fights, stabbings, and shootings over crack, the price of crack, the quantity and quality of crack, and the use and sharing of crack; any manner and variety of sexual activity—by individuals and/or groups, with members of the opposite sex, the same sex, or both, or with animals, in private or public, in exchange for crack. I also saw "drug hounds" and "rock monsters" (some of the "regulars" in a crack house) crawling on their hands and knees, inspecting the floors for slivers of crack that may have dropped; beatings and gang rapes of small-time drug couriers—women, men, girls, and boys—as punishment for "messing up the money"; people in convulsions and seizures, brought on by crack use, cocaine use, the use of some other drug, or whatever; users of both sexes, so dependent on crack, so desperate for more crack, that they would do anything for another hit, eagerly risking the full array of sexually transmitted diseases, including AIDS; imprisonment and sexual slavery, one of the ultimate results of crack addiction. . . .

Many crack users engage in sexual behaviors with extremely high frequency. However, to suggest that crack turns men into "sex-crazed fiends" and women into "sex-crazed whores," as sensationalized media stories imply, is anything but precise. The situation is far more complex than that.

. . . Medical authorities generally concede that because of the disinhibiting effects of cocaine, its use among new users does indeed enhance sexual enjoyment and improve sexual functioning, including more intense orgasms (Weiss and Mirin 1987; Grinspoon and Bakalar 1985). These same reports maintain, however, that among long-term addicts, cocaine decreases both sexual desire and performance.

Going further, the crack-sex association involves the need of female crack addicts to pay for their drug. Even this connection has a pharmacological component—crack's rapid onset, extremely short duration of effects, and high addiction liability combine to result in compulsive use and a willingness to obtain the drug through any means.... Prostitution has long been the easiest, most lucrative, and most reliable means for women to finance drug use (Goldstein 1979).

The combined pharmacological and sociocultural effects of crack use can put female users in severe jeopardy. Because crack makes its users ecstatic and yet is so short-acting, it has an extremely high addiction potential. Use rapidly becomes compulsive use. Crack acquisition thus becomes enormously more important than family, work, social responsibility, health, values, modesty, morality, or self-respect....

A benefit of its current criminalization is that since it *is* against the law, it doesn't have widespread availability, so proportionately few people use it.

So where does all of this take us? My point is this. Within the context of reversing the human suffering that crack has helped to exacerbate, what purpose is served by arguing for its legalization? Will legalizing crack make it less available, less attractive, less expensive, less addictive, or less troublesome? Nobody really knows for sure, but I doubt it.

Drugs-Crime Connections

For the better part of this century there has been a concerted belief that addicts commit crimes because they are "enslaved" to drugs, that because of the high prices of heroin, cocaine, and other illicit chemicals on the black market, users are forced to commit crimes in order to support their drug habits. I have often referred to this as the "enslavement theory" of addiction (Inciardi 1986, 147–49; Inciardi 1992, 263–64)....

Research since the middle of the 1970s with active drug users in the streets of New York, Miami, Baltimore, and elsewhere has demonstrated that enslavement theory has little basis in reality, and that the contentions of the legalization proponents in this behalf are mistaken (see Inciardi 1986, 115–43; Johnson et al. 1985; Nurco et al. 1985; Stephens and McBride 1976; McBride and McCoy 1982). All of these studies of the criminal careers of heroin and other drug users have convincingly documented that while drug use tends to intensify and perpetuate criminal behavior, it usually does not initiate criminal careers. In fact, the evidence suggests that among the majority of street drug users who are involved in crime, their criminal careers were well established prior to the onset of either narcotics or cocaine use....

Postscript

... [L]et me reiterate the major points I have been trying to make.

The arguments *for* legalization are seemingly based on the fervent belief that America's prohibitions against marijuana, cocaine, heroin, and other drugs impose far too large a cost in terms of tax dollars, crime, and infringements on civil rights and individual liberties. And while the overall argument may be well-intended and appear quite logical, I find it to be highly questionable in its historical, sociocultural, and empirical underpinnings, and demonstrably naive in its understanding of the negative consequences of a legalized drug market. In counterpoint:

1. Although drug-prohibition policies have been problematic, it would appear that they have managed to keep drugs away from most people. High school and general population surveys indicate that most Americans don't use drugs, have never even tried them, and don't know where to get them. Thus, the numbers "at risk" are dramatically fewer than is the case with the legal drugs. Or stated differently, there is a rather large population who might be at risk if illicit drugs were suddenly available.

2. Marijuana, heroin, cocaine, crack, and the rest are not "benign" substances. Their health consequences, addiction liability, and/or abuse potential are considerable.

3. There is extensive physiological, neurological, and anthropological evidence to suggest that people are of a species that has been honed for pleasure. Nearly all people want and enjoy pleasure, and the pursuit of drugs—whether caffeine, nicotine, alcohol, opium, heroin, marijuana, or cocaine—seems to be universal and inescapable. It is found across time and across cultures. Moreover, history and research has demonstrated that "availability creates demand."

4. Crack cocaine is especially problematic because of its pharmacological and sociocultural effects. Because crack makes its users ecstatic and yet is so short-acting, it has an extremely high addiction potential. *Use* rapidly becomes *compulsive use....*

5. The research literature on the criminal careers of heroin and other drug users have convincingly documented that while drug use tends to intensify and perpetuate criminal behavior, it usually does not initiate criminal careers.

6. There is also a large body of work suggesting that drug abuse is overdetermined behavior. That is, physical dependence is secondary to the wide range of influences that instigate and regulate drug-taking and drug-seeking. Drug abuse is a disorder of the whole person, affecting some or all areas of functioning. In the vast majority of drug offenders, there are cognitive problems, psychological dysfunction is common, thinking may be unrealistic or disorganized, values are misshapen, and frequently there are deficits in educational and employment skills. As such, drug abuse is a response to a series of social and psychological disturbances. Thus, the goal of treatment should be "habilitation" rather than "rehabilitation." Whereas *rehabilitation* emphasizes the return to a way of life previously known and perhaps forgotten or rejected, *habilitation* involves the client's initial socialization into a productive and responsible way of life.

7. The focus on the war on drugs can be shifted. I believe that we do indeed need drug enforcement, but it is stressed far too much in current policy. Cut it in half, and shift those funds to criminal justice-based treatment programs.

8. Drug control should remain within the criminal justice sector for some very good reasons. The Drug Use Forecasting (DUF) program clearly demonstrates that the majority of arrestees in urban areas are drug-involved. Moreover,

recent research has demonstrated not only that drug abuse treatment works, but also that coerced treatment works best. The key variable most related to success in treatment is "length of stay in treatment," and those who are forced into treatment remain longer than volunteers. By remaining longer, they benefit more. As such, compulsory treatment efforts should be expanded for those who are dependent on drugs and are involved in drug-related crime.

9. Since the "war on drugs" will continue, then a more humane use of the criminal justice system should be structured. This is best done through treatment in lieu of incarceration, and corrections-based treatment for those who do end up in jails and prisons....

American drug policy as it exists today is not likely to change drastically anytime soon. Given that, something needs to be kept in mind. While the First Amendment and academic freedom enable the scholarly community to continue its attack on American drug policy, verbal assault and vilification will serve no significant purpose in effecting change. Calls for the legalization or decriminalization of marijuana, heroin, cocaine, and other illicit drugs accomplish little more than to further isolate the legalizers from the policy-making enterprise.

Finally, there is far too much suffering as the result of drug abuse that is not being addressed. Many things warrant discussion, debate, and prodding on the steps of Capitol Hill and the White House lawn. More drug abuse treatment slots, a repeal of the statutes designed to prosecute pregnant addicts and prohibit needle-exchange programs, the wider use of treatment as an alternative to incarceration—all of these are worthy of vigorous consideration and lobbying. But not legalizing drugs. It is an argument that is going nowhere.

POSTSCRIPT

Is the Drug War Harming Blacks?

For some (such as Szasz) the drug war is only part of a larger war on individual freedom. Blacks, according to this reasoning, are simply a convenient conduit for establishing greater legal, medical, and psychological control over citizens. The media and politicians are successful in linking Blacks and crime, crime and drugs, and drugs and Blacks. This makes a war on drugs and the alleged concomitant loss of basic freedoms for all of us more palpable. Szasz implies that few people understand this other than the medical and criminal justice establishments, especially the former. Moral do-gooders, some Black leaders, and criminological scholars, in supporting the drug war and claims of Black genocide, unwittingly acquiesce to the charade.

To Szasz, Inciardi's position of calling for treatment over incarceration is dangerous semantics and conceptual surrender to the medical experts, who Szasz sees as grabbing a monopoly on the issue. That is, to define drug use as an illness in need of treatment simply reinforces medical hegemony and maintains the myth that individuals who make drug-related choices are sick and in need of help.

Although Inciardi agrees with Szasz that Blacks have been discriminated against in drug arrests, he also feels that arrests do help Black communities. Naturally, differential racial arrest rates, if undeserved, should be remedied. For Inciardi, the solution is more rehabilitation programs for everyone. He insists that the drug problem is real and that it is not simply a matter of labeling, as Szasz suggests.

Among the outstanding historical-cultural delineations of drugs, drug policies, and controversies are *Hep-Cats, Narcs, and Pipe Dreams: A History of America's Romance With Illegal Drugs* by Jill Jonnes (Johns Hopkins University Press, 1999); *Forces of Habit: Drugs and the Making of the Modern World* by David T. Courtwright (Harvard University Press, 2001); and *Drugs and Drug Policy in America: A Documentary History* by Steven R. Belenko (Greenwood Press, 2000).

A recent discussion of America's reaction to the drug war is "The War Against the War on Drugs," by M. Roosevelt, *Time* (May 2, 2001). A fascinating account of U.S. involvement in Latin America's war on drugs can be found in *Killing Pablo: The Hunt for the World's Greatest Outlaw* by Mark Bowden (Atlantic Monthly Press, 2001). Several useful articles on justice and African Americans can be found in the issue of *Journal of Contemporary Criminal Justice* entitled "Crime, Justice, and the African American Community" (May 2000). Anita Kalunta-Crumpton offers an account of the drug war in England in *Race and Drug Trials: The Social Construction of Guilt and Innocence* (Ashgate, 1999). Finally, several commercial films that critically examine the drug war, such as *Traffic,* have recently been released on videotape and are worth seeing.

Contributors to This Volume

EDITOR

RICHARD C. MONK is a professor of criminal justice at Coppin State College in Baltimore, Maryland. He received a Ph.D. in sociology from the University of Maryland in 1978, and he has taught sociology, criminology, and criminal justice at Morgan State University, San Diego State University, and Valdosta State College. He has received two NEH fellowships, and he coedited the May 1992 issue of the *Journal of Contemporary Criminal Justice,* which dealt with race, crime, and criminal justice. Among his edited works are *Baltimore: A Living Renaissance* (Historic Baltimore Society, 1982) and *Structures of Knowing* (University of America Press, 1986), which partially deals with theories and research methods related to ethnic minorities. He coedited a special issue entitled "Police Training and Violence" for the *Journal of Contemporary Criminal Justice* (August 1996) and coauthored two articles on issues in philosophy of science for the *Journal of Social Pathology* (Fall 1995 and Winter 1997). Professor Monk's research article "Some Unanticipated Consequences of Women Guarding Men in Prison" was published in Nijole Benokraitis, ed., *Subtle Sexism: Current Practice and Prospects for Change* (Sage Publications, 1998). He is also the editor of *Taking Sides: Clashing Views on Controversial Issues in Crime and Criminology* (McGraw-Hill/ Dushkin), now in its sixth edition. He is currently completing a coauthored book on theory and policies in crime and crime control.

STAFF

Theodore Knight   List Manager
David Brackley   Senior Developmental Editor
Juliana Gribbins   Developmental Editor
Rose Gleich   Administrative Assistant
Brenda S. Filley   Director of Production/Design
Juliana Arbo   Typesetting Supervisor
Diane Barker   Proofreader
Richard Tietjen   Publishing Systems Manager
Larry Killian   Copier Coordinator

AUTHORS

ROBERT APONTE is an assistant professor of sociology in the James Madison College at Michigan State University in East Lansing, Michigan, and a research associate at the Julian Samora Research Institute.

VICTORIA BARNETT, a graduate of Union Theological Seminary in New York City, is a professional writer whose articles have appeared in *Christianity and Crisis, The Christian Century,* and *The Witness.* She is the author of *Bystanders: Conscience and Complicity During the Holocaust* (Greenwood Press, 1999).

MAITRAYEE BHATTACHARYYA is an editor and a researcher at the Institute for Research on the African Diaspora in the Americas and the Caribbean (IRADAC).

DEREK BOK is president emeritus at Harvard University and the 300th Anniversary University Professor in the Kennedy School of Government. He is the author of *The State of the Nation: Government and the Quest for a Better Society, 1960–1995* (Harvard University Press, 1998).

WILLIAM G. BOWEN is president of the Andrew W. Mellon Foundation. He is coauthor, with Derek Bok, of *The Shape of the River: Long-Term Consequences of Considering Race in College and University Admissions* (Princeton University Press, 1998).

JOHN V. BRAIN is a columnist for *The Sentinel* in Baltimore, Maryland.

PETER BRIMELOW is senior editor at *Forbes* and *National Review* magazines. He is the author of *Alien Nation: Common Sense About America's Immigration Disaster* (Random House, 1995).

CHRISTOPHER R. BROWNING teaches at Pacific Lutheran University. He is the author of *Ordinary Men: Reserve Police Battalion 101 and the Final Solution in Poland* (HarperCollins, 1993).

ROBERT D. BULLARD is the Ware Professor of Sociology and director of the Environmental Justice Resource Center at Clark Atlanta University. He served on President Bill Clinton's Transition Team in the Natural Resources and Environmental Cluster (Department of Energy, Interior, Agriculture, and Environmental Protection Agency), and he currently serves on the U.S. EPA National Environmental Justice Advisory Council (NEJAC), where he chairs the Health and Research Subcommittee. His many publications include *Sprawl City: Race, Politics, and Planning in Atlanta* (Island Press, 2000).

LINDA CHAVEZ, a political commentator, policy analyst, and author, is the John M. Olin Fellow of the Manhattan Institute for Policy Research in Washington, D.C., and chairperson of the National Commission on Migrant Education. Her articles have appeared in such publications as *Fortune,* the *Wall Street Journal,* and the *Los Angeles Times.*

DAVID COLE is a professor at Georgetown University Law Center and a volunteer staff attorney for the Center for Constitutional Rights.

JAMES CRAWFORD is an independent writer and lecturer specializing in the politics of language. He is the former Washington editor of *Education Week* and the author of *At War With Diversity: U.S. Language Policy in an Age of Anxiety* (Multilingual Matters, 2000).

OLGA IDRISS DAVIS is an assistant professor of speech communication at Kansas State University in Manhattan, Kansas. A Rockefeller Humanities Fellow for summer 1997, she conducted research on a project entitled *Piecing Ourselves Together: The Rhetoric of Coalition-Building in Black Women's Slave Narratives.*

LELIA LOMBA DE ANDRADE is an assistant professor of sociology and Africana studies at Bowdoin College. Her current research focuses on the connections that Cape Verdean Americans maintain with the homeland and the uses of these connections in their formation of community and identity. She holds an M.A. and a Ph.D. from Syracuse University.

DINESH D'SOUZA, a former senior domestic policy analyst for the Reagan administration, is the John M. Olin Research Fellow at the American Enterprise Institute in Washington, D.C. He is the author of *The End of Racism: Principles for a Multiracial Society* (Free Press, 1995).

JON ENTINE is a writer and an Emmy-winning television news reporter and producer. His book *Taboo: Why Black Athletes Dominate Sports and Why We Are Afraid to Talk About It* (Public Affairs, 2001) was based on his 1989 NBC documentary *Black Athletes: Fact and Fiction.* He won a National Press Club award in 1995 for "Shattered Image: Is The Body Shop Too Good to Be True?" which was published in *Business Ethics* magazine. Entine was a producer for the television series *20/20* and for *PrimeTime Live* at ABC News, and he was Tom Brokaw's producer on NBC's *Nightly News.* He currently writes an award-winning business journal column entitled "The Ethical Edge."

JEFF FERRELL is an associate professor of criminal justice at Northern Arizona University in Flagstaff, Arizona. He is the author of *Crimes of Style: Urban Graffiti and the Politics of Criminology* (Garland, 1993).

OWEN FISS is the Sterling Professor of Law at Yale University and the author of *A Community of Equals: The Constitutional Protection of New Americans* (Beacon Press, 1999). He holds a B.A. from Dartmouth University and an LL.B. from Harvard University.

DAVID FRIEDMAN is a writer, an international consultant on environmental policy, and a fellow in the MIT Japan program.

DANIEL JONAH GOLDHAGEN teaches political science at Harvard University. He is the author of *Hitler's Willing Executioners: Ordinary Germans and the Holocaust* (Alfred A. Knopf, 1996).

EDMUND W. GORDON is the John M. Musser Professor of Psychology Emeritus at Yale University and a professor of psychology at City College of New York. He is also director of the Institute for Research on the African Diaspora in the Americas and the Caribbean (IRADAC).

LANI GUINIER is a professor of law at Harvard Law School. She is the author of *Every Little Voice* (Simon & Schuster, 1998) and *The Miner's Canary* (Harvard University Press, 2002). Guinier is a graduate of Radcliffe College and Yale University Law School.

MARK S. HAMM is a professor of criminology at Indiana State University in Terre Haute, Indiana. He is the author of *American Skinheads: The Criminology and Control of Hate Crime* (Praeger, 1993).

JAMES A. HARMON is chairman of the U.S. Export-Import Bank.

SHEILA E. HENRY is affiliated with the School of Arts and Sciences at National University in Costa Mesa, California. Her research interests include ethnic identity, the African diaspora, ethnic inequality, and historical sociology.

JOHN HOBERMAN is a professor of Germanic studies at the University of Texas at Austin. He is the author of several books on race and sports, including *Darwin's Athletes: How Sport Has Damaged Black America and Preserved the Myth of Race* (Houghton Mifflin, 1997). Hoberman holds an M.A. and a Ph.D. from the University of California, Berkeley.

JAMES A. INCIARDI is director of the Center for Drug and Alcohol Studies at the University of Delaware in Newark, Delaware, and an adjunct professor in the Comprehensive Drug Research Center at the University of Miami School of Medicine in Miami, Florida.

KENNETH LASSON is a professor of law at the University of Baltimore and director of its Haifa Summer Law Institute. He holds an M.A. from the Johns Hopkins University and a J.D. from the University of Maryland.

SUSAN LEDLOW is a faculty associate for the University Program for Faculty Development at Arizona State University in Tempe, Arizona. She was also involved with teacher training in bilingual education progams for the University of Arizona's Mountain State Multifunctional Resource Center for eight years.

GLENN C. LOURY is a professor of economics at Boston University in Boston, Massachusetts. He has been actively involved in public debate and analysis of the problems of racial inequality and social policy toward the poor in the United States, which is reflected in his publication *Achieving the Dream* (Heritage Foundation, 1990).

DENNIS R. MARTIN is a former president of the National Association of Chiefs of Police in Arlington, Virginia.

ROBERT K. MERTON is an adjunct professor at Rockefeller University, a resident scholar at the Russell Sage Foundation, and a professor emeritus at Columbia University, all located in New York City. His publications include *The Sociology of Science: Theoretical and Empirical Investigations* (University of Chicago Press, 1973).

JON REYHNER is an associate professor in the Department of Curriculum and Instruction at Eastern Montana College, where he teaches education and Native American studies. His publications include *Teaching American Indian Students* (University of Oklahoma, 1992).

KEITH B. RICHBURG is the Southeast Asia correspondent for the *Washington Post*. He is the author of *Out of America: A Black Man Confronts Africa* (Basic Books, 1997).

EUGENE F. RIVERS III is the founder and pastor of Azusa Christian Community and a Harvard Divinity School guest lecturer.

JAMES RON is an assistant professor of sociology at the Johns Hopkins University whose research interests include political sociology, social and revolutionary movements, ethnic conflict, state violence, human rights, and humanitarian assistance. His forthcoming book from the University of California Press, *Frontier and Ghetto,* explores the institutional underpinnings of state violence in the Balkans and the Middle East. He holds a Ph.D. from the University of California, Berkeley.

PAUL RUFFINS is executive editor of *Crisis* magazine.

JACK G. SHAHEEN is a journalist, a former professor of mass communications at Southern Illinois University in Edwardsville, Illinois, and a recipient of two Fulbright-Hayes Lectureship Grants.

KALUMBI SHANGULA is the permanent secretary of health and social services for the Republic of Namibia.

THOMAS SOWELL is a senior fellow of the Hoover Institution at Stanford University. He has taught economics at a number of universities, including Brandeis University, and he is the author of several books, including *Conquests and Cultures* (Basic Books, 1998).

STEPHEN STEINBERG is assistant chair for day studies at Queen's College in New York City and a writer on race and ethnicity in the United States. His book *Turning Back: The Retreat From Racial Justice in American Thought and Policy* (Beacon Press, 1995) was awarded the Oliver Cromwell Cox Award for Distinguished Anti-Racist Scholarship by the Race and Ethnicity Section of the American Sociological Association. He holds a Ph.D. from the University of California, Berkeley.

SUSAN STURM is a professor of law at Columbia Law School and the coprincipal investigator, with Lani Guinier, of the Racetalks project. She holds a B.A. from Brown University and a J.D. from Yale University.

THOMAS SZASZ is a psychiatrist, a psychoanalyst, and a professor in the Department of Psychiatry at the State University of New York's Upstate Medical Center at Syracuse, New York. His publications include *Pharmacracy: Medicine and Politics in America* (Greenwood, 2001) and *Fatal Freedom: The Ethics and Politics of Suicide* (Greenwood, 1999).

J. PHILLIP THOMPSON is an assistant professor of political science at Barnard College and an assistant professor of management at the Columbia University Business School. He holds a B.A. from Harvard University, an M.C.P. from Hunter College, and a Ph.D. from the City University of New York.

LAWRENCE WRIGHT is a staff writer for *The New Yorker* magazine and the author of *Twins: And What They Tell Us About Who We Are* (John Wiley, 1997).

Index